Celtic Christian Spirituality

Also by Oliver Davies and Fiona Bowie
and published by SPCK

The Rhineland Mystics 1989
Beguine Spirituality 1989
Hildegard of Bingen 1990
Meister Eckhart: Mystical Theologian 1991

Celtic
Christian Spirituality

MEDIEVAL AND MODERN

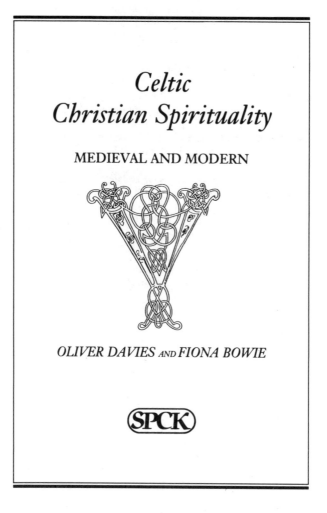

OLIVER DAVIES AND FIONA BOWIE

SPCK

First published 1995
SPCK
Holy Trinity Church
Marylebone Road
London
NW1 4DU

British Library Cataloguing in Publication Data
A catalogue record for this book is available from the British Library

ISBN 0-281-04765-0

Photoset by Rowland Phototypesetting Limited,
Bury St Edmunds, Suffolk
Printed in Great Britain by
the Cromwell Press, Melksham, Wiltshire

Cyflwynir y llyfr hwn i

Huw a Nancy, Meilyr ac Allison,
Catrin Haf ac Alun Gwynedd.

CONTENTS

ACKNOWLEDGEMENT

Our thanks go to Rachel Boulding, Brendan Walsh and Judith Long-man, all of whom, in their capacity as editors, have waited patiently for this book, and to the many friends and colleagues whose encouragement and criticisms have been invaluable.

Oliver Davies and Fiona Bowie,
Lampeter

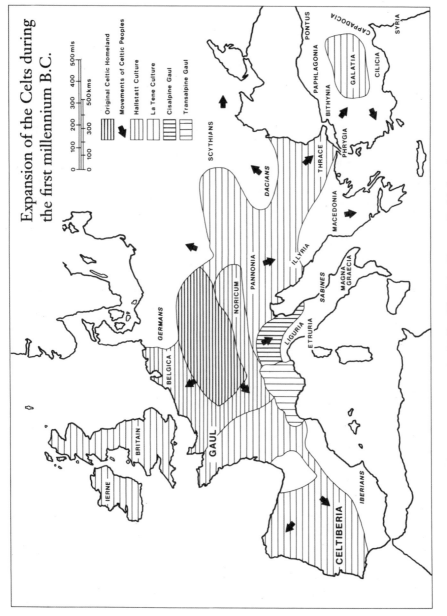

Expansion of the Celts during the first millennium B.C.

Original Celtic Homeland
Movements of Celtic Peoples
Hallstatt Culture
La Tene Culture
Cisalpine Gaul
Transalpine Gaul

0 100 200 300 400 500 mls
0 100 300   500 kms

IERNE

BRITAIN

GERMANS

BELGICA

GAUL

NORICUM

PANNONIA

SCYTHIANS

DACIANS

ILLYRIA

LIGURIA

ETRURIA

SABINES

MAGNA
GRAECIA

MACEDONIA

THRACE

PHRYGIA

BITHYNIA

PAPHLAGONIA

PONTUS

GALATIA

CAPPADOCIA

CILICIA

SYRIA

CELTIBERIA

IBERIANS

Adapted from Peter Beresford Ellis, *The Celtic Empire*, Guild, London, 1990.

Introducing Celtic Christianity

Recent decades have witnessed an extraordinary revival of interest in the Celtic inheritance of Britain and Ireland.[1] The modern 'Celtic' prayers of David Adam (a priest from Lindisfarne), which draw inspiration from the collection of Gaelic religious literature known as the *Carmina Gadelica*, as well as the many anthologized editions of this work, have reached a wide and appreciative audience. An awareness of the Celtic past of these islands has been awakened in others by the medieval high crosses, often striking in both their execution and location, and rich in iconographic symbolism. The beauty, intricate detail and complexity of medieval gospel books such as the Book of Kells are a further tribute to the past genius of a Celtic Christian culture, hinting at values far removed from our modern consumerist society.

The revival of 'Celtic' arts, the development of neo-druidic groups and of 'Celtic Christian Churches' all testify to a desire to link the present to a past which is perceived as more ecological, imaginative, intuitive and theologically sound. For those who feel themselves to be modern Celts, particularly people who speak Celtic languages (Welsh, Irish and Scots Gaelic, Breton, and even Manx or Cornish), there is the added dimension of a search for roots, a sense of continuity and the validation of a separate and coherent identity, which is not merely the exotic 'other' of English or French culture.

There are numerous, often excellent, introductions to the Celtic world, pitched at different levels of interest and focusing on its various aspects (such as archaeology, mythology, literature). One may well ask, therefore, why yet another introduction to Celtic Christianity is thought necessary. But despite the growing number of publications in this field this book does, we believe, attempt something rather different. As with the other volumes in this series (*The Rhineland Mystics, Beguine Spirituality* and *Hildegard of Bingen*) our aim is to disseminate up-to-date scholarship to a non-specialist readership. In a field which abounds with popular representations and misrepresentations, feeding off a wide public interest in all things Celtic, it can become increasingly difficult to tell fact from fiction. We hope that the introductory essays will provide the reader with a map through this difficult terrain. In contrast to most other books on Celtic religion, the passages in this anthology cover a period of many centuries and come from many parts of the Celtic world. In moving from early medieval poetry and prose to nineteenth century oral literature and modern poetry we are seeking to demonstrate both the variety and the threads of continuity within the Celtic Christian world. The existence of 'Celtic Christianity' is, however, disputed by many reputable scholars. Understanding the complex web of desires, emotions and intuitions which lead some people to 're-discover' what others deny exists, will require some knowledge of the context of the study of Celtic history, and it is to this that we now turn.

The Search for Celtic Christianity

The retrieval of the Celtic Christian past is a process fraught with particular difficulties. In the first place, the very term 'Celtic' is essentially a recent invention. Although the Greeks and Romans used names such as *Keltoi*, *Galli* and *Celtae* to denote a wide range of different peoples, the term is first used in a more precise sense by linguists of the early eighteenth and nineteenth centuries who began to recognize a distinctive 'Celtic' family of languages.[2] Gradually, with an increase in knowledge, the term began to cover a diversity of artistic, social and cultural phenomena which appeared, to a greater or lesser degree, to be characteristic of the 'Celtic' peoples. The sense of a common Celtic identity among many in Ireland, Scotland, Wales, Brittany, Cornwall and the Isle of Man (and even Galicia), though real enough today, is decidedly a modern phenomenon, generated by economic and political factors which are far removed from the early and late medieval world. The monastic artists who produced the Book of Kells and carved the high crosses would not have thought of themselves as Celts.

The question at least needs to be asked therefore whether it is legitimate for us to talk of medieval 'Celtic' Christianity at all when the term 'Celtic' would itself have had no meaning in the Middle Ages. But in fact most of the ethnic terms habitually used by historians of early European history would not have been recognized, or would at least have been understood differently, by the peoples to whom they refer. While many of us may feel a European identity today, the Goths,

Lombards and Anglo-Saxons of the early Middle Ages emphatically did not. And yet these peoples will certainly feature in any study of 'European' history. The truth is that such broad ethnic categories constantly evolve and are useful to the historian precisely because they combine geographical and chronological meanings, as well as cultural and linguistic ones. In other words, they function well as tools with which to discuss and analyse the complex realities of human history precisely because they are inclusive and vague.

Great care must be taken with the term 'Celtic' however since all too often it is used in a way which suggests that nineteenth-century Scotland and pre-Christian Gaul, eighth-century Ireland and modern Brittany all somehow form a unified cultural unit: a single world populated by 'Celts'. In reality, of course, each period and each geographical area is distinct. The Celtic peoples, though related by language and aspects of culture, have all experienced different histories, and have had to negotiate their own identity with respect to dominant powers in diverse ways. Their spiritualities are also varied and we should beware of extracting specific elements that catch our eye from periods which are as far apart as, for instance, modern Italy and ancient Rome and presenting these together as if they all constituted a single and timeless phenomenon called 'Celtic spirituality'. In almost two thousand years of Celtic Christian history, we should expect to see more divergence and difference than continuity.

The view that the Celts had their own distinctive Church is one of the chief ways in which Celtic Christianity has been misread. We live in a Christian world governed by denominations, and it is natural that we should project this into the past. In truth however the Western Church was united as one Church until the Reformation, and what might be construed as a conflict between the 'Celtic Church' and the 'Roman Catholic Church' was in fact competition between different trends and traditions within a single and still united Church. A number of prominent historians have refuted the idea of the existence in any way of 'a Celtic Church' as a distinct institutional body, pointing also to the differences in church organization among the different Celtic peoples.[3] In attempting to come to an authentic understanding of medieval Celtic Christianity, our legitimate desire to find an alternative Christian model for today must be matched by a close and informed reading of historical sources.

It was in fact inter-denominational rivalry which formed the context for the earliest systematic explorations into the field of Celtic Christianity. Both English and Welsh Reformers believed that they had discovered in the Ancient British (i.e. Celtic) Church of old a body which was both ancient and episcopal and evidently not to be identified with the Roman Catholic Church of the Counter-Reformation.[4] Indeed, this remained the paramount point of interest with regard to Celtic Christianity for several centuries, and the desire to discover an ancient alternative to Roman Catholicism is still a factor in the minds even of some modern commentators, who like to point, with some justification, to its affinities with the Orthodox East.

Despite the ambiguity over the term 'Celtic' and the lack of any consensus as to what it actually designates, we feel justified in using the term 'Celtic Christianity' for two reasons. First, because there undoubtedly are some distinctive and important Christian emphases which thread their way through the religious imagination of Celtic-speaking peoples, and second, though just as important, many Christians living in Celtic countries today choose to regard themselves as Celts. Such an identity is to some extent, like all ethnicities, based on a mythologized reading of the past, but it has its own reality and exigencies, and should not be dismissed too lightly.

The Origins of the Celts

Peoples speaking Celtic languages once covered much of Europe. The earliest traces of Celtic-language groups date from the late Urnfield culture of the first millennium BC, although the first visible expression of a grouping which has been unequivocally identified as Celtic on linguistic grounds is the Hallstatt culture, which developed in what is modern Austria in 700–500 BC.[5] It was the war-like, iron-using people of the late Hallstatt period, together with the La Tène culture which evolved from it, with which the classical civilizations of Greece and Rome came into immediate contact and who are remembered in their literature as wild, scantily clad warriors. The fine and distinctive metalwork of La Tène is the surviving expression of a widespread and sophisticated culture which straddled Europe in the period from around 500 BC to the time of the subjugation of the continental Celtic peoples by Julius Caesar in the first century BC. Celtic remains have been found as far afield as southern Italy, Portugal and Spain, Denmark and modern Turkey (the home of the Galatians who may have spoken a Celtic language when St Paul wrote to them in around 54 AD). Roman conquest, and then migration by Germanic tribes into central and southern Europe, brought to an end the high period of continental Celtic civilization which we can glimpse today only in the more spectacular archaeological finds of deposits in river, shaft and lake, and by the remarks of their classical contemporaries, curious as to the nature and customs of the peoples they were set to conquer.

Ancient Celtic society, at least as we see it through the eyes of contemporary Greek and Roman writers, was one which had the values of the earliest heroic age of Greece and Rome.[6] This means to say that it was a warrior culture in which the greatest value was placed upon achievement in war and upon the qualities of self-denying strength and fearless valour by which it was achieved. But the power of the warrior was balanced in Celtic society by other no less important elements. There are signs of great ingenuity and dexterity in the design and manufacture of tools, such as ploughs and spoked wheels, as well as in the magnificent torques and brooches which have been discovered all over Europe. Indeed, the inventiveness of the Celt is apparent not only in high art but also in the more popular and widespread forms of decoration and craftsmanship that are typical even of everyday objects. The Celtic designer delighted in riddles and ambiguity, in rhythm and fluidity of form, and in abstract harmonies at the expense of the naturalism and idealism of the Greeks. But Celtic art also showed its vigour in the ability of the craftsmen to absorb and transform foreign influences at different stages of history, whether from Greece or Rome, Etruria or Scythia, while maintaining a distinctively Celtic continuity of form and style.

Pre-Christian Celtic Religion

Early Celtic societies, with their characteristic division into king, druidic class, bardic class, law-givers and artisans, seem also to have found their common focus in religion. Celts, as the Romans observed, were very religious people.[7] There was no aspect of life which was not in some way touched by the intricate webs of ritual and belief that gave life and meaning to the Celtic world. Time and seasons were calculated according to religious criteria, with the druids pronouncing upon the most auspicious moment for undertakings. Divination was common-place, including perhaps divination by human sacrifice, as was the reading of auguries within the natural world, especially involving the behaviour of birds. Religion demanded sacrifice, particularly in times of war when victory was paid for by dedicating the spoils of victory to the relevant god. Indeed, much Celtic wealth seems to have found its way for cultic reasons into the earth, rivers or lakes to be swiftly retrieved by Roman soldiers or, centuries later, by the painstaking work of archaeologists.

Indeed, there are notable differences between the religiosity of the Celts and that of the Romans, who were methodically destroying continental Celtic civilization during the first century BC. In the first place, we find among the Celts an absence of the written word, which contrasts with the philosophically sophisticated religious writings of the Mediterranean world. Celtic society had clearly not begun to emulate the standards of literacy of Greece and Rome, and shows all the signs of having been vigorously oral. Power was invested in the druidic class, who protected traditional knowledge ranging from cosmology to genealogy and law, by an oral system of learning which was based, as such systems are, on simple and repetitive poetic forms in order to facilitate the task of memory. Although traditional knowledge among the Celts may have been — and probably was — very sophisticated, its oral character suggests its decidedly unphilosophical (in the modern sense) nature, and its indebtedness to poetry, mythology and imagery.

Second, there is a tribal dimension. Caesar mentions the fact that a Celt who was banned by his or her own community from partaking in the sacrifices suffered total social isolation. It would be difficult to parallel this in the contemporary classical world, but similarly closed social communities can be found among some of the technologically less developed societies that exist today.

Third, Celtic religion appeared to be a markedly local phenomenon. The cult of a particular deity was generally linked to a specific location, whether this was a river or lake or one of the dark forest groves that so shocked the Romans. The gods of the classical peoples, on the other hand, were more mobile and their temples might appear anywhere within the Empire. We see among the Celts an interpenetration of religion and landscape in a way that surpasses anything we might find in the late classical world. This is an important point. It means that, for the Celt, God, or the transcendent, did not speak to the human community outside and beyond its natural environment. Rather, God spoke to humanity precisely *within* the natural world. In other words, nature, the cosmos, was taken up into and formed part of the dialogue between human beings and God. This is in stark contrast to the tendency we find in the late classical world to abstract human community from its environment and to confine religious dialogue to the realm of the spirit. We might note here however that there are certain parallels between this Celtic approach and the religious consciousness of the Hebrews with their promised land.

The attempt to recreate early Celtic religion is precarious and is based upon the evidence of archaeology, historical linguistics and place-names, combined with anecdotes and snippets of information recorded by some of the writers of antiquity. To this must be added perspectives that can be discerned in the earliest Irish and Welsh writings which, although they date from a later period, are likely in some degree to reflect the beliefs and practices of earlier centuries. We can imagine that early Celtic religion offered society a means of manipulating the powerful spirit forces that were everywhere present in their world. It is likely that the early Celt lived in a domain that was filled with unseen presences, including possibly those of potentially hostile ancestor spirits whose skulls may have been carefully tended by their living relatives, as they are in many sub-Saharan African and other societies today.[8] There may also have been particular individuals who, dressed in skins, entered trance-like states in which they believed that they were carried on a spirit journey into the bodies of animals in order to effect an act of healing, like the shamans of the Arctic north or of South America.[9] We can imagine too that the topography of the tribal area would have been filled with religious resonances, particular places (such as springs and lakes) being passage-ways to the unseen world where humans could contact, supplicate or control the hidden forces that seemed to determine the health and prosperity of individuals and the community.

Although we can point to many continental Celtic representations of the horned god Cernunos (who may after all simply be a shamanic figure dressed as a stag), to early Irish inspirational bards who may have dressed in bird feathers, and to goddess-like muses such as the Welsh Ceridwen or Ogyrfen who were the source of bardic inspiration and song, we can be neither specific nor certain on any of these matters.[10] It is surely the case however that by looking at the full range of contemporary human societies, we can glimpse at least the possibilities of what early Celtic religion may have been.

The Roots of Celtic Christianity

An account of the history of Christianity among the Celtic-speaking peoples must consider the forms of religious and spiritual life that predominated at that time. Prior to the arrival of Christianity the Celtic peoples had a dynamic and vital indigenous religion. The religious outlook, sensibilities and practices of British, and later Irish, converts would not have changed overnight, but would have fused in various ways with the new faith. Insular Christianity (that is, Christianity in Britain and Ireland) therefore took on a distinctively 'Celtic' colour, and it is this which interests so many observers today.[11]

The Celtic inhabitants of Britain and Ireland during this period were divided into two main groups who spoke distinct but related languages. In what is now England, Wales and southern Scotland there lived Brythonic Celts, who spoke the 'Brythonic' or 'British' language (related to Welsh and Cornish, from which Breton is also derived). Although divided into numerous, often warring, tribes the Brythonic Celts also maintained close links with one another, intermarried and spoke mutually comprehensible dialects. In Ireland, western Scotland and the Isle of Man were the Goedelic Celts (who spoke languages which evolved into Irish, Scots Gaelic and Manx). These two branches of the Celtic-speaking family never lost contact with one another. Many individuals (like St Patrick in the fifth century AD) moved easily between the two cultural areas which were linked by sea routes. Extensive Irish settlements have been found in Wales, particularly on the coasts, and the existence of common place-names and church dedications confirm the narrative evidence of continued contact between Britain and Ireland.

The experience of Roman occupation in what is now known as England, southern Scotland and much of Wales did, however, mean that the Brythonic and Goedelic Celts followed different historical paths. It is usual to regard early Ireland as the model for insular Celtic civilization since of all the Celtic societies of north western Europe, Ireland alone represents a Celtic tradition which was virtually untouched by *latinitas* and *romanitas*, which is to say the culture and civilization of the Roman Empire. The Irish were never conquered by the Roman armies that put an end to continental Celtic civilization. But it is in fact to mainland Britain that we must look for the earliest signs of Celtic Christianity, precisely because the Brythonic Celts, the forerunners of the modern Welsh, Cornish and southern Scots, suffered defeat at the hands of Caesar's troops and remained for several centuries an integral part of the late Roman world.

BRITAIN

The new faith came to the British Isles through the Roman forces and administrators, and from the numerous traders and other wanderers who traversed the Roman domains. The first signs of a Christian presence in Britain date from some two hundred years after the death of Jesus. The martyrdoms of Aaron and Julius, probably in Caerleon in Gwent (south east Wales), and Alban can be dated to the middle of the third century,[12] and British bishops were present at the Council of Arles in 314. Two archaeological finds from this period suggest a relatively peaceful coexistence of the new religion with some of the symbols and practices of the older pagan way of life. The hoard of silver church plate which dates from around 350 AD, found in 1975 at Water Newton near Peterborough, includes Christian votive tablets, while the Hinton St Mary mosaic seems to combine an image of Christ detailed upon the floor with pagan religious motifs.[13]

Very little is known about the character and quality of the Christian life in Britain in this early period, but the scant evidence we have points to the existence of a strongly Romanized Church, most prevalent among the Romano-British elite, the wealthy and entrepreneurial Brythonic Celts who were the people most directly in contact with the occupiers. It was a Church whose language was overwhelmingly Latin and whose diocesan structure, based upon local centres of population, reflected the Roman pattern of civil organization. The three British bishops who attended the Council of Arles came from London, York and either Lincoln or Colchester. Romano-British Christians suffered with the rest of Christendom during the persecutions of the mid-third century and rejoiced when in 313 the Edict of Milan marked a new period of liberation and security for the Christian Church.

Although the remoteness of the Romano-British Church from the continental sources of ecclesiastical power needs to be stressed (it was little more than an off-shore appendage to the Church in Gaul), it did at least produce a theology which caused a considerable stir in the great centres of the Christian world. Pelagius, who was probably a Brythonic Celt by birth, lent his name to the heresy which appears to have arisen in monastic circles and which was particularly influential in Britain and southern Gaul. Prosper of Aquitaine tells us that Pope Celestine was prompted to send Germanus, Bishop of Auxerre, on a mission to Britain in 429 in order to counter the Pelagians, which he did successfully, though only temporarily.

It is not easy to reconstruct Pelagianism in detail today, since many of the relevant texts are lost and much of what survives is Catholic polemic, but the movement characteristically stressed the role of the human will in the process of redemption. Pelagius himself believed that God-given human nature was itself capable of distinguishing the good from the bad, thus of initiating the movement of the individual towards God. In theological terms this was to emphasize nature at the expense of grace, or at least to confine the operation of grace to an external sphere, denying that it acted also within the human will. This view evoked an emphatic response from the great Augustine, Bishop of Hippo, who developed his own theory of grace in his many anti-Pelagian writings. Pelagianism, in the form it took among the most eager supporters of Pelagius' position, was repeatedly condemned by church councils, not least for denying the concept of original sin and opposing the baptism of infants. We can postulate that such a positive view of human nature may itself have been a reflection of a greater optimism towards the created world in early Celtic culture than was the case in that of the Mediterranean and North Africa, although, without knowing more about Pelagius' relation to native culture, such a hypothesis must remain speculative.[14] The themes of nature, freedom and grace became a perennial concern, of course, and were to reappear forcefully during the Reformation when, ironically, it could be said that the Protestants generally adopted a quasi-Augustinian position and the Catholics a quasi-Pelagian one.

The Romano-British Church survived until the first half of the fifth century when, after the withdrawal of the Roman forces in 409, the Romanized, Celtic areas of Britain came under increasing pressure from the vigorous assaults of the Irish from the west, the Picts from the north and, most importantly, from the early English peoples who were seizing land from the east. Over a period of time the territory of the Romano-British Church sharply contracted in the face of such pagan advances. The Brythonic lands, largely to the west of the country, which offered the invaders most resistance did so on account of the generally remote and inaccessible character of their terrain, which had served also to restrict the degree of Roman influence in these parts. The Romano-British Church therefore, which sent no more bishops to continental councils, was cut off from the continental well-springs of the Christian religion and increasingly took on the aspect of an insular and archaic foundation. It was not necessarily the case that Christianity was completely extinguished in the eastern, English parts of Britain (nor that the indigenous Brythonic-speaking inhabitants of these parts actually moved west), but evidence for its survival there, prior to the evangelization of the English in the seventh century, is meagre.[15]

With the collapse of the Romano-British Church in the fifth century, Christianity was restricted to Strathclyde and Cumbria in the north, through Wales and the borders to Devon and Cornwall in the south. In addition, there increasingly occurred the movement of peoples from the south west of Britain to Armorica or Brittany in north west France. But despite the presence of figures such as St Ninian at Whithorn in the north, it is to the Welsh church that we must turn for the most numerous British sources in the early period, since we possess almost no literary sources for Christian life in Brythonic Scotland, Cornwall and Brittany until the later Middle Ages.[16] Indeed, the early Welsh were keen to stress their historical links with the old Roman civilization and with the religion that it had introduced, and it is worth noting that the very term 'Welsh' is an early English word which means 'Romanized Celt'.[17] There is much evidence to support continuity moreover, since there are almost no accounts of conversion in the earliest Welsh literature, the Welsh/British Church that Gildas berates in the early sixth century is apparently already hopelessly corrupt, and there is evidence for at least one sixth-century territorial diocese (along the lines of the Romano-British Church) in either Welsh Bicknor or near Kenderchurch in south east Wales.[18]

The spiritual inspiration for the early Welsh Church seems to have come in the main from the monks of the Middle East and their counterparts in southern Gaul. The *Lives* of the early Welsh saints are full of references and allusions to the monasticism of the desert; the Eastern monastic ascetic ideal, particularly as this was mediated by the works of Cassian, evidently provided a powerful role model in Wales, as it did in other Celtic lands.[19] It is likely that during the fifth and sixth centuries individuals inspired by these ideals sought solitude and a life of work and prayer, attracting to themselves like-minded followers who established communities about them, as had been the pattern in fourth-century Egypt. In course of time, some such communities developed into small townships while other sites retained their original ascetical and eremetical character. There is some evidence to suggest that the communities of the far west (such as Bardsey to the north, Caldy and St David's in the south west), which were closer to Ireland, may have reflected a more ascetical lifestyle, while those of the east (such as Llantwit Major), which were closer to England, may have laid greater stress upon learning.[20]

Perhaps the most important single feature about the Welsh Church during the early Middle Ages is its remoteness from the urban centres of ecclesiastical power and hence its tendency to retain customs that elsewhere were rapidly overtaken by the harmonization process that was characteristic of the Christian Church throughout Europe at this time. The belated acceptance by the Celtic churches of the Roman method of calculating the date of Easter at the Synod of Whitby in 664 is but one example of this. The Welsh medieval Church reflects earlier ways therefore, and is not neatly organized into monks, clergy and laity. Rather the *clasau*, or religious communities, were probably based on a proliferation of local rules, variously adhered to. 'Monasticism' was widespread, if not the norm, even if it was only a small minority that were celibate, committed to a rigorous lifestyle and, perhaps, living in solitude like the 'saints of old'.

It was in this environment, however, that something of the distinctive Christianity, which resulted from the fusion of the old religion with the new, could survive. And in fact there is much that is original in a body of literature which occurs in a thirteenth-century manuscript, based on earlier sources, known as the *Black Book of Carmarthen*. First, we find in these works an unusually positive attitude to the creation and, second, they constitute in themselves a phenomenon which cannot be paralleled outside the Celtic world. It was the convention during the Middle Ages for monks to communicate with other monks in Latin prose, for this was the appropriate medium of the Church. The fact that these works from the *Black Book of Carmarthen*, which date from the ninth or tenth centuries, were poems and were written in Welsh, although they were composed by monks and are often expressly concerned with monastic life, is itself an indication of how different the Welsh religious tradition could be (pages 28–31). Specifically, it shows the central place that poetry enjoyed in medieval Welsh Christianity. In fact one poem from this corpus lists the devotional practices that are required of a pious soul and includes 'listening to the songs of clear-speaking poets'.[21] The poetic tradition, then, was one of the principal ways in which a distinctive spiritual sensibility was maintained in Wales, a fact which is less surprising when we remember that the earliest Christian poetic tradition must have emerged from the bardism which was central to the religion of the pre-Christian Celtic world.

The 'archaic' period in Wales came to an end with the arrival of the Normans, who brought with them many of the norms of continental Christianity. For the first time the major religious Orders of the Catholic Church, principally the Cistercians, took root in Wales. The ancient Celtic foundations either gave way to the new Orders or themselves conformed, frequently by adopting the Augustinian Rule and becoming Canons. It would be wrong to view this time as marking the end of the existence of a 'Celtic Church' in Wales (and Ireland), however, since the Church in the Celtic countries never constituted a separate entity but rather a geographical and cultural area in which the rationalization and reorganization of the Catholic Church were slow to arrive. The new integration into European ways brought change, but also quickened a Welsh national consciousness and represented a welcome expansion of Welsh cultural horizons. Nor did it necessarily prove entirely inimical to the indigenous religion, since a number of the Welsh Cistercian houses became bastions of Welsh culture and tradition. A Franciscan such as Madog ap Gwallter, and the anonymous Dominican author of *Food for the Soul* still reflect a deeply Celtic sensibility in their work despite the European character of their religious formation.

IRELAND

If the earliest origins of Celtic Christianity are to be found on mainland Britain, then its flowering was in Ireland. But the coming of Christianity to Ireland was markedly different from that of most of Europe in that Christianity was not a religion fostered or even approved by the state, since Ireland lay outside the confines of the Roman Empire. There is only scant and contradictory evidence for the earliest period of evangelization. Prosper of Aquitaine stated in his chronicle for the year 431 that 'Palladius was ordained by Pope Celestine and sent to the Irish believers in Christ as their first bishop'.[22] This has been taken to indicate the existence of a sizeable Christian community in Ireland prior to the missionary activity of Patrick, and indeed, it is entirely reasonable that just such a community existed, evolving through contact with the Celtic Christians of western Britain. It is notable that the foundations that are linked with the name of Palladius by tradition are all in Leinster, in the eastern part of Ireland, and thus a short sea journey away from the north western coast of Wales.

The most important documents for the life and work of Patrick are those by his own hand, the *Declaration* and the *Letter to Coroticus*, although these offer us only an uncertain picture of his provenance and background. It seems likely however that he was from a Christian family and came from western Britain (perhaps around Carlisle), from where he was snatched by an Irish raiding party and taken into slavery. He then escaped and made his way back to Britain, but returned later to Ireland with a deep commitment to work as a missionary there. It is likely that he carried out his ministry mainly in the north of Ireland, among the Ulaid, around the middle of the fifth century. Muirchú's *Life of Patrick* was written in Ireland in the seventh century and marks an upsurge of interest in the figure of Patrick after some two hundred years of silence. This trend culminates in the *Book of Armagh*, written in the north of Ireland in 807, which juxtaposes the writings of Patrick with Muirchú's *Life* and the prestigious *Life of St Martin of Tours*, in order to reinforce the claim of Armagh to the Primacy of all Ireland.

Although Patrick and Palladius were both bishops, and therefore represented the conventional diocesan structure of the Church of Gaul and elsewhere, the early evangelization of Ireland was largely marked by the spread of monasticism. From the beginning of the sixth century onwards we find an abundance of monastic foundations which are linked with individual saints such as Buithe (Monasterboice), Brigid (Kildare), Finnian (Clonard), Ciarán (Clonmacnois), Colum mac Crimthainn (Terryglass) and Brendan (Clonfert). The immediate origins of this monastic movement remain obscure, although the monastic and ascetical ideals which originated in Egypt in the fourth century may have come to Ireland from Gaul and Wales in the fifth. One reason that has been put forward for the rapid spread of monasticism in Ireland is that the monasteries were taken over into the kinship pattern of the ruling families. Certainly foundations often remained within the possession of a single family, and different monasteries within the same confederations were linked by the ties of kinship, as well as by more spiritual bonds. Early Irish society was deeply tribal in its structure, and it is very likely this that both prepared the ground for the ideal of spiritual community that came with the advent of monasticism, and influenced its form. It is certainly the case that we can observe in early Ireland diocesan structures which are based either upon the bishop, or upon the abbot or upon individuals who fulfill the office of both.

Among the many figures of early Irish monasticism, two in particular stand out. The first is Colum Cille (also known as Columba, 521/22–597), whose *Life* was written by his relative Adomnán some one hundred years after his death. Colum Cille was linked with the powerful Uí Néill tribe of northern Ireland and with the royal dynasty of Leinster. He founded monasteries in Derry and Durrow and, in 563, left Ireland to found a community off the Scottish coast at Iona. The island of Iona was still in the sphere of influence of the Picts at this point, although in course of time Irish language and culture would come to dominate the whole of the western part of Scotland. Iona itself became a greatly influential centre of Irish Christianity from where the religion of the Irish passed to Northumbria, where it took root at Lindisfarne and elsewhere, and even extended down into parts of East Anglia. The happy coalescence of Irish and early English culture and Christianity during this period, which led to what is termed the 'Insular' tradition, suffered a blow with the Synod of Whitby in 664 and controversy over the calculation of Easter. Nevertheless, even after this time, there was still much travel and interchange, with Irishmen holding senior posts in the English Church, Englishmen studying in Ireland or at Irish foundations, and visible co-operation in the fields of learning and art.[23]

The second leading figure of this period was Columbanus (543–615), who was born in Leinster, trained in Bangor (County Down) and left Ireland in 587 for Gaul. In contrast to Colum Cille, we have a good number of works from the pen of Columbanus which convey the picture of a passionate and able Christian leader. The works of Columbanus include a *Rule* and a *Penitential* (for monks and laity) and several impressive sermons and letters (pages 74–77). Columbanus was a principal mediator of Irish Christianity to the Continent and was the founder of important monasteries such as Luxeuil in south east France and Bobbio in northern Italy. The life-long and voluntary commitment of Columbanus to exile from his homeland is an outstanding example of *peregrinatio pro Christo*, or 'wandering for the sake of Christ', whereby a monk would cut himself off from his own extended family as an act of ascetical discipline. It is these wandering Irish monks in exile who were responsible for bringing Christianity to large areas of central Europe, as well as introducing to many other parts the advantages of Irish Christianity with its discipline, commitment and devotion to learning and the arts.

The religious vocation of these early monks was an ideal which was to reappear time and again in the history of the Irish Church. Its first and major resurgence occurred in the eighth century with the emergence of a movement known as the *Célí Dé*, or 'servants/friends of God'. The reform spread out from Munster in southern Ireland to other parts of the country and even beyond, to the western seaboard of Britain. It found its centre however in the Dublin area where leaders such as Maelrúain of Tallaght and Dublittir of Finglas inspired their followers with a love of renunciation and radical monasticism. The movement is associated also with the flowering of Irish religious poetry, especially the hermit poetry, and with the Stowe Missal, which is one of our chief sources for the early Irish liturgical tradition.

The Irish Church was badly disrupted from the ninth century onwards by Viking attacks, as was the case elsewhere in Europe, but it was the advent of the English and the Normans in the twelfth century which, as we have seen with Wales, led to the greater integration of Ireland into the forms and ways of continental Christianity.

THE MODERN PERIOD

Both the Reformation and the Catholic Counter-Reformation proved inimical to much that was distinctive in early Celtic Christianity. In addition, literacy and more developed technology, mobility of populations and of ideas lessened the remoteness and isolation of the Celtic countries. And yet important social, geographical and cultural forces have combined to ensure a far greater degree of continuity for the Celtic peoples than has been the case for their major European neighbours. In the first place, social change has come more slowly in the remote western parts of Scotland, Ireland, Brittany and Wales. It is here that the Celtic languages have been preserved, ensuring the survival of a vigorous oral culture for much of the modern period. Oral and geographically isolated cultures can be peculiarly shielded from the more radical change engendered by books and the written word within an urban environment, especially if — as has increasingly been the case in recent centuries — the very identity of a people is bound up with an oral, Celtic-language culture surviving in precarious opposition to the cultural innovation of the English or French-speaking world. In such a cultural milieu, moreover, especially when the English (or French) world is outrightly hostile to the survival of the oral medium, the forces of cultural conservatism can become far greater than in secure urban centres of cultural power. In that case there is a tendency for the bearers of the oral tradition precisely to anchor themselves in the past, as a form of self-definition, and as a secure point of orientation in a generally hostile cultural landscape.

It is legitimate to speak of the survival of a Celtic Christian tradition in the modern period therefore, but it is to the oral traditions that we must turn, generally those of poetry and song. In the case of Wales there are surprising parallels between the early monks, with their sense of community and emphasis upon religious poetry, and the culture of popular Methodism in the eighteenth century and later, when the chapels became the focus for a strongly communal spirituality which found its prime expression in powerful hymns such as those of Williams Pantycelyn (1717–1791) and Ann Griffiths (1776–1805). A Calvinist Methodist poet such as Thomas Jones (1756–1820) still stands within an identifiable poetic tradition going back to the Middle Ages. But it is the religious songs of the Highlands and Western Isles of Scotland, which were gathered by Alexander Carmichael (1832–1912) during the second half of the nineteenth century and published initially in two volumes in 1900 as the *Carmina Gadelica*, which are perhaps the finest example of the survival of a distinctively Celtic religious spirit in the modern world.

Alexander Carmichael, a Gaelic speaker from the Island of Lismore near Oban in Scotland, worked for the Customs and Excise Department, which gave him an extensive familiarity with the western Highlands and Islands of the Outer and Inner Hebrides where, between 1855 and 1899, he collected an enormous amount of oral Gaelic material. After Carmichael's death, a further three volumes of the *Carmina Gadelica* were published at intervals, all of which were based upon Carmichael's original notes.[24] In order to evaluate his achievement it is important to remember the social and historical context in which Carmichael worked. He lived at a time when the status of Gaelic culture was particularly low and he belonged to a literary and national movement which was keen both to protect the interests of Gaelic culture and to establish its credentials. If the items in the *Ortha na Gaidheal/Carmina Gadelica* sometimes seem more literary and polished than might be expected in oral material of this kind, then this probably reflects the editor's extensive editing due to his understandable desire that the material be accorded its own dignity.

The situation in Ireland with respect to Irish language culture showed certain parallels. Douglas Hyde (1860–1949), born into an Anglican family in County Roscommon, was founder and President of the Gaelic League; he served also as the first President of an independent Ireland (1938–45). A man of extensive interests and talents, Hyde published plays, poetry (historical and literary), as well as academic works. He is, however, perhaps best remembered for the bilingual collection of songs and stories, originally printed in various journals, which comprise *The Songs of Connacht*. These included love songs, drinking songs, songs in praise of women, various tales and religious material. *The Religious Songs of Connacht*, from which the selections in this volume are taken, was first published in book form in 1906. Like Carmichael, Hyde was an admirer of the Gaelic-speaking peasantry, and recognized the wealth of oral literature which was commonly disregarded by the educated, and in danger of disappearing along with the Irish language itself.

One marked difference between the Irish and Scottish situation was that many more Irish texts were recorded in manuscript, and so the line of demarcation between a purely oral and a written culture in Ireland is not always easily drawn. Some poems by the thirteenth-century bard Donagha More O'Daly, for instance, were still learnt and recited orally by people in the nineteenth century. As Hyde comments, 'They were as well known in the province of Munster as they were in Connacht, and some of them are in the mouths of the people to this very day.' In terms of content, there are both similarities and differences between the *Carmina Gadelica* and the *Religious Songs of Connacht*. Both include charms, prayers for protection against the evil eye or fairies, herbal cures, curses, tales concerning Irish mythological characters such as Ossian and Fionn, and saints, and both contain a number of the same traditional Catholic prayers. But the *Religious Songs of Connacht* also contains a large body of literature concerning priests, a genre absent from the *Carmina Gadelica*. There is also far more sentimental Catholic piety in the Irish material, and long moralistic tales which, if known in Scotland, Carmichael either failed or chose not to record.

The final section of this volume is an anthology of modern poetry from the Celtic countries, which is set in context with an introductory essay. For many, it is in poems that something vital remains of an ancient tradition, and poets, more than most, often have reason to explore the roots of the tradition of which they themselves are a part. The Celtic cultures remain surprisingly responsive to the work of poets, who enjoy a popularity and a fame that living English or French poets can only envy. Their work can thus become a point of transmission to a community of an earlier way of seeing the world, revitalized and transformed by the personal art and creativity of the individual poet.

Celtic Christianity Today

There is a widespread interest throughout the Western world in the spirituality of indigenous peoples, from Native Americans to the highland culture of the Philippines. But a personal engagement with such religious systems leads to precisely the same problem facing those who are attracted to the spirituality of the Celtic peoples. How can we share in something we much admire when we ourselves are not part of that particular culture which is the very foundation of the spirituality? How can one participate in a 'Celtic Christianity' if one is living in New York or London, and therefore unable to engage with the particular spirituality of place which is so characteristic a part of the Celtic tradition? For the majority of people who actually live through the medium of a Celtic language the great Celtic Christian civilizations of the Middle Ages, even if ever present in place and personal names, are far removed from the daily concerns of finding work, coping with unemployment, dealing with English- (or French-)speaking inward migration, and the continual struggle to preserve a language and community life in the face of sometimes seemingly overwhelming odds. And yet, even if an authentic Celtic Christian culture is in a certain sense exclusive, and to a large degree a thing of the past, there are still all kinds of ways in which we may learn from this inheritance and make its wisdom our own.

The first thing we can learn from Celtic Christianity concerns its physicality. Many early monks were inspired by the monastic and ascetical ideals of the Egyptian desert and sought to re-enact the achievements of Anthony and his followers on the islands and mountains of their homeland. Many took themselves into exile, 'crucifying their body on the blue waves', like Columba. But perhaps the chief expression of this spirit was the penitential tradition, which laid great stress upon the voluntary acceptance of physical discomfort and deprivation as a way to God. Although penance is altogether out of favour today, the typically Celtic emphasis upon it has something important to teach us. In the first place, it reminds us that we are embodied beings. There is much within traditional Christianity, particularly in some of its Protestant forms, which seems to stress the reception of the gospel in the mind to the exclusion of the body. Yet neither is early Celtic penitential discipline to be identified with the refinements of self-mortification that we associate with Post-Tridentine Catholicism. It is not so much the unwholesome desire to punish oneself or one's body that we encounter in early Celtic penitential texts (although this certainly also exists) but rather a sense of spiritual opportunity — that glory is the reward of 'long penance, daily' (page 53). Penance then is a way of including the body in our dialogue with God. The dynamic here is different from our own. We generally have little sense of the need for penance today, and equally little sense of the reality of glory.

Linked perhaps with the stress upon physicality, there is a persistent emphasis in the Celtic texts upon the place of nature within the Christian revelation. We see this in a number of saints' *Lives*, where creatures spontaneously offer their services to the Christian saint, or seek refuge with him or her (page 65); but it is no less evident in early Irish and Welsh poems which may well have been written by monks. There the natural world is the context in which the poet delights and for which and with which he offers praise (page 28). It is certainly this acknowledgement and affirmation of nature which is one of the most distinctive aspects of Celtic Christianity. In the classical model, by way of contrast, the natural world, if it is mentioned at all, is in nearly every instance that which the Christian saint merely *controls*. The Celtic Christian recognition of the place of nature, and refusal to set up sharp oppositions between the worlds of grace and humanity and the natural realm, is undoubtedly of great importance to those who seek to restore a more positive and responsible relation between human beings and the environment in our own day.

Furthermore, we find in Celtic Christianity a valuing of the creative imagination of the individual, evident in a particular way in the High Crosses, in the tradition of illumination which culminates in the Book of Kells and in the Christian bardic tradition. Of course, other cultures have produced religious art of the highest quality, but the place of the scribe within early Irish society and the belief of Welsh poets that the Holy Spirit was their direct inspiration remind us that the creative arts stood not at the margins of the Church but at its very centre.

Finally, Celtic Christianity is filled with the spirit of community, whether in terms of monasticism or the close-knit rural societies of the post-medieval world. The bards too had a public function and spoke directly to a community, as many poets still do. And from a theological point of view the Trinity, which is the ultimate ground and model of community, held a special place in Celtic religious life, being the primary way in which most Celtic thinkers and artists understood the Godhead. Although the sense of community of the early Celts was rooted primarily in the extended family and tribe, there are hints also of a more universalist understanding, mediated through the Church and contained in particular in reflections upon the origins of the human body. We can read texts such as the *Creation of Adam* and *The Evernew Tongue* (pages 79–81) as conveying an understanding of the human person as being essentially in community with the natural world, with the whole of humanity and with the body of the resurrected Christ. Community is of vital concern for us too, on both a local and a universal level, since Western society has so often been caught between rampant individualism on the one hand and aggressive nationalism on the other.

In sum therefore, the distinctive tenor of Celtic Christianity is one of a life-affirming integration which finds its theological centre in the vision of God as divine creativity and community, which is the Christian doctrine of the Trinity. Just as they were eclectic in their art and their learning, the early Celts perceived themselves to be participants within a total environment in which the cosmic and the human, the natural and the divine, strive towards a visible unity. It is this vision that survives, albeit fitfully, in the Celtic cultures after the decline of the golden age. Of course, not all aspects of Celtic Christianity appeal to us equally today. We have less time for the apocalyptic tradition, which was so strong and in which the Celtic imagination engaged powerfully with Judgement and the end of time. Their severe asceticism can also seem harsh to us. And we are often too optimistic regarding the place of women in Celtic society which, despite the wholesome affirmation of the feminine through powerful female figures such as Brigid, was probably only marginally less patriarchal than other societies of the day. But, finally, we still turn to an earlier age, to the remote margins of north west Europe, and find there precious *possibilities* of Christian consciousness and existence which yet retain their power and which the churches of Christ have neglected for far too long.

A Note on the Selection

The sources for Celtic Christianity are very diverse, and certainly much still remains in manuscript awaiting the attention of editors. The pieces included here represent an attempt to reflect something of that diversity, but the present authors are well aware of the inevitable inadequacy of any such anthology. Much has been left out which others perhaps would have wished to include, but many pieces appear here in new translation, some indeed appearing in English for the first time. In the case of the *Carmina Gadelica*, already well anthologized, Carmichael's own notes have often been included since these cast an important light upon the lived, social context of the pieces. We have also chosen not to emend Carmichael's slightly outdated style in the belief that these self-consciously literary translations have themselves become part of the Celtic inheritance. In the case of the modern poetry, our selection has been pared down due to the substantial costs of reprinting the work of established poets. In making our selection of texts, from all periods, we have chosen the work of authors who either spoke a Celtic language or who can be said to have had a first-hand familiarity with a Celtic-language tradition. Our choice of texts also inevitably reflects our own interests and, unashamedly, the understanding of Celtic Christianity that we have evolved. The fact that an alternative selection of texts could be made which would cast Celtic Christianity in a very different, and probably less positive, light does not undermine the authenticity of our texts but is a reminder that the Celtic tradition we have attempted to identify is more a patterning of spiritual images and ideas than an institutionalized entity with firm boundaries.

Notes

1 This interest is not new. In the late eighteenth century, for instance, the Welsh bard and antiquarian Edward Williams (1747–1826), who is better known by his bardic name, Iolo Morganwg, 'discovered' documents purporting to contain ancient druidic traditions, and on the strength of these writings instituted the 'Gorsedd of the Bards of the Island of Britain'. The *Gorsedd*, consisting of Wales' leading literary figures, still plays a central role in the Welsh National Eisteddfod. In Scotland we have the parallel of James 'Ossian' Macpherson's 'translations' of the Gaelic poetry, published as *Fingal* in 1761, which were also fictitious, owing more to the Romantic Movement than to any extant oral literature. By way of contrast, the serious comparative study of Celtic languages and peoples published by Edward Lhuyd half a century earlier in 1707 (*Archaeologia Britannica*) aroused very little popular interest. It is the *need* to establish links with a Celtic past, real or imagined, which determines the level of public interest and enthusiasm at a particular point in time. (For an account of the search for 'Celticity' in a Scottish context see Malcolm Chapman, *The Gaelic Vision in Scottish Culture*, Croom Helm, London 1978).
2 Colin Renfrew, *Archaeology and Language* (Harmondsworth 1987), pp. 211–249, and Edward Lhuyd (above). The *Grammatica Celtica*, a comparative grammar of the Celtic languages by Johann Kaspar Zeuss, appeared in 1853.
3 See especially Kathleen Hughes, 'The Celtic Church: is this a valid Concept?' in *Cambridge Medieval Celtic Studies* 1 (1981), pp. 1–20 and Wendy Davies, 'The Myth of the Celtic Church' in Nancy Edwards and Alan Lane, eds., *The Early Church in Wales and the West* (Oxbow 1992), pp. 12–21.
4 Matthew Parker, the Archbishop of Canterbury, published his *De Antiquitate Britannicae Ecclesiae* in 1572 in which he argued for a continuity between the British Church in the Celtic period and the Church of the Reformation. This was one of the earliest such works, and many similar volumes were to follow. For an overview of the field, see Glanmor Williams' essay 'Some Protestant Views of Early British Church History' in his *Welsh Reformation Essays* (Cardiff 1967), pp. 207–219.
5 On Celtic society in general, see T. G. E. Powell, *The Celts* (London 1958), Nora Chadwick, *The Celts* (London 1971) and Barry Cunliffe, *The Celtic World* (London 1992).
6 Classical accounts of the Celts are reproduced in J. J. Tierney, *The Celtic Ethnography of Posidonius*, Proceedings of the Royal Irish Academy, Vol. 60, Section C, No. 5 (Dublin 1960), pp.189–275.
7 There are good discussions of Celtic religion in the general studies noted above, to which may be added: Graham Webster, *The British Celts and their Gods under Rome* (London 1986), Jean Louis Brunaux, *The Celtic Gauls: Gods, Rites and Sanctuaries* (English translation London 1988) and Miranda Green, *The Gods of the Celts* (Stroud 1986).
8 Fiona Bowie, 'African Traditional Religions' in *Contemporary Religions: A World Guide*, edited by Ian Harris, Stuart Mews, Paul Morris and John Shepherd (London 1992), pp. 70–72. It is equally possible that the skulls preserved by early Celts were war trophies, kept for their inherent powers (see, for instance, G. W. Trompf, *Melanesian Religion* (Cambridge 1991) pp.45–46).

9 There is more than a hint of the divine possession of bards in the Taliesin tradition, particularly as we find this in the 'druidic' poems from the *Book of Taliesin*. See also Patrick K. Ford's introduction to *Ystoria Taliesin* (Cardiff 1992), and J. E. Caerwyn Williams, *The Irish Literary Tradition* (Cardiff and Belmont, Mass. 1992), pp. 21–49.

10 *Dictionary of the Irish Language*, Royal Irish Academy, s.v. *tuigen*.

11 The Sri Lankan theologian, Aloysius Pieris, has described this process of *inculturation* in which he makes the observation that world (which he calls 'metacosmic') religions spread by fusing with indigenous (or 'cosmic') religions, and are thus to some extent transformed by them.

12 Charles Thomas, *Christianity in Roman Britain to AD 500* (London 1981), pp. 42–50.

13 Ibid., pp. 113–122 and pp. 104–106.

14 M. Forthomme Nicholson seeks to place Pelagius within the Celtic tradition in his article 'Celtic Theology: Pelagius' in James P. Mackey, ed., *An Introduction to Celtic Christianity* (Edinburgh 1989), pp. 386–413.

15 But there is an interesting account in the *Life of Beuno* of how the saint left a disciple *in situ* before fleeing from the advancing Saxons. See also Patrick Sims-Williams, *Religion and Literature in Western England, 600–800* (Cambridge 1990), pp. 79–83 and Charles Thomas, *Christianity in Roman Britain*, pp. 249–294.

16 Kathleen Hughes (ed. D. Dumville), *Celtic Britain in the Early Middle Ages* (Suffolk 1980), pp. 1–21.

17 Dafydd Jenkins, 'Gwalch-Welsh' in *Cambridge Medieval Celtic Studies* 19 (1990), pp. 56–67.

18 Wendy Davies, *Wales in the Early Middle Ages* (Leicester 1982), p. 158.

19 The hermits of the Egyptian desert, Paul of Thebes and Anthony the Great, were popular iconographic figures on High Crosses in Ireland.

20 Nora Chadwick, 'Intellectual Life in West Wales in the Last Days of the Celtic Church' in K. Hughes, C. Brooke, K. Jackson, N. K. Chadwick, eds., *Studies in the Early British Church* (Cambridge 1958), p. 161.

21 A. O. H. Jarman, ed., *Llyfr Du Caerfyrddin* (Cardiff 1982), p. 9.

22 For this and other relevant texts, see Liam de Paor, *St Patrick's World* (Four Courts Press, Co. Dublin 1993), p. 79.

23 Michael Richter, *The Enduring Tradition* (London 1988), p. 95.

24 See Appendix on 'Sources and Acknowledgements', pp. 233–37.

Medieval Religious
Poetry

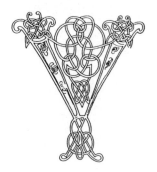

1 ALMIGHTY CREATOR

A poem of praise to the Creator in which the poet proclaims his own celebratory gift. It is worth noting the cosmic dimension of the poem and the poet's dismissive attitude to literacy in the third stanza. Circa ninth century. Old Welsh.

Almighty Creator, it is you who have made
the land and the sea . . .

The world cannot comprehend in song bright and melodious,
even though the grass and trees should sing,
all your wonders, O true Lord!

The Father created the world by a miracle;
it is difficult to express its measure.
Letters cannot contain it, letters cannot comprehend it.

Jesus created for the hosts of Christendom,
with miracles when he came,
resurrection through his nature.

He who made the wonder of the world,
will save us, has saved us.
It is not too great a toil to praise the Trinity.

Clear and high in the perfect assembly,
Let us praise above the nine grades of angels
The sublime and blessed Trinity.

Purely, humbly, in skilful verse,
I should love to give praise to the Trinity,
according to the greatness of his power.

God has required of the host in this world
who are his, that they should at all times,
all together, fear the Trinity.

The one who has power, wisdom and dominion
above heaven, below heaven, completely;
it is not too great toil to praise the Son of Mary.

2 GLORIOUS LORD

Another cosmic poem of praise in which the author shows an awareness of his own role as praise-poet. This poem is evidently dependent upon Psalm 148 or the Benedicite of Daniel 3.23ff, or both. The 'three springs' — sun, moon and sea — of line 5 belong to native Celtic cosmology. We should note also the combination of motifs from the world of nature, human society and the Church. Tenth to eleventh century. Early Middle Welsh.

Hail to you, glorious Lord!
May church and chancel praise you,
May chancel and church praise you,
May plain and hillside praise you,
May the three springs praise you,
Two higher than the wind and one above the earth,
May darkness and light praise you,
May the cedar and sweet fruit-tree praise you.
Abraham praised you, the founder of faith,
May life everlasting praise you,
May the birds and the bees praise you,
May the stubble and the grass praise you.
Aaron and Moses praised you,
May male and female praise you,
May the seven days and the stars praise you,
May the lower and upper air praise you,
May books and letters praise you,
May the fish in the river praise you,
May thought and action praise you,
May the sand and the earth praise you,
May all the good things created praise you,
And I too shall praise you, Lord of glory,
Hail to you, glorious Lord!

3 *THE SCRIBE IN THE WOODS*

The following was written in the margin of a manuscript of the Latin grammarian Priscian, which was copied by Irish monks at St Gall in the first half of the ninth century. Old Irish.

A hedge of trees surrounds me, a blackbird's lay sings to me, praise I
    shall not conceal,
Above my lined book the trilling of the birds sings to me.
A clear-voiced cuckoo sings to me in a grey cloak from the tops of
    bushes,
May the Lord save me from Judgement; well do I write under the
    greenwood.

4 *A HYMN OF PRAISE*

The ultimate origin of these stanzas is the doxology found in Revelation 7.12, where we are told that the angels who surround the throne of God worship him and sing: 'Praise and glory and wisdom, thanksgiving and honour, power and might, be to our God for ever and ever.' Circa ninth century. Old Irish.

Blessing and brightness,
Wisdom, thanksgiving,
Great power and might
To the King who rules over all.

Glory and honour and goodwill,
Praise and the sublime song of minstrels,
Overflowing love from every heart
To the King of Heaven and Earth.

To the chosen Trinity has been joined
Before all, after all, universal
Blessing and everlasting blessing,
Blessing everlasting and blessing.

5 THE LORD OF CREATION

This beautifully crafted poem dates from the ninth century. Old Irish.

> Let us adore the Lord,
> Maker of marvellous works,
> Bright heaven with its angels,
> And on earth the white-waved sea.

6 PRAISE TO THE TRINITY

This is a hymn which may possibly have had some kind of para-liturgical usage. Again the cosmic dimension of praise is stressed, as is God the Creator. The reference at the end of the second stanza is to Paul of Thebes and Anthony the Great, two early Fathers of the Egyptian desert. In this poem we again see the interweaving of the social, natural and Christian world. The 'five cities' are the 'cities of the plain', which include Sodom and Gomorrah from Genesis 9.29. Tenth to eleventh century. Early Middle Welsh.

> I praise the threefold
> Trinity as God,
> Who is one and three,
> A single power in unity,
> His attributes a single mystery,
> One God to praise.
> Great King, I praise you,
> Great your glory.
> Your praise is true;
> I am the one who praises you.
> Poetry's welfare
> Is in Elohim's care.
> Hail to you, O Christ,
> Father, Son
> And Holy Ghost,
> Our Adonai.
>
> I praise two,
> Who is one and two,

Who is truly three,
To doubt him is not easy,
Who made fruit and flowing water
And all variety,
God is his name as two,
Godly his words,
God is his name as three,
Godly his power,
God is his name as one,
The God of Paul and Anthony.

I praise the one,
Who is two and one,
Who is three together,
Who is God himself,
He made Mars and Luna.
Man and woman,
The difference in sound between
Shallow water and the deep.
He made the hot and the cold,
The sun and the moon,
The word in the tablet,
And the flame in the taper,
Love in our senses,
A girl, dear and tender,
And burned five cities
Because of false union.

7 PRAISE TO GOD

In the following poem Christ is depicted as a conquering hero, and the text consciously imitates the language of the secular heroic tradition. Words denoting action and achievement are repeatedly used. In the 'perfect rite' and the anticipation of the 'feast . . . in Paradise' there also seem to be echoes of the Eucharistic sacrifice. The opening phrase of the poem, with its mix of Welsh and Latin, also has specifically liturgical associations. The theological erudition of the poem suggests that its author may well have been a priest. Tenth to eleventh century. Early Middle Welsh.

In the name of the Lord, mine to praise, of great praise,
I shall praise God, great the triumph of his love,
God who defended us, God who made us, God who saved us,
God our hope, perfect and honourable, beautiful his blessing.
We are in God's power, God above, Trinity's king.
God proved himself our liberation by his suffering,
God came to be imprisoned in humility.
Wise Lord, who will free us by Judgement Day,
Who will lead us to the feast through his mercy and sanctity
In Paradise, in pure release from the burden of sin,
Who will bring us salvation through penance and the five wounds.
Terrible grief, God defended us when he took on flesh.
Man would be lost if the perfect rite had not redeemed him.
Through the cross, blood-stained, came salvation to the world.
Christ, strong shepherd, his honour shall not fail.

8 PRAISING GOD AT THE BEGINNING
AND END

This poem shows a typical concern with the inevitability of death, and is an appeal to God for mercy. The poet urges his monastic audience to follow their ascetical lifestyle more vigorously. Tenth to eleventh century. Early Middle Welsh.

He shall not refuse or reject whoever strives
To praise God at the beginning and end of the day,
Mary's only son, the Lord of kings.
Like the sun he shall come, from east to north.
Mary, Christ's mother, chief of maidens,
Call for the sake of your great mercy
Upon your son to chase away our sin.
God above us, God before us, may the God who rules,
Heaven's king, grant us a share of his mercy.
Royal-hearted one, peace between us
Without rejection, may I make amends
For the wrong I have done before going
To my tomb, my green grave,
My place of rest, in the dark without candle,
My burial place, my recess, my repose,

After enjoying the horses and new mead,
Feasting and women's company.
I shall not sleep; I shall consider my end.
We live in a world of wretched vanity,
Which shall pass away like leaves from a tree.
Woe to the miser who gathers great wealth.
Though the world's course lets him be,
He shall, unless he gives all to God,
Face peril at his end.
The fool does not know how to tremble in his heart,
Nor to rise early in the morning, pray and prostrate,
Nor to chant prayers or petition mercy.
He will pay in the end bitterly
For his pomp, his pride and arrogance.
For the toads and snakes he feeds his body,
And for lions, and he performs iniquity,
But death shall enter in and greedily
Devour him, bearing him away.
Old age draws near and senility;
Your hearing, your sight, your teeth grow weak,
And the skin of your fingers is wrinkly,
It is old age and grey hairs that cause this.
May Michael intercede for us with the Lord of Heaven
For a share of his mercy.

9 GRANT ME TEARS, O LORD

The tears of compunction are the theme of this poem, which underlines the extent to which the true monastic vocation is based on personal conversion and repentance. Circa tenth century, or later. Old Irish, with later features.

Grant me tears, O Lord, to blot out my sins; may I not cease from them, O God, until I have been purified.

May my heart be burned by the fire of redemption; grant me tears with purity for Mary and Íte.

When I contemplate my sins, grant me tears always, for great are the claims of tears on cheeks.

Grant me tears when rising, grant me tears when resting, beyond your every gift altogether for love of you, Mary's Son.

Grant me tears in bed to moisten my pillow, so that his dear ones may help to cure the soul.

Grant me contrition of heart so that I may not be in disgrace; O Lord, protect me and grant me tears.

For the dalliance I had with women, who did not reject me, grant me tears, O Creator, flowing in streams from my eyes.

For my anger and my jealousy and my pride, a foolish deed, in pools from my inmost parts bring forth tears.

My falsehoods and my lying and my greed, grievous the three, to banish them all from me, O Mary, grant me tears.

10 *ALL ALONE IN MY LITTLE CELL*

This poem conveys the spirit of asceticism that motivated many of the early monks. Death is here pictured both as the inevitable end of life, and as a release from sin and penance. Eighth or ninth century. Old Irish.

All alone in my little cell, without the company of a single person; precious has been the pilgrimage before going to meet death.

A hidden secluded little hut, for the forgiveness of my sins: an upright, untroubled conscience towards holy heaven.

Sanctifying the body by good habits, trampling like a man upon it: with weak and tearful eyes for the forgiveness of my passions.

Passions weak and withered, renouncing this wretched world; pure and eager thoughts; let this be a prayer to God.

Heartfelt lament towards cloudy heaven, sincere and truly devout confessions, swift showers of tears.

A cold and anxious bed, like the lying down of a doomed man: a brief, apprehensive sleep; invocations frequent and early.

My food as befits my station, precious has been the captivity: my dinner, without doubt, would not make me full-blooded.

Dry bread weighed out, well we bow the head; water of the many-coloured hillside, that is the drink I would take.

A bitter meagre dinner; diligently feeding the sick; keeping off strife and visits; a calm, serene conscience.

It would be desirable, a pure and holy blemish: cheeks withered and sunken, a shrivelled leathery skin.

Treading the paths of the gospel; singing psalms at every Hour; an end of talking and long stories; constant bending of knees.

May my Creator visit me, my Lord, my King; may my spirit seek him in the everlasting kingdom in which he is.

Let this be the end of vice in the enclosures of churches; a lovely little cell among the graves, and I alone therein.

All alone in my little cell, all alone thus; alone I came into the world, alone I shall go from it.

If on my own I have sinned through pride of this world, hear me wail for it all alone, O God!

11 *ON THE FLIGHTINESS OF THOUGHT*

This poem is taken from the manuscript known as the Leabhar Breac, *or* 'Speckled Book' *of the early fifteenth century. The poem again conveys the theme of monastic repentance as the monk regrets the inconstancy of his thought and entreats God to save him. The sevenfold Spirit is a reference to the gifts of the Holy Spirit, which are the virtues. Circa tenth century. Middle Irish.*

Shame on my thoughts, how they stray from me! I fear great danger from this on the Day of Eternal Judgement.

During the psalms they wander on a path that is not right: they run, they distract, they misbehave before the eyes of the great God.

Through eager gatherings, through companies of lewd wowen, through woods, through cities — swifter they are than the wind.

One moment they follow ways of loveliness, and the next ways of riotous shame — no lie!

Without a ferry or a false step they cross every sea: swiftly they leap in one bound from earth to heaven.

They run — not a course of great wisdom — near, far: following paths along paths of great foolishness they reach their home.

Though one should try to bind them or put shackles on their feet, they are neither constant nor inclined to rest a while.

Neither the edge of a sword nor the stripe of lash will subdue them; as slippery as an eel's tale they elude my grasp.

Neither lock nor well-constructed dungeon, nor any fetter on earth, neither stronghold nor sea nor bleak fastness restrains them from their course.

O beloved truly chaste Christ, to whom every eye is clear, may the grace of the sevenfold Spirit come to keep them, to hold them in check!

Rule this heart of mind, O swift God of the elements, that you may be my love, and that I may do your will!

That I may reach Christ with his chosen companions, that we may be together: they are neither fickle nor inconstant — they are not as I am.

12 *MAYTIME IS THE FAIREST SEASON*

The author of this poem again contemplates death and the fragility of life. His 'brothers' are probably his fellow-monks who may also be members of his own family. Tenth to eleventh century. Early Middle Welsh.

Maytime is the fairest season,
With its loud bird-song and green trees,
When the plough is in the furrow
And the oxen under the yoke,
When the sea is green,
And the land many colours.

But when cuckoos sing on the tops
Of the lovely trees, my sadness deepens,
The smoke stings and my grief is clear
Since my brothers have passed away.

On the hill and in the valley,
On the islands of the sea,
Whichever path you take,
You shall not hide from blessed Christ.

It was our wish, our Brother, our way,
To go to the land of your exile.
Seven saints and seven score and seven hundred
Went to the one court with blessed Christ,
And were without fear.

The gift I ask, may it not be denied me,
Is peace between myself and God.
May I find the way to the gate of glory,
May I not be sad, O Christ, in your court.

13 *THE PATH I WALK*

This very early accentual poem survives in a fifteenth century manuscript where it is attributed to Colum Cille: 'This is the protection of Colum Cille. And it is to be said at bed-time and on rising, and when going on a journey, and is of marvellous avail.' It is full of the language of trade and, whether by Colum Cille or not, may reflect the experience of a pilgrim priest, seeking souls for God. Sixth to eighth century. Old Irish.

The path I walk, Christ walks it. May the land in which I am be without
  sorrow.
May the Trinity protect me wherever I stay, Father, Son and Holy
  Spirit.
Bright angels walk with me — dear presence — in every dealing.
In every dealing I pray them that no one's poison may reach me.
The ninefold people of heaven of holy cloud, the tenth force of the stout
  earth.
Favourable company, they come with me, so that the Lord may not be
  angry with me.
May I arrive at every place, may I return home; may the way in which I
  spend be a way without loss.
May every path before me be smooth, man, woman and child welcome
  me.
A truly good journey! Well does the fair Lord show us a course, a path.

14 *MAY THIS JOURNEY BE EASY*

The following is a blessing for a journey. Tenth century or later. Middle Irish.

May this journey be easy, may it be a journey of profit in my hands!
  Holy Christ against demons, against weapons, against killings!

May Jesus and the Father, may the Holy Spirit sanctify us!
May the mysterious God be not hidden in darkness, may the bright
  King save us!

May the cross of Christ's body and Mary guard us on the road!
May it not be unlucky for us, may it be successful and easy!

15 *THE SAINTS' CALENDAR OF ADOMNÁN*

The following is a prayer to the saints who preside over the different seasons. Adomnán, to whom the work is attributed in one manuscript tradition, was the

ninth abbot of Iona and the author of the Life of Columba. *'God's fosterling'*
is a reference to Christ, and the 'other calendar' is that of Oengus, with which
the poet favourably compares his own. The final stanza may be a later addition.
Old Irish, with some Middle Irish forms.

The saints of the four seasons,
I long to pray to them,
May they save me from torments,
The saints of the whole year!

The saints of the glorious springtime,
May they be with me
By the will
Of God's fosterling.

The saints of the dry summer,
About them is my poetic frenzy,
That I may come from this land
To Jesus, son of Mary.

The saints of the beautiful autumn,
I call upon a company not unharmonious,
That they may draw near to me,
With Mary and Michael.

The saints of the winter I pray to,
May they be with me against the throng of demons,
Around Jesus of the mansions,
The Sprit holy, heavenly.

The other calendar,
Which noble saints will have,
Though it has more verses,
It does not have more saints.

I beseech the saints of the earth,
I beseech all the angels,
I beseech God himself, both when rising and lying down,
Whatever I do or say, that I may dwell in the heavenly land.

16 *A PRAYER TO THE ARCHANGELS FOR EVERY DAY OF THE WEEK*

This early poem again invokes supernatural protection and well shows the importance of the Archangels to the early medieval Irish mind, as beings who exercised benign influence upon human life. Circa ninth century. Old Irish.

May Gabriel be with me on Sundays, and the power of the King of
    Heaven.
May Gabriel be with me always that evil may not come to me nor injury.

Michael on Monday I speak of, my mind is set on him,
Not with anyone do I compare him but with Jesus, Mary's son.

If it be Tuesday, Raphael I mention, until the end comes, for my help.
One of the seven whom I beseech, as long as I am on the field of the
    world.

May Uriel be with me on Wednesdays, the abbot with high nobility,
Against wound and against danger, against the sea of rough wind.

Sariel on Thursday I speak of, against the swift waves of the sea,
Against every evil that comes to a man, against every disease that seizes
    him.

On the day of the second fast, Rumiel — a clear blessing — I have loved,
I say only the truth, good the friend I have taken.

May Panchel be with me on Saturdays, as long as I am in the yellow-
    coloured world,
May sweet Mary, together with her friend, deliver me from strangers.

May the Trinity protect me! May the Trinity defend me!
May the Trinity save me from every hurt, from every danger.

17 *THREE WISHES I ASK*

This short poem is beautifully expressive of the spirit of renunciation which characterized early Irish monasticism. Circa ninth century. Old Irish.

Three wishes I ask of the King when I part from my body: may I have
   nothing to confess, may I have no enemy, may I own nothing!

Three wishes I ask this day of the King, ruler of suns: may I have no
   dignity or honours that may lead me into torment!

May I do no work without reward before the Christ of this world! May
   God take my soul when it is most pure! Finally, may I not be guilty
   when my three wishes have been spoken!

18 ST PATRICK'S BREASTPLATE

*The following stanzas are from a text which has long been attributed to St
Patrick and is sometimes known as* The Deer's Cry. *It actually dates in its
present form from a period several centuries after the death of the saint and it is
the classic example of a* Lorica *or 'breastplate' prayer which invokes divine
protection for the speaker's life and body. This is an ancient monastic practice
which reflects the words of St Paul in Ephesians 6.11–18. Eighth century. Old
Irish.*

> I rise today
>> in power's strength, invoking the Trinity,
>> believing in threeness,
>> confessing the oneness,
>> of creation's Creator.

> I rise today
>> in the power of Christ's birth and baptism,
>> in the power of his crucifixion and burial,
>> in the power of his rising and ascending,
>> in the power of his descending and judging.

> I rise today
>> in the power of the love of cherubim,
>> in the obedience of angels
>> and service of archangels,
>> in hope of rising to receive the reward,
>> in the prayers of patriarchs,
>> in the predictions of prophets,

in the preaching of apostles,
in the faith of confessors,
in the innocence of holy virgins,
in the deeds of the righteous.

I rise today
in heaven's might,
in sun's brightness,
in moon's radiance,
in fire's glory,
in lightning's quickness,
in wind's swiftness,
in sea's depth,
in earth's stability,
in rock's fixity.

I rise today
with the power of God to pilot me,
God's strength to sustain me,
God's wisdom to guide me,
God's eye to look ahead for me,
God's ear to hear me,
God's word to speak for me,
God's hand to protect me,
God's way before me,
God's shield to defend me,
God's host to deliver me:
from snares of devils,
from evil temptations,
from nature's failings,
from all who wish to harm me,
far or near,
alone and in a crowd.

Around me I gather today all these powers
against every cruel and merciless force
to attack my body and soul,
against the charms of false prophets,
the black laws of paganism,
the false laws of heretics,

the deceptions of idolatry,
against spells cast by women, smiths and druids,
and all unlawful knowledge
that harms the body and soul.

May Christ protect me today
against poison and burning,
against drowning and wounding,
so that I may have abundant reward;
Christ with me, Christ before me, Christ behind me;
Christ within me, Christ beneath me, Christ above me;
Christ to right of me, Christ to left of me;
Christ in my lying, Christ in my sitting, Christ in my rising;
Christ in the heart of all who think of me,
Christ on the tongue of all who speak to me,
Christ in the eye of all who see me,
Christ in the ear of all who hear me.

I rise today
in power's strength, invoking the Trinity,
believing in threeness,
confessing the oneness,
of creation's Creator.

For to the Lord belongs salvation,
and to the Lord belongs salvation
and to Christ belongs salvation.

May your salvation, Lord, be with us always.

19 *ALEXANDER'S BREASTPLATE*

The following poem is described as a Lorica, *or 'breastplate', and is— wrongly—attributed to Alexander the Great, whose exploits were made known in the medieval world through the writings of the historian Orosius. The poem is typical in its evocation of the power of Christ as a defence against all ills. Twelfth or thirteenth century. Middle Welsh.*

On the face of the world
There was not born
His equal.
Three-person God,
Trinity's only Son,
Gentle and strong.
Son of the Godhead,
Son of humanity,
Only Son of wonder.
The Son of God is a refuge,
Mary's Son˜a blessed sanctuary,
A noble child was seen.
Great his splendour,
Great Lord and God,
In the place of glory.
From the line of Adam
And Abraham
We were born.
From David's line,
The fulfilment of prophecy,
The host was born again.
By his word he saved the blind and the deaf,
From all suffering,
The ragged,
Foolish sinners,
And those of impure mind.
Let us rise up
To meet the Trinity,
Following our salvation.
Christ's cross is bright,
A shining breastplate
Against all harm,
Against all our enemies may it be strong:
The place of our protection.

20 THE HOLY MAN

These words occur on the margin of Codex S. Pauli *and are spoken by the Devil to St Moling. Eighth century. Old Irish.*

He is a bird round which a trap closes,
He is a leaky ship to which peril is dangerous,
He is an empty vessel, he is a withered tree,
Whoever does not do the will of the King above.
He is pure gold, he is the radiance round the sun,
He is a vessel of silver with wine,
He is happy, beautiful and holy,
Whoever does the will of the King.

21 PRAYER

From the Litany of Confession. The place of litanies in early Irish devotional and liturgical life is unclear, but there are a significant number of such texts written in both Latin and Irish. The following has been attributed to the sixth century saint, Ciaran of Clonmacnois, but must date from a later period. The first line is Latin, otherwise Irish.

'According to the multitude of your mercies, cleanse my iniquity.'

O star-like sun,
O guiding light,
O home of the planets,
O fiery-maned and marvellous one,
O fertile, undulating, fiery sea,
        Forgive.

O fiery glow,
O fiery flame of Judgement,
        Forgive.

O holy story-teller, holy scholar,
O full of holy grace, of holy strength,
O overflowing, loving, silent one,
O generous and thunderous giver of gifts,
        Forgive.

O rock-like warrior of a hundred hosts,
O fair crowned one, victorious, skilled in battle,
        Forgive.

22 NININE'S PRAYER

This prayer is traditionally attributed to the poet Ninine or to Fiacc, Bishop of Sletty. It occurs in the eleventh century Irish Book of Hymns, but is of earlier date. It is a fine example of the place of the saints in the devotional life of the early Celts. Old Irish.

We invoke holy Patrick, Ireland's chief apostle.
Glorious is his marvellous name, a flame that baptized heathen.
He warred against hard-hearted druids.
He thrust down the proud with the help of our Lord of fair heaven.
He cleansed Ireland's meadowlands, a great birth.
We pray to Patrick, chief apostle; his judgement shall save us on
    Doomsday from the evil of dark devils.
God be with us, and the prayer of Patrick, chief apostle.

23 PRAYER

This prayer is traditionally attributed to the Columbanus (c.543–615), although the attribution is doubted. Latin.

O Lord God, destroy and root out whatever the Adversary plants in me, that with my sins destroyed you may sow understanding and good work in my mouth and heart; so that in act and in truth I may serve only you and know how to fulfil the commandments of Christ and to seek yourself. Give me memory, give me love, give me chastity, give me faith, give me all things which you know belong to the profit of my soul. O Lord, work good in me, and provide me with what you know that I need. Amen.

24 LITANY OF THE VIRGIN AND ALL SAINTS

The following litany includes references to the organs of sense, as the places where sin occurs, and is thus reminiscent of the tradition of the 'breastplate'. It reflects a monastic and celibate milieu and occurs in manuscripts of the fifteenth century, though it may be earlier.

May Mary and John the youth and John the Baptist and all the saints of the world intercede with the fount of true purity and true innocence, Jesus Christ, Son of the Virgin, that the grace and compassion of the Holy Spirit may come to forgive us all our past sins, and protect us from future sins, to subdue our fleshly desires, and to control our unseemly thoughts;

> To kindle the love and affection of the Creator in our hearts, that it may be he that our mind searches for, desires and meditates upon for ever;
>
> That our eyes may not be deceived by idle glances, and by the profitless beauty of perishable things;
>
> That our hearing may not be perverted by idle songs, nor by the harmful persuasion of devils and evil men.
>
> That our senses of taste may not be beguiled by dainties and many savours.
>
> That he may free our tongues from denigration and insult and unkind chatter.
>
> That we may not barter the true light and true beauty of the life eternal for the deceitful fantasy of the present life.
>
> That we may not forsake the pure wedlock and marriage of our husband and noble bridegroom, Jesus Christ, Son of the King of Heaven and Earth, for the impure wedlock of a servant of his, so that our soul and body may be a consecrated temple to the Holy Spirit,
>
> That we may accompany the blameless lamb,
>
> That we may sing the song that only the virgins sing,
>
> That we may merit the crown of eternal glory in the unity of the company of heaven, in the presence of the Trinity, for ever and ever. Amen.

25 MY SPEECH — MAY IT PRAISE YOU

This poem expresses the author's desire to praise God in perfect form. Note the triadic structure. Twelfth century or later. Middle Irish.

My speech — may it praise you without flaw: may my heart love you, King of Heaven and of earth.

My speech — may it praise you without flaw: make it easy for me, pure Lord, to do you all service and to adore you.

My speech — may it praise you without flaw: Father of all affection,
   hear my poems and my speech.

26 *TO THE TRINITY*

*The theme of death again dominates this poem, and the poet speculates whether
he will be found worthy on the Day of Judgement. His religious task in this life
is to sing the praises of God and to entreat his mercy, and it is this that will
finally give him a place in 'the land of Heaven'. Twelfth or thirteenth century.
Middle Welsh.*

> To the Trinity I make my prayer,
> O Lord, grant me the skill to sing your praise,
> For the way of this world is perilous,
> Our deeds and decisions a wild tumult.
> Among the family of the saints, in their society,
> King of Heaven, may I be ready to praise you.
> Before my soul parts from my body,
> Grant me, for my sins, the means to worship you,
> To sing entreaty before your glory.
> May I be part of the merciful Trinity,
> My plea to you is like a battle cry,
> Nine orders of heaven, he made the hosts,
> The tenth is the blessed company of the saints,
> Wonderful glory of the peoples,
> A great host, their noble victory is clear,
> A company who see God . . .
> In heaven, on earth, at my end,
> In times of joy and sorrow, in tribulation,
> In my body, in my soul, in austerity,
> Long preparation before the approach of glory,
> I shall beseech you, Lord of the land of peace,
> That my soul may dwell
> For all eternity, in the highest place,
> In the land of heaven, I shall not be refused.

27 THE DEATHBED SONG OF MEILYR BRYDYDD

Meilyr Brydydd was the first of the 'Poets of the Princes'. He was court poet to Gruffudd ap Cynan, the prince most closely associated with the rise of the province of Gwynedd in North Wales. In this poem he reflects upon the inevitability of his own death, and entreats God for his mercy. Enlli, or Bardsey Island, was a major centre of pilgrimage, where 20,000 saints were reputed to be buried. Early twelfth century. Middle Welsh.

King of kings, leader easy to praise,
I ask this favour of my highest Lord:
Realm-mastering ruler of the sublime and blessed land,
Noble chief, make peace between you and me.
Feeble and empty is my mind, since
I have provoked you, and full of regret.
I have sinned before the Lord my God,
Failing to attend to my due devotion;
But I shall serve my Lord King
Before I am laid in the earth, stripped of life.
A true foretelling (to Adam and his offspring
The prophets had declared
That Jesus would be in the womb of martyrs),
Mary gladly received her burden.
But a burden I have amassed of unclean sin
And have been shaken by its clamour.
Lord of all places, how good you are to praise,
May I praise you and be purified before punishment.
King of all kings, who know me, do not refuse me,
On account of wickedness, for the sake of your mercy.
Many a time I had gold and brocade
From fickle kings for praising them,
And after the gift of song of a superior power,
Poverty-stricken is my tongue on the prospect of its silence.
I am Meilyr the Poet, pilgrim to Peter,
Gate-keeper who measures right virtue.
When the time of our resurrection comes,
All who are in the grave, make me ready.
As I await the call, may my home be
The monastery where the tide rises,

49

A wilderness of enduring glory,
Around its cemetery the breast of the sea,
Island of fair Mary, sacred isle of the saints,
Awaiting resurrection there is lovely.
Christ of the prophesied cross, who knows me, shall guide me
Past hell, the isolated abode of agony.
The Creator who made me shall receive me
Among the pure parish, the people of Enlli.

28 MEILYR AP GWALCHMAI'S ODE TO GOD

*The following stanzas are taken from a poem by Meilyr ap Gwalchmai, who
came from Anglesey and was the grandson of Meilyr Brydydd. We again see
the poet's sense that his own salvation depends upon the proper use of his art:
'May being righteous on account of my gift cleanse me.' In fact, by his use of
imagery, the poet deftly succeeds in identifying faith as right or 'skilled' belief,
with the 'skills' of his poetic art, and the divine 'gift' of grace with the 'gift' of
his inspiration and art. Late twelfth century. Middle Welsh.*

May God grant me, may I be granted mercy,
May no evil lack defeat me,
May being righteous on account of my gift cleanse me
And the world, which I know well, be shaken.
May I deserve God's favour, the Lord glorify me,
And give me entrance to the home of heaven.

Heaven shall be sure for those who seek freely
The royal growth of the religion of the Creed.
May the king of seas and stars hear me,
Privileged is the cause of one who petitions.
May the honour of the land of Paradise admit me;
That is the genuine kingdom and true.

With fullness of wisdom may my spirit reflect
On the wise fusion of skills that shall make me skilful.
A skilled man does not approach him who speaks
The glib and lying word, for all he may preach it.
I believe in Christ, blessed teacher,
No skilled believer it is who does not believe in him.

May I believe and reflect, and may the wise one see that
I believe in God and the saints and their land's honour,
A Christian am I with unshakeable right to a gift;
Christ, may I be granted gifts when he gives.
May Christianity's nurture release me,
The Lord Christ my King bring me freedom.

And may heaven's king protect me from error;
May his gift and his understanding cure my faults.
May God, who is flawless, not destroy me;
Undarkened is the mind that praises him,
Undeceived is the love that loves him,
Unblemished glory for all who believe in him.

May God, creator and ruler, guide me till judgement,
May he desire the ways of sinlessness for me,
And may it be his majestic desire to give me
Bright gifts that can purify me:
May rites of remission accompany my end,
And gifts of counsel guide me.

The counsellor of man, gentle to all who desire him,
Bears no ill-will to those who love him.
Love for me it is that can clear my blame;
May love and his concern for me not fail.
May the friend of our true cause elect me,
May I have the friendship of the Lord for ever.

29 THE DEATHBED SONG OF CYNDDELW THE GREAT POET

Cynddelw, from Powys in mid-Wales, is generally regarded as the greatest of the 'Poets of the Princes'. In these stanzas from the Black Book *Cynddelw shows again that the poet wins salvation through the quality of his praise and the skill of his verse, both of which have their source in God. Late twelfth century. Middle Welsh.*

Greatest Lord, take to yourself
This tribute of praise and well-formed poetry.

Perfect is the speech-skill and shape
Of my extolling song, candle of a hundred lands;
For you are master and great monarch,
You are counsellor and light's lord,
You are the heart of the prophet, and judge,
You are my generous ruler, the giver,
You are teacher to me; drive me not from your heights,
In your wrath, or from your lovely land,
Nor deny me your favour, my Lord Creator,
Nor refuse my submission and lowly plea.
Nor deliver me by your hand to a wretched home,
Nor let me run with the black host of the rejected.

Greatest Lord, when I sang of you,
Not without worth were my words,
Nor bereft of fair features,
Not wanting the grace wherever I received it.
Unshakeable God did not make me
To pursue folly, deceit or violence.
Such a one, I considered, shall not be woken,
Nor be given heaven, who seeks it not.
I did not serve too keenly,
Nor profit too greatly,
Nor let arrogance grow in my breast,
Nor did I pursue too much penance,
But to be in my Lord's dwelling was my desire,
And freedom for the soul, the need for which I prayed.

30 *FRAGMENT OF THE DISPUTE BETWEEN BODY AND SOUL*

These stanzas are part of a lost dialogue poem of a type found in many different cultures in medieval Europe. Normally, the soul castigates the body as the seat of sin. In this case however the body takes its rightful place beside the soul as its 'companion in glory' — since physical penance is the path to Heaven. Tenth to eleventh century. Early Middle Welsh.

While we walk together, companion in glory,
Be perfect in what you do.

Let us seek salvation
Through faith, religion and creed.

Companions in faith, by the friendship of faith
Comes great and long penance daily;
Soul, when you ask me what my end shall be:
The grave or eternity.

31 THE MASS OF THE GROVE

This poem was written in the fourteenth century by Dafydd ap Gwilym, who is widely regarded as the greatest Welsh poet. It presents a delicate fusion of natural imagery and Christian liturgy, as well as touches of courtly love. Morfudd here is the name of the poet's beloved. The 'englyn' referred to in the fifth line is a type of short Welsh poem in strict metre. It is the lyrical cock thrush who is the central figure; and he will return in a much later poem entitled 'The Mistle Thrush' given below. Middle Welsh.

I was in a pleasant place today
Beneath mantles of fine, green hazel,
Listening at break of day
To the skilful cock thrush
Singing a splendid englyn
Of fluent signs and lessons.
He is a stranger here, of wise nature,
Love's brown go-between from afar,
From fair Carmarthenshire he came
At my golden girl's command.
Full of words, without password,
He makes his way to Nentyrch valley;
It was Morfudd who sent him,
Foster son of May, skilled in the arts of song,
Swathed in the vestments
Of flowers of the sweet boughs of May,
His chasuble was of the wings,
Green mantles of the wind.
By the great God, there was here
Only gold for the altar's canopy.
In bright language I heard

A long and faultless chanting,
An unfaltering reading to the people
Of the gospel without haste,
And on the hill for us there
Was raised a well-formed leaf as wafer,
And the slender, eloquent nightingale
From the corner of a nearby grove,
Poetess of the valley, rings out to the many
The Sanctus bell in her clear whistle,
Raising the sacrifice on high
To the sky above the bush,
With adoration to God the Father,
And with a chalice of ecstasy and love.
This psalmody pleases me:
Bred it was by a gentle grove of birch trees.

32 THE LOVES OF TALIESIN

This is one of the greatest works of medieval Welsh religious literature. It conveys a comprehensive view of human life by interweaving the social, natural and religious worlds. Penance, and the desire for penance, which is the thematic heart of the poem, seems remarkably free of the negative connotations it generally bears in the modern world. Penance, rather, is the possibility of glory. Circa thirteenth century. Middle Welsh.

The beauty of the virtue in doing penance for excess,
Beautiful too that God shall save me.
The beauty of a companion who does not deny me his company,
Beautiful too the drinking horn's society.
The beauty of a master like Nudd, the wolf of God,
Beautiful too a man who is noble, kind and generous.
The beauty of berries at harvest time,
Beautiful too the grain on the stalk.
The beauty of the sun, clear in the sky,
Beautiful too they who pay Adam's debt.
The beauty of a herd's thick-maned stallion,
Beautiful too the pattern of his plaits.
The beauty of desire and a silver ring,
Beautiful too a ring for a virgin.

The beauty of an eagle on the shore when tide is full,
Beautiful too the seagulls playing.
The beauty of a horse and gold-trimmed shield,
Beautiful too a bold man in the breach.
The beauty of Einion, healer of many,
Beautiful too a generous and obliging minstrel.
The beauty of May with its cuckoo and nightingale,
Beautiful too when good weather comes.
The beauty of a proper and perfect wedding feast,
Beautiful too a gift which is loved.
The beauty of desire for penance from a priest,
Beautiful too bearing the elements to the altar.
The beauty for a minstrel of mead at the head of the hall,
Beautiful too a lively crowd surrounding a hero.
The beauty of a faithful priest in his church,
Beautiful too a chieftain in his hall.
The beauty of a strong parish led by God,
Beautiful too being in the season of Paradise.
The beauty of the moon shining on the earth,
Beautiful too when your luck is good.
The beauty of summer, its days long and slow,
Beautiful too visiting the ones we love.
The beauty of flowers on the tops of fruit trees,
Beautiful too covenant with the Creator.
The beauty in the wilderness of doe and fawn,
Beautiful too the foam-mouthed and slender steed.
The beauty of the garden when the leeks grow well,
Beautiful too the charlock in bloom.
The beauty of the horse in its leather halter,
Beautiful too keeping company with a king.
The beauty of a hero who does not shun injury,
Beautiful too is elegant Welsh.
The beauty of the heather when it turns purple,
Beautiful too moorland for cattle.
The beauty of the season when calves suckle,
Beautiful too riding a foam-mouthed horse.
And for me there is no less beauty
In the father of the horn in a feast of mead.
The beauty of the fish in his bright lake,
Beautiful too its surface shimmering.

The beauty of the word which the Trinity speaks,
Beautiful too doing penance for sin.
But the loveliest of all is covenant
With God on the Day of Judgement.

33 *from 'THE MIRROR OF DEATH'*

The following is from a sixteenth century Breton poem by Mestre Jehan an Archer Coz entitled 'The Mirror of Death'. It well shows the fascination with the brevity of life and certainty of divine judgement which is so characteristic of Celtic writings. Middle Breton.

Birds are caught in snares during the time of ice, when they are in search of food, and fish are caught in nets, and, though they had never thought of dying, are now being cooked for supper over the charcoal fire. Such is your life too, from beginning to end, which you spend in this world in the midst of many sins, and if you do not put them right before your time comes after all your pleasures, then you will remain caught in the snares . . .

34 *from 'THE MISTLE THRUSH'*

Thomas Jones (1756–1820) was an early Methodist minister. A close friend of Thomas Charles, he was a leading author and figure in eighteenth century Wales. Although written by a convinced Calvinist, the interpenetration of the themes of nature and grace that we find in the following poem seems to owe as much to the spirit of medieval poets such as Dafydd ap Gwilym and Rhys Goch ap Rhiccert as it does to the theology of Geneva.

Lowly bird, beautifully taught,
You enrich and astound us,
We wonder long at your song,
Your artistry and your voice.
In you I see, I believe,
The clear and excellent work of God.
Blessed and glorious is he,
Who shows his virtue in the lowest kind.
How many bright wonders (clear note of loveliness)

Does this world contain?
How many parts, how many mirrors of his finest work
Offer themselves a hundred times to our gaze?
For the book of his art is a speaking light
Of lines abundantly full,
And every day one chapter after another
Comes among us to teach us of him.

The smallest part of his most lovely hand
Finely taught our teacher,
A winged and lively bird,
Who gave an impromtu sermon,
Who taught us much
Of the Lord who is Master,
Of right measure, his power and wealth,
And wisdom, great and true.
Let us come to receive his learning,
Unmerited, from this learned bird:
Let the Lord be praised (by his own right),
Holy and pure, and no idol.
If our Lord is great, and great his praise
From just this one small part of earth,
Then what of the image of his greatness
Which comes from the whole of his fine work?
And through the image of the ascending steps
Of his gracious work, which he has made,
(Below and above the firmament,
Marvellously beyond number),
What of the greatness and pure loveliness,
Of God himself?

35 SELECTED VERSES FROM THE HYMNS OF ANN GRIFFITHS

Ann Griffiths was born in 1776 and died soon after the birth of her first child, in 1805. Although lacking in formal education, she became one of the greatest hymn writers of Welsh revivalism. Her passionate and lyrical hymns combine perfect mastery of form — in the original — with a profound and personal reflection upon her faith. Welsh.

Wholly counter to my nature
Is the path ordained for me;
Yet I'll tread it, yes, and calmly
while thy precious face I see.

Pilgrim, faint and tempest-beaten,
lift thy gaze, behold and know
Christ the Lamb, our Mediator,
My sole pleasure, my sole comfort
Is thy glorious face to see.

His left hand, in heat of noon-day,
lovingly my head upholds.
And his right hand, filled with blessings,
tenderly my soul enfolds.

Thou thine all-excelling glory
Over all things dost display.
Let me drink for ever deeply
of salvation's mighty flood,
Till I thirst no more for ever
after any earthly good.

Thanks for ever,
and a hundred thousand thanks,
thanks while there is breath in me,
that there is an object to worship.

What more have I to do
with the base idols of earth?
O to abide
in his love all the days of my life.

O to have faith to look
with the angels above,
into the plan of salvation.

O to spend my whole life
sanctifying the holy name of God.

*Medieval Religious
Prose*

36 *from* 'ON THE CHRISTIAN LIFE'

Pelagius, who wrote this text, was either a British- or Irish-born monk of the fourth and fifth century who advocated views on grace and freedom which attracted the charge of heresy. He was accused of preaching that grace operated only externally, through Scripture and the teachings of the Church, and not within the human heart. His chief opponent was Augustine. Whatever views he may have held on grace, Pelagius advocated a strongly moral Christianity and exercised a stern critique of the half-hearted and fashionable Christianity of the late Roman world. The following extract is the opening passage to On the Christian Life *in which the author appears to acknowledge both his own humility and the humble nature of the rural and unsophisticated culture from which he comes. Latin.*

It is purely the occasion of your love (which I have grasped in heart and mind by God's power) and not faith in my own righteousness, nor the experience of wisdom, nor the glory of knowledge that has compelled me, a sinner first and last, more foolish than others and less experienced than all, to dare to write to you at length in order to counsel you to continue along the path of holiness and justice. And it is this too that so drives me and challenges me to speak, though I am sinful and ignorant, that even if I lack the knowledge to speak, still I may not remain silent. And so it is my desire and wish that you should be introduced to those whose wisdom is more abundant, whose eloquence is greater and knowledge fuller, whose conscience is freer from stain of sin, and who can rightly instruct you with words and examples. For not only has the darkness of foolishness and ignorance so blinded our mind that it can neither sense nor utter anything divine, but also conscience has convicted it of all sins, so that even if our mind may have some light, still it conceals it. And so it is not only that we have nothing to say but also that we lack the confidence to offer what it is that we do have, since conscience prevents us. But you should nevertheless be content with our crude counsels, for as long as it seems wiser to you and better to do so, and consent to love. Do not weigh what he offers you, or inquire into what it is that he lacks; all that he has, he willingly shares. Do not look at the appearance of his gift so much as the intent of his soul, and note that he could have denied you all that he has and that he wishes to give you. He has offered you all that he can, and would have offered you what he does not have, had he been able to. And so they thirst, but too little, who cannot be content with the water of a shallow stream but must come to a purer and more abundant spring. Nor do I believe them to feel hunger enough who, when they have coarse bread, still wait for bread that is white and refined. And so you too, most beloved sister, who, I am sure, hunger and thirst immeasurably for the things of heaven: eat coarse bread for the moment, until you find bread of the whitest wheat, and drink the water of a shallow and muddy stream, until such time as you find one that is purer and more abundant. And do not for the moment disdain our bread, although it may seem rustic to you. For although rustic bread seems less refined, it is more substantial and more swiftly fills a hungry stomach, restoring strength to the weak, than white bread made from finely ground flour. I shall now give an account, to the best of my abilities, and an explanation, as far as I am able, of how a Christian should act. I can find no better preface to my treatise than first to discuss the very word 'Christian' and why it is that anyone should bear this name . . .

37 from 'TO A YOUNG MAN'

In this passage from his letter 'To a Young Man', we see Pelagius' frustration with the nominal Christian and a lukewarm Church. Latin.

First, then, get to know God's will, as contained in his law, so that you may be able to do it, since you can be certain that you are a true Christian only when you have taken the trouble to keep all God's commandments. I do not want you to pay any attention to the examples set by the majority, who claim the honour of belonging to this religion for themselves in name alone; for a prize so great belongs to only a few. How straight and narrow is the road that leads to life! And those who enter by it are few (Matthew 7.14). It is not the name but the deed which makes a Christian; you will find it harder to discover the essence of something than its title. For those who think they are Christians merely because they possess the name of 'Christian' are making a very serious mistake: they do not know that it is the name which belongs to the thing and not the thing to the name, and that it is right to call a man what he is but foolish to call him what he is not.

But perhaps you want to know what it means to be a Christian? A Christian is a man or woman in whom can be found these three attributes which all Christians should possess: knowledge, faith, obedience; knowledge by which we know God, faith by which we believe in him whom we know, obedience by which we render our allegiance and service to him in whom we believe.

38 *from* 'TO CELANTIA'

In the letter 'To Celantia', Pelagius stresses the moral and also deeply communitarian character of his ideal Christianity. Latin.

You should take out and write over your heart that sentence of the Gospel which is offered to us from the mouth of the Lord as the epitome of all righteousness: 'Whatever you wish that others should do to you, do also to them'; and to express the full force of this precept, he adds the statement: 'For this is the law and the prophets' (Matthew 7.12). The types and categories of righteousness are infinite, and it is most difficult not only to record them with the pen but also to grasp them in thought; but he includes them all in one brief sentence and either acquits or condemns the hidden consciences of men and women by the secret judgement of the mind.

With every act, therefore, with every word, even with every thought let this sentence be re-examined, since, like a mirror ready and always to hand, it reveals the nature of your will and also either exposes the wrong in the case of an unrighteous deed or shows cause for rejoicing in the case of a righteous one. For whenever you have the kind of attitude to another that you wish another to have towards you, then you are keeping to the way of righteousness; but whenever you are the kind of person to another that you want no one to be to you, you have abandoned the way of righteousness. See how demanding, how difficult is this whole business of keeping the divine law! See what it is that makes us protest against the Lord for giving us hard commands and say that we are being overwhelmed either by the difficulty or by the impracticability of these commands! Nor does it suffice that we do not carry out the commands without also pronouncing the one who gives them unfair, while we complain that the author of righteousness himself has imposed commands upon us which are not only difficult and arduous but even quite impossible. Whatever you wish, he says, that others would do to you, do also to them. He wants love between us to be established and maintained by mutual acts of kindness, and all to be united to one another by mutual love; so that, while each one provides for the other what all want provided for themselves, total righteousness, as in this commandment of God, may be the common benefit of humankind. And — how wonderful is God's mercy! how ineffable his kindness! — he promises us a reward if we love each other, that is, if we give to each other those things of which each one of us has need in return. But with a proud and ungrateful spirit, we oppose his will, when even his command is an act of kindness.

39 *from Cogitosus' LIFE OF BRIGID*

The following passages are taken from the Life of Brigid *by Cogitosus, which was written in the middle of the seventh century and is the earliest Life of an Irish saint. While Brigid of Kildare was almost certainly the foundress of a major monastic house in the late fifth or early sixth century, it is likely that imagery and themes associated with a powerful pre-Christian goddess figure became associated with her. In the passages which follow, the first is a classic instance of the Celtic saint's control over the elements, in this case fire and the power of the sun, while the final two show the particular interrelation between creatures and the Celtic saint, who appear to discover in each other the special presence of God.*

What I recount here is another episode which demonstrates her sanctity; one in which the action of her hand corresponded to the quality of her pure and virginal mind.

It happened that she was pasturing her sheep on a grassy spot on the plain when she was soaked by heavy rain, and she returned home in wet clothes. The sun shining through a gap in the building cast a ray which, at first glance, seemed to her to be a solid wooden beam fixed across the house. She placed her wet cloak upon it as if it were indeed solid, and the cloak hung securely from the incorporeal sunbeam. When the inhabitants of the house spread the word of this great miracle among the neighbours, they extolled the incomparable Brigid with fitting praise . . .

Once a solitary wild boar which was being hunted ran out from the woods, and in its headlong flight was brought suddenly into the herd of pigs that belonged to the most blessed Brigid. She noticed its arrival among her pigs and she blessed it. Thereupon it lost its fear and settled down among the herd. See how brute beasts and animals could oppose neither her bidding nor her wish, but served her tamely and humbly . . .

On another day the blessed Brigid felt a tenderness for some ducks that she saw swimming on the water and occasionally taking wing. She commanded them to come to her. A great flock of them flew on feathered wings towards her, without any fear, as if they were humans under obedience. When she had touched them with her hand and caressed them, she released them and let them fly into the sky. She praised the Creator of all things greatly, to whom all life is subject, and for the service of whom — as has already been said — all life is given . . .

40 *from the* LIFE OF MELANGELL

The version of the Life of Melangell *from which this translation was made is contained in a seventeenth century manuscript. Melangell (Latin: Monacella) is an important Welsh saint who was the foundress of Pennant Melangell in Montgomeryshire. Her feast day fell on May 27. Latin.*

In Powys there was once a certain most illustrious prince by the name of Brychwel Ysgithrog, who was the Earl of Chester and who at that time lived in the town of Pengwern Powys (which means in Latin the head of Powys marsh and is now known as Shrewsbury) and whose home or abode stood in that place where the college of St Chad is now situated. Now that very same noble prince gave his aforesaid home or mansion for the use of God as an act of almsgiving both by his own free will and from a sense of religious duty, making a perpetual grant of it for his own sake and for the sake of his heirs. When one day in the year of our Lord 604, the said prince had gone hunting to a certain place in Britain called Pennant, in the said principality of Powys, and when the hunting dogs of the same prince had started a hare, the dogs pursued the hare and he too gave chase until he came to a certain thicket of brambles, which was large and full of thorns. In this thicket he found a girl of beautiful appearance who, given up to divine contemplation, was praying with the greatest devotion, with the said hare lying boldly and fearlessly under the hem or fold of her garments, its face towards the dogs.

Then the prince cried 'Get it, hounds, get it!', but the more he shouted, urging them on, the further the dogs retreated and, howling, fled from the little animal. Finally, the prince, altogether astonished, asked the girl how long she had lived on her own on his lands, in such a lonely spot. In reply the girl said that she had not seen a human face for these fifteen years. Then he asked the girl who she was, her place of birth and origins, and in all humility she answered that she was the daughter of King Jowchel of Ireland and that 'because my father had intended me to be the wife of a certain great and generous Irishman, I fled from my native soil and with God leading me came here in order that I might serve God and the immaculate Virgin with my heart and pure body until my dying day'. Then the prince asked the girl her name. She replied that her name was Melangell. Then the prince, considering in his innermost heart the flourishing though solitary state of the girl, said: 'O most worthy virgin Melangell, I find that you are a handmaid of the true God and a most sincere follower of Christ. Therefore, because it has pleased the highest and all-powerful God to give refuge, for your merits, to this little wild hare with safe conduct and protection from the attack and pursuit of these savage and violent dogs, I give and present to you most willingly these my lands for the service of God, that they may be a perpetual asylum, refuge and defence, in honour of your name, excellent girl. Let neither king nor prince seek to be so rash or bold towards God that they presume to drag away any man or woman who has escaped here, desiring to enjoy protection in these your lands, as long as they in no way contaminate or pollute your sanctuary or asylum. But, on the other hand, if any wrongdoer who enjoys the protection of your sanctuary shall set out in any direction to do harm, then the free tenants known as abbots of your sanctuary, who alone know of their crimes, shall, if they find them guilty and culpable, ensure that they are released and handed over to the Powys authorities in order to be punished.'

This virgin Melangell, who was so very pleasing to God, led her solitary life, as stated above, for thirty-seven years in this very same place. And the hares, which are little wild creatures, surrounded her every day of her life, just as if they had been tame or domesticated animals, through which, by the aid of divine mercy, miracles and various other signs are not lacking for those who call upon her help and the grace of her favour with an inner motion of the heart.

After the death of the said most illustrious prince Brochwel, his son Tyssilio held the principality of Powys, followed by Conan, the brother of Tyssilio, Tambryd, Gurmylk and Durres the lame, all of whom sanctioned the said place of Pennant Melangell to be a perpetual sanctuary, refuge or safe haven for the oppressed (thereby confirming the acts of the said prince). The same virgin Melangell applied herself to establish and instruct certain virgins with all concern and care in the same region in order that they might persevere and live in a holy and modest manner in the love of God, and should dedicate their lives to divine duties, doing nothing else by day or by night. After this, as soon as Melangell herself had departed this life, a certain man called Elissa came to Pennant Melangell and wishing to debauch, violate and dishonour the same virgins, suddenly perished and died there in the most pitiful manner. Whoever has violated the above-mentioned liberty and sanctity of the said virgin has been rarely seen to escape divine vengeance on this account, as may be seen every day. Praises be to the most high God and to Melangell, his virgin.

41 *from the LIFE OF BEUNO*

The following extract is taken from the Life of Beuno, *which was perhaps written sometime during the twelfth century and was probably based on a Latin Life of this saint now lost. It is remarkable for containing a number of pagan motifs and for presenting the Christian saint essentially as a man of supernatural power. The second passage is interesting in that it links Beuno's lineage to Christ himself, rather in the manner of medieval Welsh genealogies of kings. Middle Welsh.*

One day Temic and his wife came to the church in order to hear Mass and Beuno's sermon, leaving his daughter behind to guard their home. She was the most beautiful girl in the world, and had not yet been given to a man. And as she remained on guard, she saw the king, who ruled that place, approaching her. His name was Caradoc. She rose up to greet him and was pleasant to him while the king, for his part, asked her where her father had gone. 'He went', she said, 'to the church. If you have any business with him, wait for him and he will soon be here.' 'I will not wait,' he said, 'unless you become my mistress.' The girl said: 'I am not fit to become your mistress since you are a great king and are from a line of kings. My blood is not noble enough for me to be your mistress. But wait here,' she said 'until I come from my room and I shall do what you desire.' Pretending to go to her room, she fled and made for the church where her father and mother were. The king saw her fleeing, and gave chase. As she reached the door of the church, he caught her up and struck off her head with his sword, which fell into the church while her body remained outside. Beuno, her mother and father saw what had happened, and Beuno stared into the face of the king and said: 'I ask God not to spare you and to respect you as little as you respected this good girl.' And in that moment the king melted away into a lake, and was seen no more in this world.

Then Beuno took the girl's head and placed it back with the body, covering the body with his cloak and saying to her mother and father who were mourning for her: 'Be quiet for a little while and leave her as she is until the Mass is over.' Then Beuno celebrated the sacrifice to God. When the Mass was finished, the girl rose up entirely healed and dried the sweat from her face; God and Beuno healed her. Where her blood fell to the earth, a spring was formed, which even today still heals people and animals from their illnesses and injuries. And that spring is called after the girl and is known as Ffynnon Wenfrewi. Many who had seen what had happened began to believe in Christ. One of those who believed was Cadfan, King of Gwynedd. He gave much land to Beuno . . .

And as Beuno's life was drawing to an end and his day approaching, on the seventh day after Easter he saw the heavens opening and the angels descending and ascending. Then Beuno said: 'I see the Trinity, the Father, the Son and the Holy Spirit, Peter and Paul and pure David, Deiniol, the saints and the prophets, the apostles and the martyrs appearing to me. And in the midst there I see seven angels standing before the throne of the highest Father and all the fathers of heaven, singing: "Blessed is the one you have chosen and have received and who shall dwell with you always." I hear the cry of the horn of the highest Father summoning me and saying to me: "My son, cast off your burden of flesh. The time is coming, and you are invited to share the feast that shall not end with your brothers. May your body remain in the earth while the armies of heaven and the angels bear your soul to the kingdom of heaven, which you have merited here through your works."

'This hour shall be the Day of Judgement when the Lord says to the saints: "Blessed sons of my Father, come to the kingdom that was prepared for you from the beginning of the world, where there shall be life without death, youth without old age and health without suffering, joy without grief, the saints in the highest rank with God the Father, in unity with the angels and archangels, in unity with the disciples of Jesus Christ, in unity with the nine grades of heaven, who did not sin, in the unity of the Father and the Son and the Holy Spirit, Amen."'

Let us too beseech the mercy of the all-powerful God by the help of St Beuno so that we may receive with him everlasting life in all eternity. Amen.

This is the line of Beuno. Beuno, son of Bugi, son of Gwynlliw, son of Tegid, son of Cadell Drynlluc, son of Categyrn, son of Gortheyrn, son of Gorthegyrn, son of Rhyddegyrn, son of Deheuwynt, son of Eudegan, son of Eudegern, son of Elud, son of Eudos, son of Eudoleu, son of Afallach, son of Amalech, son of Belim, son of Anna. The mother of that Anna was cousin to Mary the Virgin, the mother of Christ.

42 *from the* LIFE OF DAVID

This is the conclusion to the Life of David, *written in Latin by Rhigyfarch in around 1095. Although Rhigyfarch tells us that his work is based upon earlier manuscripts 'written in the manner of the elders', his work reflects the demands of a later and more sophisticated ecclesiastical establishment. This* Life of David *may well have been used to further the metropolitan claims of the see of St David in modern Pembrokeshire. In its final form it includes an account of the raising of David to the state of Archbishop and the claim that his successors inherit his primacy as spiritual leader of 'the entire British race'. Latin.*

Immediately after partaking of the Lord's Body and Blood, [David] was seized with pains and became ill. The service ended, he blessed the people and addressed everyone in these words: 'My brethren, persevere in those things which you have learned from me and have seen in me. On the third day, the first day of March, I shall go the way of my fathers. As for you, fare well in the Lord. I shall depart.' From that Sunday night until the fourth day after his death, all who had come remained weeping, fasting and keeping watch. Accordingly, when the third day arrived, the place was filled with choirs of angels, and was melodious with heavenly singing, and replete with the most delightful fragrance. At the hour of matins, while the monks were singing hymns, psalms and canticles, our Lord Jesus Christ deigned to bestow his presence for the consolation of the father [David], as he had promised by the angel. On seeing him, and entirely rejoicing in spirit, he said: 'Take me with you.' With these words, with Christ as his companion, he gave up his life to God, and, attended by the escort of angels, sought the gates of heaven. And so his body, borne on the arms of holy brethren, and accompanied by a great crowd, was committed to the earth with all honour and buried in the grounds of his own monastery; but his soul, set free from the bounds of this transitory life, is crowned throughout endless ages. Amen.

These and many other works the father did, while a mortal body weighed down the soul which it carried. We have provided only a few of the many examples that exist in order to satisfy the thirst of the ardent, by means of the vessel of my humble narrative. For, as one can never drain dry a river issuing forth from an everlasting spring with a narrow vessel of too limited capacity, so can no one commit to writing all the father's signs and miracles, his most devout practice of virtues and observance of precepts, even if he were to use a pen of iron. But as I have stated, these few I have gathered together as an example to all, and the father's glory, out of the very many that are scattered in the oldest manuscripts of our country, and chiefly of his own monastery. These, though eaten away along their edges and backs by the continuous gnawing of worms and the ravages of passing years, and written in the manner of the elders, have survived until now, and are gathered together and collected by me to the glory of the great father and for the benefit of others, that they shall not perish, as the bee sucks delicately with its mouth from the different blooms in a garden filled with flowers. And indeed, as for those works which, in the passing of time, he performs and has carried out more effectively since, having laid aside the burden of the flesh and having gazed upon the Deity face to face, he cleaves more closely to God, he who will may discover them through the witness of many. Moreover, as for myself, Rhigyfarch by name, who have somewhat rashly applied my slender mental abilities to this task, may those who read this work with a devout mind assist me with their prayers; so that, since the Father's mercy, like that of spring, has carried me through the summer heat of the flesh to the scanty flowering of my understanding, it may in the end, when the vapours of desire have vanished and before my course is ended, bring me the fruit of a good harvest through due and proper works. Then, when the tares of the enemy are separated, and the reapers shall have filled heaven's garners with purified sheaves, they may find a place for me, as a gleaning of the latest harvest, within the portals of the celestial gates, there endlessly to behold God, who is blessed above all things, for ever and ever. Amen.

43 *from the LIFE OF NINIAN*

The following is an extract from the Life of Ninian. *Ninian was a saint associated with the evangelization of the Picts and Britons of southern Scotland in the fourth and fifth centuries. He is said to have founded the 'white' or 'shining church' of Whithorn, dedicated to St Martin of Tours. This is a relatively late Life, although the passage given here can be paralleled with a number of other such accounts from the earlier Irish and Welsh hagiographical tradition.*

Wherever he went, he raised his soul to the things of heaven, either by prayer or contemplation. But whenever he rested from his journey, either for his own sake or for that of the animal he rode, he took out a book which he carried for the very purpose and liked to read or sing something, for he felt with the prophet: 'How sweet are your words in my throat, sweeter they are than honey in the mouth'. Therefore the divine power granted him such grace that even when resting in the open air, when reading in the heaviest rain, no dampness ever touched the book upon which his mind was concentrated. When everything around him was soaked, he sat alone with his little book in the downpour, as if protected by the roof of a house. Now it happened that when this most devout man was making a journey with one of his brothers (who was then still alive), also a very holy person by the name of Plebia, he rested from the fatigue of his journey, as was his custom, with the Psalms of David. And so, when they had gone some way, they left the road to rest and refreshed their souls with their psalters. But soon black clouds covered the clear sky, pouring back to earth those waters whch they had taken from it. What more can I say? The light air, like a room surrounding the servants of God, resisted the downpour like an impenetrable wall. But as they sang, the most blessed Ninian took his eyes from the book as an unlawful thought stirred in him and desire prompted by the devil. Immediately the rain fell upon him and his book, thus revealing what was hidden. Then the brother who was sitting beside him and who knew what had taken place, rebuked him gently, reminding him of his order and age and showing him how unseemly such things were in someone such as he. Straight away the man of God came to himself and blushing at having been overtaken by a vain thought, he banished it from his mind . . .

44 *from the* PENITENTIAL OF CUMMEAN

The Irish Penitential of Cummean *is the most comprehensive of the Celtic penitentials, and it makes use both of John Cassian's 'healing through opposites' principle and his eight cardinal sins. Its author was Cummaine Fota, Bishop of Clonfert, who died in 662. This penitential circulated widely on the*

Continent during the eighth and ninth centuries, and contributed, with other texts, to the adoption by the Catholic Church of the regular practice of private confession. Latin.

Here begins the prologue on the medicine for the salvation of souls.

1. As we are about to speak of the cure of wounds according to the precepts of the fathers before us, of sacred utterance to you, my most faithful brother, let us first indicate in a concise manner the medicines of Holy Scripture. 2. The first remission then is that by which we are baptized in water, according to this passage: 'Unless a man be born again of water and of the Holy Spirit, he cannot see the Kingdom of God'. 3. The second is the feeling of charity, as this text has it: 'Many sins are remitted unto her for she has loved much'. 4. The third is the fruit of almsgiving, according to this: 'As water quenches fire, so too do alms extinguish sin'. 5. The fourth is the shedding of tears, as the Lord says: 'Since Ahab wept in my sight and walked sad in my presence, I will not bring evil things in his days'. 6. The fifth is the confession of crimes, as the Psalmist testifies: 'I said, I will confess against myself my injustice to the Lord and you have forgiven the iniquity of my sin'. 7. The sixth is the affliction of heart and body, as the Apostle comforts us: 'I have given such a man to Satan for the destruction of his flesh, that his spirit may be saved in the day of our Lord Jesus Christ'. 8. The seventh is the amending of our ways, that is, the renunciation of vices, as the Gospel testifies: 'Now you are whole, sin no more, in case something worse happens to you'. 9. The eighth is the intercession of the saints, as this text states: 'If any be sick, let him bring the priests of the church and let them pray for him and lay their hands upon him, and anoint him with oil in the name of the Lord, and the prayer of faith shall save the sick man and the Lord shall raise him up, and if he be in sins, they shall be forgiven him,' and so forth, and: 'The continual prayer of a just man avails much before the Lord'. 10. The ninth is the reward of mercy and faith, as this says: 'Blessed are the merciful for they shall obtain mercy'. 11. The tenth is the conversion and salvation of others, as James assures us: 'He who causes a sinner to be converted from the error of his life shall save his soul from death and cover a multitude of sins'; but it is better for you, if you are weak, to lead a solitary life than to perish with many. 12. The eleventh is our pardon, as he that is the truth has promised, saying: 'Forgive and you shall be forgiven'.

13. The twelfth is the passion of martyrdom, as the one hope of our salvation then grants us pardon; and God replies to the cruel robber: 'Truly I say to you this day you shall be with me in Paradise'.

14. Therefore since these things are quoted on the authority of the Canon, it is right for you also to seek out the decrees of the fathers who were chosen by the mouth of the Lord, according to this passage: 'Ask your father and he will declare unto you, your elders and they will tell you'; indeed, 'Let the matter be referred to them'. And so they determine that the eight principal vices contrary to human salvation shall be healed by the eight remedies that are their contraries. For it is an old proverb: Contraries are cured by contraries. For he who without restraint commits what is forbidden ought to restrain himself even from what is permissible . . .

1. But this is to be carefully observed in all penance: the length of time anyone remains in his faults, what education he has received, with what passion he is assailed, with what courage he resists, with what intensity of weeping he seems to be afflicted, with what pressure he is driven to sin. 2. For almighty God, who knows the hearts of all and has made us all different, will not weigh the weight of sins in an equal scale of penance, as this prophecy says: 'For the gith shall not be threshed with saws, neither shall the cart wheel turn about upon the cummin; but the gith shall be beaten with a rod and the cummin with a staff, but bread corn shall be broken small' (Isaiah 28: 27–28), or as in this passage: 'The mighty shall be mightily tormented' (Wisdom 6.7). 3. For which reason a certain man, wise in the Lord, said: 'To whom more is entrusted, from him more shall be exacted' (cf. Luke 12.48). Thus the priests of the Lord who preside over the churches should learn that their share is given to them together with those whose faults they have caused to be forgiven. 4. What does it mean to cause a fault to be forgiven then unless, when you receive the sinner, by warning, exhortation, teaching and instruction you lead him to penance, correcting him from error, improving him from his vices, and making him such a person that God becomes favourable to him after his conversion, you are then said to cause his faults to be forgiven. 5. When you are a priest like this therefore, and this is your teaching and your word, there is given to you the share of those whom you have corrected, that their merit may be your reward and their salvation your glory.

Here ends this book written by Cummean.

45 *HOW THE MONK SHOULD PLEASE GOD*

This passage is taken from the third sermon of Columbanus and contains some of this great saint's reflections upon the monastic vocation. Columbanus, who was born in around 543, was the chief emissary of Irish monasticism on the Continent of Europe and was involved in the foundation of a number of important monastic sites there. Latin.

What is the best thing in the world? To please its Creator. What is his will? To fulfil what he commanded, that is, to live justly and devotedly to seek the eternal; for devotion and justice are the will of God who is himself devout and just. How do we reach this goal? By application. Then we must apply ourselves in devotion and justice. What helps to sustain this? Understanding which, while it winnows the remainder and finds nothing solid to remain in amongst those things which the world possesses, turns in wisdom to the one thing which is eternal. For the world will pass, and daily passes, and revolves towards its end (for what does it have to which it does not assign an end?) and somehow it is supported upon the pillars of vanity. But when vanity comes to an end, then it will fall and will not stand. But it cannot be said of the world that it shall not end. Thus by death and decline all things pass away and abide not. What then should the wise man love? A dull fiction, partly silent and partly sounding, which he sees and does not understand. For if he understood it, perhaps he would not love it, but it offends also in that it does not show itself as it is. For who understands, either in himself or another, being a flower of the earth and being earth from earth, by what deserving a child of God and citizen of heaven is made from what shall soon be earth and dust and from that which would never thrive without the help of the soul?

If anyone to whom God has granted it understands what life he should live in order to become eternal and not mortal, wise and not stupid, heavenly and not earthly, he should first keep his reason pure in order to use it for right living, and look not upon what is but upon what shall be. For that which is not shall be, and he should consider what he sees not by means of what he sees, and attempt to be what he was created and summon God's grace to assist his striving; for it is impossible for anyone to gain by his own efforts what he lost in Adam. But what help is it to gain discernment and not to use it well? He uses it well who lives in such a way that he need never repent but never forgets that he has repented, for a late repentance proves that we have had bad habits, while a good conscience commends our way of life. So what should a good discernment learn to love? Certainly that which makes it love all else besides, which always remains and never grows old. No other external thing should be loved, according to the reckoning of truth, except eternity and the eternal will, which is inspired and enlivened by the Eternal, Wonderful, Ineffable, Invisible, Incomprehensible, who fills all things and transcends all things, who is present to us and yet beyond our grasp.

46 *from Columbanus' 'SERMON THIRTEEN'*

An extract from a further sermon by Columbanus in which we see something of the mystical inspiration of early Irish monasticism. Latin.

Dearest brothers, do listen attentively to our words in the belief that you will hear something that needs to be heard, and refresh the thirst of your mind from the waters of the divine spring of which we now wish to speak. But do not quench that thirst; drink, but do not be filled. For now the living fountain, the fountain of life, calls us to himself and says: 'Let him who is thirsty come to me and drink.' And take note of what it is that you shall drink. Let Isaiah tell you, let the fountain himself tell you: 'But they have forsaken me the fountain of living water,' says the Lord. Thus the Lord himself, our God Jesus Christ, is the fountain of life, and so he calls us to himself, the fountain, that we may drink of him. He who loves drinks of him, he drinks who is filled with the word of God, who loves enough, who desires enough, he drinks who burns with the love of wisdom. Then let us Gentiles eagerly drink what the Jews have forsaken. For perhaps it was said of us with the Gentiles: 'He breaks off in amazement of mind, the heads of the mighty shall be moved, while they open not their jaws, like a poor man eating in secret'; and as if it were said of us also with all the perfect, of whom this was written, let us open the jaws of our inner man, as when eating that bread which came down from heaven, that we may eat hungrily and swiftly, in case anyone should see us, as if we ate in secret. Let us eat the same Lord Jesus Christ as bread, let us drink him as a fountain, who calls himself the 'living bread, who gives life to this world', as if to be eaten by us, and who likewise shows himself to be a fountain when he says: 'Let him who is thirsty come to me and drink', of which fountain the prophet also says: 'since with you is the fountain of life'.

Observe from where that fountain flows; for it comes from that place from where the bread also came down, since he is the same who is bread and fountain, the only Son, our God Christ the Lord, for whom we should always hunger. Although we eat him when we love him, though we feast on him when we desire him, let us still desire him like people who are ravenous. Likewise with the fountain, let us always drink of him with an overflowing love, let us always drink of him with a fullness of longing, and let the sweet savour of his loveliness ravish us. For the Lord is sweet and lovely; and although we eat and drink of him, let us still always hunger and thirst, since our food and drink can never be completely consumed, for though he is eaten, he is not eaten up, though he is drunk, he is not drained, since our bread is eternal and our fountain is everlasting, our fountain is sweet. Therefore the Prophet says: 'Go you who thirst to the fountain'; for that is the fountain of those who thirst, not of those who are replete, and so he calls to himself the hungry and the thirsty, whom he blessed elsewhere, who never have enough of drinking, but who thirst the more, the more they consume. We are right, my brothers, to desire the fountain of wisdom, the Word of God on high, to seek him, always to love him, in whom are hid, according to the Apostle's words, 'all the treasures of wisdom and knowledge', which he calls those who thirst to enjoy. If you thirst, drink the fountain of life; if you hunger, eat the bread of life, blessed are they who hunger for this bread and thirst for this fountain; though they are always eating and drinking, they still long to eat and drink. For that is lovely to excess which is always eaten and drunk, for which there is always a hunger and a thirst, always tasted and always desired. Therefore the Prophet-King says, 'taste and see how lovely, how pleasant is the Lord'. Therefore, my brothers, let us follow this calling, by which we are called to the fountain of life by the life who is the fountain, not only the fountain of living water, but also of eternal life, the fountain of light, indeed the fountain of glory; for from him come all these things, wisdom, life and eternal light. The Author of life is the fountain of life, the Creator of light, the fountain of glory. Therefore, spurning the things that are seen, journeying through the world, let us seek the fountain of glory, the fountain of life, the fountain of living water, in the upper regions of the heavens, like rational and most wise fishes, that there we may drink the living water which springs up to eternal life.

If only you would deign to admit me to that fountain, merciful God, righteous Lord, so that there I too might drink with your thirsting ones the living stream of the living fount of the living water and, ravished by his too great loveliness, might hold to him always on high and say: 'How lovely is the fount of living water, whose water does not fail, springing up to life eternal.' O Lord, you are yourself that fountain ever and again to be desired, although ever and again to be consumed. Give this water always, Lord Christ, that it may be in us too a fountain of water that lives and springs up to eternal life. I ask for great things; who does not know that. But you, King of Glory, know how to give great things and have promised great things. Nothing is greater than you yourself, and you have given yourself to us, you gave yourself for us. Therefore we ask that we may know what we love, for we ask for nothing other than that you should be given to us; for you are our all, our life, our light, our salvation, our food, our drink, our God. I ask that you inspire our hearts, our Jesus, with that breath of your Spirit, and wound our souls with your love, so that the soul of each one of us may be able to say in truth, 'show me him whom my soul has loved', for by love am I wounded. I desire that those wounds may be in me, O Lord. Blessed is such a soul which is thus wounded by love. Such a soul seeks the fountain, such a one drinks, but always thirsts when drinking, it always drinks when desiring, and always drinks when thirsting. Thus it always seeks by loving and is always healed by its wounding. And with this healing wound may our God and Lord Jesus Christ, that Physician of right-eousness and health, deign to wound the inward parts of our soul, who with the Father and the Holy Spirit is one for ever and ever. Amen.

47 AN OLD IRISH HOMILY

This sermon dates from around the ninth century and contains many of the themes of Celtic Christianity, including the giving of blessings, a concern with hell and judgement, and a truly cosmic sense of the meaning of religion which is visible in the listing of earthly analogues for heaven and hell. Later Old Irish.

We give thanks to almighty God, Lord of heaven and earth, for his mercy and forgiveness, for his love and his blessings which he has bestowed upon us in heaven and on earth. It is of him that the Prophet says: 'Confitentur tibi, Domine, omnia opera tua et sancti tui confiten-tur tibi'. For it is the duty of all the elements to give thanks to God and to bless him, as it is said: 'Benedicite omnia opera Domini Domino'. For God does not deny his present blessings even to sinners, as Scripture says: 'Bonus est Deus qui dat iustis et iniustis bona terrae in commune', that is, God is devoted and excellent who gives to the good and the evil the good things of the earth equally. For he is the one excellent God who is without beginning or end. He it is who has created all things, who has formed them and sustains them by the might of his power. He it is who nourishes and preserves and gladdens and illuminates and rules and has redeemed and renews all things. In him they trust; he it is for whom they wait, for he is King of kings and Lord of lords, Creator of heaven and earth, Maker of the angels, Teacher of the prophets, Master of the apostles, Giver of the Law, Judge of the men and women of the world. He is higher than the heavens, lower than the earth, wider than the seas.

It is our duty to give thanks to that Lord for his gifts. For the grateful soul who gives thanks to God for his grace is a temple and dwelling-place of God; as Peter says: 'Animam gratias agentem ac familiarem sibi facit deus'. That is, the man or woman who gives thanks to God for his blessings is an estate that belongs to the King of all. But they who are not grateful for the blessings of God are a temple and dwelling-place of the Devil; as Peter says: 'Ingratam animam malum possidet demon'. The evil demon possesses and inhabits the soul of the ungrateful who do not give thanks to God for his blessings. It is that thanksgiving which is meant when they say: 'Tibi gratias agunt animae nostrae pro innumeris beneficiis tuis'. That is, our souls give thanks to you, O Lord, for your blessings without number on heaven and earth.

And so may the blessing of the Lord of heaven and earth be on everyone with whom we have come into contact, on their possession of field and house, on their property both animate and inanimate, and on everyone who serves them and is obedient to them. May the earth give its fruits, may the air give its rainfall, may the sea give its fishes, may there be more grain and milk, more honey and wheat for everyone whose labour and goodwill we enjoy. May God give them a hundred-fold on this earth and the kingdom of heaven in the life to come. For they who receive Christ's people actually receive Christ, as he himself says: 'Qui vos recipit me recipit, qui vos spernit, me spernit'. That is, he who receives you, receives me, he who despises you, despises me.

But there are analogies to the kingdom of heaven and to hell in this world. First the analogy to hell, that is winter and snow, stormy weather and the cold, old age and decay, disease and death. The analogy to the kingdom of heaven however is summer and fair weather, flower and leaf, beauty and youth, feasts and feastings, prosperity and an abundance of every good thing.

But it is into hell that God shall cast sinners on Judgement Day, saying: 'Ite maledicti in ignem aeternum qui praeparatus est Diabolo et angelis eius', that is, 'Go, you cursed ones, into the everlasting fire which has been prepared for the Devil and his vile vassals'. Woe to them to whom the Lord shall say on the Day of Judgement that they shall dwell for ever in hell with its many and great torments. For its setting is deep, its surrounds are solid, its jaws are dark, its company are sorrowful, its stench is great, its monsters are everlasting, its earth is sunken, its surface is poisonous, it is an abyss to restrain, it is a prison to hold, it is a flame to burn, it is a net to hold fast, it is a scourge to lash, it is a blade to maim, it is a night to blind, it is smoke to suffocate, it is a cross to torture, it is a sword to punish.

In this way then these punishments are to be avoided: by hard work and study, by fasting and prayer, by righteousness and mercy, by faith and love. For whoever fulfils these commandments, God shall call them to himself on the Day of Judgement, saying to them: 'Venite benedicti patris mei, possidete regnum quod vobis paratum est ab origine mundi', which is 'Come, you blessed of my Father, possess the kingdom which has been prepared for you from the beginning of the world.'

We should strive then for the kingdom of heaven which is unlike the human dominion of the present world which earthly kings love. It blinds like mist, it slays like sleep, it wounds like a point, it destroys like a blade, it burns like fire, it drowns like a sea, it swallows like a pit, it devours like a monster. But not like that is the kingdom which the saints and the righteous strive for. It is a bright flower in its great purity, it is an open sea in its great beauty, it is a heaven full of candles in its true brilliance, it is the eye's delight in its great loveliness and pleasantness, it is a flame in its fairness, it is a harp in its melodiousness, it is a feast in its abundance of wine, it is a . . . in its true radiance. Blessed are they who shall come into the Kingdom where God himself is, a King, great, fair, powerful, strong, holy, pure, just, knowing, wise, merciful, loving, beneficent, old, young, wise, noble, glorious, without beginning, without end, without age, without decay. May we enter the kingdom of that King, may we merit it and may we dwell there *in saecula saeculorum*. Amen.

48 *from 'THE EVERNEW TONGUE'*

This is part of an apocryphal work possibly based on a lost Latin Apocalypse of Philip. 'Evernew Tongue' is the apostle Philip whose tongue has been cut out nine times and has been nine times miraculously restored. The text is essentially a dialogue between him and the Hebrew sages who are assembled on Mount Sion on Easter Eve, during which Philip explains to them the secrets of the creation. Of particular interest is the understanding of the cosmic significance of the resurrection since the body of Christ, like any other human body, contained within it all the elements of which the world is made. In the passage below, the two instances of angelic language are gibberish. Tenth or eleventh century. Old Irish with some Middle Irish forms.

Then suddenly, when it was the end of Easter Eve, something was heard: the sound in the clouds like the noise of thunder, or it was like the crash of an oak-tree bursting into flame. Meanwhile there was a thunderous blast, and suddenly a solar glow was seen like a radiant sun in the midst of the sound. That radiant solar glow turned round and round, so that eyesight could not comprehend it, for it was seven times more radiant than the sun.

Then suddenly something was heard, when the eyes of the company were expecting the sound; for they thought it was a sign of the Judgement. Something was heard: the clear voice that spoke in the language of angels: *Haeli habia felebe fae niteia temnibisse salis sal*, that is: 'Hear this story, you sons of men! I have been sent by God to speak with you'.

Then suddenly fainting and fear fell upon the hosts. Nor were they frightened without cause. The sound of the voice was like the shout of an army, except that it was clearer and plainer than the voices of human beings. It rang out over the multitude like the cry of a mighty wind, and yet was not louder than the conversation of friends in each other's ears; and it was sweeter than the melodies of the world.

The sages of the Hebrews answered and said: 'Tell us your name, your substance, your appearance.' Something was heard and the Ever-new Tongue spoke with an angelic voice: *Nathire uimbae o lebiae ua uh nimbisse tiron tibia am biase sau fimblia febe ab le febia fuan*, that is: 'Truly, it was among the tribes of the earth that I was born; and by the conception of man and woman I was conceived. This is my name: Philip the Apostle. The Lord sent me to the tribes of the heathen to preach to them. Nine times my tongue has been cut out of my head and nine times I continued to preach again. Therefore my name among the people of heaven is the Evernew Tongue.'

The sages of the Hebrews said: 'Tell us what language it is that you speak to us.'

He said: 'There is a language of angels, and the language I speak to you is that of all the ranks of heaven. As for the beasts of the sea, reptiles, quadrupeds, birds, snakes and demons, they know it, and this is the language that all will speak at the Judgement.

'This then is what has driven me to you: to explain to you the wonderful tale which the Holy Spirit declared through Moses, son of Amram, of the creation of heaven and earth with all that exists in them. For it is of the making of heaven and earth that that tale speaks, and of the formation of the world, which was effected by Christ's resurrection from the dead on this eve of Easter. For every kind of matter, every element and every essence which is seen in the world were all combined in the body in which Christ arose, that is, in the body of every human being.

'In the first place there is the matter of wind and air. From this there came the afflation of breath in the human body. Then there is the matter of heat and boiling from fire. It is this that makes the red heat of blood in bodies. Then there is the matter of the sun and the other stars of heaven, and it is this that makes colour and light in the eyes of men and women. Then there is the matter of bitterness and saltness, and it is this that makes the bitterness of tears and the gall of the liver and the abundance of wrath in the hearts of men and women. Then there is the matter of the stones and of the clay of earth, and it is this that makes the mingling of flesh and bone and limbs in human beings. Then there is the matter of flowers and the beautiful hues of the earth, and it is this that makes the variegation and whiteness of faces and colour in the cheeks.

'All the world rose with him, for the essence of all the elements dwelt in the body which Jesus assumed. For if the Lord had not suffered on behalf of Adam's race, and if he had not risen after death, the whole world together with Adam's race would be destroyed on Judgement Day, and no creature of sea or land would be reborn, but the heavens, as far as the third heaven, would blaze. With the exception of only three of the high heavens, none would survive without being burned. There would be neither earth nor kindred, alive or dead, in the whole world, only hell and heaven, had the Lord not come to ransom them. All would have perished without renewal.

'For this,' says Philip, 'I have come to you, that I may make this known to you, for the fashioning of the world is obscure to you, as it has been recounted of old.'

49 *THE PRIEST AND THE BEES*

This story comes from the fifteenth century Liber Flavus Fergusiorum. *Middle Irish.*

There was a good, noble and reverend priest, who was God's own servant and bore the yoke of devotion to Christ. One day he went to tend a sick man, and as he was there, a swarm of bees came upon him. He had the sacred Host with him, and when he saw the swarm, he laid the sacred Host on the ground and gathered the swarm into his chest. He forgot the sacred Host lying there, and so went his way. And so it was that the bees went back again from him, and they found the Host and bore it away among them to the home where they lived. And they revered it lovingly, and made for it a lovely chapel of wax and an altar and a Mass chalice and a pair of priests, fashioning them finely of wax, to stand over the Host.

But as for the priest, he remembered the Host and went searching for it in anxiety and contrition, but could not find it anywhere. He was filled with sorrow and went to confession, and with the great contrition that seized him, he spent a whole year in penance. But an angel came to him at the end of the year and told him where the Host was, under reverent protection. And the angel told the priest to bring many people with him to see it. They went and saw it, and when they saw it, many of the people believed in it.

50 *from 'LETTER TO THE BELOVED WELSH'*

Morgan Llwyd (1619–1656) was a Welsh minister and author who, as a Puritan, fought with the Parliamentary forces during the Civil War. Towards the end of his life he read and translated the work of Jakob Böhme, and acquired from him an emphasis upon the presence of God within the human soul. The following extract was written in 1653.

Books are like springs of water, and for some today they are learned teachers who are like so many lights. And so, beloved Welshman, receive these few brief words in truth as an address to you in your own Welsh language.

Publishing many books is pointless; too many thoughts lead to fatigue; speaking many words is dangerous; playing host to many spirits is discomforting, and trying to answer all the reasonings of humankind is folly. But, dear reader, strive to know your own heart, and to enter through the narrow gate.

Many say no; few enter into life. Many dream, few awake; many loose their arrows, few strike their target; everyone speaks of God and gazes upon the work of his hands, but they do not see how near he is to them, giving breath to all and to us life of the spirit.

Almost everyone honours bats more than eagles, seeking to raise the human spirit above that of God, following their own lights without seeing the heavenly sun from the vantage point of the heights.

And, alas, how many Welshmen too, both wise and foolish, live in the sieve of vanity and in the gall of bitterness; they lie bound with untruth in the bed of Babel and feed their flesh in the devil's meadow, not knowing the invisible God who made them or the marvellous God who saved them, or the merciful God who cries out at their door to be let in and to make his dwelling in them.

But each one fumbles their way like a blindman along the wall and the borders looking (in their minds) for something to fill their eyes, to soften their hearts and to cool the burning desire within them, and they live as if on the edge of a shore, where the ebb and flow of flesh and blood ceaselessly beat upon them, who have no thought that they are poised on the edge of a precipice and the cliff of eternity, about to enter the world that shall last for ever, as they sleep beneath the paws of the cat of hell, murmering fondly in their slumber.

'If I had', says one, 'the native wit to know how the spinning wheel turns and to discover depths, then I would be happy and wise among people.'

Another says, 'If I were allowed to enjoy the origin of youth, even if I had to go through the hellish fire of adultery to find it, I would have what I wanted.' And another: 'If everyone were to bow to me as to God, then I would be a fine man.' A fourth says: 'If I had the bowels of the earth for my coffer, I would sleep easily and would be happy.' There is only the occasional one who enquires into the nature of the sun and moon and the appearance of the planets to his mind, and their orbits to his intelligence; but then an animal of a man says: 'If I had good food and strong drink and soft clothes, offspring and leisure and comfort, I would be content.' And the person whose mind is weary says: 'If I were in the grave, in the womb of my first mother, she would hold me and hide me from hell and the tribulation of life on earth.' That person is dreaming who says in their heart, 'If only I could be a scholar, a preacher, a doctor, a traveller, a soldier, a lawyer, a magistrate, or a treasurer, an aristocrat and a gentleman of character in my country, then I would be happier than ever before.'

But, O Welshman (I do not know your name though, by God's light, I know your nature), not one of these knows goodness, nor follows godliness, nor soars beyond the sun to the dweller in eternity, nor sees through faith the rock which produced it; but people try to live among the dead, seeking the sun in the pits of the earth, and you desire the rose, without wishing to come to the garden to fetch it, but die on your feet as you peep across the wall.

You are chasing the wind; you are eating the chaff. And the more you have of it, the more distress there is in your bowels and your mind; desire has deceived you and has imprisoned you in the chains of sin. You are eating grass with the animals, while the dew and power of the firmament rule you in the darkness and pride of Lucifer, who is the prince and root of evil angels, father of sin and torment. You knew neither yourself, poor thing, nor the one who made you, nor him who was sent to create you anew: Christ is the heart of God. If the Son were in your heart, he would destroy your sins, burn your desires, and fill your thoughts with wonderful light in heavenly love and unspeakable joy. Your soul is the image and likeness of God, and nothing can satisfy you but the fullness and image of the Highest, who is Son of the Father, Lamb of God, the First and the Last, the Source of Life, the Beauty of Angels, the Head of the Heavenly Ones, Root of the Universe, Centre of the Lights, Father of Spirits, the Word of God, the Craftsman who made Heaven and Earth, the Light of Men and Women, the Sun of the Scriptures, the Lover of Sinners, the Judge of Devils, the fifth King on the earth, the Ruler within God and humankind. He has one foot on the sea and the other on the shore. He obtains what he wills, and finishes what he begins, and no one can stop him.

He has filled the mind of God, and God is eternal mind, spirit both glorious and wonderful. He can fill your own mind too: he is always close to you, he sees you, hears you, tastes you, smells you, feels your presence everywhere day and night. But you are far from him; that is, you neither see nor hear him, and although he is constantly with you, you are not yet a companion to him. You cannot rest upon him, although he ever bears you in his arms, and though God listens to you at every moment, you have not yet succeeded in speaking a single word to him, in him and before him.

84

Although God takes care of you, filling your mouth with food, your body with life, your nostrils with air, your mind with reason, and your limbs with movement, you have not yet succeeded in conceiving of God in his Son, nor of his Son in his Spirit, nor of his Spirit in his word, nor of his word in your heart, nor of your heart within yourself, nor of yourself in this world, nor of this world in God, nor of God who is glorious in himself.

You should know that the universe which you see is like the bark of a tree, or a crust of bread, or a bone among dogs. It is the spirit or moistness within the creature which unites with your nature and causes desire in you, but beyond the life of nature within you your spirit walks and runs with the angels at all times. And beyond that within you there is the Blessed and Infinite Trinity, the Father, the Word and the Spirit (that is, will, delight and power, the three of these being one), and this far the human mind can penetrate through the spirit. But further than this and deeper there is the root and the ground in the immense, eternal and still unity that no eye can look upon and no mind grasp but his alone . . .

51 *from the WRITINGS OF HOWEL HARRIS*

Although he remained an Anglican, Howel Harris (1714–1773) was one of the most prominent leaders of the Methodist revival in eighteenth century Wales, which was strongly marked by a spirituality of pietism and mass conversion. In the first passage, which is taken from his diary, he speaks of his own conversion, while in the second, he gives spiritual advice to an acquaintance.

June 18th, 1735, being in secret prayer, I felt suddenly my heart melting within me like wax before the fire with love to God my Saviour; and I also felt not only love, peace, etc. but longing to be dissolved, and to be with Christ; then was a cry in my inmost soul, which I was totally unacquainted with before, Abba Father! Abba Father! I could not help calling God my Father; I knew that I was his child, and that he loved me, and heard me. My soul being filled and satiated, crying, 'Tis enough, I am satisfied. Give me strength, and I will follow thee through fire and water.' I could say I was happy indeed! There was in me a well of water, springing up to everlasting life, John 4.14. The love of God was shed abroad in my heart by the Holy Ghost, Romans 5.5 . . .

*

Rest not till you have the Spirit of God continually bearing witness with your spirit that you are born of God, till you can say I know on whom I have believed; — see that faith grows, and then love, meekness, brokenness of heart, godly sorrow, resignation of will, humility, holy fear, watchfulness, tenderness of conscience, and all other graces will grow, which are all destroyed by unbelief and doubts: — O beware of this hellish root, this hardens the heart, and alienates the soul from God. Still look up to Jesus, in him alone salvation is laid up, and can be conveyed to us by faith alone. — O glorious faith, when shall I hear thee preached up fully? All talking of holiness before faith is fruitless; but let us first lay the spring of it in our hearts, Christ living in us by faith, and the tree being once made good, the fruit will be so of course; and without this heart-purifying faith, this world-overcoming newborn creature of God, we may strive, and watch, and pray, but we shall be whited sepulchres at last. O see to the growth of this heavenly flower, and then all the wheels in your soul will keep a regular motion. Beware of false rests, and false peace. Rather, be wounded and mourning, till Christ speaks peace to your soul.

The Oral Tradition:
Gaelic Oral Literature
from Scotland and
Ireland

Carmina Gadelica: Hymns and Incantations
With Illustrative Notes on Words, Rites, and
Customs, Dying and Obsolete: Orally Collected
in the Highlands and Islands of Scotland

by Alexander Carmichael

INVOCATIONS

52 RUNE BEFORE PRAYER

Old people in the Isles sing this or some other short hymn before prayer. Sometimes the hymn and the prayer are intoned in low tremulous unmeasured cadences like the moving and moaning, the soughing and the sighing, of the ever-murmuring sea on their own wild shores.

They generally retire to a closet, to an out-house, to the lee of a knoll, or to the shelter of a dell, that they may not be seen nor heard of men. I have known men and women of eighty, ninety, and a hundred years of age continue the practice of their lives in going from one to two miles to the seashore to join their voices with the waves and their praises with the praises of the ceaseless sea.

> I am bending my knee
> In the eye of the Father who created me,
> In the eye of the Son who purchased me,
> In the eye of the Spirit who cleansed me,
> In friendship and affection.
> Through Thine own Anointed One, O God,
> Bestow upon us fullness in our need,
> Love towards God,
> The affection of God,
> The smile of God,

The wisdom of God,
The grace of God,
The Fear of God,
And the will of God
To do on the world of the Three,
As angels and saints
Do in heaven;
    Each shade and light,
    Each day and night,
    Each time in kindness,
    Give Thou us Thy Spirit.

53 GOD WITH ME LYING DOWN

This poem was taken down in 1866 from Mary Macrae, Harris. She came from Kintail when young, with Alexander Macrae, whose mother was one of the celebrated daughters of Macleod of Rararsay, mentioned by Johnson and Boswell. Mary Macrae was rather under than over middle height, but strongly and symmetrically formed. She often walked with companions, after the work of the day was done, distances of ten and fifteen miles to a dance, and after dancing all night walked back again to the work of the morning fresh and vigorous as if nothing unusual had occurred. She was a faithful servant and an admirable worker, and danced at her leisure and carolled at her work like 'Fosgag Mhoire,' Our Lady's lark, above her.

The people of Harris had been greatly given to old lore and to the old ways of their fathers, reciting and singing, dancing and merry-making; but a reaction occurred, and Mary Macrae's old-world ways were abjured and condemned.

    'The bigots of an iron time
    Had called her simple art a crime.'

But Mary Macrae heeded not, and went on in her own way, singing her songs and ballads, intoning her hymns and incantations, and chanting her own 'port-a-bial,' mouth music, and dancing to her own shadow when nothing better was available.

I love to think of this brave kindly woman, with her strong Highland characteristics and her proud Highland spirit. She was a true type of a grand people gone never to return.

God with me lying down,
God with me rising up,
God with me in each ray of light,
Nor I a ray of joy without Him,
    Nor one ray without Him.

Christ with me sleeping,
Christ with me waking,
Christ with me watching,
Every day and night,
    Each day and night.

God with me protecting,
The Lord with me directing,
The Spirit with me strengthening,
For ever and for evermore,
    Ever and evermore, Amen.
    Chief of chiefs, Amen.

54 *THE INVOCATION OF THE GRACES*

Duncan Maclellan, crofter, Carnan, South Uist, heard this poem from
Catherine Macaulay in the early years of his century. When the crofters
along the east side of South Uist were removed, many of the more frail
and aged left behind became houseless and homeless, moving among
and existing upon the crofters left remaining along the west side of the
island.

Among these was Catherine Macaulay. Her people went to Cape
Breton. She came from Mol-a-deas, adjoining Corradale, where Prince
Charlie lived for several weeks when hiding in South Uist after
Culloden [in 1746]. Catherine Macaulay had seen the Prince several
times, and had many reminiscences of him and of his movements
among the people of the district, who entertained him to their best
when much in need, and who shielded him to their utmost when sorely
harassed.

Catherine Macaulay was greatly gifted in speaking, and was marvellously endowed with a memory for old tales and hymns, runes and
incantations, and for unwritten literature and traditions of many kinds.

She wandered about from house to house, and from townland to townland, warmly welcomed and cordially received wherever she went, and remained in each place longer or shorter according to the population and the season, and as the people could spare the time to hear her. The description which Duncan Maclellan gave of Catherine Macaulay, and of the people who crowded his father's house to hear her night after night, and week after week, and of the discussions that followed her recitations, were realistic and instructive. Being then but a child he could not follow the meaning of this lore, but he thought many times since that much of it must have been about the wild beliefs and practices of his people of the long ago, and perhaps not so long ago either. Many of the poems and stories were long and weird, and he could only remember fragments, which came up to him as he lay awake, thinking of the present and the past, and of the contrast between the two, even in his own time.

I heard versions of this poem in other islands and in districts of the mainland, and in November 1888 John Gregorson Campbell, minister of Tiree, sent me a fragment taken down from Margaret Macdonald, Tiree. The poem must therefore have been widely known. In Tiree the poem was addressed to boys and girls, in Uist to young men and maidens. Probably it was composed to a maiden on her marriage. The phrase 'cala dhonn,' brown swan, would indicate that the girl was young — not yet a white swan.

> I bathe thy palms
> In showers of wine,
> In the lustral fire,
> In the seven elements,
> In the juice of the rasps,
> In the milk and honey,
> And I place the nine pure choice graces
> In thy fair fond face,
>> The grace of form,
>> The grace of voice,
>> The grace of fortune,
>> The grace of goodness,
>> The grace of wisdom,
>> The grace of charity,
>> The grace of choice maidenliness,
>> The grace of whole-souled loveliness,
>> The grace of godly speech.

Dark is yonder town,
Dark are those therein,
Thou art the brown swan,
Going in among them.
Their hearts are under thy control,
Their tongues are beneath thy sole,
Nor will they ever utter a word
        To give thee offence.

A shade art thou in the heat,
A shelter art thou in the cold,
Eyes art thou to the blind,
A staff art thou to the pilgrim,
An island art thou at sea,
A fortress art thou on land,
A well art thou in the desert,
        Health art thou to the ailing.

Thine is the skill of the Fairy Woman,
Thine is the virtue of Bride the calm,
Thine is the faith of Mary the mild,
Thine is the tact of the woman of Greece,
Thine is the beauty of Emir the lovely,
Thine is the tenderness of Darthula delightful,
Thine is the courage of Maebh the strong,
        Thine is the charm of Binne-bheul.

Thou art the joy of all joyous things,
Thou art the light of the beam of the sun,
Thou art the door of the chief of hospitality,
Thou art the surpassing star of guidance,
Thou art the step of the deer of the hill,
Thou art the step of the steed of the plain,
Thou art the grace of the swan of swimming,
        Thou art the loveliness of all lovely desires.

The lovely likeness of the Lord
Is in thy pure face,
The loveliest likeness that
Was upon earth.

The best hour of the day be thine,
The best day of the week be thine,
The best week of the year be thine,
The best year in the Son of God's domain be thine.

Peter has come and Paul has come,
James has come and John has come,
Muriel and Mary Virgin have come,
Uriel the all-beneficent has come,
Ariel the beauteousness of the young man has come,
Gabriel the seer of the Virgin has come,
Raphael the prince of the valiant has come,
And Michael the chief of the hosts has come,
    And Jesus Christ the mild has come,
    And the Spirit of true guidance has come,
    And the King of kings has come on the helm,
    To bestow on thee their affection and their love,
        To bestow on thee their affection and their love.

55 JESUS WHO OUGHT TO BE PRAISED

The reciter said that this poem was composed by a woman in Harris. She was afflicted with leprosy, and was removed from the community on the upland to dwell alone on the sea-shore, where she lived on the plants of the plains and on the shell-fish of the strand. The woman bathed herself in the liquid in which she had boiled the plants and shell-fish. All her sores became healed and her flesh became new — probably as the result of the action of the plants and shell-fish.

Leprosy was common everywhere in mediaeval times. In Shetland the disease continued till towards the end of the last century. Communities erected lazar-houses to safeguard themselves from persons afflicted with leprosy. Liberton, now a suburb of Edinburgh, derives its name from a lazaretto having been established there.

The shrine of St James of Compostello in Spain was famous for the cure of leprosy. Crowds of leper pilgrims from the whole of Christendom resorted to this shrine, and many of them were healed to the glory of the Saint and the enrichment of his shrine. In their gratitude, pilgrims offered costly oblations of silks and satins, of raiments and vestments, of silver and gold, of pearls and precious stones, till the shrine of St James of Compostello became famous throughout the world. The bay of Compostello was famed for fish and shell-fish, and the leper pilgrims who came to pray at the altar of the Saint and to bestow gifts at his shrine were fed on those and were healed — according to the belief of the period, by the miraculous intervention of the Saint. As the palm was the badge of the pilgrims to Jerusalem, the scallop-shell was the badge of the pilgrims to Compostello: 'My sandal shoon and scallop-shell'.

> It were as easy for Jesu
> To renew the withered tree
> As to wither the new
> Were it His will so to do.
>> Jesu! Jesu! Jesu!
>> Jesu! meet it were to praise Him.

> There is no plant in the ground
> But is full of His virtue,
> There is no form in the strand
> But is full of His blessing.
>> Jesu! Jesu! Jesu!
>> Jesu! meet it were to praise Him.

> There is no life in the sea,
> There is no creature in the river,
> There is naught in the firmament,
> But proclaims His goodness.
>> Jesu! Jesu! Jesu!
>> Jesu! meet it were to praise Him.

> There is no bird on the wing,
> There is no star in the sky,
> There is nothing beneath the sun,
> But proclaims His goodness.
>> Jesu! Jesu! Jesu!
>> Jesu! meet it were to praise Him.

56 *THE GUARDIAN ANGEL*

Thou angel of God who hast charge of me
From the dear Father of mercifulness,
The shepherding kind of the fold of the saints
To make round about me this night;

Drive from me every temptation and danger,
Surround me on the sea of unrighteousness,
And in the narrows, crooks and straits,
Keep thou my coracle, keep it always.

Be thou a bright flame before me,
Be thou a guiding star above me,
Be thou a smooth path below me,
And be a kindly shepherd behind me,
To-day, to-night, and for ever.

I am tired and I a stranger,
Lead thou me to the land of angels;
For me it is time to go home
To the court of Christ, to the peace of heaven.

57 *DESIRES*

May I speak each day according to Thy justice,
Each day may I show Thy chastening, O God;
May I speak each day according to Thy wisdom,
Each day and night may I be at peace with Thee.

Each day may I count the causes of Thy mercy,
May I each day give heed to Thy laws;
Each day may I compose to Thee a song,
May I harp each day Thy praise, O God.

May I each day give love to Thee, Jesu,
Each night may I do the same;
Each day and night, dark and light,
May I laud Thy goodness to me, O God.

58 *INVOCATION FOR JUSTICE*

The administration of law and justice throughout the Highlands and Islands before the abolition of heritable jurisdictions was inadequate — men being too often appointed to administer justice not from their fitness but from their influence. Probably the feeling of distrust engendered by this absence of even-handed justice evoked these poems from the consciousness of the people and led them to appeal their cause to a Higher Court.

The litigant went at morning dawn to a place where three streams met. And as the rising sun gilded the mountain crests, the man placed his two palms edgeways together and filled them with water from the junction of the streams. Dipping his face into this improvised basin, he fervently repeated the prayer, after which he made his way to the court, feeling strong in the justice of his cause. On entering the court and looking round the room, the applicant for justice mentally, sometimes in an undertone, said —

> God sain the house
> From site to summit;
> My word above every person,
> The word of every person below my foot.

The ceremonies observed in saying these prayers for justice, like those observed on many similar occasions, are symbolic. The bathing represents purification; the junction of three streams, the union of the Three Persons of the Godhead; and the spreading rays of the morning sun, divine grace. The deer is symbolic of wariness, the horse of strength, the serpent of wisdom, and the king of dignity.

> I will wash my face
> In the nine rays of the sun,
> As Mary washed her Son
>> In the rich fermented milk.

> Love be in my countenance,
> Benevolence in my mind,
> Dew of honey in my tongue,
>> My breath as the incense.

97

Black is yonder town,
Black are those therein,
I am the white swan,
     Queen above them.

I will travel in the name of God,
In likeness of deer, in likeness of horse,
In likeness of serpent, in likeness of king:
     Stronger will it be with me than with all persons.

59 SLEEP BLESSING

The night prayers of the people are numerous. They are called by
various names, as: 'Beannachadh Beinge' — Bench-Blessing, 'Beannachadh Bobhstair' — Bolster Blessing, 'Beannachadh Cluasaig' —
Pillow Blessing, 'Beannachadh Cuaiche' — Couch Blessing, 'Coich
Chuaiche' — Couch Shrining, 'Altachadh Cadail' — Sleep Prayer; and
other terms. Many of these prayers are become mere fragments and
phrases, supplemented by the people according to their wants and
wishes at the time.

It is touching and instructive to hear these simple old men and
women in their lowly homes addressing, as they say themselves, 'Dia
mor nan dul, Athair nan uile bheo,' the great God of life, the Father of
all living. They press upon Him their needs and their desires fully and
familiarly, but with all the awe and deference due to the Great Chief
whom they wish to approach and attract, and whose forgiveness and aid
they would secure. And all this in language so homely yet so eloquent,
so simple yet so dignified, that the impressiveness could not be greater
in proudest fane.

60 SLEEP CONSECRATION

I lie down to-night
With fair Mary and with her Son,
With pure-white Michael,
And with Bride beneath her mantle.

I lie down with God,
And God will lie down with me,
I will not lie down with Satan,
Nor shall Satan lie down with me.

O God of the poor,
Help me this night,
Omit me not entirely
From thy treasure-house.

For the many wounds
That I inflicted on Thee,
I cannot this night
Enumerate them.

Thou King of the blood of Truth,
Do not forget me in Thy dwelling-place,
Do not exact from me for my transgressions,
Do not omit me in Thine ingathering.
          In Thine ingathering.

61 *THE SOUL-SHRINE*

The Soul-Shrine is sung by the people as they retire to rest. They say
that the angels of heaven guard them in sleep and shield them from
harm. Should any untoward event occur to themselves or to their flocks,
they avow that the cause was the deadness of their hearts, the coldness
of their faith, and the fewness of their prayers.

God, give charge to Thy blessed angels,
     To keep guard around this stead to-night,
A band sacred, strong, and steadfast,
     That will shield this soul-shrine from harm.

Safeguard Thou, God, this household to-night,
     Themselves and their means and their fame,
Deliver them from death, from distress, from harm,
     From the fruits of envy and of enmity.

Give Thou to us, O God of peace,
Thankfulness despite our loss,
To obey Thy statutes here below,
And to enjoy Thyself above.

62 *A RESTING PRAYER*

God shield the house, the fire, the kine,
Every one who dwells herein to-night.
Shield myself and my beloved group,
Preserve us from violence and from harm;
Preserve us from foes this night,
For the sake of the Son of the Mary Mother,
In this place, and in every place wherein they dwell to-night,
On this night and on every night,
This night and every night.

63 *THE BAPTISM BLESSING*

It is known that a form of baptism prevailed among the Celts previous to the introduction of Christianity, as forms of baptism prevail among pagan people now. Whenever possible the Celtic Church chris-tianized existing ceremonies and days of special observance, grafting the new on the old, as at a later day Augustine did in southern Britain. Immediately after its birth the nurse or other person present drops three drops of water on the forehead of the child. The first drop is in the name of the Father, representing wisdom; the second drop is in the name of the Son, representing peace; the third drop is in the name of the Spirit, representing purity. If the child be a male the name 'Maol-domhnuich,' if a female the name 'Griadach,' is applied to it temporarily. 'Maol-domhnuich' means tonsured of the Lord, and 'Griadach' is rendered Gertrude. When the child is ecclesiastically baptized — generally at the end of eight days — the temporary is super-seded by the permanent name. This lay baptism is recognized by the Presbyterians, the Anglican, the Latin, and the Greek Churches. If the child were not thus baptized it would need to be carefully guarded lest the fairies should spirit it away before the ecclesiastical baptism took place, when their power over it ceased. The lay baptism also ensured that in the event of death the child should be buried in consecrated ground.

> Thou Being who inhabitest the heights
> Imprint Thy blessing betimes,
> Remember Thou the child of my body,
> In Name of the Father of peace;
> When the priest of the King
> On him puts the water of meaning,
> Grant him the blessing of the Three
> Who fill the heights.
> The blessing of the Three
> Who fill the heights.

> Sprinkle down upon him Thy grace,
> Give Thou to him virtue and growth,
> Give Thou to him strength and guidance,
> Give Thou to him flocks and possessions,
> Sense and reason void of guile,
> Angel wisdom in his day,
> That he may stand without reproach
> In Thy presence.
> He may stand without reproach
> In Thy presence.

64 *THE SOUL LEADING*

Death blessings vary in words but not in spirit. These death blessings are known by various names, as: 'Beannachadh Bais,' Death Blessing, 'Treoraich Anama,' Soul Leading, 'Fois Anama,' Soul Peace, and other names familiar to the people.

The soul peace is intoned, not necessarily by a cleric, over the dying, and the man or the woman who says it is called 'anam-chara,' soul-friend. He or she is held on special affection by the friends of the dying person ever after. The soul peace is slowly sung — all present earnestly joining the soul-friend in beseeching the Three Persons of the God-head and all the saints of heaven to receive the departing soul of earth. During the prayer the soul-friend makes the sign of the cross with the right thumb over the lips of the dying.

The scene is touching and striking in the extreme, and the man or woman is not to be envied who could witness unmoved the distress of these lovable people of the West taking leave of those who are near and dear to them in their pilgrimage, as they say, of crossing 'abhuinn dubh a bhais' — the black river of death; 'cuan mor na duibhre' — the great ocean of darkness; and 'beanntaibh na bith-bhuantachd' — the mountains of eternity. The scene may be a lowly cot begrimed with smoke and black with age, but the heart is not less warm, the tear is not less bitter, and the parting is not less distressful, than in the court of the noble or in the palace of royalty . . .

When a person gives up the ghost the soul is seen ascending like a bright ball of light into the clouds. Then it is said: —

> The poor soul is now set free
> Outside the soul-shrine;
> O kindly Christ of the free blessings,
> Encompass Thou my love in time . . .

65 *THE DEATH BLESSING*

God, omit not this woman from Thy covenant,
And the many evils which she in the body committed,
That she cannot this night enumerate.
> The many evils that she in the body committed,
> That she cannot this night enumerate.

Be this soul on Thine own arm, O Christ,
Thou King of the City of Heaven,
And since Thine it was, O Christ, to buy the soul,
At the time of the balancing of the beam,
At the time of the bringing of judgement,
Be it now on Thine own right hand,
> Oh! on Thine own right hand.

And be the holy Michael, king of angels,
Coming to meet the soul,
And leading it home
To the heaven of the Son of God.
> The Holy Michael, high king of angels,

Coming to meet the soul,
And leading it home
To the heaven of the Son of God.

66 *THE NEW MOON*

This little prayer is said by old men and women in the islands of Barra.
When they first see the new moon they make their obeisance to it as to a
great chief. The women curtsey gracefully and the men bow low,
raising their bonnets reverently. The bow of the men is peculiar,
partaking somewhat of the curtsey of the women, the left knee being
bent and the right drawn forward towards the middle of the left leg in a
curious but not inelegant manner.

The fragment of moon-worship is now a matter of custom rather
than of belief, although it exists over the whole British Isles.

In Cornwall the people nod to the new moon and turn silver in their
pockets. In Edinburgh cultured men and women turn the rings on their
fingers and make their wishes. A young English lady told the writer that
she had always been in the habit of bowing to the new moon, till she had
been bribed out of it by her father, a clergyman, putting money in her
pocket lest her lunar worship should compromise him with his bishop.
She naively confessed, however, that among the free mountains of Loch
Etive she reverted to the good customs of her fathers, from which she
derived great satisfaction!

In name of the Holy Spirit of grace,
In name of the Father of the City of peace,
In name of Jesus who took death off us,
Oh, in name of the Three who shield us in every need,
If well thou hast found us to-night,
Seven times better mayest thou leave us without harm,
Thou bright white Moon of the seasons,
Bright white Moon of the seasons.

67 *AUGURY OF MARY*

The 'frith,' augury, was a species of divination enabling the 'frithir,'
augurer, to see into the unseen. This divination was made to ascertain

the position and condition of the absent and the lost, and was applied to man and beast. The augury was made on the first Monday of the quarter and immediately before sunrise. The augurer, fasting, and with bare feet, bare head, and closed eyes, went to the doorstep and placed a hand on each jamb. Mentally beseeching the God of the unseen to show him his quest and to grant him his augury, the augurer opened his eyes and looked steadfastly straight in front of him. From the nature and position of the objects within his sight, he drew his conclusions.

Many men in the Highlands and Islands were famed augurers, and many stories, realistic, romantic, and extremely curious, are still told of their divinations.

The people say that the Virgin made an augury when Christ was missing, and that it was by means of this augury that Mary and Joseph ascertained that Christ was in the Temple disputing with the doctors. Hence this divination is called 'frith Mhoire,' — the augury of Mary; and 'frithircachd Mhoire,' — the auguration of Mary.

The 'frith' of the Celt is akin to the 'frett' of the Norsemen. Probably the surnames Freer, Frere, are modifications of 'frithir,' augurer. Persons bearing this name claim that their progenitors were astrologers to the kings of Scotland.

> God over me, God under me,
> God before me, God behind me,
> I on Thy path, O God,
> Thou, O God, in my steps.
>
> The augury made of Mary to her Son,
> The offering made of Bride through her palm,
> Sawest Thou it, King of life? —
> Said the King of life that He saw.
>
> The augury made by Mary for her own offspring,
> When He was for a space amissing,
> Knowledge of truth, not knowledge of falsehood,
> That I shall truly see all my quest.
>
> Son of beauteous Mary, King of life,
> Give Thou me eyes to see all my quest,
> With grace that shall never fail, before me,
> That shall never quench nor dim.

68 *OMENS*

The people believed in omens of birds and beasts, fishes and insects, and of men and women. These omens were innumerable, and a few only can be mentioned.

The fisher would deem it a bad omen to meet a red-haired woman when on his way to fish; and were the woman defective in mind or body, probably the man would return home muttering strong adjectives beneath his breath. On the other hand, it was lucky for a girl to find the red hair of a woman in the nest of certain birds, particularly in the nest of the wheatear . . .

69 *OMENS*

I heard the cuckoo with no food in my stomach,
I heard the stock-dove on the top of the tree,
I heard the sweet singer in the copse beyond,
And I heard the screech of the owl of the night.

I saw the lamb with his back to me,
I saw the snail on the bare flag-stone,
I saw the foal with his rump to me,
I saw the wheatear on a dyke of holes,
I saw the snipe while sitting bent,
And I forsaw that the year would not
        Go well with me.

SEASONS

70 *THE GENEALOGY OF BRIDE*

The Genealogy of Bride was current among people who had a latent belief in its efficacy. Other hymns to Bride were sung on her festival, but nothing now remains except the name and fragments of the words. The names are curious and suggestive, as: 'Ora Bhride,' Prayer of Bride, 'Lorg Bhride,' Staff of Bride, 'Luireach Bhride,' Lorica of Bride, 'Lorig

Bhride,' Mantle of Bride, 'Brot Bhride,' Corslet of Bride, and others. La Feill Bhride, St Bridget's Day, is the first of February, new style, or the thirteenth according to the old style, which is still much in use in the Highlands. It was a day of great rejoicing and jubilation in olden times, and gave rise to innumerable sayings, as —

Feast of the Bride, feast of the maiden.

Melodious Bride of the fair palms.

Thou Bride fair charming,
Pleasant to me the breath of thy mouth,
When I would go among strangers
Thou thyself wert the hearer of my tale.

There are many legends and customs connected with Bride. Some of these seem inconsistent with one another, and with the character of the Saint of Kildare. These seeming inconsistencies arise from the fact that there were several Brides, Christian and pre-Christian, whose personalities have become confused in the course of centuries — the attributes of all being now popularly ascribed to one. Bride is said to preside over fire, over art, over all beauty, 'fo cheabhar agus fo chuan,' beneath the sky and beneath the sea. And man being the highest type of ideal beauty, Bride presides at his birth and dedicated him to the Trinity. She is the Mary and the Juno of the Gael. She is much spoken of in connection with Mary — generally in relation to the birth of Christ. She was the aid-woman of the Mother of Nazareth in the lowly stable, and she is the aid-woman of the mothers of Uist in their humble homes.

It is said that Bride was the daughter of poor pious parents, and the serving-maid in the inn of Bethlehem. Great drought occurred in the land, and the master of the hostel went away with his cart to procure water from afar, leaving with Bride, 'faircil buirn agus breacag arain,' a stoup of water and a bannock of bread to sustain her till his return. The man left injunctions with Bride not to give food or drink to any one, as he had left only enough for herself, and not to give shelter to any one against his return.

As Bride was working in the house two strangers came to the door. The man was old, with brown hair and grey beard, and the woman was young and beautiful, with oval face, straight nose, blue eyes, red lips, small ears, and golden brown hair, which fell below her waist. They asked the serving-maid for a place to rest, for they were footsore and weary, for food to satisfy their hunger, and for water to quench their thirst. Bride could not give them shelter, but she gave them of her own bannock and of her own stoup of water, of which they partook at the door; and having thanked Bride the strangers went their way, while Bride gazed wistfully and sorrowfully after them. She saw that the sickness of life was on the young woman of the lovely face, and her heart was sore that she had not in her power to give them shade from the heat of the sun, and cover from the cold of the dew. When Bride returned into the house in the darkening of the twilight, what was stranger to her to see than that the bannock of bread was whole, and the stoup of water full, as they had been before! She did not know under the land of the world what she would say or what she would do. The food and the water of which she herself had given them, and had seen them partake, without a bit or a drop lacking from them! When she recovered from her wonderment Bride went out to look after the two who had gone their way, but she could see no more of them. But she saw a brilliant golden light over the stable door, and knowing that it was not a 'dreag a bhais,' a meteor of death, she went into the stable and was in time to aid and minister to the Virgin Mother, and to receive the Child into her arms, for the strangers were Joseph and Mary, and the child was Jesus Christ, the Son of God, come to earth, and born in the stable of the hostel of Bethlehem. . . . When the Child was born Bride put three drops of water from the spring of pure water on the tablet of His forehead, in the name of God, in the name of Jesus, in the name of the Spirit. When the master of the inn was returning home, and ascending the hill on which his house stood, he heard the murmuring music of a stream flowing past his house, and he saw the light of a bright star above his stable door. He knew from these signs that the Messiah was come and that Christ was born . . . for it was in the seership of the people that Jesus Christ, the Son of God, would be born in Bethlehem, the town of David. And the man rejoiced with exceeding joy at the fulfilment of the prophecy, and he went to the stable and worshipped the new Christ, whose infant cradle was the manger of the horses.

Thus Bride is called 'ban-chuideachaidh Moire,' the aid-woman of Mary. In this connection, and in consequence thereof, she is called 'Muime Chriosda,' foster-mother of Christ; 'Bana-ghoistidh Mhic De,' the god-mother of the Son of God; 'Bana-ghoistidh Iosda Criosda nam bann agus nam beannachd,' god-mother of Jesus Christ of the bindings and blessings. Christ again is called 'Dalta Bride,' the foster-son of

Bride; 'Dalta Bride bith nam beannachd,' the foster-son of Bride of the blessings; 'Daltan Bride,' little fosterling of Bride, a term of endearment.

John the beloved is called 'Dalta Moire,' foster-son of Mary, and 'Comhdhalta Chriosda,' the foster-brother, literally co-foster, of Christ. Fostership among the Highlanders was a peculiarly close and tender tie, more close and more tender even than blood. There are many proverbs on the subject, as '. . . blood to the twentieth, fostership to the hundredth degree'. A church in Islay is called 'Cill Daltain,' the Church of the Fosterling.

When a woman is in labour, the midwife or the woman next to her in importance goes to the door of the house, and standing on the 'fad-buinn,' sole-sod, door-step, with her hands on the jambs, softly beseeches Bride to come:

> Bride! Bride! come in,
> Thy welcome is truly made,
> Give thou relief to the woman,
> And give the conception to the Trinity.

When things go well, it indicates that Bride is present and is friendly to the family; and when they go ill, that she is absent and offended. Following the action of Bride at the birth of Christ, the aid-woman dedicates the child to the Trinity by letting three drops of clear cold water fall on the tablet of his forehead.

The aid-woman was held in reverence by all nations. Juno was worshipped with greater honour than any other deity of ancient Rome, and the Pharaohs paid tribute to the aid-women of Egypt. . . .

On Bride's Eve the girls of the townland fashion a sheaf of corn into the likeness of a woman. They dress and deck the figure with shining shells, sparkling crystals, primroses, snowdrops, and any greenery they may obtain. In the mild climate of the Outer Hebrides several species of plants continue in flower during winter, unless the season be exceptionally severe. The gales of March are there the destoyers of plant-life. A specially bright shell or crystal is placed over the heart of the figure. This is called 'reul-iuil Bride,' the guiding star of Bride, and typifies the star over the stable door of Bethlehem, which led Bride to the infant Christ. The girls call the figure 'Bride,' 'Brideag,' Bride, Little Bride, and carry it in procession, singing the song of 'Bride bhoidheach oigh nam mile beus,' Beauteous Bride, virgin of a thousand charms. The 'banal Bride,' Bride maiden band, are clad in white, and have their hair down, symbolising purity and youth. They visit every house, and every person is expected to give a gift to Bride and to make obeisance to her. The gift may be a shell, a spar, a crystal, a flower, or a bit of greenery to decorate the person of Bride. Mothers, however, give 'bonnach Bride,' a Bride bannock, 'cabag Bride,' a Bride cheese, or 'rolag Bride,' a Bride roll of butter. Having made the round of the place the girls go to a house to make the 'feis Bride,' Bride feast. They bar the door and secure the windows of the house, and set Bride where she may see and be seen by all. Presently the young men of the community come humbly asking permission to honour Bride. After some parleying they are admitted and make obeisance to her.

Much dancing and singing, fun and frolic, are indulged in by the young men and maidens during the night. As the grey dawn of the Day of Bride breaks they form a circle and sing the hymn of 'Bride bhoidheach muime chorr Chriosda,' Beauteous Bride, choice foster-mother of Christ. They then distribute 'fuidheal na feisde,' the fragments of the feast — practically the whole, for they have partaken very sparingly, in order to have the more to give — among the poor women of the place.

A similar practice prevails in Ireland. There the churn staff, not the corn sheaf, is fashioned into the form of a woman, and is called 'Brideog,' little Bride. The girls come clad in their best, and the girl who has the prettiest dress gives it to Brideog. An ornament something like a Maltese cross is affixed to the breast of the figure. The ornament is composed of straw, beautifully and artistically interlaced by the deft fingers of the maidens of Bride. It is called 'rionnag Brideog', the star of little Bride. Pins, needles, bits of stone, bits of straw, and other things are given to Bride as gifts, and food by the mothers.

Customs assume the complexion of their surroundings, as fishes, birds, and beasts assimilate the colours of their habitats. The seas of the 'Garbh Chriocha,' Rough Bounds in which the cult of Bride has longest lived, abound in beautiful iridescent shells, and the mountains in bright sparkling stones, and they are utilised to adorn the ikon of Bride. In other districts where the figure of Bride is made, there are no shining shells, no brilliant crystals, and the girls decorate the image with artistically interlaced straw.

The older women are also busy on the Eve of Bride, and the great preparations are made to celebrate her Day, which is the first day of spring. They make an oblong basket in the shape of a cradle, which they call 'leaba Bride,' the bed of Bride. It is embellished with much care. They take a choice sheaf of corn, generally oats, and fashion it into the form of a woman. They deck this ikon with gay ribbons from the loom, sparkling shells from the sea, and bright stones from the hill. All the sunny sheltered valleys around are searched for primroses, daisies, and other flowers that open their eyes in the morning of the year. This lay figure is called Bride, 'dealbh Bride,' the ikon of Bride. When it is dressed and decorated with all the tenderness and loving care the women can lavish upon it, one woman goes to the door of the house, and standing on the step with her hands on the jambs, calls softly into the darkness, 'Tha leaba Bride deiseal,' Bride's bed is ready. To this a ready woman behind replies, 'Thigeadh Bride steach, is e beatha Bride,' Let Bride come in, Bride is welcome. The woman at the door again addresses Bride, . . . Bride, come thou in, thy bed is made. Preserve the house for the Trinity. The women then place the ikon of Bride with great ceremony in the bed they have so carefully prepared for it. They place a small straight white wand (the bark being peeled off) beside the figure. This wand is variously called 'slatag Bride,' the little rod of Bride, 'slachdan Bride,' the little wand of Bride, and 'barrag Bride,' the birch of Bride. The wand is generally of birch, broom, bramble, white willow, or other sacred wood, 'crossed' or banned wood being carefully avoided. A similar rod was given to the kings of Ireland at their coronation, and to the Lords of the Isles at their installment. It was straight to typify justice, and white to signify peace and purity — bloodshed was not to be needlessly caused. The women then level the ashes on the hearth, smoothing and dusting them over carefully. Occasionally the ashes, surrounded by a roll of cloth, are placed on a board to safeguard them against disturbance from draughts or other contingencies. In the early morning the family closely scan the ashes. If they find the marks of the wand of Bride they rejoice, but if they find 'lorg Bride,' the footprint of Bride, their joy is very great, for this is a sign that Bride was present with them during the night, and is favour-able to them and that there is increase in a family, in flock, and in field during the coming year. Should there be no marks on the ashes, and no trace of Bride's presence, the family are dejected. It is to them a sign that she is offended, and will not hear their call. To propitiate her and gain her ear the family offer oblations and burn incense. The oblation generally is a cockerel, some say a pullet, buried alive near the junction of three streams, and the incense is burnt on the hearth when the family retire for the night.

In the Highlands and Islands St Bride's Day was called 'La Cath Choileach,' Day of Cock-fighting. The boys brought cocks to the school to fight. The most successful cock was called 'coileach buadha,' victor cock, and its proud owner was elected king of the school for the year. A defeated bird was called 'fuidse,' craven, 'coileach fuidse,' craven cock. All the defeated, maimed, and killed cocks were the perquisites of the schoolmaster. In the Lowlands, 'La Coinnle,' Candlemas Day, was the day thus observed.

It is said in Ireland that Bride walked before Mary with a lighted candle in each hand when she went up to the Temple for purification. The winds were strong on the Temple heights, and the tapers were unprotected, yet they did not flicker nor fall. From this incident Bride is called 'Bride boillsge,' Bride of brightness. This day is occasionally called 'La Fheill Bride nan Coinnle,' the Feast Day of Bride of the Candles, but more generally 'La Fheill Moire nan Coinnle,' the Feast Day of Mary of the Candles — Candlemas Day.

The serpent is supposed to emerge from its hollow among the hills on St Bride's Day, and a propitiatory hymn was sung to it. Only one verse of this hymn has been obtained, apparently the first. It differs in different localities: —

> Early on Bride's morn
> The serpent shall come from the hole,
> I will not molest the serpent,
> Nor will the serpent molest me.

Other versions say: —

> The Feast Day of the Bride,
> The daughter of Ivor shall come from the knoll,
> I will not touch the daughter of Ivor,
> Nor shall she harm me.

*

> On the Feast Day of Bride,
> The head will come off the 'caiteanach,'
> The daughter of Ivor will come from the knoll
> With tuneful whistling.

*

The serpent will come from the hole
On the brown Day of Bride,
Though there should be three feet of snow
On the flat surface of the ground.

The 'daughter of Ivor' is the serpent; and it is said that the serpent will not sting a descendant of Ivor, he having made 'tabhar agus tuis,' offering and incense, to it, thereby securing immunity from its sting for himself and his seed for ever.

On the day of Bride of the white hills
The noble queen will come from the knoll,
I will not molest the noble queen,
Nor will the noble queen molest me.

These lines would seem to point to serpent-worship. One of the most curious customs of Bride's Day was the pounding of the serpent in effigy. The following scene was described to the writer by one who was present: —

I was one of several guests in the hospitable house of Mr John Tolmie of Uignis, Skye. One of my fellow guests was Mrs Macleod, widow of Major Macleod of Stein, and daughter of Flora Macdonald. Mrs Macleod was known among her friends as 'Major Ann'. She combined the warmest of hearts with the sternest of manners, and was the admiration of old and young for her wit, wisdom, and generosity. When told that her son had fallen in a duel with the celebrated Glengarry — the Ivor MacIvor of Waverley *— she exclaimed, '. . . Good thou art my son! good thou art my son! thou the white love of thine own mother! Better the hero's death than the craven's life; the brave dies but once, the coward many times.' In a company of noblemen and gentlemen at Dunvegan Castle, Mrs Macleod, then in her 88th year, danced the reel of Tullock and other reels, jigs, and strathspays as lightly as a girl in her teens. Wherever she was, all strove to show Mrs Macleod attention and to express the honour in which she was held. She accepted all these honours and attentions with grace and dignity, and without any trace of vanity or self-consciousness. One morning at breakfast at Uignis some one remarked that this was the Day of Bride. 'The Day of Bride,' repeated Mrs Macleod meditatively, and with a dignified bow of apology rose from the table. All watched her movements with eager curiosity. Mrs Macleod went to the fireside and took up the tongs and a bit of* *peat and walked out to the doorstep. She then took off her stocking and put the peat into it, and pounded it with the tongs. And as she pounded the peat on the step, she intoned a 'rann,' rune, only one verse of which I can remember:*

> *This is the day of Bride,*
> *The Queen will come from the mound,*
> *I will not touch the queen,*
> *Nor will the queen touch me.*

Having pounded the peat and replaced her stocking, Mrs Macleod returned to the table, apologising for her remissness in not remembering the Day earlier in the morning. I could not make out whether Mrs Macleod was serious or acting, for she was a consummate actress and the delight of young and old. Many curious ceremonies and traditions in connection with Bride were told that morning but I do not remember them.

The pounding in the stocking of the peat representing the serpent would indicate destruction rather than worship, perhaps the bruising of the serpent's head. Probably, however, the ceremony is older, and designed to symbolise something now lost.

Gaelic lore is full of sayings about serpents. These indicate close observation, 'Tha cluas nathrach aige,' — he has the ear of a serpent (he hears keenly but does not speak); 'Tha a bhana-bhuitseach lubach mar an nathair,' — the witch-woman is crooked as a serpent; 'Is e an t-iorball is neo-chronail dhiot, cleas na nathrach nimhe,' — the tail is the least harmful of thee, the trick of the serpent venomous.

> Though smooth be thy skin,
> Venomous is the sting of thy mouth;
> Thou art like the dun serpent,
> Take thine own road.

> The beauteous woman, ungenerous,
> And she full of warm words,
> Is like the brindled serpent,
> And the sting of greed is in her.

[. . .]

In Barra, lots are cast for the 'iolachan iasgaich,' fishing-banks, on Bride's Day. These fishing banks of the sea are as well known and as accurately defined by the fishermen of Barra as are the qualities and boundaries of their crofts on land, and they apportion them with equal care. Having ascertained among themselves the number of boats going to the long-line fishing, the people divide the banks accordingly. All go to church on St Bride's Day. After reciting the virtues and blessings of Bride, and the examples to be drawn from her life, the priest reminds his hearers that the great God who made the land and all thereon, also made the sea and all therein, and that . . . the wealth of the sea and the plenty of the land, the treasury of Columba and the treasury of Mary, are His gift to them that follow Him and call upon His name, on rocky hill or on crested wave. The priest urges upon them to avoid disputes and quarrels over their fishing, to remember the poor, the widow and the orphan, now left to the fatherhood of God and to the care of His people. Having come out of church, the men cast lots for the fishing-banks at the church door. After this, they disperse to their homes, all talking loudly and discussing their luck or unluck in the drawing of the lots. A stranger would be apt to think that the people were quarrelling. But it is not so. The simultaneous talking is their habit, and the loudness of their speaking is the necessity of their living among the noise of winds and waves, whether on sea or on shore. Like the people of St Kilda, the people of Barra are warmly attached to one another, the joy of one and the grief of another being the joy and grief of all.

The same practice of casting lots for their fishing-banks prevails among the fisher-folks of the Lofodin Islands, Norway.

From these traditional observations, it will be seen that Bride and her services are near to the hearts and lives of the people. In some phases of her character she is much more to them than Mary is.

Dedications to Bride are common throughout Great Britain and Ireland.

GENEALOGY OF BRIDE

The genealogy of the holy maiden Bride,
Radiant flame of gold, noble foster-mother of Christ.
Bride the daugher of Dugall the brown,
Son of Aodh, son of Art, son of Conn,
Son of Crearar, son of Cis, son of Carmac, son of Carruin.

Every day and every night
That I say the genealogy of Bride,
I shall not be killed, I shall not be harried,
I shall not be put in cell, I shall not be wounded,
Neither shall Christ leave me in forgetfulness.

No fire, no sun, no moon shall burn me,
No lake, no water, nor sea shall drown me,
No arrow or fairy dart of fay shall wound me,
And I under the protection of my Holy Mary,
And my gentle foster-mother is my beloved Bride.

71 *BRIDE THE AID-WOMAN*

There came to me assistance,
Mary fair and Bride;
As Anna bore Mary,
As Mary bore Christ,
As Eile bore John the Baptist
Without flaw in him,
Aid thou me in mine unbearing,
        Aid me O Bride!

As Christ was conceived of Mary
Full perfect on every hand,
Assist thou me, foster-mother,
The conception to bring from the bone;
And as thou didst aid the Virgin of joy,
Without gold, without corn, without kine,
Aid thou me, great is my sickness,
        Aid me, O Bride!

72 *THE BELTANE BLESSING*

Bealltain, Beltane, is the first day of May. On May Day all the fires of the district were extinguished and 'tein eigin,' need-fire, produced on the knoll. This fire was divided in two, and people and cattle rushed through for purification and safeguarding against 'ealtraigh agus dosgaidh,' mischance and murrain, during the year. The people obtained fires for their homes from this need-fire. The practice of producing the need-fire came down in the Highlands and Islands to the first quarter of this century. The writer found traces of it in such distant places as Arran, Uist, and Sutherland. In 1895 a woman in Arran said that in the time of her father the people made the need-fire on the knoll, and then rushed home and brought out their 'creatairean,' creatures, and put them round the fire to safeguard them, 'bho 'n bhana bhuitsich mhoir Nic-creafain,' from the arch-witch Crawford.

The ordeal of passing through the fires gave rise to a proverb which I heard used by an old man in Lewis in 1873: — . . . Ah Mary! sonnie, it were worse for me to do that for thee, than to pass between the two great fires of Beall. . . .

73 THE BELTANE BLESSING

Mary, thou mother of saints,
Bless our flocks and bearing kine;
Hate nor scath nor let come near us,
Drive from us the ways of the wicked.

Keep thine eye every Monday and Tuesday
On the bearing kine and the pairing queys;
Accompany us from hill to sea,
Gather thyself the sheep and their progeny.

Every Wednesday and Thursday be with them,
Be thy gracious hand always about them;
Tend the cows down to their stalls,
Tend the sheep down to their folds!

Every Friday be thou, O Saint, at their head,
Lead the sheep from the face of the bens,
With their innocent little lambs following them,
Encompass them with God's encompassing.

Every Saturday be likewise with them,
Bring the goats in with their young,
Every kid and goat to the sea side,

And from the Rock of Aegir on high,
With cresses green about its summit.

The strength of the Triune be our shield in distress,
The strength of Christ, His peace and His Pasch,
The strength of the Spirit, Physician of health,
And of the precious Father, the King of grace.

[. . .]

And of every other saint who succeeded them
And who earned the repose of the kingdom of God.

Bless ourselves and our children,
Bless every one who shall come from our loins,
Bless him whose name we bear,
Bless, O God, her from whose womb we came.

Every holiness, blessing and power,
Be yielded to us every time and every hour,
In name of the Holy Threefold above,
Father, Son, and Spirit everlasting.

Be the Cross of Christ to shield us downward,
Be the Cross of Christ to shield us upward,
Be the Cross of Christ to shield us roundward,
Accepting our Beltane blessing from us,
       Accepting our Beltane blessing from us.

74 *THE FEAST DAY OF MARY*

The Feast Day of Mary the Great is the 15th day of August. Early in the
morning of this day the people go into their fields and pluck ears of
corn, generally bere, to make the 'Moilean Moire.' These ears are laid
on a rock exposed to the sun, to dry. When dry, they are husked in the
hand, winnowed in a fan, ground in a quern, kneaded on a sheep-skin,
and formed into a bannock, which is called 'Moilean Moire,' the fatling
of Mary. The bannock is toasted before a fire of fagots of rowan, or
some other sacred wood. Then the husbandman breaks the bannock

and gives a bit to his wife and to each of his children, in order according to their ages, and the family raise the 'Iolach Mhoire Mhathar,' the Paean of Mary Mother who promised to shield them, and who did and will shield them from scath till the day of death. While singing thus, the family walk sunwide round the fire, the father leading, the mother following, and the children following according to age.

After going round the fire, the man puts the embers of the faggot-fire, with bits of old iron, into a pot, which he carries sunwise round the outside of his house, sometimes round his steadings and his fields, and his flocks gathered in for the purpose. He is followed without as within by his household, all singing the praise of Mary Mother the while.

The scene is striking and picturesque, the family being arrayed in their brightest and singing their best.

> On the feast day of Mary the fragrant,
> Mother of the Shepherd of the flocks,
> I cut me a handful of the new corn,
> I dried it gently in the sun,
> I rubbed it sharply from the husk
> > With mine own palms.
>
> I ground it in a quern on Friday,
> I baked it on a fan of sheep-skin,
> I toasted it to a fire of rowan,
> And I shared it round my people.
>
> I went sunways round my dwelling,
> In the name of the Mary Mother,
> Who promised to preserve me,
> Who did preserve me,
> And who will preserve me,
> In peace, in flocks,
> In righteousness of heart,
> In labour, in love,
> In wisdom, in mercy,
> For the sake of Thy Passion.
> Thou Christ of grace
> Who till the day of my death
> Wilt never forsake me!
> > Oh, till the day of my death
> > Wilt never forsake me!

75 *MICHAEL, THE VICTORIOUS*

St Michael is spoken of as 'brian Michael,' god Michael.

> Thou wert the warrior of courage
> Going on the journey of prophecy,
> Thou wouldst not travel on a cripple,
> Thou didst take the steed of the god Michael,
> He was without bit in his mouth,
> Thou didst ride him on the wing,
> Thou didst leap over the knowledge of Nature.

St Michael is the Neptune of the Gael. He is the patron saint of the sea, and of maritime lands, of boats and boatmen, of horses and horsemen thoughout the West. As patron saint of the sea St Michael had temples dedicated to him round the coast wherever Celts were situated. Examples of these are Mount St Michael in Brittany and in Cornwall, and Aird Michael in South and in North Uist, and elsewhere. Probably Milton had this phase of St Michael's character in view. As patron saint of the land St Michael is represented riding a milk-white steed, a three-pronged spear in his right hand and a three-cornered shield in his left. The shield is inscribed 'Quis ut Deus,' a literal translation of the Hebrew Mi-cha-el. Britannia is substituted for the archangel on sea and St George on land.

On the 29th September a festival in honour of St Michael is held throughout the Western Coasts and Isles. This is much the most imposing pageant and much the most popular demonstration of the Celtic year. Many causes conduce to this — causes which move the minds and hearts of the people to their utmost tension. To the young the Day is a day of promise, to the old a day of fulfilment, to the aged a day of retrospect. It is a day when pagan cult and Christian doctrine meet and mingle like the lights and shadows on their own Highland hills.

The Eve of St Michael is the eve of bringing in the carrots, of baking the 'struan,' of killing the lamb, of stealing the horses. The Day of St Michael is the Day of the early mass, the day of the sacrificial lamb, the day of the oblation 'struan,' the day of the distribution of the lamb, the day of the distribution of the 'struan,' the day of pilgrimage to the burial-ground of their fathers, the day of the burial-ground service, the day of the burial-ground circuiting, the day of giving and receiving the carrots with wishes and acknowledgements, and the day of the 'oda' — the athletics of the men and the racing of the horses. And the Night of Michael is the night of the dance and the song, of the merry-making, of the love-making, and of the love-gifts. . . .

As may be seen from some of the poems, the duty of conveying the souls of the good to the abode of bliss is assigned to Michael. When the soul has parted from the body and is being weighed, the archangel of heaven and the archangel of hell preside at the beam, the former watching that the latter does not put . . . claw of hand nor talon of foot near the beam. Michael and all the archangels and angels of heaven sing songs of joy when the good in the soul outweighs the bad, while the devil howls as he retreats.

MICHAEL, THE VICTORIOUS

Thou Michael the victorious,
I make my circuit under thy shield,
Thou Michael of the white steed,
And of the bright brilliant blades,
Conqueror of the dragon,
Be thou at my back,
Thou ranger of the heavens,
Thou warrior of the King of all,
O Michael the victorious,
My pride and my guide,
O Michael the victorious,
The glory of mine eye.

I make my circuit
In the fellowship of my saint,
On the machair, on the meadow,
On the cold heathery hill;
Though I should travel ocean
And the hard globe of the world
No harm can e'er befall me
'Neath the shelter of thy shield;
O Michael the victorious,
Jewel of my heart,
O Michael the victorious,
God's shepherd thou art.

Be the sacred Three of Glory
Aye at peace with me,
With my horses, with my cattle,
With my woolly sheep in flocks.
With the crops growing in the field
Or ripening in the sheaf,
On the machair, on the moor,
In cole, in heap, or stack.
>Every thing on high or low,
>Every furnishing and flock,
>Belong to the holy Triune of glory,
>And to Michael the victorious.

LABOUR

76 *BLESSING OF THE KINDLING*

The kindling of the fire is a work full of interest to the housewife. When 'lifting' the fire in the morning the woman prays, in an undertone, that the fire may be blessed to her and to her household, and to the glory of God who gave it. The people look upon fire as a miracle of Divine power provided for their good — to warm their bodies when they are cold, to cook their food when they are hungry, and to remind them that they too, like the fire, need constant renewal mentally and physically.

I will kindle my fire this morning
In presence of the holy angels of heaven,
In presence of Ariel of the loveliest form,
In presence of Uriel of the myriad charms,
Without malice, without jealousy, without envy,
Without fear, without terror of any one under the sun,
But the Holy Son of God to shield me.
>Without malice, without jealousy, without envy,
>Without fear, without terror of any one under the sun,
>But the Holy Son of God to shield me.

God, kindle Thou in my heart within
A flame of love to my neighbour,

To my foe, to my friend, to my kindred all,
To the brave, to the knave, to the thrall,
O Son of the loveliest Mary,
From the lowliest thing that liveth,
To the Name that is highest of all.
> O Son of the loveliest Mary,
> From the lowliest thing that liveth,
> To the Name that is highest of all.

77 SMOORING THE FIRE

Peat is the fuel of the Highlands and Islands. Where wood is not obtainable the fire is kept in during the night. The process by which this is accomplished is called in Gaelic smaladh; in Scottish, smooring; and in English, smothering, or more correctly, subduing. The ceremony of smooring the fire is artistic and symbolic, and is performed with loving care. The embers are evenly spread on the hearth — which is generally in the middle of the floor — and formed into a circle. This circle is then divided into three equal sections, a small boss being left in the middle. A peat is laid between each section, each peat touching the boss, which forms a common centre. The first peat is laid down in the name of the God of Life, the second in the name of the God of Peace, the third in the name of the God of Grace. The circle is then covered over with ashes sufficient to subdue but not to extinguish the fire, in the name of the Three of Light. The heap slightly raised in the centre is called 'Tula nan Tri', the Hearth of the Three. When the smooring operation is complete the woman closes her eyes, stretches her hand, and softly intones one of the many formulae current for these occasions.

Another way of keeping embers for morning use is to place them in a pit at night. The pit consists of a hole in the clay floor, generally under the dresser. The pit may be from half a foot to a foot in depth and diameter, with a flag fixed in the floor over the top. In the centre of this flag there is a hole by which the embers are put in and taken out. Another flag covers the hole to extinguish the fire at night, and to guard against accidents during the day. This extinguishing fire-pit is called 'slochd guail', coke or coal-pit. This coke or charcoal is serviceable in kindling the fire.

The sacred Three
To save,
To shield,
To surround
The hearth,
The house,
The household,
This eve,
This night,
Oh! this eve,
This night,
And every night,
Each single night.
                    Amen.

78 *THE QUERN BLESSING*

The quern songs, like all the labour songs of the people, were composed in a measure suited to the special labour involved. The measure changed to suit the rhythmic motion of the body at work, at times slow, at times fast, as occasion required. I first saw the quern at work in October 1860 in the house of a cottar at Fearann-an-leatha, Skye. The cottar woman procured some oats in the sheaf. Roughly evening the heads, and holding the corn over an old partially-dressed sheep-skin, she switched off the grain. This is called 'gradanadh,' quickness, from the expert handling required in the operation. The whole straw of the sheaf was not burnt, only that part of the straw to which the grain was attached, the flame being kept from proceeding further. The straw was tied up and used for other purposes.

Having fanned the grain and swept the floor, the woman spread out the sheep-skin again and placed the quern thereon. She then sat down to grind, filling and relieving the quern with one hand and turning it with the other, singing the while to the accompaniment of the 'whirr! whirr! whirr! birr! birr! birr!' of the revolving stone. Several strong sturdy boys in scant kilts, and sweet comely girls in nondescript frocks, sat round the peat fire enjoying it fully, and watching the work and listening to the song of their radiant mother. . . .

When the mills were erected the authorities destroyed the querns in order to compel the people to go the mills and pay multure, mill dues.

This wholesale and inconsiderate destruction of querns everywhere entailed untold hardships on thousands of people living in roadless districts and in distant isles without mills, especially during storms. Among other expedients to which the more remote people resorted was the searching of ancient ruins for the 'pollagan,' mortar mills, of former generations. The mortar is a still more primitive instrument for preparing corn than the quern. . . .

The quern and mortar are still used in outlying districts of Scotland and Ireland, though isolatedly and sparingly.

THE QUERN BLESSING

On Ash Eve
We shall have flesh,
We should have that
We should have that.

The cheek of hen,
Two bits of barley,
That were enough
That were enough.

We shall have mead,
We shall have spruce,
We shall have wine,
We shall have feast.
We shall have sweetness and milk produce,
Honey and milk,
Wholesome ambrosia,
Abundance of that,
Abundance of that.

We shall have harp,
We shall have harp,
We shall have lute,
We shall have horn.
We shall have sweet psaltery
Of the melodious strings
And the regal lyre,
Of the songs we shall have,
Of the songs we shall have.

The calm fair Bride will be with us,
The gentle Mary mother will be with us.
Michael the chief
Of glancing glaves,
And the King of kings
And Jesus Christ,
And the Spirit of peace
And of grace will be with us,
Of grace will be with us.

79 *MILKING CROON*

The milking songs of the people are numerous and varied. They are sung to pretty airs, to please the cows and to induce them to give their milk. The cows become accustomed to these lilts and will not give their milk without them, nor, occasionally, without their favourite airs being sung to them. The fondness of Highland cows for music induces owners of large herds to secure milkmaids possessed of good voices and some 'go'. It is interesting and animating to see three or four comely girls among a fold of sixty, eighty, or a hundred picturesque Highland cows on meadow or mountain slope. The moaning and heaving of the sea afar, the swish of the wave on the shore, the carolling of the lark in the sky, the unbroken song of the mavis on the rock, the broken melody of the merle in the brake, the lowing of the kine without, the response of the calves within the fold, the singing of the milkmaids in unison with the movement of their hands, and of the soft sound of the snowy milk falling into the pail, the gilding of hill and dale, the glowing of the distant ocean beyond, as the sun sinks into the sea of golden glory, constitute a scene which the observer would not, if he could, forget.

Come, Brendan, from the ocean,
Come, Ternan, most potent of men,
Come, Michael valiant, down
And propitiate to me the cow of my joy.
    Ho my heifer, ho heifer of my love,
    Ho my heifer, ho heifer of my love.
    My beloved heifer, choice cow of every shieling,
    For the sake of the High King take to thy calf.

Come, beloved Colum of the fold,
Come, great Bride of the flocks,
Come, fair Mary from the cloud,
And propitiate to me the cow of my love.
      Ho my heifer, ho heifer of my love.

The stock-dove will come from the wood,
The tusk will come from the wave,
The fox will come but not with wiles,
To hail my cow of virtues.
      Ho my heifer, ho heifer of my love.

80 *HUNTING BLESSING*

A young man was consecrated before he went out to hunt. Oil was put on his head, a bow was placed in his hand, and he was required to stand with bare feet in the bare grassless ground. The dedication of the young hunter was akin to those of the 'maor,' the judge, the chief, and the king, on installation. Many conditions were imposed on the young man, which he was required to observe throughout his life. He was not to take life wantonly. He was not to kill a bird sitting, nor a beast lying down, and he was not to kill the mother of a brood, nor the mother of a suckling. Nor was he to kill an unfledged bird nor a suckling beast, unless it might be the young of a bird, or of a beast, of prey. It was at all times permissible and laudable to destroy certain clearly defined birds and beasts of prey and evil reptiles, with their young.

From my loins begotten wert thou, my son,
May I guide thee the way that is right,
In the holy name of the apostles eleven
In the name of the Son of God torn of thee.

In the name of James, and Peter, and Paul,
John the baptist, and John the apostle above,
Luke the physician, and Stephen the martyr,
Muriel the fair, and Mary mother of the Lamb.

In the name of Patrick, holy of the deeds,
And Carmac of the rights and tombs,

Columba beloved, and Adamnan of laws,
Fite calm, and Bride of the milk and kine.

In the name of Michael chief of hosts,
In the name of Ariel youth of lovely hues,
In the name of Uriel of the golden locks,
And Gabriel seer of the Virgin of grace.

The time thou shalt have closed thine eye,
Thou shalt not bend thy knee nor move,
Thou shalt not wound the duck that is swimming,
Never shalt thou harry her of her young.

The white swan of the sweet gurgle,
The speckled dun of the brown tuft,
Thou shalt not cut a feather from their backs,
Till the doom-day, on the crest of the wave.

On the wing be they always
Ere thou place missile to thine ear,
And the fair Mary will give thee of her love,
And the lovely Bride will give thee of her kine.

Thou shalt not eat fallen fish nor fallen flesh,
Nor one bird that thy hand shall not bring down,
Be thou thankful for the one,
Though nine should be swimming.

The fairy swan of Bride of the flocks,
The fairy duck of Mary of peace.

81 *PRAYER FOR TRAVELLING*

This hymn was sung by a pilgrim in setting out on his pilgrimage. The family and friends joined the traveller in singing the hymn and starting the journey, from which too frequently, for various causes, he never returned.

Life be in my speech,
Sense in what I say,
The bloom of cherries on my lips,
Till I come back again.

The love Christ Jesus gave
Be filling every heart for me,
The love Christ Jesus gave
Filling me for every one.

Traversing corries, traversing forests,
Traversing valleys long and wild.
The fair white Mary still uphold me,
The Shepherd Jesu be my shield,
The fair white Mary still uphold me,
The Shepherd Jesu be my shield.

82 *THE OCEAN BLESSING*

Sea prayers and sea hymns were common amongst the seafarers of the Western Islands. Probably these originated with the early Celtic missionaries, who constantly traversed in their frail skin coracles the storm-swept, strongly tidal seas of those Hebrid Isles, oft and oft sealing their devotion with their lives.

Before embarking on a journey the voyagers stood round their boat and prayed to the God of the elements for a peaceful voyage over the stormy sea. The steersman led the appeal, while the swish of the waves below, the sough of the sea beyond, and the sound of the wind around blended with the voices of the suppliants and lent dignity and solemnity to the scene. . . .

83 *SEA PRAYER*

HELMSMAN	Blest be the boat.
CREW	God the Father bless her.
HELMSMAN	Blest be the boat.
CREW	God the Son bless her.

HELMSMAN	Blest be the boat.
CREW	God the Spirit bless her.
ALL	God the Father,
	God the Son,
	God the Spirit,
	Bless the boat.
HELMSMAN	What can befall you
	And God the Father with you?
CREW	No harm can befall us.
ALL	God the Father,
	God the Son,
	God the Spirit,
	With us eternally.
HELMSMAN	What can cause you anxiety
	And the God of the elements over you?
CREW	No anxiety can be ours.
HELMSMAN	What can cause you anxiety
	And the King of the elements over you?
CREW	No anxiety can be ours.
HELMSMAN	What can cause you anxiety
	And the Spirit of the elements over you?
CREW	No anxiety can be ours.
ALL	The God of the elements,
	The King of the elements,
	The Spirit of the elements,
	Close over us,
	Ever eternally.

MORNING PRAYERS

84 *THANKSGIVING*

Thanks to Thee, O God, that I have risen to-day,
    To the rising of this life itself;
May it be to Thine own glory, O God of every gift,
    And to the glory of my soul likewise.

O great God, aid Thou my soul
    With the aiding of Thine own mercy;
Even as I clothe my body with wool,
    Cover Thou my soul with the shadow of Thy wing.

Help me to avoid every sin,
    And the source of every sin to forsake;
And as the mist scatters on the crest of the hills,
    May each ill haze clear from my soul, O God.

85 GOD'S AID

God to enfold me,
    God to surround me,
God in my speaking,
    God in my thinking.

God in my sleeping,
    God in my waking,
God in my watching,
    God in my hoping.

God in my life,
    God in my lips,
God in my soul,
    God in my heart.

God in my sufficing,
    God in my slumber,
God in mine ever-living soul,
    God in mine eternity.

86 SUPPLICATION

The following poem was taken down from the recitation of Dugall
MacAulay, cottar, Creagorry, Benbecula. MacAulay is an old man, full
of old songs and hymns, runes and incantations, fairy stories and
strange beliefs. These he heard from his aunt and mother, who were full

of song and story, natural and supernatural, and of old lore of the most curious kind. . . .

> O Being of life!
> O Being of peace!
> O Being of time!
> > O Being of eternity!
> > O Being of eternity!
>
> Keep me in good means,
> > Keep me in good intent,
> Keep me in good estate,
> > Better than I know to ask,
> > Better than I know to ask.
>
> Shepherd me this day,
> > Relieve my distress,
> Enfold me this night,
> > Pour upon me Thy grace,
> > Pour upon me Thy grace!
>
> Guard for me my speech,
> > Strengthen for me my love,
> Illume for me the stream,
> > Succour Thou me in death,
> > Succour Thou me in death!

PRAYERS FOR PROTECTION

87 *THOU MY SOUL'S HEALER*

> Thou, my soul's Healer,
> Keep me at even,
> Keep me at morning,
> Keep me at noon,
> On rough course faring,
> Help and safeguard
> My means this night.

I am tired, astray, and stumbling,
Shield Thou me from snare and sin.

88 *ENCOMPASSING*

'Caim', encompassing, is a form of safeguarding common in the west. The encompassing of any of the Three Persons of the Trinity, or of the Blessed Virgin, or of any of the Apostles or of any of the saints may be invoked, according to the faith of the suppliant. In making the 'caim' the suppliant stretches out the right hand with the forefinger extended, and turns round sunwise as if on a pivot, describing a circle with the tip of the forefinger while invoking the desired protection. The circle encloses the suppliant and accompanies him as he walks onward, safeguarded from all evil without or within. Protestant or Catholic, educated or illiterate, may make the 'caim' in fear, danger or distress, as when some untoward noise is heard or some untoward object seen during the night.

The caim is called . . . the encompassing of God, of Christ, of the Spirit, of Mary, of the Holy Rood, of the Holy Rood and of the saints in heaven, of Michael, of the nine angels, of the saints and the nine angels, of Columba; and to these may be added the customary epithets, as . . . the encompassing of the God of the creatures, of Michael militant the victorious, of Columba the kindly. It is also called . . . the encompassing of the forefinger, and . . . the encompassing of righteousness.

The compassing of God and His right hand
Be upon my form and upon my frame;
The compassing of the High King and the grace of the Trinity
Be upon me abiding ever eternally,
    Be upon me abiding ever eternally.

May the compassing of the Three shield me in my means,
The compassing of the Three shield me this day,
The compassing of the Three shield me this night
From hate, from harm, from act, from ill,
    From hate, from harm, from act, from ill.

89 *ENCOMPASSING*

The compassing of God be on thee,
  The compassing of the God of life.

The compassing of Christ be on thee,
  The compassing of the Christ of love.

The compassing of the Spirit be on thee,
  The compassing of the Spirit of Grace.

The compassing of the Three be on thee,
  The compassing of the Three preserve thee,
  The compassing of the Three preserve thee.

JOURNEY PRAYERS, BLESSINGS AND INVOCATIONS

90 *THE GOSPEL OF CHRIST*

Reciter: Malcolm Sinclair, fisherman, Baile Phuill, Tiree.

This was the name of a charm worn upon the person to safeguard the wearer against drowning at sea, against disaster on land, against evil eye, evil wish, evil influences, against the wrongs and oppressions of man and the wiles and witcheries of woman, against being lifted by the hosts of the air, and against being waylaid by the fairies of the mound.

Such a charm might consist of a word, a phrase, a saying, or a verse from one of the Gospels, and from this came the name 'Gospel of Christ'. The words were written upon paper or parchment, and were often illuminated and ornamented in Celtic design, the script being thus rendered more precious by the beauty of its work and the beauty of its words.

The script was placed in a small bag of linen and sewn into the waistcoat of a man and the bodice of a woman, under the left arm. In the case of a child the bag was suspended from the neck by a linen cord. Linen was sacred because the body of Christ was buried in a linen shroud, and there are many phrases which indicate the special esteem in which lint was held. The blue flax was used medicinally, especially for stomach complaints, and also as a safeguard against invisible dangers. . . .

May God bless thy cross
　　Before thou go over the sea;
Any illness that thou mayest have,
　　It shall not take thee hence.

*

May God bless thy crucifying cross
　　In the house-shelter of Christ,
Against drowning, against peril, against spells,
　　Against sore wounding, against grisly fright.

As the King of kings was stretched up
　　Without pity, without compassion, to the tree,
The leafy, brown, wreathed topmost Bough,
　　As the body of the sinless Christ triumphed,

And as the woman of the seven blessings,
　　Who is going in at their head,
May God bless all that are before thee
　　And thee who art moving anear them.

*

Grace of form,
　　Grace of voice be thine;
Grace of charity,
　　Grace of wisdom be thine;
Grace of beauty,
　　Grace of health be thine;
Grace of sea,
　　Grace of land be thine;
Grace of music,
　　Grace of guidance be thine;
Grace of battle-triumph,
　　Grace of victory be thine;
Grace of life,
　　Grace of praise be thine;

Grace of love,
  Grace of dancing be thine;
Grace of lyre,
  Grace of harp be thine;
Grace of sense,
  Grace of reason be thine;
Grace of speech,
  Grace of story be thine;
Grace of peace,
  Grace of God be thine.

*

A voice soft and musical I pray for thee,
 And a tongue loving and mild:
Two things good for daughter and for son,
 For husband and for wife.

The joy of God be in thy face,
 Joy to all who see thee;
The circling of God be keeping thee,
 Angels of God shielding thee.

*

Nor sword shall wound thee,
Nor brand shall burn thee,
Nor arrow shall rend thee,
Nor seas shall drown thee.

*

Thou art whiter than the swan on miry lake,
Thou art whiter than the white gull of the current,
Thou art whiter than the snow of the high mountains,
Thou art whiter than the love of the angels of heaven.
Thou art the gracious red rowan
That subdues the ire and anger of all men,
 As a sea-wave from flow to ebb,
 As a sea-wave from ebb to flow.

*

The mantle of Christ be placed upon thee,
　　To shade thee from thy crown to thy sole;
The mantle of the God of life be keeping thee,
　　To be thy champion and thy leader.

*

Thou shalt not be left in the hand of the wicked,
Thou shalt not be bent in the court of the false;
Thou shalt rise victorious above them
As rise victorious the arches of the waves.

*

　　Thou art the pure love of the clouds,
　　Thou art the pure love of the skies,
　　Thou art the pure love of the stars,
　　Thou art the pure love of the moon,
　　Thou art the pure love of the sun,
　　Thou art the pure love of the heavens,
　　Thou art the pure love of the angels,
　　Thou art the pure love of Christ Himself,
　　Thou art the pure love of the God of all life.

91 *BLESSINGS*

Be each saint in heaven,
Each sainted woman in heaven,
Each angel in heaven
Stretching their arms for you,
Smoothing the way for you,
When you go thither
　　Over the river hard to see;
Oh when you go thither home
　　Over the river hard to see.

*

May the Father take you
　　In His fragrant clasp of love,
When you go across the flooding streams
　　And the black river of death.

*

The love of your Creator be with you.

*

Be the eye of God dwelling with you,
The foot of Christ in guidance with you,
The shower of the Spirit pouring on you,
    Richly and generously.

*

The love and affection of the heavens be to you,
The love and affection of the saints be to you,
The love and affection of the angels be to you,
The love and affection of the sun be to you,
The love and affection of the moon be to you,
    Each day and night of your lives,
        To keep you from haters, to keep you from harmers,
            to keep you from oppressors.

92 SUN

Old men in the Isles still uncover their heads when they first see the sun
on coming out in the morning. They hum a hymn not easily caught up
and not easily got from them. The following fragments were obtained
from a man of ninety-nine years in the south end of Uist, and from
another in Mingulay, one of the outer isles of Barra.

The eye of the great God,
The eye of the God of glory,
The eye of the King of hosts,
The eye of the King of the living,
    Pouring upon us
        At each time and season,
    Pouring upon us
        Gently and generously.

Glory to thee,
    Thou glorious sun.

Glory to thee, thou sun,
        Face of the God of life.

93 *CHARM FOR FEAR BY NIGHT*

This rune is said by travellers at night. Any person saying it from the heart will be sained and safeguarded from harm. He will not be molested by the 'fuath,' the 'gruagach,' the 'peallag,' the 'ban-sith,' the 'bean-nighidh,' nor by 'fridich nan creag,' not by any spirit in the air, in the earth, under the earth, in the sea, nor under the sea. The imprecation, 'Guma h-anmoch dhuit!', 'May you be late!' is still reckoned as specially evil. . . .

'Do you see anything, little son?' 'I see nothing, father.' 'Do you see anything now, little son?' 'I see nothing, father.' 'Do you see anything at all now, little son?' 'I see nothing at all, father.' 'By Mary, you see nothing! There is not so much sense in your head or in your snout or in your eye that you would see a bogle or anything else of the ill work of the night!'

This conversation took place between a father and the little son on his back as they were passing through a spot of evil reputation. When the father passed the dreaded hollow he put down his boy and ran as hard as he could. The boy overtook and passed him. When he reached home, the boy fell in the door exhausted. Immediately after the father came up and stumbled over the motionless boy lying in the doorway. Thinking that this was the bogle at last, the father yelled, rousing the boy without and the mother within. The frightened man gave his son a cuffing and a severe scolding for leaving him to the mercy of the bogles. . . . 'You little sack of hide, to go and leave your father to be eaten by the bogles of Lag Onair and the marsh-spirit of the night!'

God before me, God behind me,
God above me, God below me;
I on the path of God,
God upon my track.

*

Who is there on land?
Who is there on wave?
Who is there on billow?
Who is there by door-post?

━━━━━━

Who is along with us?
  God and Lord.

*

I am here abroad,
I am here in need,
I am here in pain,
I am here in straits
I am here alone,
      O God, aid me.

94 *NIGHT PRAYER*

From Peigidh Nic Cormaig (Peggy MacCormack), *neé* MacDonald, Aird Bhuidhe, Loch Boisdale, Uist.

The reciter said that this and similar hymns used to be sung in her father's house at Airigh nam Ban in Uist. Crofters then held the land now occupied by sheep. The people were strong, healthy, and happy, and enjoyed life to the full in their simple homely ways. They had sheep and cattle, corn, potatoes, and poultry, milk, cheese, butter and fish, all in sufficiency. They were good to the poor, kind to the stranger, and helpful to one another, and there was nothing amiss. There were pipers and fiddlers in almost every house, and the people sang and danced in summer time on the green grass without, and in winter time on the clay floor within.

How we enjoyed ourselves in those far-away days — the old as much as the young. I often saw three and sometimes four generations dancing together on the green grass in the golden summer sunset. Men and women of fourscore or more — for they lived long in those days — dancing with boys and girls of five on the green grass. Those were the happy days and the happy nights, there was neither sin nor sorrow in the world for us. The thought of those young days makes my old heart both glad and sad, even at this distance of time. But the clearances came upon us, destroying all, turning our small crofts into big farms for the stranger, and turning our joy into misery, our gladness into bitterness, our blessing into blasphemy, and our Christianity into mockery. . . . O dear man, the tears come on my eyes when I think of all we suffered and of the sorrows, hardships, oppressions we came through.

In Thy name, O Jesu Who wast crucified,
    I lie down to rest;
Watch Thou me in sleep remote,
    Hold Thou me in Thy one hand;
        Watch Thou me in sleep remote,
        Hold Thou me in Thy one hand.

Bless me, O my Christ,
    Be Thou my shield protecting me,
Aid my steps in the pitful swamp,
    Lead Thou me to the life eternal;
        Aid my steps in the pitful swamp,
        Lead Thou me to the life eternal.

Keep Thou me in the presence of God,
    O good and gracious Son of the Virgin,
And fervently I pray Thy strong protection
    From my lying down at dusk to my rising at day;
        And fervently I pray Thy strong protection
        From my lying down at dusk to my rising at day.

95 *I LIE DOWN THIS NIGHT*

I lie down this night with God
    And God will lie down with me;
I lie down this night with Christ,
    And Christ will lie down with me;
I lie down this night with the Spirit,
    And the Spirit will lie down with me;
God and Christ and the Spirit
    Be lying down with me.

96 *REST BENEDICTION*

Reciter: Dugall MacAulay, cottar, Hacleit, Benbecula.

Bless to me, O God, the moon that is above me,
Bless to me, O God, the earth that is beneath me,

Bless to me, O God, my wife and my children,
And bless, O God, myself who have care of them;
      Bless to me my wife and my children,
      And bless, O God, myself who have care of them.

Bless, O God, the thing on which mine eye doth rest,
Bless, O God, the thing on which my hope doth rest,
Bless, O God, my reason and my purpose,
Bless, O bless Thou them, Thou God of life;
      Bless, O God, my reason and my purpose,
      Bless, O bless Thou them, Thou God of life.

Bless to me the bed-companion of my love,
Bless to me the handling of my hands,
Bless, O bless Thou to me, O God, the fencing of my defence,
And bless, O bless to me the angeling of my rest;
      Bless, O bless Thou to me, O God, the fencing of my defence,
      And bless, O bless to me the angeling of my rest.

97 *HAPPY DEATH*

. . . In the Roman Catholic communities of the west, 'bas sona,' 'happy death,' is a phrase frequently heard among the people. When these words are used they imply that the dying person has been confessed and anointed, and the death-hymn has been intoned over him. Under these conditions the consolation of the living in the loss of the loved one is touching. The old people speak of 'bas sona' with exultant satisfaction, and would wish above all things on earth that 'bas sona' may be their own portion when the time comes for them to go . . .

98 *JOYOUS DEATH*

      Death with oil,
      Death with joy,
      Death with light,
      Death with gladness,
          Death with penitence.

Death without pain,
Death without fear,
Death without death,
Death without horror,
    Death without grieving.

May the seven angels of the Holy Spirit
    And the two guardian angels
Shield me this night and every night
    Till light and dawn shall come;

        Shield me this night and every night
        Till light and dawn shall come.

The Religious Songs of Connacht:
A Collection of Poems, Stories, Prayers, Satires, Ranns, Charms etc.
being the Sixth and Seventh Chapters of
The Songs of Connacht

by Douglas Hyde

99 *MY SON REMEMBER*

After this necessary preface, we turn to the poems and religious songs themselves, which the people of Connacht had and have amongst them. That province gave to the nation the greatest and best religious poet that perhaps Erin has ever had, Donough O'Daly, who was, it was said, Abbot of Boyle, in the county of Roscommon, though this is not certain. The monastery of Boyle was a large and important institution; it scattered its branches east and west. The fine Abbey of Knockmoy, in the west of Galway, was only a branch from the Abbey of Boyle. But if the fame of the monastery was great, greater still was the fame of the Abbot who ruled over it in the beginning of the thirteenth century. The Abbot was called the Ovid of Erin, not for the freedom of his poetry, but for its sweetness. All Erin was proud of its splendid poet, Donagha More O'Daly. O'Reilly gives us the names of more than thirty of his extant poems, in which there are about 4,200 lines, and it is likely that there are more of his works which may yet be found. Most of these are religious poems, and they were held in high esteem throughout the Island. They were as well known in the province of Munster as they were in Connacht, and some of them are in the mouths of the people to this very day. I have heard from old people in the County Roscommon, his own county as it is believed, more than one of his pieces. He died in the year 1244. I shall here give only pieces of his that were very common in Ireland at the beginning of this century, and which are to be found in many of the manuscripts which, until lately, the people treasured in every part of Ireland, but which are now lost or banished.

Here, to begin, is a poem which he made, and which lived in the memory of the people for five hundred years; I got part of it from a "travelling-man" near Belmullet, in the west of the County Mayo, ten years ago. It is composed in the metre or measure called Great Rannuigheacht, [Rann-ee-ăcht]. There are seven syllables in the line, and each line must end with a monosyllable. There is no "Uaim" or alliteration in it, as there is in most of the poems which the true bards composed in this metre. Shaun O'Daly transcribed this poem from a collection which Father O'Keeffe (a learned man, and an accurate Irish scholar, born about the year 1655) made in Munster. Some of the lines of the original have eight syllables instead of seven, which is incorrect, but in my translation I have given each line this number.

MY SON REMEMBER

My son, remember what I *say*,
    That in the *day* of Judgment's shock,
When men go stumbling down the *Mount*,
    The sheep may *count* thee of their flock.

And narrow though thou find the path
    To heaven's high rath, and hard to gain,
I warn thee shun yon broad white road
    That leads to the abode of pain.

For us is many a snare designed,
    To fill our mind with doubts and fears;
Far from the land where lurks no sin
    We dwell within our vale of tears.

Not on the world thy love bestow,
    Passing as flowers that blow and die;
Follow not thou the specious track
    That turns thy back to God most high.

But oh! let faith, let Hope, let love
    Soar far above the cold world's way;
Patience, humility, and awe —
    Make them thy law from day to day.

And love thy neighbour as thyself,
 (Not for his pelf thy love should be),
But a greater love than every love
 Give God above who loveth thee.

He shall not see the abode of pain
 Whose mercies rain on poor men still;
Arms, fastings, prayers, must aid the soul;
 Thy blood control, control thy will.

The seven shafts wherewith the Unjust
 Shoots hard, to thrust us from our home,
Can'st thou avoid their fiery path,
 Dread not the wrath that is to come.

Shun sloth, shun greed, shun sensual fires,
 (Eager desires of men enslaved),
Anger and pride and hatred shun,
 Till heaven be won, till man be saved.

To Him, our King, to Mary's son,
 Who did not shun the evil death,
Since He our goal is, He alone,
 Commit thy soul, thy life, thy breath.

Since Hell each man pursues each day,
 Cleric and lay, till life be done,
Be not deceived, as others may,
 Remember what I say, my son.

100 *THE WORMS, THE CHILDREN, AND THE DEVIL*

Although O'Reilly gives us this poem amongst those of Donogha More's he says that he has cause for believing that it was not he who composed it. The following is my version of it. Shaun O'Daly printed a different copy of it in his book of the songs of "Teig O Sullivan the Gaelic," and he says it was Donogha O'Daly wrote it. It is in the Great Rannuigheacht metre.

THE WORMS, THE CHILDREN, AND THE DEVIL

There be three — my heart it saith —
    Wish the death of me infirm,
Would that they were hanged on tree,
    All three, Children, Devil, Worm.

The worms — it is a sad thought —
    When I am brought under clay,
My body they make their goal,
    For wealth or soul nought care they.

My children care for my wealth
    More than my health, when all's done,
They'd give, to get its control,
    My body and soul in one.

The loathly devil, I wis,
    Whose business is to sow tares,
Not for body, not for gold,
    Only for my soul he cares,

Now O Christ, for us who died,
    Crucified upon the tree,
These three wait for me to die,
    Swing them high in death all three.

101 *BRIDGET'S COUNSEL*

. . . most of the religious poems which I have got from the people in Connacht are giving us advice to do good works, and saying that there is no road but this by which a man may go to the heaven of God. Here for example is a poem which I wrote down from the mouth of a man in the county Galway. Martin Rua O Gillarná (Forde! in English) was his name. He was from Lisanishka near Monivea. He had no English.

BRIDGET'S COUNSEL

The teaching of Breed for his good to the sinner,
To take his father's advice and blessing,
To plead for ever with Mary Mother,
A guiding-star to our foolish women.

The Son of the Woman who earned no scandal,
The Son who never forgot the Father,
It was He himself who made our purchase,
And through His side that the lance's thrust went.

The poem goes on to say of those who have no pleasure in alms or in
mercy: —

The darkest night in this world at present
Dark without mist or stars or moonlight,
Is brighter than their day when brightest.

Could you come with me but once, and see it,
You would sooner be hacked in little pieces,
Be boiled, be burned, and be roasted,

Be put in an oven till you had perished,
Be ground in a quern with hundreds grinding,
— Sooner than live in a sin that is mortal.

Go to Mass when you rise at morning,
As you should do, regard the altar.
See, Christ Jesus is thereby standing,
In the priest's hand is His sacred body.

Go home again when that is finished,
Give wanderers lodging until the morning,
Food and drink to him who is empty.

Is your friend ill, or on sick-bed lying,
Bring him whatever will give him comfort,
— Never earn the curse of widow.

When to your bed you get at night-time
Go on your knees your prayers repeating,
Do the same when you rise next morning.

What the poem chiefly teaches is to do good deeds: —

Do good deeds without lie or falsehood,
Do without lie good deeds on earth here,
That is the one straight way to follow,
That is the road, and go not off it.

102 *MARY'S WELL*

If we look around us, over the lands of Christendom today, we shall scarcely see another place in which the love and respect of their people for the priesthood is greater than in Erin. I am not now speaking of any cause of quarrel that may have lately come between them, but if we examine the history of the country during the last couple of hundred years we find that the priest clung to his people, and the people to their priest.

The long years, full of ruin and poverty, which the Irish suffered after the downfall of their natural protectors, the native nobles, without anyone to stand up for them but their own priests, bound them to the heart of the nation, strongly, firmly, inseparably. The people saw during two hundred years their priests in poverty and misery, standing in the gap of danger, seeking to fulfil their sacred office, coming in and going out amongst them, anointing those who were on the point of death, tying young couples, assuaging the grief of the poor, and administering the sacraments of the church, although they themselves often met suffering and persecution and death in doing so. If what I have just said is true, namely, that there is scarce another country in Europe in which the respect for and power of the Roman Catholic priests is as great as it is in Erin, and if we seek what is the cause, we shall easily understand that it is because Erin has not yet forgotten all the misfortunes and persecutions which she and her priests suffered to-gether during the penal laws. She has not yet quite forgotten it; and if the priesthood of Erin has so good a position, in comparison with the Roman Catholic priests of other countries, it is not on account of Celtic blood being in the people, nor on account of anything else of the sort, but on account of the comfort, the satisfaction, the aid, and the continuous- help which the poor people of Erin received from their priests in the last two centuries, when there was not other person of education taking their part, but they only.

The wiles which the priests of Erin had to practice in order to save their lives are not yet forgotten. But these old stories are passing into dis-remembrance since the priests and the people begin to cast away from them the Irish language, in which they were told. There were people at one time in Ireland who had no other business than to find out priests and gain from the law a reward on account of their dirty work, as we see from this rann which Father O'Leary heard from some one.

> There is no use in my speaking [encomiums on you]
> Seeing your kinsip with Donogha-of-the-priest,
> And with Owen-of-the-cards, his father,
> With the people of the cutting off of the heads,
> To put them into leather bags,
> To bring them down with them to the city,
> and to bring home the gold [they got for them]
> For sustenance of wives and children.

Here is a story, for example, which I got from Próinsias O'Conor, in Athlone, who heard it from an old woman who was herself from Ballintubber, in the County Mayo. So long as Irish was spoken, and these stories told in it it was small wonder that the people should have a regard for their priests.

MARY'S WELL

Long ago there was a blessed well in Ballintubber (i.e., the town of the well), in the county Mayo. There was once a monastery in the place where the well is now, and it was on the spot where stood the altar of the monastery that the well broke out. The monastery was on the side of a hill, but Cromwell and his band of destroyers came to this country, they overthrew the monastery, and never left stone on top of stone in the altar that they did not throw down.

A year from the day that they threw down the altar — that was Lady Day in spring — the well broke out on the site of the altar, and it is a wonderful thing to say, but there was not one drop of water in the stream that was at the foot of the hill from the day that the well broke out.

There was a poor friar going down the road the same day, and he went out of his way to say a prayer upon the site of the blessed altar, and there was great wonder on him when he saw a fine well in its place. He fell on his knees and began to say his paternoster, when he heard a voice saying: 'Put off your brogues, you are upon blessed ground, you are on the brink of Mary's well, and there is the curing of thousands of blind in it; there shall be a person cured by the water of that well for every person who heard mass in front of the altar that was in the place where the well is now, if they be dipped three times in it, in the name of the Father, the Son, and the Holy Spirit.'

When the friar had his prayers said, he looked up and saw a large white dove upon a fir tree near him. It was the dove who was speaking. The friar was dressed in false clothes, because there was a price on his head, as great as on the head of a wild-dog.

At any rate, he proclaimed the story to the people of the little village, and it was not long till it went out through the country. It was a poor place, and the people in it had nothing [to live in] but huts, and these filled with smoke. On that account there were a great many weak-eyed people amongst them. With the dawn, on the next day, there were above forty people at Mary's Well, and there was never a man nor woman of them but came back with good sight.

The fame of Mary's Well went through the country, and it was not long till there were pilgrims from every county coming to it, and nobody went back without being cured; and at the end of a little time even people from other countries used to be coming to it.

There was an unbeliever living near Mary's Well. It was a gentleman he was, and he did not believe in the cure. He said there was nothing in it but pishtrogues (charms), and to make a mock of the people he brought a blind ass, that he had, to the well, and he dipped its head under the water. The ass got its sight, but the scoffer was brought home as blind as the sole of your shoe.

At the end of a year it so happened that there was a priest working as a gardener with the gentleman who was blind. The priest was dressed like a workman, and nobody at all knew that it was the priest who was in it. One day the gentleman was sickly, and he asked his servant to take him out into the garden. When he came to the place where the priest was working he sat down. 'Isn't it a great pity,' says he, 'that I cannot see my fine garden?'

The gardener took compassion on him, and said, 'I know where there is a man who would cure you, but there is a price on his head on account of his religion.'

'I give my word that I'll do no spying on him, and I'll pay him well for his trouble,' said the gentleman.

'But perhaps you would not like to go through the mode of curing that he has,' says the gardener.

'I don't care what mode he has, if he gives me my sight,' said the gentleman.

Now, the gentleman had an evil character, because he betrayed a number of priests before that. Bingham was the name that was on him. However, the priest took courage, and said, 'Let your coach be ready on to-morrow morning, and I will drive you to the place of the cure; neither coachman nor anyone else may be present but myself, and do not tell to anyone at all where you are going, or give anyone a knowledge of what is your business.'

On the morning of the next day Bingham's coach was ready, and he himself got into it, with the gardener driving him. 'Do you remain at home this time,' he says to the coachman, 'and the gardener will drive me.' The coachman was a villain, and there was plenty of jealousy on him. He conceived the idea of watching the coach to see what way they were to go. His blessed vestments were on the priest, inside of his outer clothes. When they came to Mary's Well the priest said to him, 'I am going to get back your sight for you in the place where you lost it.' Then he dipped him three times in the well, in the name of the Father, the Son, and the Holy Spirit and his sight came to him as well as ever it was.

'I'll give you a hundred pounds,' said Bingham, 'as soon as I go home.'

The coachman was watching, and as soon as he saw the priest in his blessed vestments, he went to the people of the law, and betrayed the priest. He was taken and hanged, without judge, without judgment. The man who was after getting back his sight could have saved the priest, but he did not speak a word on his behalf.

About a month after this, another priest came to Bingham, and he dressed like a gardener, and he asked work of Bingham, and got it from him; but he was not long in his service until an evil thing happened to Bingham. He went out one day walking through his fields, and there met him a good-looking girl, the daughter of a poor man, and he assaulted her, and left her half dead. The girl had three brothers, and they took an oath that they would kill him as soon as they could get hold of him. They had not long to wait. They caught him in the same place where he had assaulted the girl, and hanged him on a tree, and left him there hanging.

On the morning of the next day millions of flies were gathered like a great hill round about the tree, and nobody could go near it on account of the foul smell that was round the place, and anyone who would go near it the midges would blind him.

Bingham's wife and son offered a hundred pounds to anyone who would bring out the body. A good many people made an effort to do that, but they were not able. They got dust to shake on the flies, and boughs of trees to beat them with, but they were not able to scatter them, nor to go as far as the tree. The foul smell was getting worse, and the neighbours were afraid that the flies and noisome corpse would bring a plague upon them.

The second priest was at this time a gardener with Bingham, but the people of the house did not know that it was a priest who was in it, for if the people of the law or the spies knew, they would take him and hang him. The Catholics went to Bingham's wife and told her that they knew a man who would banish the flies. 'Bring him to me,' said she, 'and if he is able to banish the flies, that is not the reward he'll get, but seven times as much.'

'But,' said they, 'if the people of the law knew, they would take him and hang him, as they hung the man who got back the sight of his eyes for him before.' 'But,' said she, 'could not he banish the flies without the knowledge of the people of the law?'

'We don't know,' said they, 'until we take counsel with him.'

That night they took counsel with the priest and told him what Bingham's wife said.

'I have only an earthly life to lose,' said the priest, 'and I shall give it up for the sake of the poor people, for there will be a plague in the country unless I banish the flies. On to-morrow morning I shall make an attempt to banish them in the name of God, and I have hope and confidence in God that he will save me from mine enemies. Go to the lady now, and tell her that I shall be near the tree at sunrise to-morrow morning, and tell her to have men ready to put the corpse in the grave.'

They went to the lady and told her all the priest said.

'If it succeeds with him,' said she, 'I shall have the reward ready for him, and I shall order seven men to be present.'

The priest spent that night in prayer, and half an hour before sunrise he went to the place where his blessed vestments were hidden; he put these on, and with a cross in one hand, with the holy-water in the other, he went to the place where were the flies. He then began reading out of his book and scattering holy-water on the flies, in the name of the Father, the Son, and the Holy Ghost. The hill of flies rose, and flew up into the air, and made the heaven as dark as night. The people did not know where they went, but at the end of half an hour there was not one of them to be seen.

There was great joy on the people, but it was not long until they saw the spy coming, and they called to the priest to run away as quick as it was in him to run. The priest gave to the butts (took to his heels), and the spy followed him, and with a knife in each hand with him. When he was not able to come up with the priest he flung the knife after him. As the knife was flying out past the priest's shoulder he put up his left hand and caught it, and without ever looking behind him he flung it back. It struck the man and went through his heart, so that he fell dead and the priest went free.

The people got the body of Bingham and buried it in the grave, but when they went to bury the body of the spy they found thousands of rats round it, and there was not a morsel of flesh on his bones that they had not eaten. They would not stir from the body, and the people were not able to rout them away, so that they had to leave the bones over-ground.

The priest hid away his blessed vestments and was working in the garden when Bingham's wife sent for him, and told him to take the reward that was for banishing the flies, and to give it to the man who banished them, if he knew him.

'I do know him, and he told me to bring him the reward to-night, because he has the intention of leaving the country before the law-people hang him.'

'Here it is for you,' she said, and she handed him a purse of gold.

On the morning of the next day the priest went to the brink of the sea, and found a ship that was going to France. He went on board, and as soon as he had left the harbour he put his priest's-clothes on him, and gave thanks to God for bringing him safe. We do not know what happened to him from that out.

After that, blind and sore-eyed people used to be coming to Mary's Well, and not a person of them ever returned without being cured. But there never yet was anything good in this country that was not spoilt by somebody, and the well was spoilt in this way.

There was a girl in Ballintubber and she was about to be married, when there came a half-blind old woman to her asking alms in the honour of God and Mary.

'I've nothing to give an old blind-thing of a hag, it's bothered with them I am,' said the girl.

'That the marriage ring may never go on you until you're as blind as myself,' says the old woman.

Next day, in the morning, the young girl's eyes were sore, and the morning after that she was nearly blind, and the neighbours said to her that she ought to go to Mary's Well.

In the morning, early, she rose up and went to the well, but who should she see at it but the old woman who asked the alms of her, sitting on the brink, combing her head over the blessed well.

'Destruction on you, you nasty hag, is it dirtying Mary's well you are?' said the girl, 'Get out of that or I'll break your neck.'

'You have no honour nor regard for God or Mary, you refused to give alms in honour of them, and for that reason you shall not dip yourself in the well.'

The girl caught hold of the hag, trying to pull her from the well, and with the dragging that was between them, the two of them fell into the well and were drowned.

From that day to this there has been no cure in the well.

103 *GREAT MARY*

Mary Mother bears a great part in the religious poetry of the Gaels. It was she who put the curing of the blind in the well, it was she who showed herself to the poor friar under the form of a dove, and it is she who gives a cure to the poor of the world through her intercession with her Son. It was no wonder, then, that the heart of the Gaels, the heart of a nation that especially respected and honoured its women, should give itself up particularly to Mary.

'Good is the woman, Great Mary,'
says Owen O'Duffy,
'A Woman who give sight to the blind.'

GREAT MARY

Good is the woman, Great Mary,
The mother of the High-king of the eternal hosts,
They are her graces which are ever full,
A woman who put a hedge around each country.

A woman to whom right inclines,
A woman greatest in strength and power,
A woman softest (i.e., most generous) in red gold,
A woman by whom is quenched the anger of the king.

A woman who gives sight to the blind,
A woman who is most powerful beyond in heaven,
A woman who has taken away my enemies from me,
A woman who is a defence to me in every battle.

[. . .]

Mary is not like women,
[Great Mary of good deeds],
Balsam is not like to myrrh,
To salt ale, wine is not like.

Gall is not like honey,
And brass is not like gold,
The lily is not like the thorn,
And to smooth plain, bog is not like.

104 *CHARM AGAINST EVIL EYE*

The belief is very common in Ireland and in Scotland that there are people in it who can cast an evil eye on anything that they please. If they cast an evil eye on your churn there will be no butter in the churning, if they cast it on your cow perhaps she will fall and be hurt, if they cast it on yourself perhaps it is a heavy disease or sickness that will come upon you. Here is a charm against the evil eye that Mr. Lyons wrote from the mouth of a man from Donegal, and Father O'Growney found the same charm in Aran.

CHARM AGAINST EVIL EYE

God's Son hath given a charm of charms,
 (First on thy knees thy *pater* say),
Shed was His blood by cruel arms,
 Faultless and fair his righteous sway.

When Mary saw him, as she stood,
　　High on the Cross all torn and rent,
Rained from her eyes three showers of blood
　　And at its foot she made lament.

An Evil Eye hath me undone
　　Paling my face in dule and dree,
I cry to Mary and her Son
　　Take the ill eye away from me.

105 *I PRAY GOD'S RIGHT-HAND ANGEL*

Father Eugene O'Growney, of a day, met a little child in Aran, and they were talking to one another, until at last they talked about fairies, and the child spoke to him exactly thus, 'It is said Father,' says he, 'anything that is seen on your left-hand side, — that it is a bad thing, but anything that will rise up on your right-hand side — it is no danger to you. But, whatever side they rise on, here is a charm to be said against them going the way, of you.'

I PRAY GOD'S RIGHT-HAND ANGEL

I pray the Right-hand Angel of God
That he may put me on the best-way for me,
I pray for God's sake
The Left-hand Spirits
　　All of them, so let me be.

106 *CHARM AGAINST FAIRIES*

Here is another little charm I heard from Father O'Growney against the fäerie of the fairies.

We accept their protection
And we refuse their removal,
Their back to us,
Their face from us,
Through the death and passion
Of our Saviour Jesus Christ.

107 *TO SAINT PATRICK*

Here is another melodious little song in honour of St. Patrick, which I got from the same Patrick O'Donnell. I do not remember that I ever heard any other verses in honour of St. Patrick amongst the people except this one — a thing which surprises me.

O Patrick in the Paradise
　　Of God on high,
Who lookest on the poor man
　　With a gracious eye,
See me come before thee
　　Who am weak and bare,
O help me into Paradise
　　To find thee there.

108 *A BLIND MAN'S CURSE*

A curse is a sort of prayer also; it is an evil prayer. I have not up to this given any example of these; but it is worth while to put down a few of them, and — 'may God increase the good, and diminish the evil' — it is out of no bad intention I am doing it, but only to preserve a specimen of every kind. This book would not be complete without one or two of them being in it. Curses are not numerous. When a person frames a prayer for himself, praying to God and Mary, his prayer is suitable for thousands of other people; but it is not so with the curse. It only appertains to the person who shaped it, and the person against whom it is loosed. The prayer suits the public; the curse concerns only the special person. I never heard any rhymed curse in the mouths of the people — a curse going the country, so to speak, and it ready to be launched at the enemy. I do not think there is such a thing. But here is an example or two of how people composed their own curses for themselves, when they sought to overthrow their opponents.

　　There was a poor blind man seeking alms in the County Galway, and he came to the door of a big house, and asked for a drink. The woman of the house was an English (or English-speaking?) woman, and since she did not understand him, she asked the servant what was the blind man asking for. The servant told her that he was asking for a drink. '*Water is good enough for the blind beggar,'* said she. The blind man understood the thing she said, and answered: —

A BLIND MAN'S CURSE

Your milk may no butter crown,
On your ducks may there come no down,
May your child never walk the ground,
  Be your cows where the flayer flays.
May more hot be in the flames that shall roll
One day through your wicked soul
Than the mountains of Connemara
  And they be in one blaze.

109 *THE BED CONFESSION*

Here is a version of the 'Bed Confession' that I heard in the county Mayo. There is a good deal of this that I had not got before, and it is worth while putting it down entirely.

May we lie down with God, and may God lie with us.
A Person from God with us. The two hands of God with us.
The Three Marys with us.
God and Columcille with us.
Is it not strong the fortress in which we are!
Between Mary and her Son,
Brigit and her mantle,
Michael and his shield,
God and His right hand,
Going between us and every evil.
May we not lie down with evil,
May evil not lie down with us.
The protection of the Three Trees,
The tree of the Cross,
The tree of the blood,
The tree on which Christ was hanged
And from which He rose again alive.
O King of the *cathair* in heaven,
Keep the spirit of my soul
From the real-temptations of the adversary.

110 *A HEALTH*

Here is a curious health from the County Mayo which I got from my friend Philip Waldron of Drombaun, about three miles from Ballyhaunis: —

> A health let us drink. Our glass we clink it,
>> May the King of the Graces to us be near.
> We will drink this glass as Patrick would drink it,
>> With a grace made salt by a mingled tear,
> Without sadness or sorrow or passion or pain,
>> — None knowing to-morrow that we were here.

Here is another little prayer in which Patrick is mentioned: —

THE LUCK OF GOD AND PROSPERITY OF PATRICK

> The luck of God and the prosperity of Patrick on all I shall see, and on all I shall touch, from the time I rise at morning until I sleep at night.

111 *HOW THE FIRST CAT WAS CREATED*

Here is a curious story that I got from my friend Dr. Connor Maguire, of Claremorris. I believe he got it from Ned Gibbons, the same old man from whom I got that fine poem, 'The Joyce's Repentance.' This story explains how the first cat and the first mouse were created. I heard many of such stories from the Red Indians in Canada, giving us to understand how this thing or the other thing was first made, but none of them had anything to say to Christianity! It is impossible to tell what is the age of this story, but it is certain that stories of this kind were common in early pagan times, even as they are common now amongst the Red men, and other wild tribes; and it may be that the story is older than the Christian religion itself, and that a saint was first put in the place of an enchanter when people began to become Christians. I think it is certain that this story originally concerned only the flour — the food of man — and the mice — the enemy of the flour — and the cat — the enemy of the mice; and the mention of the sow and her litter is a late and stupid introduction. This is only a supposition, and I shall set down the story here without saying any more and without altering anything in it.

HOW THE FIRST CAT WAS CREATED

One day Mary and her Son were travelling the road, and they heavy and tired, and it chanced that they went past the door of a house in which there was a lock (a small quantity) of wheat being winnowed. The Blessed Virgin went in, and she asked an alms of wheat, and the woman of the house refused her.

'Go in again to her,' said the Son, 'and ask her for it in the name of God.'

She went, and the woman refused her again.

'Go into her again,' said He, 'and ask her to give you leave to put your hand into the pail of water, and to thrust it down into the heap of wheat, and to take away with you all that shall cling to your hand.'

She went, and the woman gave her leave to do that. When she came out to our Saviour He said to her, 'Do not let one grain of that go astray, for it is worth much and much.'

When they had gone a bit from the house they looked back, and saw a flock of demons coming towards the house, and the Virgin Mary was frightened lest they might do harm to the woman. 'Let there be no anxiety on you,' said Jesus to her; 'since it has chanced that she has given you all that of alms, they shall get no victory over her.'

They travelled on, then, until they reached as far as a place where a man named Martin had a mill. 'Go in,' said our Saviour to his mother, 'since it has chanced that the mill is working, and ask them to grind that little grain-*een* for you.'

She went. 'O musha, it's not worth while for me,' said the boy who was attending the querns, 'to put that little lock*een* a-grinding for you.' Martin heard them talking and said to the lout, 'Oh, then, do it for the creature, perhaps she wants it badly,' said he. He did it, and he gave her all the flour that came from it.

They travelled on then, and they were not gone any distance until the mill was full of flour as white as snow. When Martin perceived this great miracle he understood well that it was the Son of God and His Mother, who chanced that way. He ran out and followed them, at his best, and he made across fields until he came up with them, and there was that much haste on him in going through a scunce (a thick-set double ditch) of hawthorns that a spike of the hawthorn met his breast and wounded him greatly. There was that much zeal in him that he did not feel the pain, but clapt his hand over it, and never stopped until he came up with them. When our Saviour beheld the wound upon poor Martin He laid his hand upon it, and it was closed, and healed upon the spot. He said to Martin then that he was a fitting man in the presence of God, 'and go home now,' said He, 'and place a fistful of flour under a dish, and do not stir it until morning.'

When Martin went home and did that, and he put the dish, mouth under, and the fistful of flour beneath it.

The servant girl was watching him, and thought that maybe it would be a good thing if she were to set a dish for herself in the same way, and signs on her, she set it.

On the morning of the next day Martin lifted his dish, and what should run out from under it but a fine sow and a big litter of bonhams with her. The girl lifted her own dish, and there ran out a big mouse and a clutch of young mouselets with her. They ran here and there, and Martin at once thought that they were not good, and he plucked a big mitten off his hand and flung it at the young mice, but as soon as it touched the ground it changed into a cat, and the cat began to kill the young mice. That was the beginning of cats. Martin was a saint from that time forward, but it is not known which of the saints he was of all who were called Martin.

Modern Poetry

INTRODUCTION

Artistic inspiration is often born from tension, the attempt of individuals to make sense of, articulate and come to terms with disparate elements of their experience. For 'Celtic' poets writing today the relationship between the past and present is a rich, if somewhat vexed, vein to tap. Questions of identity, language, nationhood and of one's relationship to the land and community pose particular conundrums in an increasingly cosmopolitan world. A nostalgic sentimentality, evident in some nineteenth-century verse, is usually eschewed, and we see an often ambivalent attitude towards the past and the ties of family and tribal loyalty. There are also, however, aspects of contemporary poetry from the Celtic countries which echo themes evident in the medieval period. An attachment to the land, not in general, but to a particular country, hill, valley, rock, island or town, is striking; not a romanticized, idealized landscape, but actual places which the poets know and value for their own sake. There is no doubting, for instance, that Ian Crichton Smith, born on the Hebridean island of Lewis, is writing of a specific place and a familiar experience in his poem 'By Ferry to the Island':[1]

> We crossed by ferry to the bare island
> where sheep and cows stared coldly through the wind —
> the sea behind us with its silver water,
> the silent ferryman standing in the stern
> clutching his coat about him like old iron.

There is ambivalence about these island roots, however, evident in Crichton Smith's poem 'Going Home':[2]

> Tomorrow I shall go home to my island . . .
> I will lift a fistful of its earth in my hands
> or I will sit on a hillock of the mind
> watching 'the shepherd at his sheep'.

> There will arise (I presume) a thrush.
> A dawn or two will break . . .

Ian Crichton Smith, like so many of his fellow Gaelic language poets in Scotland, is in exile from his home, and to some extent from the language community that raised him. The forces described by Alexander Carmichael which drove the Gaels from their native villages, valleys and islands are still operating. The old saying that Glasgow is the capital of the Highlands and Islands of Scotland (and Liverpool and London respectively of north and south Wales) are not without meaning today. The same is not true, however, of the Breton poet Anjela Duval. She lived almost all her life in the family farmhouse, working the same few acres of land. Some of her more nationalistic verse shares with Anglo-Welsh poet, R. S. Thomas, a deep anxiety at the encroachment of foreigners into that beloved land, as in 'Work of the Foreigner':[3]

> Strip. Despoil our Country
> Sweep away the sacred oaks of the Druids
> The birches of the Celts and the yew-trees
> — And the chestnuts of our youth —
> In which our birds sang.

More characteristic of Duval's poems, however, is a celebration of her relationship with nature, a ubiquitous subject for what are in the main rural poets, as in her poem 'Lindens'. Having described the thirteen giant trees, already full grown in her youth, Duval reveals her inner attitude to the land she inherited from her parents:

> These lindens are not my possession
> Yet I possess the right
> To cut them down
> They are sucking the sap of my land
> With their roots so long. But I won't.
> I would miss them
> For they are part of that living tableau
> That forms the framework of my life.

Nature is characteristically allowed to be just that, the natural world. Where it is invested with meaning beyond its surface appearance, this is usually the sense of wonder and astonishment invoked in the human observer by the simple fact that it exists, and exists not just in the eyes and minds of human beings but for its own sake. The Scottish poet Edwin Muir in 'Horse' describes his fascination with the shire horses he used to watch ploughing the rocky fields of his childhood:[4]

> Those lumbering horses in the steady plough
> On the bare field — I wonder why, just now,
> They seemed terrible, so wild and strange,
> Like magic power on the stony grange.

In her poem 'A Marvellous Hour', Duval describes the tranquillity of evening after a day's work, 'The hour of prayer, hour of study./Hour of dreaming, of fantasy,/Hour divine, full of ecstasy'. All that the poet misses to perfect the moment is the singing of a cricket in the hearth. Gillian Clarke's description of the birth of a calf on a hot summer's day, in her poem 'Birth', has the quiet and empathetic observation of something that is in itself a miracle: the gift of new life.[5]

> . . . Hot and slippery, the scalding
> Baby came, and the cow stood up, her cool
> Flanks like white flowers in the dark.
> We waited while the calf struggled
> To stand, moved as though this
> Were the first time. I could feel the soft sucking
> Of the new-born, the tugging pleasure
> Of bruised reordering, the signal
> Of milk's incoming tide, and satisfaction
> Fall like a clean sheet around us.

One of the tensions evident in medieval verse is the relationship between Christianity and the pre-Christian past or 'pagan' elements in the present. This relationship between the past and present, and the Christian/pagan mixture of religious traditions and sensibilities, is sometimes evoked through a sense of place. The topographical features of the landscape and human endeavours which leave their mark for later generations can be 'read' by those sensitive to them. Gillian Clarke and Seamus Heaney were both struck by the little squat carved stone figure of a fertility goddess (Sheelagh na Gig) on the twelfth-century church at Kilpeck in Herefordshire. In Gillian Clarke's memorable words (in her poem 'Sheila na Gig at Kilpeck'):[6]

Pain's a cup of honey in the pelvis.
She burns in the long, hot afternoon, stone
among the monstrous nursery faces
circling Kilpeck church.

Ruth Bidgood in her poem 'Hoofprints' describes the way in which
'carved hoofprints on a rock' acquire mythological significance:[7]

The legend was always here,
at first invisible, poised above the hill,
stiller than any kestrel . . .

And so it remains until people recognize in the marks the leap of a magic
horse, 'the print of miracle'. Similarly in 'Green Man at the Bwlch',
Bidgood describes the serendipity which brought the Green Man to her
conscious attention until at last she discovers him in a remote half-
crumbled house:[8]

In a central room, on the beam
over the great hearth, royally
he spreads his mouth-borne branches,
meets my unsurprised eyes . . .

The terror is in his utter
neutrality. Yet somewhere
in his kingdom of possibilities
is a tree whose leaves give shelter,
whose boughs know songs, whose sap
flows gold through our veins.

A sense of community, not only with the living, but also with the
dead, is another recurrent motif in both medieval and contemporary
Celtic verse. Death, in fact, seems to hold a particular fascination for the
Celts. George Mackay Brown's extraordinarily evocative poem 'The
Jars' recalls a man's life in a dream-like state which hovers between the
living and the dead. His family, his loves and labours are distilled into
jars found in a deserted house. For Euros Bowen the Christian theology
of death and resurrection, sometimes perceived in terms of failure and
triumph, are subsumed into an older, more ecologically balanced,
affirmation that life and death belong together, and that all life depends

upon the earth which sustains us. 'The earth keeps the tap root of death awake . . . /Without a root in the earth death's finality is our death . . . /

There is no resurrection where there is no earth.' Brendan Kennelly is another poet keenly aware of the continuity between the living and the dead. At the end of his poem 'House' he writes:[9]

> Listen! You can hear the dance
> Starting on the kitchen floor.
> They are learning the steps
> Becoming the music
> Reaching the skill, the fever,
> Doing what I've always wanted.
> Dancing through me, dancing their beginning,
> They are learning to be haunted.

For Ruth Bidgood keeping faith with the dead involves a recitation of the names of farms and houses, now mainly deserted. In 'All Souls' this act of remembrance takes on the strains of a litany:[10]

> From the hill Clyn ahead
> Glangwesyn's lively shout of light
> celebrates old Nant Henfron, will not let
> Cenfaes and Blaennant be voiceless.
> I am a latecomer, but offer
> speech to the nameless, those
> who are hardly a memory, those
> whose words were always faint
> against the deafening darkness
> of remotest hills.

Anjela Duval describes her heart as a cemetery containing the countless graves of friends and relatives but, like Ruth Bidgood, transforms the finality of the past through remembrance. The poem 'My Heart' ends with this transformation:

> My heart is a Cemetery
> But no!
> My heart is a Sanctuary
> Wherein live My Dear Departed!

Contemporary Celtic poets also deal with the living community, often with those marginalized and ignored by our modern society which values outward achievements and material success above all. In 'Down Syndrome, in memory of Joseph Leary', Bernard O'Donaghue writes 'Take consolation that it won't be you/That has to declare strategy/Or give the order to burn sprawling/Ranks of soldiers.' Joseph Leary, instead, had 'a weakness for the truth', and an ability to bring out the best in those who knew him.[11] In 'St Magnus Day in the Island' and 'Feast of Candles' George Mackay Brown celebrates the community, ordinary working Orkney people with their rough hands and faces, long-suffering and enduring, who gather together for ritual, pilgrimage and worship.[12]

> (And the monk gathered the folds of his cloak
>   together at the altar and bent
>   and prayed between two tall
>   set apart candles: in Latin
>   whispers and a boy replied,
>   hesitant with the Latin syllables,
>   in country whispers)
> And a flame set, and a flame set, and a flame
>   set . . .

An emphasis on community is linked, very often, to an awareness of presence (or absence). Space is not empty but resonant. Material objects which might at first sight appear fixed yield to subtler dimensions, change form and take on meanings beyond their surface solidity. Even when dealing with everyday occurrences and the most mundane realities, such as eating Christmas dinner with relatives, the poet remains sensitive to the possibility of less visible company. Angels, fairies, spirits of nature and of the dead are never far away, and whether one 'believes in' them or not, they continue to inhabit the poetic imagination. This ever present other world is strongly felt in much of Nuala Ní Dhomhnaill's powerful poetry. In 'Abduction', for instance, the housewife changes place with a fairy woman:[13]

> The fairy woman walked
> into my poem.
> She closed no door
> She asked no by-your-leave.

Knowing my place
I did not tell her to go.

Nuala Ní Dhomhnaill's 'Parthenogenesis' recalls Irish legends of the coupling of a woman with a mysterious sea creature while she is out swimming, subsequently giving birth to a child of the 'Sea People':

She and her husband so satisfied,
so full of love for this new son
forgot the shadow in the sea
and did not see what only the midwife saw —
stalks of sea-tangle in the boy's hair
small shellfish and sea-ribbons
and his two big eyes
as blue and limpid as lagoons.

For R. S. Thomas in 'The Presence' the invisible world is not named or peopled with miraculous creatures but is no less strongly felt:[14]

I feel the power
that, invisible, catches me
by the sleeve . . .
I know its ways with me;
how it enters my life,
is present rather
before I perceive it, sunlight quivering
on a bare wall.

The human community, past and present, with this Celtic admixture of ordinary human foibles and ancient mystery, is captured by John Montague in his poem 'Like Dolmens Round My Childhood, the Old People'.[15] The figures of the poet's youth are named, Jamie MacCrystal who 'sang to himself a broken song, without tune, without words'. Maggie Owens, surrounded by animals, the Nialls who 'lived along a mountain lane' and who were all blind. Mary Moore, who is remembered for her 'bag apron and boots'. This, however, seems to be a community which is failing to renew itself: 'Sometimes they were found by neighbours,/Silent keepers of a smokeless hearth,/Suddenly cast in the mould of death.' The ambivalence shown towards a rural island home in Ian Crichton Smith's poetry is echoed in Montague's observation of the dying, inward-looking community of his youth. His poem ends with a kind of exorcism which brings personal realease, but which at the same time links his present with his past, and with the past of all the people of Ireland:

> Ancient Ireland, indeed! I was reared by her bedside,
> The rune and the chant, evil eye and averted head,
> Fomorian fierceness of family and local feud.
> Gaunt figures of fear and of friendliness,
> For years they trespassed on my dreams,
> Until once, in a standing circle of stones,
> I felt their shadows pass
> Into that dark permanence of ancient forms.

Miracle, in many different guises, expresses the poet's vision of the world. It could be described in terms of the tension between the ordinary and extraordinary, everyday reality and that particular vision which makes the mundane special and the inanimate alive. Nuala Ní Dhomhnaill's poem 'Marvellous Grass' is reminiscent of the stories of miracle-working priests with supernatural powers collected by Douglas Hyde in his *Religious Songs of Connacht*.

> When you were a holy priest
> in the middle of Mass in your purple robes
> your linen mantle, your stole, your chasuble.
> You saw my face in the crowd
> approaching you for communion
> and you dropped the blessed host . . .
>
> And in the place where fell
> the sacred host you will see
> among the useless plants
> a patch of marvellous grass.

Religion as a theme in the poems selected here is interpreted broadly — a yearning of the human spirit, a proclivity to wonder and the company of a world infused with glory. As an explicit subject religion, or Christianity, is oriented less towards creeds and the dogmas of faith (which are more often expressed in hymns) than to experience and theophany — the birds, animals, flowers, and even the humble lichen

offer their sacrament of praise to the Creator. There are some poems of
more traditional piety, such as Anjela Duval's 'Saint Mary' which
echoes both the Magnificat and the Prayer of Saint Francis ('Saint
Mary, Mother of God,/Preserve for me a child's heart,/Pure and
transparent as a spring,/A heart simple and straight,/That will never
taste unhappiness . . .'), or John F. Deane's poem 'Contact'.[16]

> *When I call to you, God,*
> *it is only that I want to grasp*
> *what you can offer; when you call to me,*
> *God, I know you want*
> *all that I have to offer, so,*
> *I yield to the distractions.*
> > *. . . Now,*
> *if I can only find the silence,*
> *a sudden glance towards you*
> *can be my prayer.*

Pilgrimage, whether ancient or contemporary, and tales of Celtic
saints, are frequent subjects for many Celtic poets. Norman MacCaig
turns to Assisi, while George Mackay Brown focuses on the popular
Highland saint, St Magnus. John Irvine imagines Colm-Cille's farewell
to his native Ireland before setting sail for Iona in his poem 'Saint
Colm-Cille and the Cairn of Farewell' which, with its rather sentimental nostalgia and simple rhyme, recalls the exile of so many of Ireland's
sons and daughters today:[17]

> The oaks are green in Derry now,
> The waves break on the Irish shore,
> My grief that I must say farewell —
> Farewell for ever more . . .
>
> But row me to Iona's Isle
> Though I am weary of the sea,
> Beyond the far enpurpled hills
> That will not let me be.

Both Sheenagh Pugh, writing about St Cuthbert, and Nuala Ní
Dhomhnaill, referring to St Anthony, speculate on the hermit's relationship with women and on the narrow asceticism which feeds on

misogyny. In Nuala Ní Dhomhnaill's poem 'Monk' the torments suffered by the ascetic are not related to individual, particular women, as in Sheenagh Pugh's 'St Cuthbert and the Women', but to the feminine ('Eve' and 'the serpent') and to the very forces of life itself:[18]

> But it's not to torment you
> every day I rise —
> but to drown you
> in love's delights.
> I'm a dead hero leaping
> from the edge of the bridge of fear —
> That's the only reason I haunt you:
> my monk, my apostle, my priest.

Ambivalence in religion is a frequent contemporary preoccupation. The exuberant confidence of the medieval 'Loves of Taliesin', and of many oral invocations recorded by Alexander Carmichael, do not have the self-conscious quality which characterizes R. S. Thomas' verse. In 'Covenant' the poet states 'I feel sometimes we are his penance for having made us', and ends with the words:[19]

> Often
> I think that there is no end
> to this torment and that the electricity
> that convulses us is the fire
> in which a god
> burns and is not consumed.

Another clergyman, Euros Bowen, seems at times unsure of his loyalties to a patriarchal God who requires us to be his human servants. The goddess, in the guise of Gaia or the earth, is bemoaned now that she is all but destroyed. In 'Changing Government' Bowen writes:[20]

> We no longer put our trust
> in the masculine deity
> of the mountain and the sea
> nor in the feminine deity
> of rivers and trees . . .

> The queen of heaven has been divorced,
> she is throneless in our world
> now that the ridges of her ramparts
> are in laboratories . . .
>
> With the change to
> our government
> the writing of the four winds is on the wall,
> for the rocks cannot become bread
> and the waters
> cannot turn the air into wine.

The poetic tradition and the magic power of language sometimes evoked in medieval verse continues to preoccupy contemporary Celtic poets. The way in which the poet becomes a mere channel for a higher power is beautifully captured by W. R. Rogers in the poem 'Words'. The words arrive like 'winds', pouring like 'Atlantic gales over these ears', waiting in the darkness of the unconscious to come forth and 'speak for me — their most astonished host'.[21] In Gillian Clarke's poem 'Miracle on St David's Day' it is poetry which reawakens speech in a man long silent, joining human verse to the paeans of the flowers and the thrush:[22]

> He is suddenly standing, silently,
> huge and mild, but I feel afraid. Like slow
> movement of spring water or the first bird
> of the year in the breaking darkness,
> the labourer's voice recites 'The Daffodils'.
>
> The nurses are frozen, alert; the patients
> seem to listen. He is hoarse but word-perfect.
> Outside the daffodils are still as wax,
> a thousand, ten thousand, their syllables
> unspoken, their creams and yellows still.
>
> Forty years ago, in a Valleys school,
> the class recited poetry by rote.
> Since the dumbness of misery fell
> he has remembered there was a music
> of speech and that once he had something to say.

When he's done, before the applause, we observe
the flowers' silence. A thrush sings
and the daffodils are flame.

The harsher realities of life are not forgotten by other Celtic poets, even in their religious verse. On seeing a military jet over the west Wales countryside Gillian Clarke, in her poem 'In January', muses that:[23]

The cities can forget on days like this
all the world's wars. It's we
out on the open hill who see
the day crack under the shadow of the cross.

And in 'Fires on Llyn', Clarke describes sitting with a friend at Uwchmynydd on the edge of the Llyn Peninsula in Gwynedd, looking out towards Bardsey Island (Ynys Enlli), the resting place of 'twenty thousand saints', and to Ireland beyond:[24]

Facing west, we've talked for hours
of our history,
thinking of Ireland and the hurt
cities,
gunshot on lonely farms,

praised unsectarian saints,
Enlli open
to the broken rosary
of their coracles,
praying in Latin and Welsh.

The Ulster-born poet Louis MacNeice ends his famous poem 'Prayer Before Birth', which is a great cry for justice and truly human values, with the words:[25]

I am not yet born; O fill me
With strength against those who would freeze my
humanity, would dragoon me into a lethal automaton,
would make me a cog in a machine, a thing with
one face, a thing, and against all those

who would dissipate my entirety, would
blow me like thistledown hither and
thither or hither and thither
like water held in the
hands would spill me.

Let them not make me a stone and let them not spill me.
Otherwise kill me.

Notes

1 *Thistles and Roses*, Eyre & Spottiswode 1961.
2 *Nua-Bhardachd Ghaidhlig/Modern Scottish Gaelic Poems*, Canongate 1980. The translation is by the author.
3 All the quotations of the work of Anjela Duval are from *A Modern Breton Political Poet: Anjela Duval*, edited and introduced by L. A. Timm, Edwin Mellen 1990. The translations from Breton are by Lenora Timm.
4 From *First Poems*, 1925, reprinted in *Edwin Muir's Collected Poems, 1921-1958*, Faber & Faber.
5 *Selected Poems*, Carcanet, London 1985.
6 ibid.
7 *The Print of Miracle*, Gomer 1978.
8 Ruth Bidgood, *Selected Poems*, Seren/Poetry Wales Press 1992.
9 *Breathing Spaces*, Bloodaxe 1992.
10 *The Print of Miracle*.
11 *The Weakness*, Chatto & Windus 1991.
12 *The Wreck of the Archangel*, John Murray 1989.
13 *Selected Poems: Rogha Dánta*, Raven Arts Press 1991. English translations in this bilingual edition are by Michael Hartnett. All the poems by Nuala Ní Dhomhnaill are taken from this edition.
14 *Between Here and Now*, Macmillan 1981.
15 *The Rough Field*, Dolmen Press 1972.
16 *The Deer's Cry*, edited by Patrick Murray, Four Courts Press 1986.
17 ibid.
18 *Selected Poems*, Seren (Poetry Wales Press) 1992.
19 *Between Here and Now*.
20 *Priest-Poet/Bardd-Offeiriad*, Church in Wales Publications 1993; translation by Cynthia Davies.
21 *Collected Poems*, Oxford University Press 1971.
22 *Selected Poems*.
23 *Letting in the Rumour*, Carcanet 1989.
24 *Selected Poems*.
25 *The Deer's Cry*.

SAUNDERS LEWIS (1893–1985)

Saunders Lewis, poet, playwright, nationalist and scholar, was a somewhat enigmatic character who often occupied the lonely and anomalous position of the insider/outsider. Born and brought up in Cheshire, where his father was minister to a Welsh-speaking chapel, he was sent to a minor English public school. He studied English and French at Liverpool University, and developed a life-long love of France. Saunders Lewis' decision to join the Roman Catholic Church (in 1932) was linked to his sense of continuity with a pan-European medieval Catholic culture. From 1923–36 Saunders Lewis lectured in Welsh at the University of Wales, Swansea, and began writing plays in Welsh, despite the fact that the Welsh theatrical tradition was virtually non-existent. In 1925 Saunders Lewis was one of the founder members of the Welsh Nationalist Party, Plaid Cymru, *and its President from 1926–1939. A radio talk by Lewis on the fate of the Welsh language in 1962 was instrumental in the founding of the Welsh Language Society,* Cymdeithas yr Iaith Gymraeg. *Saunders Lewis was briefly imprisoned and was dismissed from his post at Swansea for his part in a symbolic demonstration against English rule in Wales in 1936. It was not until 1952 that the Welsh Department in Cardiff offered him work.*

112 ASCENSION THURSDAY

What is happening this May morning on the hillside?
See there, the gold of the broom and laburnum
And the bright surplice on the thorn's shoulder
And the intent emerald of the grass and the still calves;

See the candelabra of the chestnut tree alight
The bushes kneel and the mute beech, like a nun,
The cuckoo's two notes above the bright hush of the stream,
And the form of the mist that curls from the censor of the meadows.

179

Come out, you men, from the council houses
Before the rabbits run, come with the weasel to see
The elevation of the unblemished host from the earth,
The Father kiss the Son in the white dew.

EUROS BOWEN (1904–1988)

Euros Bowen was brought up in the Rhondda Valley in south Wales. He was son of a Congregationalist minister, and intended to follow his father's profession, but after studying in various places in Wales and in Oxford he joined the Anglican Church, and served as a priest of the Church in Wales. Euros Bowen was a prolific poet in Welsh. He wrote both in free verse and in cynghanedd *(strict metre), and twice won the crown at the National Eisteddfod. In 1974 Bowen translated some of his own poems into English (some of which are included here). Although widely educated in classical and French literature (which he also translated), and strongly attracted to Eastern Christianity, Euros Bowen's poetry owes more to the medieval Welsh tradition. The sacramentality of nature and the place of humanity within the world are recurrent themes in his verses.*

113 *THE ROWAN TREE*

You can see it above the river's hollow bank, on the edge,
      of gorse and wind,
A crack in bareness of rock is its earth.

The twisted form of its grey trunk stands,
      gaunt and bare,
Shaped like a wooden cross.

Its branches are arms outstretched, darkened
      by a wound in the chest,
Rough and harsh as the ribs of Christ.

And blood trickles on this tree, on the edge
      of gorse and wind,
Blood which breaks from the swell of God's pity.

114 *THIS IS PRAISE*

In my day I have often heard morning and evening
the thrush's call
on the tree's high branch,
the brook trebling in the solitude
of moor-bank and marsh,
an infant's ready laughter
at his foot's first venture on the ground,
and the children's noisy fun
on the village meadow:
And when the swallow,
its diligent nesting done,
has left for the south,
I have seen summer decay
as an acorn rolls golden
into the shadow of the country's oak,
like the smile of the departed
before burial in the earth. —
Life does not die. This is praise.

115 *REREDOS*

The reredos was not
an ecclesiastical adornment
of symbols,
but plain glass,
with the danger
of distracting the celebrant
from
the properties of the communion table.

for
in the translucence
the green earth
budded in the morning view,
the river was in bloom,
the air a joyous flight,

and the sunshine
set the clouds ablaze.

and I noticed
the priest's eyes
as it were unconsciously
placing his hand
on these gifts,
as though these
were
the bread and the wine.

116 CROWS

Crows flying to their retreat in the woods' choir,
turning away beyond the road's rushing,
old ever-with-us-things
like green, yellowish grey sins,
the generations of the leaves and the oak trees' decay,
ministers under the raucous belfry of the parish,
in their black despite the broken altars of the druids,
as it now between the surpliced walls of heaven
chanting the psalms of the day's meditations —
having long been shepherding the salt of the earth
in the light of the world on slope and on field,
listening to the treasure's seed
and pecking to the very heart
of the hidden wisdom between the rocks and the stones, —
and returning from the ravines' fragrances
to chancel and altar at nightfall
past the ebb and the flow, the ashes and the dust
with the mustard seeds of the pearl in their beak, —
the stewards of the blessed mysteries
under the hill's bells in the branched glory of the tree.

117 *CHANGING GOVERNMENT*

We no longer put our trust
in the masculine deity
of the mountain and the sea
nor in the feminine deity
of rivers and trees.

The government of the skies
we have sent to hell,
and so the throne of the sun is empty;
there is a death mask on its face
in a museum.

The queen of heaven has been divorced,
she is throneless in our world
now that the ridges of her ramparts
are in laboratories.

By now
the traces of the carriages
of their splendour
across the day
and across the night skies
have become the sphere of archaeology.

In the midst of our century
a desert of dust exploded
between us and the sceptre of light,
and we the subjects of
goodness
were found
in a heap of rubble.

Under our government
the privy council of the stars were all excommunicated.

The brightness on the sea
is the spittle of oils,

slag-heaps are filth's poison,
and the gold of the heavens is lead
that fouls lungs wings and leaves.

They are at it desecrating the sea's care,
polluting the river's cleanliness;
the wells were deprived of their healing power
and the generosity of the trees was demythologized.

Chapter and verse
the manna and the miracle
in the west and the east,
in the north and the south,
in unscriptural language
in the marrow
and the blood's mouth.

With the change to
our government
the writing of the four winds is on the wall,
for the rocks cannot become bread
and the waters
cannot turn the air into wine.

118 *A REFRIGERATOR*

A cupboard
the buttress of technology
in the kitchen,
a very material and useful
refuge:
keeping together
the mild of meadows,
the pasture's honey,
the produce of fields and forests,
the goodness
of the cream and the mill,
the generosity
of the wine vat.

All that was conceived
by the air
and the earth
in the graves of the soil
and that was nurtured
by water
and fire
in the cradle of the earth
is born anew:

The trout's resurrection
beside the descents of the valley,
the salmon's leap
by the falls of the weir,

the firmament's power
gladdens

the slopes of the lemon,
breezes
sweetening the juice of oranges.

This is the culture of the sun's galleries
and the utterance of the rain's pastures:

The store cupboard
of the anamnesis
of the images of earth.

119 *TAP ROOT*

The earth keeps the tap root of death
    awake:

The flesh covering bones will rot,
    or, if it does not, will remain
    as stone relics
    eventually
    for antiquarians,
    fragments of a city under a heap.

The flesh of leaves will descend into oblivion,
    blood filled limbs becoming clay,
    veins of branches clotting coldly.

Without a root in the earth
    death's finality is our death,
    like snowflakes on a river's current,
    like birds' designs in the sky:

There is no resurrection where there is no earth.

120 *MOUNTAINS*

We had better leave these mountains
where they are
to their fate and the wind.

If we were to shepherd them
with our years,
that would make no scrap of difference
to their shape and colour
as mountains.

Although, probably, the outcrop
of their shape and colour
would leave its mark
on the flesh and bone
of the days that belong to us.

For their outline is to us an assurance
of the stability of rock
and a warrant of the blade of tenderness
in that heritage
that is faith under the wind's roar,
the faith
that does not want to move mountains.

GEORGE MACKAY BROWN (b.1921)

George Mackay Brown comes from an old Orkney family and, apart from a period studying at Edinburgh University, has lived most of his life in Orkney. He joined the Roman Catholic Church in 1961. Some of Brown's most memorable works feature Saint Magnus, patron saint of Orkney, and detail the relationship between religion and the harsh life of the island people, as in the following passage from 'Our Lady of the Waves':

> Blessed Lady, since midnight
> We have done three things
> We have bent hooks,
> We have patched a sail.
> We have sharpened knives,
> Yet the little silver brothers are afraid.
> Bid them come to our net,
> Show them our fire, our fine round plates.
> *Per Dominum Christum nostrum*
> Look mildly on our hungers.

As well as poetry, Brown has written short stories, plays, novels, essays, books for children and a non-fictional work on Orkney. Together with religion, it is the physical environment of his island home and the interweaving of Scots and Norse myths and cultures which provide the main inspiration for his poetry.

121 *THE JARS*

> A house on the mist-shrouded moor! —
> the ghost of a house
>
> Over the lintel this carving
> HOUSE OF WOMEN

Not a woman stirred, outside
or in

He knocked. No-one answered.
He pushed open the door

It was dark and cold inside
the house

He opened a cupboard. In the
cupboard was a small clay
jar with markings on it

He tasted the stuff in the jar:
finest of honey! His flesh
glowed with lost suns and
blossoms. He sipped again

Now the window was black
as tar

He stooped. He stroked with
blind hands the shape of a bed.
He covered himself with coarse
weave

He slept at once

*   *   *

The man woke. The window
was gray. He took down the jar
to taste the honey

The single jar stood on the shelf —
the shape of it had changed, and it
was of coarser clay

He opened it. It was crammed
with salt.

(the man heard, somewhere in
the house, a small cry)

He went through the rooms
of the house in search of a
child. The house was empty still

He returned to the room with
the cupboard and jar. He said,
*Young one, whoever you are, you
won't starve because of me —
There will be fish for the salting*

He came to a room where
the hearth was cold and the
lamp empty

On a stone of the wall was
carved the shape of a fish

He looked at the rune so long
that it seemed to pass into him
and become part of him

In another room, hidden, a
girl was singing

The man said, *Lost and
darkling creature, I will bring
you oil and driftwood
always*

The song guttered out. It
stopped. It faltered into
low cries of pain

*   *   *

The man wandered again
through the rooms of the house

He saw his reflection in a
pane. Furrows in the face,
a mesh of gray through his
black beard

A poor house, he said.
There should be a bowl
on the sill, daffodils
or roses or heather, to say
what time of year it is — yes —
to spill some beauty into a
bleak place. This jar is all,
it seems

He took the jar from the shelf.
An earth smell came out of it —
it was half full of flailed corn.
His hands that held the jar were
twisted with a summer of pain

Through the corridors of the
house a contented cry came. It
must (he thought) be a woman over
new loaves and ale, well pleased,
arms and face fire-flushed

Lost one in this house, he
said, *there will always be*
cornstorks — I will see to it

He scratched an ear-of-corn
on a stone beside the stone
with the carved fish

*　　*　　*

He lay down on the bed.
He was as weary as if he
had toiled, sunrise to
sunset, in a harvest field

He lay under a green and
a gold wave

His dream was about the
one jar that flowed always
from shape to shape, and
was ripeness, keeping, care,
sorrow, delight

The man woke. He knew now
that he was old

A thin-spun silver flowed over
the blanket. His hands were like
shreds of net, or winter roots

Seven women of different
ages stood about his bed. They
all, from first to last, had the
same fleeting look: the lost
girl at the horse fair

One by one, beginning with
the youngest, they bent over
and kissed him

The mid-most woman smelt
of roses and sunlight. Her
mouth had the wild honey
taste

The oldest one dropped
tears on his face

Then the seven women
covered their faces and
went out of the room

*   *   *

He slept on into the starred
ebb of winter

    * * *

He opened his eyes

A young man was
standing in the open door. He
carried a jar on his
shoulder

The young man greeted
him — then he turned
and went out into the
sun

The man said, *That is
my son. He is carrying
away the dust of my death*

RUTH BIDGOOD (b.1922)

Ruth Bidgood was born at Seven Sisters near Neath in south Wales, and was educated in Wales and Oxford. After many years and a varied career in England she went to live in the hamlet of Abergwesyn near Llanwrtyd Wells on the eastern edge of the Cambrian Mountains. She writes with great sensitivity of people, both living and dead, known personally and through records in local archives. Her poems refer chiefly to the places and people in her immediate locality, including her own family, and to the minutiae of nature which frequently reveal the awe-inspiring wonders of the creation. Ruth Bidgood's poems are sacramental rather than sentimental. Her touch is light and often humorous and gives the impression of a writer who has made peace with herself and with life.

122 *THE SPOUT*

Rain and rain had followed snow.
Under watery sun, sluggish water
spread, slid on the hill-slope:
churned narrow, brown in ditches:
sucked our steps between tussocks.
The river went in new white violence
over the rocks and down.

The children were tired of wet plodding.
Fields were rutted, grey-brown,
a mess of plashiness; one only,
steeply tilted, showed green.
Thankful for easy walking,
we idled across it.

Just before the gate, we saw grasses
gleam and part. A newborn spout

sprang up, sparkled, flowed.
It spoke to the children. They laughed, screamed,
bathed muddy hands, patted the spout,
attacked it, tried to force it back down,
jumped on it, over it, into it.

A skyful of water, a landful of water,
a dayful of water; and the little spout
could do this! The dismal downwardness
of mud, cheating slitheriness
of surface puddles, demented downrush
of rivers, were gathered, embraced, redeemed
by the small eager spout,
the thrusting, humorous creature of water,
that irrepressibly proclaimed
upwardness, happy intransigence,
in the depth of things.

123 SOURCES
a. County History
Llangynog

Small, bleak and barren,
with a ruinous church,
wrote the historian, apologising
for noting a place devoid
of history or good soil,
whose few frugal farmers
would gaze down mortified
from their snowy hills
at the soft flocking-in of green
to the spring valley.

Cold and late in greyness,
over a field of wet red earth
I draggle to barbed wire
and a ditch. Beyond the trees
Cynog's roofless church

suffers a long shedding of stone.
I free an earthbound cross,
prop it against rubble.
Wind seeps through shelter-trees.
Consecrated silence welcomes in
a flock of prayers crying,
praises clapping their wings.

124 *RESURRECTION ANGELS*

(Kilvert was told that the people used to come to the Wild Duck Pool
on Easter morning 'to see the sun dance and play in the water and the
angels who were at the Resurrection playing backwards and forwards
before the sun'.)

These were not troubling the waters
to bring healing. They were serving
no purpose. After the watch at the tomb,
the giving of good news, they were at play.
To and fro went the wings, to and fro
over the water, playing before the sun.

Stolid-seeming villagers stared
enchanted, watching sun dance and play,
light-slivers splinter water's dark.
In dazzle they half-saw
great shining shapes swoop frolicking
to and fro, to and fro.
                              This much was shared,
expected; day and place had their
appropriateness, their certainties.
The people had no words to tell
the astonishment, the individual bounty —
for each his own dance in the veins,
brush of wings on the soul.

125 *ALL SOULS'*

Shutting my gate, I walk away
from the small glow of my banked fire
into a black All Souls'. Presently
the sky slides back across the void
like a grey film. Then the hedges
are present, and the trees, which my mind
already knows, are no longer
strangers to my eyes.
The road curves. Further along,
a conversation of lights begins
from a few houses, invisible except as light,
calling to farms that higher in darkness
answer still, though each now speaks
for others that lie dumb.
Light at Tymawr above me, muted by trees,
is all the voice Brongwesyn has,
that once called clearly enough
into the upper valley's night.
From the hill Clyn ahead
Glangwesyn's lively shout of light
celebrates old Nant Henfron, will not let
Cenfaes and Blaennant be voiceless.
I am a latecomer, but offer
speech to the nameless, those
who are hardly a memory, those
whose words were always faint
against the deafening darkness
of remotest hills.
For them tonight when I go home
I will draw back my curtains, for them
my house shall sing with light.

126 *STANDING STONE*

The stone stands among new firs,
still overtopping them. Soon

they will hide it. Their lower branches
will find its cold bulk
blocking their growth. After years,
lopped trunks will lie piled,
awaiting haulage. The stone will stand
in a cleared valley, and offer again
the ancient orientation.

The stone stores, transmits.
Against its almost-smoothness
I press my palms. I cannot ask,
having no word of power,
no question formed. Have I
anything to give? My hands offer
a dumb love, a hope towards
the day of the freed valley.
Flesh fits itself to the slow curve
of dominating stone, as prayer
takes the shape of a god's will.

A mindless ritual is not empty.
When the dark minds fails, faith lives
in the supplication of hands
on prayer-wheel, rosary, stone.
It is evening. I walk down-valley
on an old track. Behind me
the ephemeral trees darken.
Among them, the stone waits.

127 DRINKING STONE

You offer me your stories
laughing, to show I may laugh, to say
you are sure I must mock
at such old childishness.
Tonight by your fire I listen
to tales of the drinking stone
that each midsummer cockcrow
goes thirsty down to the stream.

I am not to think you credit
that shuddering heave of stone
from the suck of earth, that gliding
over still-dark fields, that long drinking.
You tell it laughing, wary of my response,
but I shall not think you credulous.
It is I who thirstily drink
wonders, I who from dawn mist mould
a grey shape, sated, going home.

128 *HOOFPRINTS*

The legend was always here,
at first invisible, poised above the hill,
stiller than any kestrel. Idle hands
carved hoofprints on a rock
by the hill path. The legend, venturing nearer,
breathed warm as blessing. At last
men recognised it. A magic horse
had leapt from hill to hill, they said,
the day the valley began. Could they not see
his prints, that had waited in the rock
till guided hands revealed them?
From the unseeable, legends leap.
In the rock of our days
is hidden the print of miracle.

129 *LAST WORDS*

They came for his last counsel,
saying 'Tell us now, tell us,
sum your life for us before you go.
we need the right question,
the sufficient answer.'

He turned his head stiffly on the pillow,
and muttered of a curving wall
and moss on stone, of wind in the hedge

by the top gate, the stir and trample
of uneasy mares. He whispered
of a russet hill across the river,
and on the bank one golden tree.
'It is too late,' they said,
'he is babbling.' They touched his hand,
and went away.

He felt the resistance of stone,
the fragile antennae of moss
and its plushy deeps. He heard
a breeze in the hazel, and soft snorting
of gentled mares. At the river,
whirl upon whirl rose over him
the golden leaves, a visual song,
balance of phrase and phrase,
question and answer.

130 *LICHEN, CLADONIA FIMBRIATA*

This little scaly thing,
fibrous lichen, taker of peat-acid
the rotten juice of dead trees,
grows lowly, slowly, on bog-earth
or the scant soil of crevices,
and holds up to the air its fruit
in tiny fantastic goblets.

Might not this pallid creeping thing,
that needs for food only the sour,
sparse and corrupt, be late to go? —
too small and too tenacious
to be torn off by the dusty wind
and offering in final celebration
its little tainted chalices?

131 *GREEN MAN AT THE BWLCH*

For a week or more
some baffling serendipity
has brought him to me
in books, journals, photographs —
a play-mouthed face,
flesh shared with leaves.

Now on a remote pass above trees
of two Radnor valleys
I come to this ancient place —
cruck house half-crumbled, lovingly encased
by scaffolding and plastic sheets, cocoon
in which goes on the work of rebirth.
He is here too.

In a central room, on the beam
over the great hearth, royally
he spreads his mouth-borne branches,
meets my unsurprised eyes.
Here is an abyss, like Nietzsche's,
into which if I look long
I find it looking into me.

The terror is in his utter
neutrality. Yet somewhere
in his kingdom of possibilities
is a tree whose leaves give shelter,
whose boughs know songs, whose sap
flows gold through our veins.

132 *LOTUS*

Bryn, the round hill,
dips to a valley that accepts
others: a place of joining.
No wind carries up

conversation of rivers.
Old sheepwalks, hardly grazed,
stretch to the verge of forest.
On this grey day
no smoke rises
from the one gaunt house.

Surely the silent utterance
of this place is 'Emptiness',
its time 'Never'?
Yet it is said
that not leaves, not petals,
but the space at the centre
of the heart's lotus
contains everything.
                        Here
rivers out of sight
have their rhythms,
like blood through the heart.
Stillness throbs with the flow
of unperceived lives.

This is a place of joining,
whose silent utterance is 'Abundance',
whose time is 'Ever'.

133 *ROADS*

No need to wonder what heron-haunted lake
lay in the other valley,
or regret the songs in the forest
I chose not to traverse.
No need to ask where other roads might have led,
since they led elsewhere;
for nowhere but this here and now
is my true destination.
The river is gentle in the soft evening,
and all the steps of my life have brought me home.

W. R. ROGERS (1909–1969)

W. R. Rogers was born in Belfast and graduated from Queen's University, before entering the Presbyterian ministry. In 1946 Rogers moved to London to work for the BBC, and spent the rest of his life in England and California. As well as poetry and his work as a journalist, Rogers wrote scripts for radio.

134 *WORDS*

Always the arriving winds of words
Pour like Atlantic gales over these ears,
These reefs, these foils and fenders, these shrinking
And sea-scalded edges of the brain-land.
Rebutted and rebounding, on they post
Past my remembrance, falling all unplanned.
But some day out of darkness they'll come forth,
Arrowed and narrowed into my tongue's tip,

And speak for me — their most astonished host.

GLADYS MARY COLES

Gladys Mary Coles was educated at Liverpool University, where she now teaches a creative writing course, travelling from her home on Deeside in north Wales. Coles has written biography as well as poetry. Places, particularly with historical or mythological significance, feature widely in her work, and the landscape of north Wales is a frequent source of inspiration.

135 *WATER POWER*

Cures and curses
and counter-curses —
this well's water
accepted all wishes:

Send a baby to Gwen's womb.
Please untie my stammer.
Cure Alun's black hairy tongue.
Make Edward Hughes love me
and let a sore spread
in the middle of Nell Parry's face.

Dropped into depths —
medieval believings.
      Stick a pin
      in a cork:
      throw it in.
      Rub a rag on rheumatics:
      dip it in.
      Rub rheumatics on the rag:
      hang it high.
Trees near the well
festooned with shreds
of hopes.

Earlier still,
a Roman at Sulis Minerva
cast his lead tablet in:
May he who carried off Vilbia
from me, become as liquid as water.
Only the God could read the curse —
its backward flow.

I come today with my own petitions,
seeking the well on Llanelian hill:
Let all terrorists' bombs
explode in their faces.
Give rapists the rot.
Protect us from Poll's evil eye.
Please clear my writer's block.

The hills are green heaven,
the sky a blue halo,
I look for the well at Llanelian —
no fold in a field yields a sign,
only weeds crowd the meadow —
Llanelian's landlord has filled it in.

I leave with my ill-wishings,
well-wishings.

BRENDAN KENNELLY (b.1936)

Brendan Kennelly was born in Ballylongford, County Kerry (Ireland), and educated in Kerry and at Trinity College Dublin, where he worked for many years, being appointed Professor of Modern Literature in 1973. Kennelly is a prolific writer in many genres, including plays and poetry. His engagement with poetry involves a wrestling with the Irish psyche. People make outcasts, he suggests, of what is most exciting and most revealing, and 'in Ireland, this outcasting, this silent, fierce partitioning of energies is so commonplace as to be unobserved'. The Irish, he suggests, fall back too readily on labels and clichés, which give a spurious sense of security, and it is the task of the poet to fight 'their muggy, cloying, complacent, sticky, distorting, stultifying, murderous and utterly reassuring embrace'.* In this Kennelly succeeds magnificently. His poetry is refreshing, surprising, moving and often haunting — always honest and never self-indulgent; carefully crafted with an easy narrative style.

136 *SCULPTED FROM DARKNESS*

It is one o'clock on a Christmas morning.
The people are passing over the bridge
On their way to scattered homes.
The darkness bears no grudge
Because the people have tasted the god
Who permits himself to be eaten
By the faithful, the militant, the mindless
And the god-forsaken
About whom the god is not mistaken.
The more he is devoured, the more he lives.
He has an appetite for appetite.
He swallows those who eat him

---

* Introduction to *Breathing Spaces*, Bloodaxe 1992, p.11.

And inspires them to eat.
How sweet is the god's flesh, how sweet!
The bridge bears the weight of the shuffling feet
And no one bothers to wonder
At the black passion of water
Spelling out its own hunger
Under the bridge, under the mill
With all its small windows
Closed like books everyone has read
And nobody knows.
And the river articulates its hunger
As it bends with the creek
Twisting like need
Over mud, sedge, weed, gravel and rock.

If the god instructed the people
To enter the blackness, drink the river, eat the mud,
They would enter, drink, eat, because mud, river, blackness
Are three words of the god.
Those who eat the god
Digest the god's language
To increase their substance, deepen their shadows.
Now as they shuffle over the bridge
Their hearts beat with a deeper heartbeat,
The fields they move towards are wrapped
About their bodies like wise cloaks,
Roofs of houses are scales tipped
In their favour, the river and its creatures
Flow and thrive for the flowing people
And the eaten god is happy, finding
Himself in blood. If all is ever well

It is well now in the enlarging darkness
For the people contained as planets
In their appointed places
Each one of them so sure he seems to find delight
In not being able to see
His own or all those other faces
Sculpted from darkness by the selfsame hand
That motions the people home again

Through the familiar, invisible land
Where the long consequences spread like rain.

137 *PLAY*

Picture the old man of seventy years
Rehearsing his death several times a day.
Between rehearsals, he calls the youngsters
To his side. If, in old men, it is possible
To speak of some belief in innocence
This old man has it in his drowsy way.
When he resigns the world for a spell
He does so only when the children promise
On pain of cross their hearts and hope to die
That they will quietly play about the chair
Where he sits staring down at heaven
Somewhere in his mind adrift in sleep.
'Angels of the earth, angels of the air,
All angels love to play about a sleeping man
And when they play, holy is the watch they keep.'

138 *THE GOOD*

The good are vulnerable
As any bird in flight,
They do not think of safety,
Are blind to possible extinction
And when most vulnerable
Are most themselves.
The good are real as the sun,
Are best perceived through clouds
Of casual corruption
That cannot kill the luminous sufficiency
That shines on city, sea and wilderness,
Fastidiously revealing
One man to another,
Who yet will not accept
Responsibilities of light.

The good incline to praise,
To have the knack of seeing that
The best is not destroyed
Although forever threatened.
The good go naked in all weathers,
And by their nakedness rebuke
The small protective sanities
That hide men from themselves.
The good are difficult to see
Though open, rare, destructible;
Always, they retain a kind of youth,
The vulnerable grace
Of any bird in flight,
Content to be itself,
Accomplished master and potential victim,
Accepting what the earth or sky intends.
I think that I know one or two
Among my friends.

139 *HOUSE*

I am youth slipping like water
From that cracked tap in the yard.
They are many. I am one.
Thinking of me, they will always be children.
Every leaving will be a return
To me who sheltered their dead.
They ran to me out of streets and fields
When I gave them the smell of hot bread.
That oven in my belly
Helped them grow in the sun.
They are many. I am one.
They will live in others,
Stare out of cities, over seas
To find me,
They will hear their noisy hearts
Beat in my silence,
They will not overcome the surprise
Of finding surprise in me,

They will scour a world for evidence
Of what never dies in me.

They happened in me.
They can happen only once.
This drives my children out-of-sense.

Listen! You can hear the dance
Starting on the kitchen floor.
They are learning the steps
Becoming the music
Reaching the skill, the fever,
Doing what I've always wanted.
Dancing through me, dancing their beginning,
They are learning to be haunted.

140 *THE SECOND TREE*

My head sore with nightmare —
The seagulls tore the crows to death
Dipped the ripped bodies in the sewers
Of the trembling city
Dropped the shite-cake corpses on my head
Till I was buried, breathing, in a heap
Of bleeding flesh of crows, their features
Fixing in my skin like hateful glances
Thrown like knives across a room
Which for someone must be home
Where he can slip the world off like an overcoat —

I walked, stiffnecked with nightmare,
Under a sky split open like my mind
Out into the small garden at the back of the house.
I closed my eyes, breathing the morning air,
Breathing the innocent air.
I opened my eyes and saw a pear on the ground
Nearly hidden in the grass.
I picked it up and felt its coolness
Thrill my fingers, then my blood, my being.

I tasted it. And I knew,
As though I were another Adam
To whom another tree, a second tree
In some small corner growing unseen,
Were shown by accident
At the moment of his deepest need,
What nightmare hungered for
As it regrouped its battering legions
Of packed, implacable assassins
To savage vulnerable sleep,
The cool, moist taste, caressed by grass,
Of sanity, clear, sweet, miraculously
Normal, so near it must always be easily
Lost.
                I could have knelt
Before the second tree, but stood in silence
While my mind rejoiced in priceless quiet
Then turned towards a human voice,
Eating the garden's flesh as I entered the house, dumb with gratitude.

NUALA NÍ DHOMHNAILL (b.1952)

Nuala Ní Dhomhnaill was born in Lancashire (England) but grew up in an Irish speaking area (Gaeltacht) in Kerry in the west of Ireland. She now lives in Dublin with her Turkish husband and four children. She writes as a woman, from her own experience, weaving Ireland's past and present, the mythological and mundane, Christian and pagan, into a rich and evocative tapestry.

141 *PARTHENOGENESIS*

Once, a lady of the Ó Moores
(married seven years without a child)
swam in the sea in summertime.
She swam well, and the day
was fine as Ireland ever saw
not even a puff of wind in the air
all the day calm, all the sea smooth —
a sheet of glass — supple, she struck out
with strength for the breaking waves
and frisked, elated by the world.
She ducked beneath the surface and there saw
what seemed a shadow, like a man's
And every twist and turn she made
the shadow did the same
and came close enough to touch.
Heart jumped and sound stopped in her mouth
her pulses ran and raced, sides near burst
The lower currents with their ice
pierced her to the bone
and the noise of the abyss numbed all her limbs
then scales grew on her skin . . .

the lure of the quiet dreamy undersea . . .
desire to escape to sea and shells . . .
the seaweed tresses where at last
her bones changed into coral
and time made atolls of her arms,
pearls of her eyes in deep long sleep,
at rest in a nest of weed,
secure as feather beds . . .
But stop!
Her heroic heritage was there,
she rose with speedy, threshing feet
and made in desperation for the beach:
with nimble supple strokes she made the sand.

Near death until the day,
some nine months later
she gave birth to a boy.
She and her husband so satisfied,
so full of love for this new son
forgot the shadow in the sea

and did not see what only the midwife saw —
stalks of sea-tangle in the boy's hair
small shellfish and sea-ribbons
and his two big eyes
as blue and limpid as lagoons.
A poor scholar passing by
who found lodging for the night
saw the boy's eyes never closed
in dark or light and when all the world slept
he asked the boy beside the fire
'Who are your people?' Came the prompt reply
'Sea People.'

This same tale is told in the West
but the woman's an Ó Flaherty
and tis the same in the South
where the lady's called Ó Shea:
this tale is told on every coast.
But whoever she was I want to say

that the fear she felt
when the sea-shadow followed her
is the same fear that vexed
the young heart of the Virgin
when she heard the angel's sweet bell
and in her womb was made flesh
by all accounts
the Son of the Living God.

142 *ABDUCTION*

The fairy woman walked
into my poem.
She closed no door
She asked no by-your-leave.
Knowing my place
I did not tell her go.
I played the woman-of-no-welcomes trick
and said:

'What's your hurry, here's your hat.
Pull up to the fire,
eat and drink what you get —
but if I were in your house
as you are in my house
I'd go home straight away
but anyway, stay.'

She stayed. Got up and pottered
round the house. Dressed the beds
washed the ware. Put the dirty clothes
in the washing-machine.
When my husband came home for his tea
he didn't know what he had wasn't me.

For I am in the fairy field
in lasting darkness
and frozen with the cold there
dressed only in white mist.

And if he wants me back
there is a solution —
get the sock of a plough
smear it with butter
and redden it with fire.

And then let him to go the bed
where lies the succubus
and press her with red iron.
'Push in into her face,
burn and brand her,

and as she fades before your eyes
I'll materialise
and as she fades before your eyes
I'll materialise.'

143 *CHRISTMAS DINNER*

The Christmas meal is over.
We were quick to knock it back.
We lapped up celery soup with zest
turkey, bacon, pies and now, mince tarts.
Our bellies full, our bones around the table.
The Christmas candle throws its little light
and the scarlet holly berries glow.

I count those present. We're all there
(seldom now together in one place.)
The fledglings are long scattered
making their own nests — we are the old clutch.
You'd swear you were caged with the tropical birds
in the Zoo with the chirping and fluttering
some mouthing, the rest up to the gunnells
with drink and jollity, with noise and crack.

Suddenly there's silence. An angel passes over
the roof. In the quietness — a sudden sneeze.
We call God's blessing on our house.
Someone farts. We laugh and say

'Better down than up!'
We're well used to the old saws
(though they have nothing to do with our lives
They come readily to our lips).

My brother stands up, goes to the door.
But there's no one there, out in the dark
not a soul, not a sinner, no Christian being.
'Dhera, an arrow struck your ear — the fairies
I'm sure are walking the hill.
You'd better come in and close the door
for fear we'll get a puck.'

Said the trickster in our midst and I hear in the babble
someone speak of 'St. Michael the Archangel
our protection in time of battle' and how
this prayer ends all fear of the dead
fear of demons of the air and all evil things.
I raise my eyes and outside the magic circle
I see Loki, a bow of mistletoe in his hand,

He offers it beguilingly to the blind old man
waffling away from the shelter
of the oak tree. Listen, tis not your ear
the next arrow will strike, Baldor, beloved brother.

144 *ISLAND*

Your body an island
in the great ocean.
Your limbs spread
on a bright sheet
over a sea of gulls.

Your forehead a spring well
mix of blood and honey —
it gave me a cooling drink
when I was burning
a healing drink
when I was feverish.

Your eyes
are mountain lakes
a lovely August day
when the sky
sparkles in the waters.
Flowing reeds your eyelashes
growing at their margins

And if I had a boat
to go to you
a white bronze boat
not a feather out of place on it
but one feather
red feather with white back
making music
to my self on board

I'd put up
the soft white billowing sails: I'd plough
through high seas
and I would come
where you lie
solitary, emerald,
insular.

145 *ANNUNCIATIONS*

She remembered to the very end
the angelic vision
in the temple:
the flutter of wings
about her —
noting the noise of doves,
sun-rays raining
on lime-white walls —
the day she got the tidings.

He —
he went away

and perhaps forgot
what grew from his loins —
two thousand years
of carrying a cross
two thousand years
of smoke and fire
of rows that reached a greater span
than all the spires of the Vatican.

Remember
O most tender virgin Mary
that never was it known
that a man came to you
in the darkness alone,
his feet bare, his teeth white
and roguery swelling in his eyes.

146 *MASCULUS GIGANTICUS HIBERNICUS*

Country lout, knife thrower (dagger-wielder)
whether in jeans or a devil at noon
all dolled up in your pinstriped suit
you're always after the one thing.

Dangerous relic from the Iron Age
you sit in pubs and devise
the treacherous plan
that does not recoil on you —
a vengeful incursion to female land.

Because you will not dare to halt the growth
of the dark-red damask rose in your mother's heart
you will have to turn the garden
to a trampled mess
pounded and ruined by your two broad hooves.

And you're frisky, prancing, antlered —
your bread is baked.
You'd live off the furze

or the heather that grows
on a young girl's sunny slopes.

147 *MARVELLOUS GRASS*

When you were a holy priest
in the middle of Mass in your purple robes
your linen mantle, your stole, your chasuble.
you saw my face in the crowd
approaching you for communion
and you dropped the blessed host.

I — I said nothing.
I was ashamed.
My lips were locked.
But still it lay on my heart
like a mud-thorn until
it penetrated my insides.
From it I nearly died.

Not long till I took to my bed:
medical experts came in hundreds
doctors, priests and friars —
not one could cure me
they abandoned me for death.

Go out, men:
take with you spades and scythes
sickles, hoes and shovels.
Ransack the ruins
cut the bushes, clear the rubble,
the rank growth, the dust, the misery
that grows on my tragic grassland.

And in the place where fell
the sacred host you will see
among the useless plants
a patch of marvellous grass.

Let the priest come and with his fingers
take dexterously the sacred host.
And it's given to me: on my tongue
it will melt and I will sit up in the bed
as healthy as I was when young.

148 *GREAT MOTHER*

Maiden and mother, oh nurse, oh atom bomb,
you will spurt on us the black liquid milk,
volcano dust will burst from your throat
from your heart the burnt smell be stripped.

We have avoided your gluttonous embrace:
arrogant angels, we built our tower of Babel
with the help of science: we leapt into the skies
with a hop and a skip and a gambol.

The seven-league boots of conscience can't keep up,
dwarfs in motion, spoilt brats apeing
adult behaviour — animals in disguise.
In this unruly house our acts have neither finish nor *finesse*.

The fringe of your cloak is on the horizon:
you will wrap us in *your* great-coat of clay,
we'll be extinguished with kisses, drenched with bitter tears
of acid rain — our own home-brewed rain.

149 *MONK*

You are St Anthony
or some other saint
sitting in your rocky hermitage.
You make the sign of the cross —
wind and sea no longer toss.
Your hands are full of larks.

I am Temptation.
You know me.
Sometimes I'm Eve,
sometimes the snake:
I slide into your reverie
in the middle of brightest day.
I shine like the sun in an orchard.

But it's not to torment you
every day I rise —
but to drown you
in love's delights.
I'm a dead hero leaping
from the edge of the bridge of fear —
That's the only reason I haunt you:
my monk, my apostle, my priest.

150 *MISCARRIAGE ABROAD*

You, embryo, moving in me —
I welcomed your emerging
I said I'd rear you carefully
in the manner of my new people —

under your pillow the holy book,
in your cot, bread and a needle:
your father's shirt as an eiderdown
at your head a brush for sweeping.

I was brimming
with happiness
until the dykes broke
and out was swept
a ten-weeks frog —
'the best-laid schemes . . .'

And now it's March
your birthday that never was —
and white ribbons of tide
remind me of baby-clothes,
an imbecile's tangled threads.

And I will not go to see
my best friend's new born child
because of the jealousy
that stares from my evil eye.

ANJELA DUVAL (1905-1981)

Anjela Duval was born into a long line of Breton peasant farmers, and as the only surviving child inherited the family smallholding in the Leger River valley, a farm which had passed down from one generation to another through the maternal line. After only four years of primary schooling Anjela worked full time on the land, as she continued to do until prevented by sickness in her old age. In her forties, after the death of her parents, Duval coped with depression and loneliness by reading Breton literature, which gave her a new goal in life — the nationalist struggle and defence of the Breton language. Her first poems were published in the 1960s, and with the resurgence of Breton nationalism in the 1970s they brought her considerable notoriety. Her poetry deals with her attachment to the land and her life as a farmer, her love of trees and of the natural world, the Roman Catholic faith in which she was raised, and the human community, be it her deceased loved ones or the Breton nation as a whole.*

151 *SAINT MARY*

Saint Mary, Mother of God,
Preserve for me a child's heart,
Pure and transparent as a spring,
A heart simple and straight,
That will never taste unhappiness.
A devoted heart,
Tender and grateful,
A heart loyal and generous,
That will not forget goodness,
And will not hold on to evil.
Make for me a humble and patient heart,

*This information is from Lenora A. Timm's Introduction to *A Modern Breton Political Poet, Anjela Duval: A Biography and An Anthology*, Edwin Mellen Press 1990.

Loving without expecting a return.
Content to leave in a beloved heart
The first place for your Son.
A lofty and invincible heart,
That no ignorance will be able to close,
That no insensitivity will be able to expend.
A heart wrought with the glory of Christ,
Pierced with His love,
Whose wound would not heal
Except in heaven.

152 *A MARVELOUS HOUR*

The day is now over.
The hour's come I was waiting for.
After labour so material,
How sweet a spiritual hour.

I'm bathed here in tranquillity.
I hear no sound around me.
But the sound of the pendulum,
Counting out the drops of time.

The hour of prayer, hour of study.
Hour of dreaming, of fantasy,
Hour divine, full of ecstasy.

In this hour there's so much happiness!
Only one thing's missing to perfect it:
— In the hearth the singing of a cricket! . . .

153 *MELANCHOLY*

I am gathering ferns,
The nicest of jobs, you might say . . .
True, but it's hot,
Let's stop for a moment.

. . .

On my arm a sickle and a pitchfork,
in my hand a fern
fine and light like a piece of lace
on the edge of the field I sit down
In the shade of the chestnut tree.

. . .

A sharp perfume, a dizzying perfume
the ferns turning
while tickling my nostrils
have gone to my head.
And here I am beginning to daydream,
my mind wandering
down the path of memories;
where before me passes
as on a brilliant screen
my bygone youth.

And I think of the past
that will never return!
The autumn of my life,
Ah, golden-brown fern,
symbol of arid and poor soil,
such a fate is ours!
Sterile. Unimportant. Meaningless.
I would at least wish to be like you,
also able to produce a perfume:
a sharp, dizzying perfume
of pure poetry.

154 *LINDENS*

Thirteen linden trees stand thick together
One against the other on a dry bank
Their heads held straight in the blue heaven
At a time when I was young
They were already grown
Thirteen lindens in a cluster

A bouquet of dark green
Immense. Giants
On the horizon.

These lindens are not my possession
Yet I possess the right
To cut them down.
They are sucking the sap of my land
With their roots so long. But I won't.
I would miss them.
They are my organ,
They are my harp,
When the wind plays on them
Its thousand different notes.
When the crow caws
On their bare winter branches
When on their dark summits
The yellow-beaked blackbird whistles,
And when from their highest limb flow
The crystal drops
Of the nightingale.

155 *MY HEART*

My heart is a Cemetery
In it are countless graves
In it always a new grave
Graves of friends and relatives
My heart is a Cemetery!

My heart is a Cemetery
But no!
My heart is a Sanctuary
Wherein live My Dear Departed!

156 *DAWN-SONG*

Would your soft cooing
Each morning in the chestnut tree
Be for me, russet dove?

No! I'd be crazy to think so!
Your song is a hymn
To the One who gave you
That nostalgic voice.

Your soft cooing
Is a dawn-song to your loving mate
And to your baby birds
And to all your winged friends.

. . . Who would sing for me?
An old woman without a relative or a mate!
Yet my heart is brimming with songs
For I love every Creature.

157 *WORK OF THE FOREIGNER*

Strip. Despoil our Country
Sweep away the sacred oaks of the Druids
The birches of the Celts and the yew-trees
— And the chestnuts of our youth —
In which our birds sang.
Start fires in the moor
In the heath. In the broom waving
Like seas of golden water
And write on the bare back
Of the old Country, in every foreign language
Poems of mourning
Ugly poems.
With their stiff letters
Rigid as their steel faces:
Long rows of lead soldiers

Tedious songs of their resin trees
With strange names!
And soon . . . if we don't pay attention
On the great organ
Of their dark and sad forests
— Fertilised with the ashes of our trees —
The Atlantic Wind
Will play while singing
        . . . The Requiem of our Country.

158 *MISUNDERSTANDING*

What's in it for you to stir up
My too tender heart?
Why do you inflame
My too active brain with madness?
You know very well
— or don't you know? —
— In spite of an invincible love —
There are too many differences between us
Between city-dwellers and peasants.

Their mockery has wounded me
And my audacity has wounded them
— Why that misunderstanding
Eternally between us?
— Why mock us
Scorn us
Make fun of us
Although we love you
The sap of your living heart
Of your bare earth — of my Country!
My Brittany. My love. My Life.
They love you too — they say —
— Yes then! Your brilliant multicoloured skirt
Your green woods. Your streams.
Your golden heath. Your alluring seas.
Your birds and your flowers.

But they should be repulsed
To hold between their white fingers
A handful of Soil of their Country
Soaked so often with the sweat
     — and blood —
Of generations of Bretons.

Because of love for you
Sacred Soil of my Country
We suffer that disrespect
     — done to you —
To be despised for loving you too much
Brittany, my only love
For you all my strength until the last spark
Until the hour when you will open my arms
On my rageless and lifeless body
While my ardent Soul passes
Toward the Paradise of our Race.

159 *IN THE FOREST*

On the soft carpet of the forest
To go on velvet footsteps
To sit at your feet
In the dappled sunlight, in silence
Far from the sounds of humans
To listen to the rustling of your leaves . . .
And to caress alternatively
With my hand and my look . . .
In a soft voice I call you
Using your magical names:
White-oak. Forest-aspen.
Maple. Hornbeam.
Black-alder. Willow. White Birch.

My thousand mute friends.

160 *YOUR PAIN IS YOURS*

You may share
With one you care for
    Your goods
    Your knowledge
    Your love
    Your happiness
There's one thing you won't share:
    Your pain
    For that's been cut
To just your measure.

161 *WHY?*

They are heedless
Those who walk on city pavements.
Heedless of killing and injuring
Small creatures moving or not . . .
Ah. How heedful I am at each step
Heedful of crushing, of smashing
Along the path or through the field
Tiny humble creatures beneath my foot:
The green beetle crouched in the moss,
The minute ant carrying
With great effort and ingenuity
The short-straw to her anthill.
Pretty little flowers half-hidden in the grass,
Trying to open their heart to the Sun.
It seems to me that I hear their lament:
— Why then, Lord, did you not give
Wings to man?
Ah! How heavy is the weight of his foot on us!

162 *A CHILD'S FEELING*

Such love as that for the trees?
From my tenderest age
When I caressed their bark
With my babyish hand.
When I glued my ear against them
To listen to the rustling of their leaves
The humming of their branches twisting in a high wind.
And the snap of their dry twigs breaking off.
      When I tried to climb high, high!
Ever higher. From limb to limb.
      A bird without wings!
And from there to marvel at the horizon.

. . . And how unpleasant the descent
To touch one's feet on the ground!

Trees of my childhood, tell me then
Where it came from so early
A love so profound for you?

Perhaps I was a tree
               at the beginning of time . . .

163 *PRAYER FOR A NEW YEAR*

Lord! Father of the Universe
And Father of all Creatures
Spirit and Matter
Today hear if she asks
The least of your children
Who loves you from the depths of her heart
Her happiness to live forever . . .
Before you like a child before his father
With neither pain nor suspicion
I start a new Year
In the beginning of the springtime.

What will I be? I am in your hands.
Respectful? . . . Yes. Obedient? Hardly . . .
But may Your Will be done
And may a morsel of wisdom descend on my old age
So that my time will not be empty or vain
Give me Love and Enlightenment
Sufficient to share with others who
Stumble and grope on the Way
The Way so narrow that leads to Eternity . . .
                                        Amen.

SOURCES AND ACKNOWLEDGEMENTS

The translations in the medieval sections are by Oliver Davies, unless otherwise indicated, although in many cases we must acknowledge a debt to previous translators.

Medieval Religious Poetry

1. Text in Ifor Williams, *The Beginnings of Welsh Poetry* (Cardiff, 1972), p. 102.
2. Text in A. O. H. Jarman, ed., *Llyfr Du Caerfyrddin* (Cardiff, 1982), p. 16. Text slightly emended.
3. Gerard Murphy, *Early Irish Lyrics* (Oxford, 1956), p. 4.
4. R. I. Best, *Ériu* 4, p. 120.
5. Murphy, p. 4.
6. Jarman, pp. 17–18.
7. Jarman, p. 9.
8. Jarman, pp. 13–14.
9. Brian ó Cuív, *Ériu* 19, pp. 4–5.
10. Kuno Meyer, *Ériu* 2, pp. 55–56.
11. Kuno Meyer, *Ériu* 3, p. 14.
12. Jarman, p. 15.
13. James Carney, *Ériu* 22, pp. 27–28.
14. Kuno Meyer, *Ériu* 6, p. 112.
15. M. E. Byrne, *Ériu* 1, pp. 226–27.
16. T. P. O'Nowlan, *Ériu* 2, pp. 92–94 and Robin Flower, *Ériu* 5, p. 112.
17. Kuno Meyer, *Ériu* 6, p. 116.
18. Text in W. Stokes and J. Strachan, eds., *Thesaurus Palaeohibernicus* vol. II, (Cambridge, 1903), pp. 354–58.
19. Marged Haycock, *Blodeugerdd Barddas o Ganu Crefyddol Cynnar* (Llandybie, 1994), pp. 23–29.
20. Stokes and Strachan, p. 294.

21. Charles Plummer, ed., *Irish Litanies* (Henry Bradshaw Society, vol. LXII, London, 1925), p. 6.

22. Stokes and Strachan, p. 322.

23. G. S. M. Walker, *Sancti Columbani Opera (Scriptores Latini Hiberniae*, vol. II, Dublin, 1970), p. 214.

24. Plummer, p. 26.

25. Murphy, p. 64.

26. Haycock, pp. 165–9.

27. Henry Lewis, *Hen Gerddi Crefyddol* (Cardiff, 1931), pp. 21–22.

28. Lewis, pp. 57–59.

29. Jarman, p. 59.

30. Jarman, p. 54 (text slightly emended).

31. Thomas Parry, ed., *Gwaith Dafydd ap Gwilym* (Cardiff, 1952).

32. Haycock, pp. 30–40.

33. E. Ernaut, ed., *Le Mirouer de la Mort* (Paris, 1914), p. 62.

34. Thomas Parry, ed., *The Oxford Book of Welsh Verse* (Oxford, 1962), pp. 332–39.

35. Brendan O'Malley, ed., *A Welsh Pilgrim's Manual* (Llandysul, 1989), pp. 32–36 (translated by Cynthia Davies). Our thanks to Gomer Press and to the editor of the volume, the Reverend Brendan O'Malley, for permission to reprint these translations.

Medieval Religious Prose

36. *Patrologia Latina* 40, 1031–46.

37. *Patrologia Latina Supplementum* I, 1375–80.

38. *Corpus Scriptorum Ecclesiasticorum Latinorum* 29, 436–59.

39. *Patrologia Latina* 72, 775–90.

40. *Archaeologia Cambrensis* (1894), 139–42.

41. Stanley Miller Dahlmann, *Critical Edition of the Buched Beuno*, PhD, Catholic University of America, Washington, 1976.

42. J. W. James, *Rhigyfarch's Life of St David*, Cardiff, 1967.

43. J. Pinkerton, *Vitae antiquae sanctorum . . . in Scotia* (London, 1789), pp. 1–23.

44. Ludwig Bieler, *The Irish Penitentials* (Dublin, 1963), pp. 108–10, 133–35. I acknowledge a debt to Bieler for my own translation.

45. Walker, pp. 72–74.

46. Walker, pp. 116–20.

47. J. Strachan, *Ériu* 3, pp. 1–10.

48. W. Stokes, *Ériu* 2, pp. 96–162.
49. E. J. Gwynn, *Ériu* 2, pp. 82–83.
50. P. J. Donovan, ed., *Ysgrifeniadau Byrion Morgan Llwyd* (Cardiff, 1985), pp. 1–3.
51. Eifion Evans, *Daniel Rowland and the Great Evangelical Awakening in Wales* (Banner of Truth Trust, 1985), pp. 51ff.

The Carmina Gadelica

The following numbers refer to the volume and item numbers of the individual pieces as printed in the 1928 edition of the first two volumes of the *Carmina Gadelica*, and the 1940 edition of Volume III, all published by Scottish Academic Press in Edinburgh. In these editions the Gaelic and English are on facing pages and the numbering is consecutive, from 1 to 351 over the three volumes. Volumes I and II were originally published in 1900 and were edited and translated by Alexander Carmichael. Volume III was edited from Carmichael's notes by his grandson, Professor James Carmichael Watson (see Appendix).

52. I, 1
53. I, 2
54. I, 3
55. I, 14
56. I, 18
57. I, 19
58. I, 20
59. I, 26
60. I, 33
61. I, 38
62. I, 43
63. I, 50
64. I, 51
65. I, 52
66. I, 54
67. II, 194
68. II, 203
69. II, 206
70. I, 70
71. I, 71
72. I, 73

73. I, 74
74. I, 76
75. I, 77
76. I, 82
77. I, 84
78. I, 92
79. I, 93
80. I, 114
81. I, 116
82. I, 118
83. I, 121
84. III, 225
85. III, 231
86. III, 232
87. III, 242
88. III, 248
89. III, 249
90. III, 272
91. III, 277
92. III, 316
93. III, 321
94. III, 327
95. III, 328
96. III, 331
97. III, 343
98. III, 350

The Religious Songs of Connacht

The following numbers refer to the volumes of *The Religious Songs of Connacht*. Volume I comprises Chapter 6 and Volume II Chapter 7 of a longer work, *The Songs of Connacht*, all edited and in the case of oral pieces translated by Douglas Hyde. The extracts in this work are from the 1972 Irish University Press edition which reproduces the original 1906 volumes in a single cover, with an Introduction by Dominic Daly.

  99–103. Volume I
104–111. Volume II

Modern Poetry

112. Translation by Oliver Davies. Welsh original, *'Difiau Dyrchafael'* is reprinted in Medwin Hughes, ed., *Blodeugerdd Barddas O Gerddi Crefyddol* (Barddas, 1993).

113. Translation by Oliver Davies. Welsh original, *'Y Griafolen'* is reprinted in *Euros Bowen, Priest-Poet/Bardd-Offeiriad*, edited by Cynthia and Saunders Davies (Church in Wales Publications, 1993). All the poems by Euros Bowen were written in Welsh.

114. Translation Euros Bowen, ibid. We acknowledge with thanks permission granted by the Board of Mission of the Church in Wales to reproduce this and the following poems by Euros Bowen (nos. 114–120) from *Priest-Poet/Bardd-Offeiriad*.

115. Translation Euros Bowen.

116–120. Translation Cynthia Davies.

121. From *The Wreck of the Archangel*, John Murray (London, 1989). Reproduced with permission of the publisher, acknowledged with thanks.

122–133. From *Selected Poems* (Seren Poetry Wales Press, 1992). Reproduced with kind permission of the author, Ruth Bidgood, and Seren.

134. From W. R. Rogers, *Poems* (The Gallery Press, 1971). By kind permission of the author and The Gallery Press.

135. From Gladys Mary Coles, *The Glass Island* (Duckworth, 1992) by kind permission of the author and Duckworth.

136–140. From Brendan Kennelly, *Breathing Spaces: Early Poems*, (Bloodaxe Books, 1992). Reprinted by permission of Bloodaxe Books Ltd.

141–150. From Nuala Ní Dhomhnaill, *Selected Poems: Rogha Dánta*, translated by Michael Hartnett (The Raven Arts Press, Dublin, 1992). Reprinted by kind permission of the author and New Island Books.

151–163. The poems by Duval were all written in Breton and translated into English by Lenora A. Timm. We are grateful to both Lenora Timm and Edwin Mellen Press for permission to reproduce them here.

APPENDIX: EDITIONS OF THE
CARMINA GADELICA

The presence of many anthologized selections from the *Carmina Gadelica*, and its widespread popularity in recent years, have given Carmichael's collection of Gaelic oral literature a notoriety unusual in the field of Victorian folklore. The following notes may be of use to readers who wish to orientate themselves with respect to the original publication of these volumes.

Alexander Carmichael published the first two volumes in 1900, being the result of some fifty years of recording the religious oral literature and folklore of the Gaelic speakers of the Highlands and Islands of Scotland. It came out under the Gaelic and Latin title *Ortha Nan Gaidheal/Carmina Gadelica: Hymns and Incantations*, with the subtitle, 'With Illustrative Notes on Words, Rites, and Customs, Dying and Obsolete: Orally Collected in the Highlands and Islands of Scotland and Translated into English by Alexander Carmichael' (published by T. & A. Constable, Edinburgh). Before his death Carmichael also started to prepare material for a third volume, which was finally edited and published by his grandson, Professor James Carmichael Watson in 1940, followed by Volume IV in 1941 (both published by Oliver & Boyd, Edinburgh). The first two volumes were reprinted by Oliver and Boyd in 1928 with minor corrections by Carmichael's daughter, Ella, a reputed Gaelic scholar in her own right. Scottish Academic Press brought out further bilingual editions in 1983/4.

Two further volumes based on Carmichael's original unpublished manuscripts were edited by Angus Matheson. Volume V consists mainly of secular poetry (Oliver & Boyd, Edinburgh, 1954) and Volume VI contains indexes and bibliographical information (Scottish Academic Press, 1971). All six volumes retain the bilingual format, with the Gaelic on the left-hand folio and the English translation facing it. Illustrative notes are in English, but with extensive Gaelic quotations.

In 1992 Floris Books (Edinburgh) produced an English paperback version of the *Carmina Gadelica* in a single volume. Most of Carmichael's notes and comments are retained but are placed at the end rather than with the passages to which they refer, and do not follow the numbering of earlier editions. In addition to these full-length versions of the *Carmina Gadelica* there are numerous English selections, usually concentrating on the more immediately accessible and less obviously 'pagan' elements of the original. While they bring the material to a wide readership a reading of the work in its entirety is to be recommended to anyone wishing to make a balanced assessment of Carmichael's extensive original collection. It is also worth pointing out, lest the nineteenth-century Highlanders be seen as excessively pious, that the religious material was only one genre of oral literature. As with Hyde's *Songs of Connacht*, Carmichael might well have included love songs, drinking songs, tales of heroic battles and of inter-clan rivalries had these been his interests.

SELECT BIBLIOGRAPHY

(For texts included in this anthology, see the references given in
Sources and Acknowledgements)

General

Allchin, A. M., *Praise above All: Discovering the Welsh Tradition*, Cardiff,
1991.
Bradley, Ian, *The Celtic Way*, London, 1993.
Davies, Oliver, *Celtic Christianity in Early Medieval Wales*, Cardiff, 1995
(forthcoming).
Davies, Oliver, *Celtic Spirituality*, Classics of Western Spirituality, New
York (forthcoming).
Davies, Wendy, 'The Myth of the Celtic Church' in Nancy Edwards
and Alan Lane, eds., *The Early Church in Wales and the West*, Oxbow,
1992, 12–21.
De Waal, Esther, *A World Made Whole*, London, 1992.
Flower, Robin, *The Irish Tradition*, Oxford, 1947.
Hughes, Kathleen, 'The Celtic Church: is this a Valid Concept?' in
Cambridge Medieval Celtic Studies, 1 (1981), 1–20.
Kenny, J. F., *The Sources for the Early History of Ireland*, Dublin, 1929.
Lapidge, M. and Sharpe, R., *A Bibliography of Celtic-Latin Literature
400-1200*, Dublin, 1985.
Mackey, J. P., ed., *An Introduction to Celtic Christianity*, Edinburgh, 1989.
Maher, Michael, ed., *Irish Spirituality*, Dublin, 1981.
O'Donoghue, Noel Dermot, *The Mountain Beyond the Mountain*, Edin-
burgh, 1993.
Piggot, Stuart, *Ancient Britons and the Antiquarian Imagination*, Thames
and Hudson, 1989.
Sims-Williams, Patrick, 'The Visionary Celt: the Construction of an
Ethnic Preconception' in *Cambridge Medieval Celtic Studies*, 11
(1986), 71–96.

Sims-Williams, Patrick, 'Some Celtic Otherworld Terms' in *Celtic Language, Celtic Culture: a Festschrift for Eric P. Hamp*, California, 1990, 6–81.

Thomas, Patrick, *Candle in the Darkness*, Llandysul, 1993.

Pre-Christian Celtic Religion

Brunaux, Jean Louis, *The Celtic Gauls: Gods, Rites and Sanctuaries*, London, 1988 (English translation).

Chadwick, Nora, *The Celts*, London, 1971.

Condran, Mary, *The Serpent and the Goddess*, San Francisco, 1989.

Cunliffe, Barry, *The Celtic World*, London, 1992.

Green, Miranda, *The Gods of the Celts*, Stroud, 1986.

Green, Miranda, *Symbol and Image in Celtic Religious Art*, London, 1989.

Hutton, Ronald, *The Pagan Religions of the Ancient British Isles*, London, 1991.

Piggot, Stuart, *The Druids*, London, 1968.

Wait, G.A., *Ritual and Religion in Iron Age Britain*, British Archaeological Reports, British Series, 149, 1985.

Webster, Graham, *The British Celts and their Gods under Rome*, London, 1986.

Church History and Archaeology

Bieler, Ludwig, *The Irish Penitentials*, Dublin, 1963.

Chadwick, Nora, *Early Brittany*, Cardiff, 1969.

N. Chadwick, K. Hughes, C. Brooke, K. Jackson, eds., *Studies in the British Church*, Cambridge, 1958.

Cowley, F. G., *A History of the Monastic Order in South Wales*, Cardiff, 1977.

Davies, Wendy, *Wales in the Early Middle Ages*, Leicester, 1982, 141–93.

de Paor, Liam, *St Patrick's World*, Co. Dublin, 1993.

Edwards, Nancy and Lane, Alan, eds., *The Early Church in Wales and the West*, Oxbow, 1992.

Hughes, Kathleen, *The Church in Early Irish Society*, London, 1966.

Hughes, Kathleen, *Early Christian Ireland: Introduction to the Sources*, London, 1972.

Pryce, Huw, 'Pastoral Care in Early Medieval Wales' in John Blair and Richard Sharpe, eds., *Pastoral Care before the Parish*, Leicester, 1991, 41–62.

Pryce, Huw, *Native Law and the Church in Medieval Wales*, Oxford, 1993.

Richter, Michael, *The Enduring Tradition*, London, 1988.

Thomas, Charles, *Christianity in Roman Britain to AD 500*, London, 1981.

Thompson, E. A., *Saint Germanus of Auxerre and the End of Roman Britain*, Woodbridge, 1984.

Walsh, J. and Bradley, T., *A History of the Irish Church 400-700 AD*, Co. Dublin, 1991.

Williams, David, *The Welsh Cistercians*, Tenby, 1984.

Williams, Glanmor, 'Some Protestant Views of Early British Church History' in *Welsh Reformation Essays*, Cardiff, 1967, 207-19.

Williams, Glanmor, *The Welsh Church from Conquest to Reformation*, Cardiff, 1976.

Williams, Glanmor, *The Welsh and their Religion*, Cardiff, 1991.

Hagiography

Baring-Gould, S. and Fisher, J., eds., *The Lives of the British Saints*, I-IV, London, 1907–1913.

Bowen, E. G., *Saints, Seaways and Settlements*, Cardiff, 1969.

Evans, D. Simon, *The Welsh Life of David*, Cardiff, 1988 (English translation).

Hawley, John Stratton, *Saints and Virtues*, California, 1987.

Heffernan, Thomas J., *Sacred Biography*, New York and Oxford, 1988.

Henken, Elissa R., *Traditions of the Welsh Saints*, Woodbridge, 1987.

Henken, Ellisa R., *The Welsh Saints: a Study in Patterned Lives*, Woodbridge, 1991.

James, J. W., *Rhigyfarch's Life of Saint David*, Cardiff, 1967.

Jones, Francis, *The Holy Wells of Wales*, Cardiff, 1954.

Kieckhefer, Richard, 'Imitators of Christ: Sainthood in the Christian Tradition' in Richard Kieckhefer and George D. Bond, eds., *Sainthood: its Manifestations in World Religions*, California, 1988.

O'Donoghue, Noel Dermot, *Aristocracy of Soul: St Patrick of Ireland*, Minnesota, 1988.

Plummer, Charles, *Vitae Sanctorum Hiberniae*, vols. I and II, Oxford, 1910.

Religious Poetry and Prose

Bloomfield, Morton W. and Dunn, Charles W., *The Role of the Poet in Early Societies*, Cambridge, 1989.

Evans, D. Simon, *Medieval Religious Literature*, Cardiff, 1986.

Haycock, Marged, *Blodeugerdd Barddas o Ganu Crefyddol Cynnar*, Llandybie, 1994.

McKenna, Catherine A., *The Medieval Welsh Religious Lyric*, Belmont, Mass., 1991.

Murphy, Gerard, ed., *Early Irish Lyrics*, Oxford, 1956.

Williams, J. E. Caerwyn, *The Irish Literary Tradition*, Cardiff and Belmont, Mass., 1992.

Art, Music and Liturgy

Edwards, Owain Tudor, *Matins, Lauds and Vespers for St David's Day*, Cambridge, 1990.

Henderson, George, *From Durrow to Kells*, London, 1987.

Henry, Francoise, *Irish Art in the Early Christian Period to A.D. 800*, London, 1965.

Travis, James, *Miscellanea Musica Celtica*, Wissenschaftliche Abhandlungen Bd. XIV, New York, 1968.

Warren, F. E., *Liturgy and Ritual of the Celtic Church* (2nd edition), Woodbridge, 1987.

Theology

Davies, Oliver, '*On Divine Love* from *Food for the Soul*: a Celtic Mystical Paradigm?' in *Mystics Quarterly*, vol. XX, no. 3 (1994), 87–95.

Dumville, David, 'Late Seventh or Eighth Century Evidence for the British Transmission of Pelagius' in *Cambridge Medieval Celtic Studies*, 10 (1985), 39–52.

Evans, R. F., *Four Letters of Pelagius*, London, 1968.

Forthomme Nicholson, M., 'Celtic Theology: Pelagius' in Mackey, J. P., ed., *An Introduction to Celtic Christianity*, Edinburgh, 1989, 386–413.

Herbert, M. and McNamara, M., *Irish Biblical Apocrypha*, Edinburgh, 1989.

Moran, Dermot, *The Philosophy of John Scottus Eriugena*, Cambridge, 1989.

Rees, B. R., *Pelagius: a Reluctant Heretic*, Woodbridge, 1988.

Rees, B. R., *The Letters of Pelagius and his Followers*, Woodbridge, 1991.

CASEBOOK SERIES

GENERAL EDITOR: A. E. Dyson

PUBLISHED

Jane Austen: *Emma* DAVID LODGE
Jane Austen: *'Northanger Abbey' and 'Persuasion'* B. C. SOUTHAM
Jane Austen: *'Sense and Sensibility', 'Pride and Prejudice' and 'Mansfield Park'*
  B. C. SOUTHAM
William Blake: *Songs of Innocence and Experience* MARGARET BOTTRALL
Charlotte Brontë: *'Jane Eyre' and 'Villette'* MIRIAM ALLOTT
Emily Brontë: *Wuthering Heights* MIRIAM ALLOTT
Browning: *'Men and Women' and Other Poems* J. R. WATSON
Bunyan: *The Pilgrim's Progress* ROGER SHARROCK
Byron: *'Childe Harold's Pilgrimage' and 'Don Juan'* JOHN JUMP
Chaucer: *Canterbury Tales* J. J. ANDERSON
Coleridge: *'The Ancient Mariner' and Other Poems* ALUN R. JONES AND
  WILLIAM TYDEMAN
Conrad: *The Secret Agent* IAN WATT
Dickens: *Bleak House* A. E. DYSON
Donne: *Songs and Sonets* JULIAN LOVELOCK
George Eliot: *Middlemarch* PATRICK SWINDEN
T. S. Eliot: *Four Quartets* BERNARD BERGONZI
T. S. Eliot: *The Waste Land* C. B. COX AND ARNOLD P. HINCHLIFFE
Farquhar: *'The Recruiting Officer' and 'The Beaux' Stratagem'*
  RAYMOND A. ANSELMENT
Henry Fielding: *Tom Jones* NEIL COMPTON
E. M. Forster: *A Passage to India* MALCOLM BRADBURY
Hardy *The Tragic Novels* R. P. DRAPER
Gerard Manley Hopkins: *Poems* MARGARET BOTTRALL
Jonson: *Volpone* JONAS A. BARISH
James Joyce: *'Dubliners' and 'A Portrait of the Artist as a Young Man'*
  MORRIS BEJA
John Keats: *Odes* G. S. FRASER
D. H. Lawrence: *Sons and Lovers* GĀMINI SALGĀDO
D. H. Lawrence: *'The Rainbow' and 'Women in Love'* COLIN CLARKE
Marlowe: *Doctor Faustus* JOHN JUMP
The Metaphysical Poets GERALD HAMMOND
Milton: *'Comus' and 'Samson Agonistes'* JULIAN LOVELOCK
Milton: *Paradise Lost* A. E. DYSON AND JULIAN LOVELOCK
John Osborne: *Look Back in Anger* JOHN RUSSELL TAYLOR
Peacock: *The Satirical Novels* LORNA SAGE
Pope: *The Rape of the Lock* JOHN DIXON HUNT
Shakespeare: *Antony and Cleopatra* JOHN RUSSELL BROWN
Shakespeare: *Coriolanus* B. A. BROCKMAN
Shakespeare: *Hamlet* JOHN JUMP
Shakespeare: *Henry IV Parts I and II* G. K. HUNTER
Shakespeare: *Henry V* MICHAEL QUINN
Shakespeare: *Julius Caesar* PETER URE
Shakespeare: *King Lear* FRANK KERMODE
Shakespeare: *Macbeth* JOHN WAIN
Shakespeare: *Measure for Measure* C. K. STEAD

Chaucer

The Canterbury Tales

A CASEBOOK

EDITED BY

J. J. ANDERSON

First edition 1974
Reprinted 1977

Published by
THE MACMILLAN PRESS LTD
London and Basingstoke
Associated companies in Delhi Dublin
Hong Kong Johannesburg Lagos Melbourne
New York Singapore and Tokyo

ISBN 0 333 14523 2 (hard cover)
      0 333 14524 0 (paper cover)

Printed in Great Britain by
UNWIN BROTHERS LIMITED
The Gresham Press, Old Woking, Surrey

CONTENTS

ACKNOWLEDGEMENTS

Ian Bishop, 'The Narrative Art of The Pardoner's Tale' from *Medium Ævum* xxxvi (1967) by permission of Basil Blackwell & Mott Ltd; Robert B. Burlin, 'The Art of Chaucer's Franklin' from *Neophilologus* li (1967) pp. 55–73; John Burrow, 'Irony in The Merchant's Tale' from *Anglia* lxxv (1957) by permission of Max Niemeyer Verlag; E. T. Donaldson, 'Idiom of Popular Poetry in the Miller's Tale' from *Speaking of Chaucer* (London, Athlone Press, 1970) and *English Institute Essays* (1950) by permission of Columbia University Press; E. T. Donaldson, 'Chaucer the Pilgrim', *PMLA* 69 (1954) reprinted by permission of the Modern Language Association of America; William Frost, 'An Interpretation of Chaucer's Knight's Tale' from the *Review of English Studies* vol. 25 (1949) by permission of The Clarendon Press, Oxford; A. W. Hoffman, 'Chaucer's Prologue to Pilgrimage: The Two Voices', *English Literary History* vol. xxi (1954) pp. 1–16, © The Johns Hopkins University Press; G. L. Kittredge, 'Chaucer's Discussion of Marriage' from *Modern Philology* ix (1911–12) by permission of The University of Chicago Press; Charles Muscatine, extract from *Chaucer and the French Tradition*, originally published by the University of California Press, reprinted by permission of the Regents of the University of California; Paul G. Ruggiers, *The Art of the Canterbury Tales* (Madison: The University of Wisconsin Press; © 1965 by the Regents of the University of Wisconsin) pp. 184–96; Tony Slade, 'Irony in The Wife of Bath's Tale', *Modern Language Review* lxiv (1969).

GENERAL EDITOR'S PREFACE

Each of this series of Casebooks concerns either one well-known and influential work of literature or two or three closely linked works. The main section consists of critical readings, mostly modern, brought together from journals and books. A selection of reviews and comments by the author's contemporaries is also included, and sometimes comments from the author himself. The Editor's Introduction charts the reputation of the work from its first appearance until the present time.

The critical forum is a place of vigorous conflict and disagreement, but there is nothing in this to cause dismay. What is attested is the complexity of human experience and the richness of literature, not any chaos or relativity of taste. A critic is better seen, no doubt, as an explorer than as an 'authority', but explorers ought to be, and usually are, well equipped. The effect of good criticism is to convince us of what C. S. Lewis called 'the enormous extension of our being which we owe to authors'. A Casebook will be justified only if it helps to promote the same end.

A single volume can represent no more than a small selection of critical opinions. Some critics have been excluded for reasons of space, and it is hoped that readers will follow up the further suggestions in the Select Bibliography. Other contributions have been severed from their original context, to which some readers may wish to return. Indeed, if they take a hint from the critics represented here, they certainly will.

A. E. Dyson

INTRODUCTION

Geoffrey Chaucer was born in the early 1340s and he died in 1400. He was a successful public servant as well as a successful writer, at the centre of the political and literary life of the London of his day. His first major work, *The Book of the Duchess*, commemorating the death of Blanche, Duchess of Lancaster and the first wife of John of Gaunt, must have been written soon after her death in 1369, when Chaucer was still in his twenties. From this time until his death in 1400, Chaucer maintained a fairly steady output of literary work, culminating in the *Canterbury Tales*, begun about 1387 and unfinished at the time of his death.

The evidence shows that, from the first, no other English writer of the later fourteenth century equalled Chaucer in prestige. Today, there exist some eighty-four fifteenth-century manuscripts of the *Canterbury Tales* (of which fifty-eight are relatively complete) – more than for any other poem of the period. In the few contemporary references to Chaucer that we have (by Deschamps, Gower and Usk), he is praised highly, and many poets who come after him (such as Hoccleve, Lydgate, James I of Scotland, Douglas, Henryson and Dunbar) not only refer admiringly to Chaucer but consciously set out to follow him in their own poetry. It is true that, as the fifteenth century goes on, Chaucer's name is frequently coupled with those of Gower and Lydgate, but his primacy is rarely in question. He is revered chiefly as a 'high philosophical' poet (especially as a poet of *fin amour*), and as one who transformed 'our rude language' with 'the gold dew-drops of rhetoric' (Lydgate, *The History, Siege, and Destruction of Troy*, 1412–20). The same points are made again and again by writers of the fifteenth and earlier sixteenth centuries (cf. Caxton, p. 19); Chaucer was regarded as the first English poet with the learning and skill of his continental counterparts, and above all the first poet to demonstrate that the English language was capable of poetic expression as elevated as anything in French or Latin. Fifteenth-century writers are, on the whole, more interested in *Troilus and Criseyde* than in the

Canterbury Tales, but the latter poem is certainly not neglected. Thus Lydgate refers appreciatively to the variety of the tales, and pays the poem the compliment of imitating its opening, in *The Siege of Thebes* (1420–2); and almost a century later, Skelton, in *Philip Sparrow* (before 1509), alludes to the 'delectable, solacious, and commendable' matter of the *Tales*. But in the course of the sixteenth century the poem seems to fall from favour to the extent that the phrase 'a Canterbury tale' is used as a term of abuse; there is a marked decline in the appreciation of Chaucer's writing generally, although *Troilus and Criseyde* retains something of its former reputation. Conventional praise of Chaucer (and of Gower and Lydgate) continues, but becomes ever more mechanical. Reformation writers, seizing on Chaucer's criticism of medieval clerics, make him out to be a moralist and reformer, at the same time as others condemn his coarseness – a feature of his writings which has persistently worried Chaucer's readers through the centuries (cf. for example Dryden, p. 27). Towards the middle of the century, one begins to come upon complaints that Chaucer's language, far from exhibiting 'gold dew-drops of rhetoric', is obsolete and rough, as is his versification; already, in *Philip Sparrow*, Skelton notes that there are those who wish to 'amend' Chaucer's language. Of the great writers of the later sixteenth and earlier seventeenth centuries, some never allude to Chaucer, others allude to him fleetingly, with respect or at least affection, but only Spenser calls him 'master' and sees himself as following in his footsteps. For most, Chaucer has become a remote figure. Perhaps the famous comment of Sir Philip Sidney, in *An Apology for Poetry* (written *c.* 1581), best sums up the informed opinion of the day: 'Chaucer, undoubtedly, did excellently in his *Troilus and Criseyde*; of whom, truly, I know not whether to marvel more, either that he in that misty time could see so clearly, or that we in this clear age walk so stumblingly after him. Yet had he great wants, fit to be forgiven in so reverend antiquity.'

In the seventeenth century, as the language problem becomes more acute, Chaucer's reputation reaches its nadir, though there are always a few who value him highly. Chaucer is not only rough and difficult to understand, but he is to be blamed for corrupting the language with French – a view the very opposite of that held

two centuries earlier. By the end of the century, Chaucer's
language and versification are given up for lost, and he is generally felt to be a once-great poet now antiquated and superseded;
if anything survives of him, it is his 'sense'. Thus Samuel Cobb
writes in *Poetae Britannici* (*c.* 1700) :

> A joking bard, whose antiquated muse
> In mouldy words could solid sense produce.
> Our English Ennius he, who claim'd his part
> In wealthy Nature, though unskill'd in Art.

The desire to do away with the 'mouldy words' so that the
sense could shine led to several translations of Chaucer into contemporary English, the most important of which was Dryden's
translation of some of the *Canterbury Tales* in *Fables Ancient
and Modern* (1700) – a work which greatly boosted the popularity of the *Canterbury Tales* as compared to *Troilus*. Part of
Dryden's long preface to his translations stands as undoubtedly
the most significant landmark in the history of Chaucer criticism.
It shares in many of the attitudes of the day, but it also contains
sane, humane appreciation of various aspects of Chaucer's work,
founded on a necessarily attentive reading of the original. Dryden
perceptively discusses, amongst other matters, Chaucer's poetic
decorum, his truth to nature, his skill in characterising the
pilgrims, and the many-sided quality of his genius, summing up
his author, as it seems, for all time : 'He is a perpetual fountain of
good sense'; 'a man of a most wonderful comprehensive nature';
'here is God's plenty'. There is adverse criticism, too, which goes
beyond the commonplaces of Dryden's contemporaries; Chaucer
'sometimes mingles trivial things, with those of greater moment',
and 'sometimes . . . knows not when he has said enough' (p. 28).
With the Preface Chaucer criticism proper may be said to begin.
To a modern reader, the translations themselves do not do
Chaucer any service, but they were hailed at the time as com-
parable to Vergil's transformation of Ennius : 'He found him
rubbish, and he left him gold' (Jabez Hughes, *c.* 1707). Dryden
himself does not have quite so high an opinion of his function;
nevertheless, he subscribes to the general low estimate of
Chaucer's language and versification, and clearly regards him-

self as improver as well as translator : 'What beauties I lose in some places, I give to others which had them not originally' (p. 30).

Translation activity continued through the eighteenth century into the nineteenth, but in the latter half of the eighteenth century the view that Chaucer was nothing unless in translation began to be seriously challenged, notably by Warton, who found that the original possessed 'what later and more refin'd ages could hardly equal in true humour, pathos, or sublimity' (*Observations on the Faerie Queene*, 1754), and Gray, who defended Chaucer's metre. In the nineteenth century the Romantics and Victorians read Chaucer in the original, most with approval (though Byron, at the age of nineteen, calls him 'obscene and contemptible'), and several have left us interesting criticism, most of it influenced by Dryden. I have selected from Blake's 'guide' to his splendid painting of the Canterbury pilgrims (1809), in which he explains the pilgrims as representatives of eternity; from a lecture by Hazlitt (1818), who emphasises Chaucer's sincerity and simplicity; and from a lecture by Arnold (1880), who endorses Dryden's approbation of Chaucer's 'truly human point of view' (p. 55), though he regards Chaucer as not being in the first rank of poets because of his lack of 'high seriousness'.

This kind of criticism, by men interested in writers and writing in general, often outstanding creative writers themselves, is, at its best, impressively large-minded, and it has given us some memorable perceptions. But, towards the end of the nineteenth century, a more 'professional' criticism begins to emerge, founded on the work of the great scholars of the last half of the century, when Chaucer scholarship comes into its own. Of course there had always been those with a scholarly interest in Chaucer, men who were concerned with establishing good texts and understanding Chaucer's work in a form as close to the original as possible. In the early days of printing there was a succession of editions – by Caxton (who published the *Canterbury Tales, c.* 1483), Pynson (1526), Thynne (the first 'complete' Chaucer, 1532), and Speght (1598). There was then a long gap, with little evidence of any scholarly activity (but see Dryden's reference to 'some old Saxon friends' who think it 'little less than profanation and sacrilege' to alter Chaucer's language, p. 29) until

Urry's well-intentioned but very unsatisfactory edition of 1721. But now a number of good scholars became involved in Chaucer studies, and eventually, in 1775, a fine edition of the *Canterbury Tales* was brought out by Thomas Tyrwhitt, an edition which helped confirm the eighteenth- and nineteenth-century view of the *Canterbury Tales* as Chaucer's masterpiece. During the nineteenth century there was a growth of scholarly interest in the language and literature of medieval England generally, and an increasing awareness of the complexity of the problems, particularly textual problems, facing the student of Chaucer. In 1868 the Chaucer Society was founded to make a concentrated attack on these problems. Its work culminated in Skeat's great six-volume edition of 1894–7, the first truly critical edition of Chaucer, still by no means entirely superseded, although the edition by Robinson (1933, revised 1957) has become the standard edition for most purposes, and the *Canterbury Tales* has been edited on the basis of all the known manuscripts by Manly and Rickert (1940).

The work of the scholars is one reason for the fact that twentieth-century Chaucer criticism is better informed than that of preceding centuries. Another reason is that twentieth-century critics are almost always academics (even the reading of Chaucer, as of other poets, is now confined largely to academic institutions), and so have a more professional concern and are better able to specialise. Their output is vast and varied, and therefore difficult to summarise, but it may be helpful to offer a distinction (not always easy to apply) between a 'central' kind of criticism, which works primarily from the text, and which, however refined it may have become, goes back ultimately to Dryden; and another kind, which works primarily from a more or less specialised point of view, by means of which it seeks to interpret the text – this latter being a distinctively twentieth-century kind of criticism. Representative of the first kind are G. L. Kittredge, in his famous article (reprinted here) 'Chaucer's Discussion of Marriage' (1912), and his book *Chaucer and his Poetry* (Cambridge, Mass., 1915), who concentrates on the drama of Chaucer's 'human comedy'; J. L. Lowes (*Geoffrey Chaucer and the Development of His Genius*, Boston, 1934), who explains Chaucer's 'realism' in terms of contemporary life and ideas; Charles Muscatine (*Chaucer and the French Tradition*, California, 1957), who examines the interplay in Chaucer's work of two complementary styles, the 'realistic' and 'conventional'; E. T. Donaldson, who in a number of essays (two of which are reprinted here) explores Chaucer's ironies and ambiguities (Donaldson has collected several of these essays in his *Speaking of Chaucer*, London, 1970), and P. M. Kean (*Chaucer and the Making of English Poetry*, London, 1972), who considers the manner in which Chaucer uses traditional styles, themes, and structures. Specialist approaches through, for example, medieval science, philosophy, rhetoric, art, and specific sources and analogues, have all made important contributions to our understanding of Chaucer, though there is always the danger, with this type of approach, of a partial or distorted reading of the text. Successful examples of this kind of criticism are W. C. Curry's much-quoted *Chaucer and the Medieval Sciences* (Oxford, 1926); Robert O. Payne, *The Key of Remembrance: A Study of Chaucer's Poetics* (Yale, 1963), a sensitive study of rhetorical traditions as they apply to Chaucer; and Robert M. Jordan, *Chaucer and the Shape of Creation* (Cambridge, Mass., 1967), a study of medieval aesthetic theory and its relation to Chaucer's 'Gothic' structures. The most important of these specialist approaches, the 'exegetical', which holds that behind Chaucer's text is a body of theological meaning to which the text is allegorically related, has attracted a number of critics. The theory is set forth most fully, if not most clearly, in D. W. Robertson, *A Preface to Chaucer* (Princeton, 1963), a book which is a rich mine of ideas and information, admirably directing attention to the potential relevance of theological and aesthetic traditions to Chaucer's work, though the thesis *in toto* is unconvincing. At the other extreme from critics such as Robertson are attempts at a more evaluative criticism, orientated towards the present, in the Leavis mould; examples are John Speirs, *Chaucer the Maker* (London, 1951) and Ian Robinson, *Chaucer and the English Tradition* (Cambridge, 1972). But the approach strikes one as basically unsuited to medieval authors, and it has produced some eccentric judgements.

It is not difficult to discern broad shifts of emphasis in Chaucer criticism through the twentieth century, often reflecting changes in critical attitudes generally. Thus criticism has become steadily more detailed, closer and closer in focus. The view of Chaucer as 'realistic' and 'dramatic', inherited from the nineteenth century, has been sharply modified by a growing awareness of the conventional aspects of his work. The view (again inherited from the nineteenth century) that Chaucer's reputation rests on the *Canterbury Tales* rather than *Troilus and Criseyde* has given way to the recognition that both are great poems in their different ways. Above all, as is obvious from my selection of essays, there is an acute contemporary awareness of the ironic dimension in Chaucer's writing, which has produced, and is producing, much fruitful criticism.

In criticism specifically of the *Canterbury Tales*, the old dramatic view of the poem still has life in it (as shown, for example, by the continuing interest in the psychological appropriateness or otherwise of tale to teller, evinced in R. M. Lumiansky, *Of Sondry Folk; The Dramatic Principle in the Canterbury Tales*, Austin, 1955, and in the articles by Slade and Burlin reprinted in this book). There has been an increasing concern to find an artistic unity in the poem as a whole. Thus Ralph Baldwin (*The Unity of the Canterbury Tales*, Copenhagen, 1955) sees an organising principle in the concept of the spiritual pilgrimage, whereby the pilgrims are journeying not only to Canterbury but also to the Heavenly City, the poem's fundamental values being set out in the Parson's concluding sermon. Baldwin in his monograph deals mainly with the beginning and end of the poem, but his view is filled out, with due attention to the tales in between, by P. G. Ruggiers in his *The Art of the Canterbury Tales* (Madison, 1965). On the other hand, Jordan in *Shape of Creation* sees the poem's unity as dependent on 'the Gothic principle of juxtaposition', a unity in diversity. But whilst interest in larger issues continues, the characteristic critical publication today is an article on a single tale, considered largely as a separate entity. Of those tales which are old favourites, the Knight's Tale continues to generate an astonishing amount of good criticism, the Nun's Priest's Tale surprisingly little. The *fabliaux* tales (Miller's Tale, Reeve's Tale, Merchant's Tale, and so on) have lately received appreciative attention, which has demonstrated that they are much more than the simple bawdy stories they were once thought to be. Other tales which have recently risen in critical esteem are the Franklin's Tale and the Canon's Yeoman's Tale; with respect to the latter, Charles Muscatine notes 'the virtual absence of previous literary criticism' (p. 237) in 1957, but there is a plethora of articles today. Only the Parson's Tale and 'Melibee' and one or two others still languish; were Dryden writing now, he would no doubt apply his phrase 'Here is God's plenty' to the critics instead of the pilgrims.

My selection of twentieth-century criticism is necessarily a very limited one. It has seemed a fair reflection of contemporary critical practice to concentrate on essays on individual tales, and I have tried to cover the range of the better-known tales. I have further limited myself to essays which deal in text-centred criticism, and my aim has been to select from the best of these, regardless of whether they are already well known or not; several have classic status. The selection is only secondarily intended to chronicle changing critical emphases, and I have not concerned myself at all with specialist approaches to criticism, though it is hoped that some of the essays, at least, will lead readers out into specialist areas.

In the *Early Appreciations* section, all the selections are extracts from longer pieces, though the extracts contain most of what their authors have to say about Chaucer. I have modernised Caxton's punctuation, capitalisation, and word-division, and have abbreviated Hazlitt's extensive quotation of Chaucer. In the *Twentieth-century Criticism* section, articles and chapters are complete as in the indicated sources, apart from Burlin's article, which is reprinted with minor revisions by the author, the notes to Kittredge's article, which I have omitted as being peripheral to his argument, occasional abbreviation of other notes, and some regularisation of conventions.

In writing the Introduction, I have made extensive use of Caroline Spurgeon, *Five Hundred Years of Chaucer Criticism and Allusion, 1357–1900* (Cambridge, 1925).

J. J. ANDERSON

PART ONE

Early Appreciations

William Caxton

Grete thankes, laude, and honour ought to be gyuen vnto the clerkes, poetes, and historiographs that haue wreton many noble bokes of wysedom, of the lyues, passions, and myracles of holy sayntes, of hystoryes of noble and famous actes and faittes, and of the cronycles sith the begynnyng of the creacion of the world vnto thys present tyme, by whyche we ben dayly enformed and have knowleche of many thynges of whom we shold not have knowen yf they had not left to vs theyr monumentis wreton. Emong whom and in especial tofore alle other we ought to gyue a synguler laude vnto that noble and grete philosopher Gefferey Chaucer, the whiche for his ornate wrytyng in our tongue may wel haue the name of a laureate poete. For tofore that he by hys labour enbelysshyd, ornated, and made faire our Englisshe, in thys royame was had rude speche and incongrue, as yet it appiereth by olde bookes whyche at thys day ought not to haue place ne be compared emong ne to hys beauteuous volumes and aournate writynges; of whom he made many bokes and treatyces of many a noble historye, as wel in metre as in ryme and prose, and them so craftyly made that he comprehended hys maters in short, quyck, and hye sentences, eschewyng prolyxyte, castyng away the chaf of superfluyte, and shewyng the pyked grayn of sentence vtteryd by crafty and sugred eloquence; of whom emonge all other of hys bokes I purpose t'emprynte, by the grace of God, the *Book of the Tales of Cauntyrburye*, in whiche I fynde many a noble hystorye of every astate and degre, fyrst rehercyng the condicions and th'arraye of eche of them as properly as possyble is to be sayd, and after theyr tales, whyche ben of noblesse, wysedom, gentylesse, myrthe, and also of veray holynesse and vertue, wherin he fynysshyth thys sayd booke; whyche book I haue dylygently ouersen and duly examyned, to th'ende that it be made acordyng vnto his owen makyng. . . .

SOURCE: Proem to Caxton's Second Edition of *The Canterbury Tales* (1484).

John Dryden

... I proceed to *Ovid*, and *Chaucer*; considering the former only in relation to the latter. With *Ovid* ended the Golden Age of the *Roman* Tongue: From *Chaucer* the Purity of the *English* Tongue began. The Manners of the Poets were not unlike: Both of them were well-bred, well-natur'd, amorous, and Libertine, at least in their Writings, it may be also in their Lives. Their Studies were the same, Philosophy, and Philology. Both of them were knowing in Astronomy, of which *Ovid's* Books of the *Roman* Feasts, and *Chaucer's* Treatise of the *Astrolabe*, are sufficient Witnesses. But *Chaucer* was likewise an Astrologer, as were *Virgil, Horace, Persius,* and *Manilius*. Both writ with wonderful Facility and Clearness; neither were great Inventors: For *Ovid* only copied the *Grecian* Fables; and most of *Chaucer's* Stories were taken from his *Italian* Contemporaries, or their Predecessors: *Boccace* his *Decameron* was first publish'd; and from thence our *Englishman* has borrow'd many of his *Canterbury* Tales: Yet that of *Palamon* and *Arcite* was written in all probability by some *Italian* Wit, in a former Age; as I shall prove hereafter: The Tale of *Grizild* was the Invention of *Petrarch*; by him sent to *Boccace*; from whom it came to *Chaucer*: *Troilus* and *Cressida* was also written by a *Lombard* Author; but much amplified by our *English* Translatour, as well as beautified; the Genius of our Countrymen in general being rather to improve an Invention, than to invent themselves; as is evident not only in our Poetry, but in many of our Manufactures. I find I have anticipated already, and taken up from *Boccace* before I come to him: But there is so much less behind; and I am of the Temper of most Kings, *who love to be in Debt,* are all for present Money, no matter how they pay it afterwards: Besides, the Nature of a Preface is rambling; never wholly out of the Way, nor in it. This I have learn'd from the Practice of honest *Montaign,* and return at my pleasure to *Ovid* and *Chaucer*, of whom I have little more to say. Both of them built on the Inventions of other Men; yet since *Chaucer* had something of his own, as *The Wife of Baths*

Tale, The Cock and the Fox, which I have translated, and some others, I may justly give our Countryman the Precedence in that Part; since I can remember nothing of *Ovid* which was wholly his. Both of them understood the Manners; under which Name I comprehend the Passions, and, in a larger Sense, the Descriptions of Persons, and their very Habits : For an Example, I see *Baucis* and *Philemon* as perfectly before me, as if some ancient Painter had drawn them; and all the Pilgrims in the *Canterbury* Tales, their Humours, their Features, and the very Dress, as distinctly as if I had supp'd with them at the *Tabard* in *Southwark* : Yet even there too the Figures of *Chaucer* are much more lively, and set in a better Light : Which though I have not time to prove; yet I appeal to the Reader, and am sure he will clear me from Partiality. The Thoughts and Words remain to be consider'd, in the Comparison of the two Poets; and I have sav'd my self one half of that Labour, by owning that *Ovid* liv'd when the *Roman* Tongue was in its Meridian; *Chaucer,* in the Dawning of our Language : Therefore that Part of the Comparison stands not on an equal Foot, any more than the Diction of *Ennius* and *Ovid*; or of *Chaucer,* and our present *English.* The Words are given up as a Post not to be defended in our Poet, because he wanted the Modern Art of Fortifying. The Thoughts remain to be consider'd : And they are to be measur'd only by their Propriety; that is, as they flow more or less naturally from the Persons describ'd, on such and such Occasions. The Vulgar Judges, which are Nine Parts in Ten of all Nations, who call Conceits and Jingles Wit, who see *Ovid* full of them, and *Chaucer* altogether without them, will think me little less than mad, for preferring the *Englishman* to the *Roman* : Yet, with their leave, I must presume to say, that the Things they admire are only glittering Trifles, and so far from being Witty, that in a serious Poem they are nauseous, because they are unnatural. Wou'd any Man who is ready to die for Love, describe his Passion like *Narcissus*? Wou'd he think of *inopem me copia fecit,* and a Dozen more of such Expressions, pour'd on the Neck of one another, and signifying all the same Thing? If this were Wit, was this a Time to be witty, when the poor Wretch was in the Agony of Death? This is just *John Littlewit* in *Bartholomew Fair,* who had a Conceit (as he tells you) left him in his Misery; a miserable Conceit. On these Occasions the Poet shou'd endeavour to raise Pity: But instead of this, *Ovid* is tickling you to laugh. *Virgil* never made use of such Machines, when he was moving you to commiserate the Death of *Dido*: He would not destroy what he was building. *Chaucer* makes *Arcite* violent in his Love, and unjust in the Pursuit of it: Yet when he came to die, he made him think more reasonably: He repents not of his Love, for that had alter'd his Character; but acknowledges the Injustice of his Proceedings, and resigns *Emilia* to *Palamon*. What would *Ovid* have done on this Occasion? He would certainly have made *Arcite* witty on his Death-bed. He had complain'd he was farther off from Possession, by being so near, and a thousand such Boyisms, which *Chaucer* rejected as below the Dignity of the Subject. They who think otherwise, would by the same reason prefer *Lucan* and *Ovid* to *Homer* and *Virgil*, and *Martial* to all four of them. As for the Turn of Words, in which *Ovid* particularly excels all Poets; they are sometimes a Fault, and sometimes a Beauty, as they are us'd properly or improperly; but in strong Passions always to be shunn'd, because Passions are serious, and will admit no Playing. The *French* have a high Value for them; and I confess, they are often what they call Delicate, when they are introduc'd with Judgment; but *Chaucer* writ with more Simplicity, and follow'd Nature more closely, than to use them. I have thus far, to the best of my Knowledge, been an upright Judge betwixt the Parties in Competition, not medling with the Design nor the Disposition of it; because the Design was not their own; and in the disposing of it they were equal. It remains that I say somewhat of *Chaucer* in particular.

In the first place, As he is the Father of *English* Poetry, so I hold him in the same Degree of Veneration as the *Grecians* held *Homer*, or the *Romans Virgil*: He is a perpetual Fountain of good Sense; learn'd in all Sciences; and therefore speaks properly on all Subjects: As he knew what to say, so he knows also when to leave off; a Continence which is practis'd by few Writers, and scarcely by any of the Ancients, excepting *Virgil* and *Horace*. One of our late great Poets is sunk in his Reputation, because he cou'd never forgive any Conceit which came in his way; but swept like a Drag-net, great and small. There was plenty enough, but the Dishes were ill sorted; whole Pyramids of

Sweet-meats, for Boys and Women; but little of solid Meat, for Men : All this proceeded not from any want of Knowledge, but of Judgment; neither did he want that in discerning the Beauties and Faults of other Poets; but only indulg'd himself in the Luxury of Writing; and perhaps knew it was a Fault, but hop'd the Reader would not find it. For this Reason, though he must always be thought a great Poet, he is no longer esteem'd a good Writer : And for Ten Impressions, which his Works have had in so many successive Years, yet at present a hundred Books are scarcely purchas'd once a Twelvemonth : For, as my last Lord *Rochester* said, though somewhat profanely, *Not being of God, he could not stand.*

Chaucer follow'd Nature every where; but was never so bold to go beyond her : And there is a great Difference of being *Poeta* and *nimis Poeta*, if we may believe *Catullus*, as much as betwixt a modest Behaviour and Affectation. The Verse of *Chaucer*, I confess, is not Harmonious to us; but 'tis like the Eloquence of one whom *Tacitus* commends, it was *auribus istius temporis accommodata*: They who liv'd with him, and some time after him, thought it Musical; and it continues so even in our Judgment, if compar'd with the Numbers of *Lidgate* and *Gower* his Contemporaries : There is the rude Sweetness of a *Scotch* Tune in it, which is natural and pleasing, though not perfect. 'Tis true, I cannot go so far as he who publish'd the last Edition of him; for he would make us believe the Fault is in our Ears, and that there were really Ten Syllables in a Verse where we find but Nine : But this Opinion is not worth confuting; 'tis so gross and obvious an Errour, that common Sense (which is a Rule in every thing but Matters of Faith and Revelation) must convince the Reader, that Equality of Numbers in every Verse which we call *Heroick*, was either not known, or not always practis'd in *Chaucer*'s Age. It were an easie Matter to produce some thousands of his Verses, which are lame for want of half a Foot, and sometimes a whole one, and which no Pronunciation can make otherwise. We can only say, that he liv'd in the Infancy of our Poetry, and that nothing is brought to Perfection at the first. We must be Children before we grow Men. There was an *Ennius*, and in process of Time a *Lucilius*, and a *Lucretius*, before *Virgil* and *Horace*; even after *Chaucer* there was a

Spencer, a *Harrington*, a *Fairfax*, before *Waller* and *Denham*
were in being : And our Numbers were in their Nonage till these
last appear'd. I need say little of his Parentage, Life, and Fortunes : They are to be found at large in all the Editions of his
Works. He was employ'd abroad, and favour'd by *Edward* the
Third, *Richard* the Second, and *Henry* the Fourth, and was
Poet, as I suppose, to all Three of them. In *Richard*'s Time, I
doubt, he was a little dipt in the Rebellion of the Commons;
and being Brother-in-Law to *John of Ghant*, it was no wonder
if he follow'd the Fortunes of that Family; and was well with
Henry the Fourth when he had depos'd his Predecessor. Neither
is it to be admir'd, that *Henry*, who was a wise as well as a valiant
Prince, who claim'd by Succession, and was sensible that his Title
was not sound, but was rightfully in *Mortimer*, who had married
the Heir of *York*; it was not to be admir'd, I say, if that great
Politician should be pleas'd to have the greatest Wit of those
Times in his Interests, and to be the Trumpet of his Praises.
Augustus had given him the Example, by the Advice of
Mæcenas who recommended *Virgil* and *Horace* to him; whose
Praises help'd to make him Popular while he was alive, and after
his Death have made him Precious to Posterity. As for the
Religion of our Poet, he seems to have some little Byas towards
the Opinions of *Wickliff*, after *John of Ghant* his Patron; some-
what of which appears in the Tale of *Piers Plowman* : Yet I can-
not blame him for inveighing so sharply against the Vices of the
Clergy of his Age : Their Pride, their Ambition, their Pomp, their
Avarice, their Worldly Interest, deserv'd the Lashes which he
gave them, both in that, and in most of his *Canterbury Tales* :
Neither has his Contemporary *Boccace*, spar'd them. Yet both
those Poets liv'd in much esteem, with good and holy Men in
Orders : For the Scandal which is given by particular Priests,
reflects not on the Sacred Function. *Chaucer*'s *Monk*, his
Chanon, and his *Fryar*, took not from the Character of his *Good
Parson*. A Satyrical Poet is the Check of the Laymen, on bad
Priests. We are only to take care, that we involve not the
Innocent with the Guilty in the same Condemnation. The Good
cannot be too much honour'd, nor the Bad too coursly us'd : For
the Corruption of the Best, becomes the Worst. When a Clergy-
man is whipp'd, his Gown is first taken off, by which the Dignity

of his Order is secur'd : If he be wrongfully accus'd, he has his Action of Slander; and 'tis at the Poet's Peril, if he transgress the Law. But they will tell us, that all kind of Satire, though never so well deserv'd by particular Priests, yet brings the whole Order into Contempt. Is then the Peerage of *England* any thing dishonour'd, when a Peer suffers for his Treason? If he be libell'd, or any way defam'd, he has his *Scandalum Magnatum* to punish the Offendor. They who use this kind of Argument, seem to be conscious to themselves of somewhat which has deserv'd the Poet's Lash; and are less concern'd for their Publick Capacity, than for their Private : At least, there is Pride at the bottom of their Reasoning. If the Faults of Men in Orders are only to be judg'd among themselves, they are all in some sort Parties : For, since they say the Honour of their Order is concern'd in every Member of it, how can we be sure, that they will be impartial Judges? How far I may be allow'd to speak my Opinion in this Case, I know not : But I am sure a Dispute of this Nature caus'd Mischief in abundance betwixt a King of *England* and an Archbishop of *Canterbury*; one standing up for the Laws of his Land, and the other for the Honour (as he call'd it) of God's Church; which ended in the Murther of the Prelate, and in the whipping of his Majesty from Post to Pillar for his Penance. The Learn'd and Ingenious Dr. *Drake* has sav'd me the Labour of inquiring into the Esteem and Reverence which the Priests have had of old; and I would rather extend than diminish any part of it : Yet I must needs say, that when a Priest provokes me without any Occasion given him, I have no Reason, unless it be the Charity of a *Christian*, to forgive him : *Prior læsit* is Justification sufficient in the Civil Law. If I answer him in his own Language, Self-defence, I am sure, must be allow'd me; and if I carry it farther, even to a sharp Recrimination, somewhat may be indulg'd to Humane Frailty. Yet my Resentment has not wrought so far, but that I have follow'd *Chaucer* in his Character of a Holy Man, and have enlarg'd on that Subject with some Pleasure, reserving to my self the Right, if I shall think fit hereafter, to describe another sort of Priests, such as are more easily to be found than the Good Parson; such as have given the last Blow to Christianity in this Age, by a Practice so contrary to their Doctrine. But this will keep cold till another time. In the mean

while, I take up *Chaucer* where I left him. He must have been
a Man of a most wonderful comprehensive Nature, because, as it
has been truly observ'd of him, he has taken into the Compass of
his *Canterbury Tales* the various Manners and Humours (as we
now call them) of the whole *English* Nation, in his Age. Not a
single Character has escap'd him. All his Pilgrims are severally
distinguish'd from each other; and not only in their Inclinations,
but in their very Phisiognomies and Persons. *Baptista Porta*
could not have describ'd their Natures better, than by the Marks
which the Poet gives them. The Matter and Manner of their
Tales, and of their Telling, are so suited to their different
Educations, Humours, and Callings, that each of them would be
improper in any other Mouth. Even the grave and serious
Characters are distinguish'd by their several sorts of Gravity:
Their Discourses are such as belong to their Age, their Calling,
and their Breeding; such as are becoming of them, and of them
only. Some of his Persons are Vicious, and some Vertuous; some
are unlearn'd, or (as *Chaucer* calls them) Lewd, and some are
Learn'd. Even the Ribaldry of the Low Characters is different:
The *Reeve*, the *Miller*, and the *Cook*, are several Men, and distinguish'd from each other, as much as the mincing Lady
Prioress, and the broad-speaking gap-tooth'd Wife of *Bathe*. But
enough of this: There is such a Variety of Game springing up
before me, that I am distracted in my Choice, and know not
which to follow. 'Tis sufficient to say according to the Proverb,
that here is God's Plenty. We have our Fore-fathers and Great
Grand-dames all before us, as they were in *Chaucer*'s Days; their
general Characters are still remaining in Mankind, and even in
England, though they are call'd by other Names than those of
Moncks, and *Fryars*, and *Chanons*, and *Lady Abbesses*, and
Nuns: For Mankind is ever the same, and nothing lost out of
Nature, though every thing is alter'd. May I have leave to do my
self the Justice, (since my Enemies will do me none, and are so
far from granting me to be a good Poet, that they will not allow
me so much as to be a Christian, or a Moral Man) may I have
leave, I say, to inform my Reader, that I have confin'd my
Choice to such Tales of *Chaucer*, as savour nothing of Immodesty.
If I had desir'd more to please than to instruct, the *Reve*,
the *Miller*, the *Shipman*, the *Merchant*, the *Sumner*, and

above all, the *Wife of Bathe*, in the Prologue to her Tale, would have procur'd me as many Friends and Readers, as there are *Beaux* and Ladies of Pleasure in the Town. But I will no more offend against Good Manners : I am sensible as I ought to be of the Scandal I have given by my loose Writings; and make what Reparation I am able, by this Publick Acknowledgment. If any thing of this Nature, or of Profaneness, be crept into these Poems, I am so far from defending it, that I disown it. *Totum hoc indictum volo. Chaucer* makes another manner of Apologie for his broad-speaking, and *Boccace* makes the like; but I will follow neither of them. Our Country-man, in the end of his Characters, before the *Canterbury Tales*, thus excuses the Ribaldry, which is very gross, in many of his Novels.

> *But first, I pray you, of your courtesy,*
> *That ye ne arrete it nought my villany,*
> *Though that I plainly speak in this mattere*
> *To tellen you her words, and eke her chere :*
> *Ne though I speak her words properly,*
> *For this ye knowen as well as I,*
> *Who shall tellen a tale after a man*
> *He mote rehearse as nye, as ever He can :*
> *Everich word of it been in his charge,*
> All speke he, never so rudely, ne large.
> *Or else he mote tellen his tale untrue,*
> *Or feine things, or find words new :*
> *He may not spare, altho he were his brother,*
> *He mote as well say o word as another.*
> Christ *spake himself full broad in holy Writ,*
> *And well I wote no Villany is it.*
> *Eke* Plato *saith, who so can him rede,*
> *The words mote been Cousin to the dede.*

Yet if a Man should have enquir'd of *Boccace* or of *Chaucer*, what need they had of introducing such Characters, where obscene Words were proper in their Mouths, but very undecent to be heard; I know not what Answer they could have made : For that Reason, such Tales shall be left untold by me. You have here a *Specimen of Chaucer*'s Language, which is so obsolete, that his Sense is scarce to be understood; and you have like-

wise more than one Example of his unequal Numbers, which
were mention'd before. Yet many of his Verses consist of Ten
Syllables, and the Words not much behind our present *English* :
As for Example, these two Lines, in the Description of the
Carpenter's Young Wife :

> *Wincing she was, as is a jolly Colt,*
> *Long as a Mast, and upright as a Bolt.*

I have almost done with *Chaucer*, when I have answer'd some
Objections relating to my present Work. I find some People are
offended that I have turn'd these Tales into modern *English*; because they think them unworthy of my Pains, and look on *Chaucer*
as a dry, old-fashion'd Wit, not worth receiving. I have often
heard the late Earl of *Leicester* say, that Mr. *Cowley* himself was
of that opinion; who having read him over at my Lord's Request,
declar'd he had no Taste of him. I dare not advance my Opinion
against the Judgment of so great an Author : But I think it fair,
however, to leave the Decision to the Publick : Mr. *Cowley* was
too modest to set up for a Dictatour; and being shock'd perhaps
with his old Style, never examin'd into the depth of his good
Sense. *Chaucer*, I confess, is a rough Diamond, and must first be
polish'd e'er he shines. I deny not likewise, that living in our early
Days of Poetry, he writes not always of a piece; but sometimes
mingles trivial Things, with those of greater Moment. Sometimes also, though not often, he runs riot, like *Ovid*, and knows
not when he has said enough. But there are more great Wits,
beside *Chaucer*, whose Fault is their Excess of Conceits, and
those ill sorted. An Author is not to write all he can, but only all
he ought. Having observ'd this Redundancy in *Chaucer*, (as it
is an easie Matter for a Man of ordinary Parts to find a Fault in
one of greater) I have not ty'd my self to a Literal Translation;
but have often omitted what I judg'd unnecessary, or not of
Dignity enough to appear in the Company of better Thoughts.
I have presum'd farther in some Places, and added somewhat of
my own where I thought my Author was deficient, and had not
given his Thoughts their true Lustre, for want of Words in the
Beginning of our Language. And to this I was the more em-
bolden'd, because (if I may be permitted to say it of my self) I
found I had a Soul congenial to his, and that I had been con-

versant in the same Studies. Another Poet, in another Age, may take the same Liberty with my Writings; if at least they live long enough to deserve Correction. It was also necessary sometimes to restore the Sense of *Chaucer*, which was lost or mangled in the Errors of the Press : Let this Example suffice at present; in the Story of *Palamon* and *Arcite*, where the Temple of *Diana* is describ'd, you find these Verses, in all the Editions of our Author :

> *There saw I* Danè *turned unto a Tree,*
> *I mean not the Goddess* Diane,
> *But* Venus *Daughter, which that hight* Danè.

Which after a little Consideration I knew was to be reform'd into this Sense, that *Daphne* the Daughter of *Peneus* was turn'd into a Tree. I durst not make thus bold with *Ovid*, lest some future *Milbourn* should arise, and say, I varied from my Author, because I understood him not.

But there are other Judges who think I ought not to have translated *Chaucer* into *English*, out of a quite contrary Notion : They suppose there is a certain Veneration due to his old Language; and that it is little less than Profanation and Sacrilege to alter it. They are farther of opinion, that somewhat of his good Sense will suffer in this Transfusion, and much of the Beauty of his Thoughts will infallibly be lost, which appear with more Grace in their old Habit. Of this Opinion was that excellent Person, whom I mention'd, the late Earl of *Leicester*, who valu'd *Chaucer* as much as Mr. *Cowley* despis'd him. My Lord dissuaded me from this Attempt, (for I was thinking of it some Years before his Death) and his Authority prevail'd so far with me, as to defer my Undertaking while he liv'd, in deference to him : Yet my Reason was not convinc'd with what he urg'd against it. If the first End of a Writer be to be understood, then as his Language grows obsolete, his Thoughts must grow obscure, *multa renascentur quæ nunc cecidere; cadentque quæ nunc sunt in honore vocabula, si volet usus, quem penes arbitrum est et jus et norma loquendi.* When an ancient Word for its Sound and Significancy deserves to be reviv'd, I have that reasonable Veneration for Antiquity, to restore it. All beyond this is Superstition. Words are not like Landmarks, so sacred as never to be remov'd :

Customs are chang'd, and even Statutes are silently repeal'd, when the Reason ceases for which they were enacted. As for the other Part of the Argument, that his Thoughts will lose of their original Beauty, by the innovation of Words; in the first place, not only their Beauty, but their Being is lost, where they are no longer understood, which is the present Case. I grant, that something must be lost in all Transfusion, that is, in all Translations; but the Sense will remain, which would otherwise be lost, or at least be maim'd, when it is scarce intelligible; and that but to a few. How few are there who can read *Chaucer*, so as to understand him perfectly? And if imperfectly, then with less Profit, and no Pleasure. 'Tis not for the Use of some old *Saxon* Friends, that I have taken these Pains with him: Let them neglect my Version, because they have no need of it. I made it for their sakes who understand Sense and Poetry, as well as they; when that Poetry and Sense is put into Words which they understand. I will go farther, and dare to add, that what Beauties I lose in some Places, I give to others which had them not originally: But in this I may be partial to my self; let the Reader judge, and I submit to his Decision. Yet I think I have just Occasion to complain of them, who because they understand *Chaucer*, would deprive the greater part of their Countrymen of the same Advantage, and hoord him up, as Misers do their Grandam Gold, only to look on it themselves, and hinder others from making use of it. In sum, I seriously protest, that no Man ever had, or can have, a greater Veneration for *Chaucer*, than my self. I have translated some part of his Works, only that I might perpetrate his Memory, or at least refresh it, amongst my Countrymen. If I have alter'd him any where for the better, I must at the same time acknowledge, that I could have done nothing without him: *Facile est inventis addere*, is no great Commendation; and I am not so vain to think I have deserv'd a greater. I will conclude what I have to say of him singly, with this one Remark: A Lady of my Acquaintance, who keeps a kind of Correspondence with some Authors of the Fair Sex in *France*, has been inform'd by them, that *Mademoiselle de Scudery* who is as old as *Sibyl*, and inspir'd like her by the same God of Poetry, is at this time translating *Chaucer* into modern *French*. From which I gather, that he has been formerly translated into the old *Provencall*, (for,

how she should come to understand Old *English*, I know not.)
But the Matter of Fact being true, it makes me think, that there
is something in it like Fatality; that after certain Periods of Time,
the Fame and Memory of Great Wits should be renew'd, as
Chaucer is both in *France* and *England*. If this be wholly
Chance, 'tis extraordinary; and I dare not call it more, for fear
of being tax'd with Superstition.

    Boccace comes last to be consider'd, who living in the same
Age with *Chaucer*, had the same Genius, and follow'd the same
Studies: Both writ Novels, and each of them cultivated his
Mother-Tongue: But the greatest Resemblance of our two
Modern Authors being in their familiar Style, and pleasing way
of relating Comical Adventures, I may pass it over, because I
have translated nothing from *Boccace* of that Nature. In the
serious Part of Poetry, the Advantage is wholly on *Chaucer*'s
Side; for though the *Englishman* has borrow'd many Tales
from the *Italian*, yet it appears, that those of *Boccace* were not
generally of his own making, but taken from Authors of former
Ages, and by him only modell'd: So that what there was of Invention in either of them, may be judg'd equal. But *Chaucer*
has refin'd on *Boccace*, and has mended the Stories which he
has borrow'd, in his way of telling; though Prose allows more
Liberty of Thought, and the Expression is more easie, when un-
confin'd by Numbers. Our Countryman carries Weight, and
yet wins the Race at disadvantage. I desire not the Reader should
take my Word; and therefore I will set two of their Discourses
on the same Subject, in the same Light, for every Man to judge
betwixt them. I translated *Chaucer* first, and amongst the rest,
pitch'd on the Wife of *Bath*'s Tale; not daring, as I have said,
to adventure on her Prologue; because 'tis too licentious: There
Chaucer introduces an old Woman of mean Parentage, whom
a youthful Knight of Noble Blood was forc'd to marry, and
consequently loath'd her: The Crone being in bed with him on
the wedding Night, and finding his Aversion, endeavours to win
his Affection by Reason, and speaks a good Word for her self,
(as who could blame her?) in hope to mollifie the sullen Bridegroom. She takes her Topiques from the Benefits of Poverty, the
Advantages of old Age and Ugliness, the Vanity of Youth, and
the silly Pride of Ancestry and Titles without inherent Vertue,

which is the true Nobility. When I had clos'd *Chaucer*, I return'd
to *Ovid*, and translated some more of his Fables; and by this time
had so far forgotten the Wife of *Bath*'s Tale, that when I took up
Boccace, unawares I fell on the same Argument of preferring
Virtue to Nobility of Blood, and Titles, in the Story of *Sigis-
monda*; which I had certainly avoided for the Resemblance of
the two Discourses, if my Memory had not fail'd me. Let the
Reader weigh them both; and if he thinks me partial to *Chaucer*,
'tis in him to right *Boccace*.

I prefer in our Countryman, far above all his other Stories, the
Noble Poem of *Palamon* and *Arcite*, which is of the *Epique*
kind, and perhaps not much inferiour to the *Ilias* or the *Æneis*:
the Story is more pleasing than either of them, the Manners as
perfect, the Diction as poetical, the Learning as deep and
various; and the Disposition full as artful: only it includes a
greater length of time; as taking up seven years at least;
but *Aristotle* has left undecided the Duration of the Action;
which yet is easily reduc'd into the Compass of a year, by a Narration of what preceded the Return of *Palamon* to *Athens*. I had
thought for the Honour of our Nation, and more particularly
for his, whose Laurel, tho' unworthy, I have worn after him, that
this Story was of *English* Growth, and *Chaucer*'s own: But I
was undeceiv'd by *Boccace*; for casually looking on the End of
his seventh *Giornata*, I found *Dioneo* (under which name he
shadows himself) and *Fiametta* (who represents his Mistress, the
natural Daughter of *Robert* King of *Naples*) of whom these
Words are spoken. *Dioneo e Fiametta gran pezza cantarono
insieme d'Arcita, e di Palamone* : by which it appears that this
Story was written before the time of *Boccace*; but the Name of its
Author being wholly lost, *Chaucer* is now become an Original;
and I question not but the Poem has receiv'd many Beauties by
passing through his Noble Hands. Beside this Tale, there is another of his own Invention, after the manner of the *Provencalls*,
call'd *The Flowers and the Leaf*; with which I was so particularly
pleas'd, both for the Invention and the Moral; that I cannot
hinder my self from recommending it to the Reader. . . .

S O U R C E : Preface to *Fables Ancient and Modern* (1700).

William Blake

. . . The characters of Chaucer's Pilgrims are the characters which compose all ages and nations: as one age falls, another rises, different to mortal sight, but to immortals only the same; for we see the same characters repeated again and again, in animals, vegetables, minerals, and in men; nothing new occurs in identical existence; Accident ever varies, Substance can never suffer change nor decay.

Of Chaucer's characters, as described in his Canterbury Tales, some of the names or titles are altered by time, but the characters themselves for ever remain unaltered, and consequently they are the physiognomies or lineaments of universal human life, beyond which Nature never steps. Names alter, things never alter. I have known multitudes of those who would have been monks in the age of monkery, who as this deistical age are deists. As Newton numbered the stars, and as Linneus numbered the plants, so Chaucer numbered the classes of men.

The Painter has consequently varied the heads and forms of his personages into all Nature's varieties; the Horses he has also varied to accord to their Riders; the costume is correct according to authentic monuments.

The Knight and Squire with the Squire's Yeoman lead the procession, as Chaucer has also placed them first in his prologue. The Knight is a true Hero, a good, great, and wise man; his whole length portrait on horseback, as written by Chaucer, cannot be surpassed. He has spent his life in the field; has ever been a conqueror, and is that species of character which in every age stands as the guardian of man against the oppressor. His son is like him with the germ of perhaps greater perfection still, as he blends literature and the arts with his warlike studies. Their dress and their horses are of the first rate, without ostentation, and with all the true grandeur that unaffected simplicity when in high rank always displays. The Squire's Yeoman is also a great character, a man perfectly knowing in his profession:

And in his hand he bare a mighty bow.

Chaucer describes here a mighty man; one who in war is the worthy attendant on noble heroes.

The Prioress follows these with her female chaplain:

> Another Nonne also with her had she,
> That was her Chaplaine, and Priests three.

This Lady is described also as of the first rank, rich and honoured. She has certain peculiarities and little delicate affectations, not unbecoming in her, being accompanied with what is truly grand and really polite; her person and face Chaucer has described with minuteness; it is very elegant, and was the beauty of our ancestors, till after Elizabeth's time, when voluptuousness and folly began to be accounted beautiful.

Her companion and her three priests were no doubt all perfectly delineated in those parts of Chaucer's work which are now lost; we ought to suppose them suitable attendants on rank and fashion.

The Monk follows these with the Friar. The Painter has also grouped with these the Pardoner and the Sompnour and the Manciple, and has here also introduced one of the rich citizens of London: Characters likely to ride in company, all being above the common rank in life or attendants on those who were so.

For the Monk is described by Chaucer as a man of the first rank in society, noble, rich, and expensively attended; he is a leader of the age, with certain humorous accompaniments in his character, that do not degrade, but render him an object of dignified mirth, but also with other accompaniments not so respectable.

The Friar is a character also of a mixed kind:

> A friar there was, a wanton and a merry.

but in his office he is said to be a 'full solemn man': eloquent, amorous, witty, and satyrical; young, handsome, and rich; he is a complete rogue, with constitutional gaiety enough to make him a master of all the pleasures of the world.

> His neck was white as the flour de lis,
> Thereto strong he was as a champioun.

It is necessary here to speak of Chaucer's own character, that I may set certain mistaken critics right in their conception of the humour and fun that occurs on the journey. Chaucer is himself the great poetical observer of men, who in every age is born to record and eternize its acts. This he does as a master, as a father, and superior, who looks down on their little follies from the Emperor to the Miller; sometimes with severity, oftener with joke and sport.

Accordingly Chaucer has made his Monk a great tragedian, one who studied poetical art. So much so, that the generous Knight is, in the compassionate dictates of his soul, compelled to cry out :

> 'Ho,' quoth the Knyght, – 'good Sir, no more of this;
> That ye have said is right ynough I wis;
> And mokell more, for little heaviness
> Is right enough for much folk, as I guesse.
> I say, for me, it is a great disease,
> Whereas men have been in wealth and ease,
> To heare of their sudden fall, alas,
> And the contrary is joy and solas.'

The Monk's definition of tragedy in the proem to his tale is worth repeating :

> Tragedie is to tell a certain story,
> As old books us maken memory,
> Of hem that stood in great prosperity,
> And be fallen out of high degree,
> Into miserie, and ended wretchedly.

Though a man of luxury, pride and pleasure, he is a master of art and learning, though affecting to despise it. Those who can think that the proud Huntsman and Noble Housekeeper, Chaucer's Monk, is intended for a buffoon or a burlesque character, know little of Chaucer.

For the Host who follows this group, and holds the center of the cavalcade, is a first rate character, and his jokes are no trifles; they are always, though uttered with audacity, and equally free with the Lord and the Peasant, they are always substantially and weightily expressive of knowledge and experience; Henry Baillie, the keeper of the greatest Inn of the greatest City, for such was the Tabarde Inn in Southwark, near London: our Host was also a leader of the age.

By way of illustration, I instance Shakspeare's Witches in Macbeth. Those who dress them for the stage, consider them as wretched old women, and not as Shakspeare intended, the Goddesses of Destiny; this shews how Chaucer has been misunderstood in his sublime work. Shakspeare's Fairies also are the rulers of the vegetable world, and so are Chaucer's; let them be so considered, and then the poet will be understood, and not else.

But I have omitted to speak of a very prominent character, the Pardoner, the Age's Knave, who always commands and domineers over the high and low vulgar. This man is sent in every age for a rod and scourge, and for a blight, for a trial of men, to divide the classes of men; he is in the most holy sanctuary, and he is suffered by Providence for wise ends, and has also his great use, and his grand leading destiny.

His companion, the Sompnour, is also a Devil of the first magnitude, grand, terrific, rich and honoured in the rank of which he holds the destiny. The uses to Society are perhaps equal of the Devil and of the Angel, their sublimity, who can dispute.

> In daunger had he at his own gise,
> The young girls of his diocese,
> And he knew well their counsel, &c.

The principal figure in the next groupe is the Good Parson; an Apostle, a real Messenger of Heaven, sent in every age for its light and its warmth. This man is beloved and venerated by all, and neglected by all; He serves all, and is served by none; he is, according to Christ's definition, the greatest of his age. Yet he is a Poor Parson of a town. Read Chaucer's description of the Good Parson, and bow the head and the knee to him, who, in every age, sends us such a burning and a shining light. Search, O ye

rich and powerful, for these men and obey their counsel, then
shall the golden age return : But alas! you will not easily distinguish him from the Friar or the Pardoner; they, also,
are 'full solemn men', and their counsel you will continue to
follow.

I have placed by his side the Sergeant at Lawe, who appears
delighted to ride in his company, and between him and his
brother, the Plowman; as I wish men of Law would always ride
with them, and take their counsel, especially in all difficult points.
Chaucer's Lawyer is a character of great venerableness, a Judge,
and a real master of the jurisprudence of his age.

The Doctor of Physic is in this groupe, and the Franklin, the
voluptuous country gentleman, contrasted with the Physician,
and on his other hand, with two Citizens of London. Chaucer's
characters live age after age. Every age is a Canterbury Pilgrimage; we all pass on, each sustaining one or other of these
characters; nor can a child be born, who is not one of these
characters of Chaucer. The Doctor of Physic is described as the
first of his profession; perfect, learned, completely· Master and
Doctor in his art. Thus the reader will observe, that Chaucer
makes every one of his characters perfect in his kind; every one
is an Antique Statue; the image of a class, and not of an imperfect individual.

This groupe also would furnish substantial matter, on which
volumes might be written. The Franklin is one who keeps open
table, who is the genius of eating and drinking, the Bacchus; as
the Doctor of Physic is the Esculapius, the Host is the Silenus, the
Squire is the Apollo, the Miller is the Hercules, &c. Chaucer's
characters are a description of the eternal Principles that exist in
all ages. The Franklin is voluptuousness itself, most nobly pour-
trayed :

It snewed in his house of meat and drink.

The Plowman is simplicity itself, with wisdom and strength for
its stamina. Chaucer has divided the ancient character of Hercules between his Miller and his Plowman. Benevolence is the
plowman's great characteristic; he is thin with excessive labour,
and not with old age, as some have supposed :

He would thresh, and thereto dike and delve
For Christe's sake, for every poore wight,
Withouten hire, if it lay in his might.

Visions of these eternal principles or characters of human life
appear to poets, in all ages; the Grecian gods were the ancient
Cherubim of Phoenicia; but the Greeks, and since them the
Moderns, have neglected to subdue the gods of Priam. These gods
are visions of the eternal attributes, or divine names, which, when
erected into gods, become destructive to humanity. They ought
to be the servants, and not the masters of man, or of society. They
ought to be made to sacrifice to Man, and not man compelled to
sacrifice to them; for when separated from man or humanity,
who is Jesus the Saviour, the vine of eternity, they are thieves
and rebels, they are destroyers.

The Plowman of Chaucer is Hercules in his supreme eternal
state, divested of his spectrous shadow; which is the Miller, a
terrible fellow, such as exists in all times and places for the trial
of men, to astonish every neighbourhood with brutal strength and
courage, to get rich and powerful to curb the pride of Man.

The Reeve and the Manciple are two characters of the most
consummate worldly wisdom. The Shipman, or Sailor, is a
similar genius of Ulyssean art; but with the highest courage
superadded.

The Citizens and their Cook are each leaders of a class.
Chaucer has been somehow made to number four citizens, which
would make his whole company, himself included, thirty-one,
But he says there was but nine and twenty in his company:

Full nine and twenty in a company.

The Webbe, or Weaver, and the Tapiser, or Tapestry Weaver,
appear to me to be the same person; but this is only an opinion,
for full nine and twenty may signify one more or less. But I dare
say that Chaucer wrote 'A Webbe Dyer', that is, a Cloth Dyer:

A Webbe Dyer, and a Tapiser.

The Merchant cannot be one of the Three Citizens, as his dress is different, and his character is more marked, whereas Chaucer says of his rich citizens :

> All were yclothed in o liverie.

The characters of Women Chaucer has divided into two classes, the Lady Prioress and the Wife of Bath. Are not these leaders of the ages of men? The lady prioress, in some ages, predominates; and in some the wife of Bath, in whose character Chaucer has been equally minute and exact, because she is also a scourge and a blight. I shall say no more of her, nor expose what Chaucer has left hidden; let the young reader study what he has said of her : it is useful as a scare-crow. There are of such characters born too many for the peace of the world.

I come at length to the Clerk of Oxenford. This character varies from that of Chaucer, as the contemplative philosopher varies from the poetical genius. There are always these two classes of learned sages, the poetical and the philosophical. The painter has put them side by side, as if the youthful clerk had put himself under the tuition of the mature poet. Let the Philosopher always be the servant and scholar of inspiration and all will be happy . . .

S o u r c e : *A Descriptive Catalogue of Pictures, Poetical and Historical Inventions, Painted by William Blake* (1809).

William Hazlitt

. . . I shall take, as the subject of the present lecture, Chaucer and Spenser, two out of four of the greatest names in poetry, which this country has to boast. Both of them, however, were much indebted to the early poets of Italy, and may be considered as belonging, in a certain degree, to the same school. The freedom and copiousness with which our most original writers, in former periods, availed themselves of the productions of their predecessors, frequently transcribing whole passages, without scruple or acknowledgement, may appear contrary to the etiquette of modern literature, when the whole stock of poetical common-places has become public property, and no one is compelled to trade upon any particular author. But it is not so much a subject of wonder, at a time when to read and write was of itself an honorary distinction, when learning was almost as great a rarity as genius, and when in fact those who first transplanted the beauties of other languages into their own, might be considered as public benefactors, and the founders of a national literature. There are poets older than Chaucer, and in the interval between him and Spenser; but their genius was not such as to place them in any point of comparison with either of these celebrated men; and an inquiry into their particular merits or defects might seem rather to belong to the province of the antiquary, than be thought generally interesting to the lovers of poetry in the present day.

Chaucer (who has been very properly considered as the father of English poetry) preceded Spenser by two centuries. He is supposed to have been born in London, in the year 1328, during the reign of Edward III, and to have died in 1400, at the age of seventy-two. He received a learned education at one, or at both of the universities, and travelled early into Italy, where he became thoroughly imbued with the spirit and excellences of the great Italian poets and prose-writers, Dante, Petrarch, and Boccace; and is said to have had a personal interview with one of these, Petrarch. He was connected, by marriage, with the famous John of Gaunt, through whose interest he was introduced into several public employments. Chaucer was an active partisan, a religious reformer, and from the share he took in some disturbances, on one occasion, he was obliged to fly the country. On his return, he was imprisoned, and made his peace with government, as it is said, by a discovery of his associates. Fortitude does not appear, at any time, to have been the distinguishing virtue of poets. There is, however, an obvious similarity between the practical turn of Chaucer's mind and restless impatience of his character, and the tone of his writings. Yet it would be too much to attribute the one to the other as cause and effect: for Spenser, whose poetical temperament was as effeminate as Chaucer's was stern and masculine, was equally engaged in public affairs, and had mixed equally in the great world. So much does native disposition predominate over accidental circumstances, moulding them to its previous bent and purposes! For while Chaucer's intercourse with the busy world, and collision with the actual passions and conflicting interests of others, seemed to brace the sinews of his understanding, and gave to his writings the air of a man who describes persons and things that he had known and been intimately concerned in; the same opportunities, operating on a differently constituted frame, only served to alienate Spenser's mind the more from the 'close-pent up' scenes of ordinary life, and to make him 'rive their concealing continents', to give himself up to the unrestrained indulgence of 'flowery tenderness'.

It is not possible for any two writers to be more opposite in this respect. Spenser delighted in luxurious enjoyment; Chaucer, in severe activity of mind. As Spenser was the most romantic and visionary, Chaucer was the most practical of all the great poets, the most a man of business and the world. His poetry reads like history. Everything has a downright reality; at least in the relator's mind. A simile, or a sentiment, is as if it were given in upon evidence. Thus he describes Cressid's first avowal of her love:

> And as the new abashed nightingale,
> That stinteth first when she beginneth sing,
> When that she heareth any herde's tale,
> Or in the hedges any wight stirring,
> And after, sicker, doth her voice outring;

Right so Cresseide, when that her dread stent,
Open'd her heart, and told him her intent.

This is so true and natural, and beautifully simple, that the two
things seem identified with each other. Again, it is said in the
Knight's Tale –

Thus passeth yere by yere, and day by day,
Till it felle ones in a morwe of May,
That Emelie that fayrer was to sene
Than is the lilie upon his stalke grene;
And fresher than the May with floures newe,
For with the rose-colour strof hire hewe :
I n'ot which was the finer of hem two.

This scrupulousness about the literal preference, as if some question of matter of fact was at issue, is remarkable. I might mention that other, where he compares the meeting between
Palamon and Arcite to a hunter waiting for a lion in a gap :

That stondeth at a gap with a spere,
Whan hunted is the lion or the bere,
And hereth him come rushing in the greves,
And breking bothe the boughes and the leves –

or that still finer one of Constance, when she is condemned to
death :

Have ye not seen somtime a pale face
(Among a prees) of him that hath been lad
Toward his deth, wheras he geteth no grace,
And swiche a colour in his face hath had,
Men mighten know him that was so bestad,
Amonges all the faces in that route;
So stant Custance, and loketh hire aboute.

The beauty, the pathos here does not seem to be of the poet's
seeking, but a part of the necessary texture of the fable. He speaks
of what he wishes to describe with the accuracy, the discrimination of one who relates what has happened to himself, or has had

the best information from those who have been eye-witnesses of it. The strokes of his pencil always tell. He dwells only on the essential, on that which would be interesting to the persons really concerned : yet as he never omits any material circumstance, he is prolix from the number of points on which he touches, without being diffuse on any one; and is sometimes tedious from the fidelity with which he adheres to his subject, as other writers are from the frequency of their digressions from it. The chain of his story is composed of a number of fine links, closely connected together, and rivetted by a single blow. There is an instance of the minuteness which he introduces into his most serious descriptions in his account of Palamon when left alone in his cell :

> Swiche sorrow he maketh that the grete tour
> Resouned of his yelling and clamour :
> The pure fetters on his shinnes grete
> Were of his bitter salte teres wete.

The mention of this last circumstance looks like a part of the instructions he had to follow, which he had no discretionary power to leave out or introduce at pleasure. He is contented to find grace and beauty in truth. He exhibits for the most part the naked object, with little drapery thrown over it. His metaphors, which are few, are not for ornament, but use, and as like as possible to the things themselves. He does not affect to show his power over the reader's mind, but the power which his subject has over his own. The readers of Chaucer's poetry feel more nearly what the persons he describes must have felt, than perhaps those of any other poet. His sentiments are not voluntary effusions of the poet's fancy, but founded on the natural impulses and habitual prejudices of the characters he has to represent. There is an inveteracy of purpose, a sincerity of feeling, which never relaxes or grows vapid, in whatever they do or say. There is no artificial, pompous display, but a strict parsimony of the poet's materials, like the rude simplicity of the age in which he lived. His poetry resembles the root just springing from the ground, rather than the full-blown flower. His muse is no 'babbling gossip of the air', fluent and redundant; but, like a stammerer, or a dumb person, that has just found the use of speech, crowds many things to-

gether with eager haste, with anxious pauses, and fond repeti-
tions to prevent mistake. His words point as an index to the objects, like the eye or finger. There were none of the commonplaces of poetic diction in our author's time, no reflected lights
of fancy, no borrowed roseate tints; he was obliged to inspect
things for himself, to look narrowly, and almost to handle the
object, as in the obscurity of morning we partly see and partly
grope our way; so that his descriptions have a sort of tangible
character belonging to them, and produce the effect of
sculpture on the mind. Chaucer had an equal eye for truth of
nature and discrimination of character; and his interest in what
he saw gave new distinctness and force to his power of observation. The picturesque and the dramatic are in him closely blended
together, and hardly distinguishable; for he principally describes external appearances as indicating character, as symbols of
internal sentiment. There is a meaning in what he sees; and it is
this which catches his eye by sympathy. Thus the costume and
dress of the Canterbury Pilgrims – of the Knight – the Squire –
the Oxford Scholar – the Gap-toothed Wife of Bath, and the rest
– speak for themselves . . .

The Serjeant at Law is the same identical individual as
Lawyer Dowling in *Tom Jones*, who wished to divide himself
into a hundred pieces, to be in a hundred places at once.

> No wher so besy a man as he ther n'as,
> And yet he semed besier than he was.

The Frankelein, in 'whose hous it snewed of mete and drinke';
the Shipman, 'who rode upon a rouncie, as he couthe'; the Doc-
tour of Phisike, 'whose studie was but litel of the Bible'; the Wif
of Bath, in

> All whose parish ther was non,
> That to the offring before hire shulde gon,
> And if ther did, certain so wroth was she,
> That she was out of alle charitee;

the poure Persone of a toun, 'whose parish was wide, and houses
fer asonder'; the Miller, and the Reve, 'a slendre colerike man' –

are all of the same stamp. They are every one samples of a kind; abstract definitions of a species. Chaucer, it has been said, numbered the classes of men, as Linnaeus numbered the plants. Most of them remain to this day : others that are obsolete, and may well be dispensed with, still live in his descriptions of them. Such is the Sompnoure :

> A Sompnoure was ther with us in that place,
> That hadde a fire-red cherubinnes face,
> For sausefleme he was, with eyen narwe,
> As hote he was, and likerous as a sparwe,
> With scalled browes blake, and pilled berd :
> Of his visage children were sore aferd.
> Ther n'as quicksilver, litarge, ne brimston,
> Boras, ceruse, ne oile of tartre non,
> Ne oinement that wolde clense or bite,
> That him might helpen of his whelkes white,
> Ne of the knobbes sitting on his chekes.
> Wel loved he garlike, onions, and lekes,
> And for to drinke strong win as rede as blood.
> Than wolde he speke, and crie as he were wood.
> And whan that he wel dronken had the win,
> Than wold he speken no word but Latin.
> A fewe termes coude he, two or three,
> That he had lerned out of som decree;
> No wonder is, he heard it all the day. –
>   In danger hadde he at his owen gise
> The yonge girles of the diocise,
> And knew hir conseil, and was of hir rede.
> A gerlond hadde he sette upon his hede
> As gret as it were for an alestake :
> A bokeler hadde he made him of a cake.
> With him ther rode a gentil Pardonere –
> That hadde a vois as smale as hath a gote.

It would be a curious speculation (at least for those who think that the characters of men never change, though manners, opinions, and institutions may) to know what has become of this character of the Sompnoure in the present day; whether or not

it has any technical representative in existing professions; into
what channels and conduits it has withdrawn itself, where it
lurks unseen in cunning obscurity, or else shows its face boldly,
pampered into all the insolence of office, in some other shape, as it
it deterred or encouraged by circumstances. *Chaucer's characters
modernized*, upon this principle of historic derivation, would be
an useful addition to our knowledge of human nature. But who
is there to undertake it?

The descriptions of the equipage, and accoutrements of the
two kings of Thrace and Inde, in the Knight's Tale, are as
striking and grand, as the others are lively and natural:

> Ther maist thou se coming with Palamon
> Licurge himself, the grete king of Trace:
> Blake was his berd, and manly was his face.
> The cercles of his eyen in his hed
> They gloweden betwixen yelwe and red,
> And like a griffon loked he about ...
>   With Arcita, in stories as men find,
> The grete Emetrius, the king of Inde,
> Upon a stede bay, trapped in stele,
> Covered with cloth of gold diapred wele,
> Came riding like the god of armes Mars ...

What a deal of terrible beauty there is contained in this description! The imagination of a poet brings such objects before
us, as when we look at wild beasts in a menagerie; their claws
are pared, their eyes glitter like harmless lightning; but we gaze
at them with a pleasing awe, clothed in beauty, formidable in the
sense of abstract power.

Chaucer's descriptions of natural scenery possess the same sort
of characteristic excellence, or what might be termed *gusto*. They
have a local truth and freshness, which gives the very feeling of
the air, the coolness or moisture of the ground. Inanimate objects are thus made to have a fellow-feeling in the interest of the
story; and render back the sentiment of the speaker's mind. One
of the finest parts of Chaucer is of this mixed kind. It is the beginning of the *Flower and the Leaf*, where he describes the
delight of that young beauty, shrouded in her bower, and listen-

ing, in the morning of the year, to the singing of the nightingale; while her joy rises with the rising song, and gushes out afresh at every pause, and is borne along with the full tide of pleasure, and still increases, and repeats, and prolongs itself, and knows no ebb. The coolness of the arbour, its retirement, the early time of the day, the sudden starting up of the birds in the neighbouring bushes, the eager delight with which they devour and rend the opening buds and flowers, are expressed with a truth and feeling, which make the whole appear like the recollection of an actual scene. . . . There is here no affected rapture, no flowery sentiment: the whole is an ebullition of natural delight 'welling out of the heart', like water from a crystal spring. Nature is the soul of art: there is a strength as well as a simplicity in the imagination that reposes entirely on nature, that nothing else can supply. It was the same trust in nature, and reliance on his subject, which enabled Chaucer to describe the grief and patience of Griselda; the faith of Constance; and the heroic perseverance of the little child, who, going to school through the streets of Jewry,

Oh *Alma Redemptoris mater,* loudly sung,

and who after his death still triumphed in his song. Chaucer has more of this deep, internal, sustained sentiment, than any other writer, except Boccaccio. In depth of simple pathos, and intensity of conception, never swerving from his subject, I think no other writer comes near him, not even the Greek tragedians. I wish to be allowed to give one or two instances of what I mean. I will take the following from the Knight's Tale. The distress of Arcite, in consequence of his banishment from his love, is thus described:

Whan that Arcite to Thebes comen was,
Ful oft a day he swelt and said Alas,
For sene his lady shall he never mo.
And shortly to concluden all his wo,
So mochel sorwe hadde never creature,
That is or shall be, while the world may dure.
His slepe, his mete, his drinke is him byraft.

That lene he wex, and drie as is a shaft.
His eyen holwe, and grisly to behold,
His hewe salwe, and pale as ashen cold,
And solitary he was, and ever alone,
And wailing all the night, making his mone.
And if he herde song or instrument,
Than wold he wepe, he mighte not be stent.
So feble were his spirites, and so low,
And changed so, that no man coude know
His speche ne his vois, though men it herd.

This picture of the sinking of the heart, of the wasting away of the body and mind, of the gradual failure of all the faculties under the contagion of a rankling sorrow, cannot be surpassed. Of the same kind is his farewell to his mistress, after he has gained her hand and lost his life in the combat:

'Alas the wo! alas the peines stronge,
That I for you have suffered, and so longe!
Alas the deth! alas min Emilie!
Alas departing of our compagnie;
Alas min hertes quene! alas my wif!
Min hertes ladie, ender of my lif!
What is this world? what axen men to have?
Now with his love, now in his colde grave
Alone withouten any compagnie.'

The death of Arcite is the more affecting, as it comes after triumph and victory, after the pomp of sacrifice, the solemnities of prayer, the celebration of the gorgeous rites of chivalry. The descriptions of the three temples of Mars, of Venus, and Diana, of the ornaments and ceremonies used in each, with the reception given to the offerings of the lovers, have a beauty and grandeur, much of which is lost in Dryden's version. For instance, such lines as the following are not rendered with their true feeling:

Why shulde I not as well eke tell you all
The purtreiture that was upon the wall

> Within the temple of mighty Mars the rede –
> That highte the gret temple of Mars in Trace
> In thilke colde and frosty region,
> Ther as Mars hath his sovereine mansion.
> First on the wall was peinted a forest,
> In which ther wonneth neyther man ne best,
> With knotty knarry barrein trees old
> Of stubbes sharpe and hidous to behold;
> In which ther ran a romble and a swough,
> As though a storme shuld bresten every bough.

And again, among innumerable terrific images of death and slaughter painted on the wall, is this one :.

> The statue of Mars upon a carte stood
> Armed, and looked grim as he were wood.
> A wolf ther stood beforne him at his fete
> With eyen red, and of a man he ete.

The story of Griselda is in Boccaccio; but the Clerk of Oxenforde, who tells it, professes to have learned it from Petrarch. This story has gone all over Europe, and has passed into a proverb. In spite of the barbarity of the circumstances, which are abominable, the sentiment remains unimpaired and unalterable. It is of that kind, 'that heaves no sigh, that sheds no tear'; but it hangs upon the beatings of the heart; it is a part of the very being; it is as inseparable from it as the breath we draw. It is still and calm as the face of death. Nothing can touch it in its ethereal purity : tender as the yielding flower, it is fixed as the marble firmament. The only remonstrance she makes, the only complaint she utters against all the ill-treatment she receives, is that single line where, when turned back naked to her father's house, she says,

> Let me not like a worm go by the way.

The story of the little child slain in Jewry (which is told by the Prioress, and worthy to be told by her who was 'all conscience and tender heart') is not less touching than that of Griselda. It is simple and heroic to the last degree. The poetry of Chaucer has a religious sanctity about it, connected with the manners and superstitions of the age. It has all the spirit of martyrdom.

It has also all the extravagance and the utmost licentiousness of comic humour, equally arising out of the manners of the time. In this too Chaucer resembled Boccaccio that he excelled in both styles, and could pass at will 'from grave to gay, from lively to severe'; but he never confounded the two styles together (except from that involuntary and unconscious mixture of the pathetic and humorous, which is almost always to be found in nature), and was exclusively taken up with what he set about, whether it was jest or earnest. The Wife of Bath's Prologue (which Pope has very admirably modernized) is, perhaps, unequalled as a comic story. The *Cock and the Fox* is also excellent for lively strokes of character and satire. *January and May* is not so good as some of the others. Chaucer's versification, considering the time at which he wrote, and that versification is a thing in a great degree mechanical, is not one of his least merits. It has considerable strength and harmony, and its apparent deficiency in the latter respect arises chiefly from the alterations which have since taken place in the pronunciation or mode of accenting the words of the language. The best general rule for reading him is to pronounce the final *e*, as in reading Italian.

It was observed in the last Lecture that painting describes what the object is in itself, poetry what it implies or suggests. Chaucer's poetry is not, in general, the best confirmation of the truth of this distinction, for his poetry is more picturesque and historical than almost any other. But there is one instance in point which I cannot help giving in this place. It is the story of the three thieves who go in search of Death to kill him, and who meeting with him, are entangled in their fate by his words, without knowing him. In the printed catalogue to Mr. West's (in some respects very admirable) picture of Death on the Pale Horse, it is observed, that 'In poetry the same effect is produced by a few abrupt and rapid gleams of description, touching, as it were with fire, the features and edges of a general mass of awful obscurity; but in painting, such indistinctness would be a defect, and imply that the artist wanted the power to portray the conceptions of his fancy. Mr. West was of opinion that to delineate a physical form, which in its moral impression would approximate to that of the visionary Death of Milton, it was necessary to endow it, if possible, with the appearance of super-human strength and energy. He has therefore exerted the utmost force and perspicuity of his pencil on the central figure.' – One might suppose from this, that the way to represent a shadow was to make it as substantial as possible. Oh, no! Painting has its prerogatives (and high ones they are), but they lie in representing the visible, not the invisible. The moral attributes of Death are powers and effects of an infinitely wide and general description, which no individual or physical form can possibly represent, but by a courtesy of speech, or by a distant analogy. The moral impression of Death is essentially visionary; its reality is in the mind's eye. Words are here the only *things*; and things, physical forms, the mere mockeries of the understanding. The less definite, the less bodily the conception, the more vast, unformed, and unsubstantial, the nearer does it approach to some resemblance of that omnipresent, lasting, universal, irresistible principle, which everywhere, and at some time or other, exerts its power over all things. Death is a mighty abstraction, like Night, or Space, or Time. He is an ugly customer, who will not be invited to supper, or to sit for his picture. He is with us and about us, but we do not see him. He stalks on before us, and we do not mind him: he follows us close behind, and we do not turn to look back at him. We do not see him making faces at us in our life-time, nor perceive him afterwards sitting in mock-majesty, a twin-skeleton, beside us, tickling our bare ribs, and staring into our hollow eye-balls! Chaucer knew this. He makes three riotous companions go in search of Death to kill him, they meet with an old man whom they reproach with his age, and ask why he does not die, to which he answers thus:

> Ne Deth, alas! ne will not han my lif.
> Thus walke I like a restless caitiff,
> And on the ground, which is my modres gate,
> I knocke with my staf, erlich and late,
> And say to hire, 'Leve mother, let me in.
> Lo, how I vanish, flesh and blood and skin,
> Alas! when shall my bones ben at reste?
> Mother, with you wolde I changen my cheste,

That in my chambre longe time hath be,
Ye, for an heren cloute to wrap in me.'
But yet to me she will not don that grace,
For which ful pale and welked is my face.

They then ask the old man where they shall find out Death
to kill him, and he sends them on an errand which ends in the
death of all three. We hear no more of him, but it is Death that
they have encountered! . . .

SOURCE: 'On Chaucer and Spenser', Lecture 2 in *Lectures
on the English Poets* (1818).

Matthew Arnold

. . . Once more I return to the early poetry of France, with which our own poetry, in its origins, is indissolubly connected. In the twelfth and thirteenth centuries, that seed-time of all modern language and literature, the poetry of France had a clear predominance in Europe. Of the two divisions of that poetry, its productions in the *langue d'oil* and its productions in the *langue d'oc*, the poetry of the *langue d'oc*, of southern France, of the troubadours, is of importance because of its effect on Italian literature; – the first literature of modern Europe to strike the true and grand note, and to bring forth, as in Dante and Petrarch it brought forth, classics. But the predominance of French poetry in Europe, during the twelfth and thirteenth centuries, is due to its poetry of the *langue d'oil*, the poetry of northern France and of the tongue which is now the French language. In the twelfth century the bloom of this romance-poetry was earlier and stronger in England, at the court of our Anglo-Norman kings, than in France itself. But it was a bloom of French poetry; and as our native poetry formed itself, it formed itself out of this. The romance-poems which took possession of the heart and imagination of Europe in the twelfth and thirteenth centuries are French; 'they are', as Southey justly says, 'the pride of French literature, nor have we anything which can be placed in competition with them.' Themes were supplied from all quarters; but the romance-setting which was common to them all, and which gained the ear of Europe, was French. This constituted for the French poetry, literature, and language, at the height of the Middle Age, an unchallenged predominance. The Italian Brunetto Latini, the master of Dante, wrote his *Treasure* in French because, he says, 'la parleure en est plus délitable et plus commune à toutes gens.' In the same century, the thirteenth, the French romance-writer, Christian of Troyes, formulates the claims, in chivalry and letters, of France, his native country, as follows:

Or vous ert par ce livre apris,
Que Gresse ot de chevalerie
Le premier los et de clergie;
Puis vint chevalerie à Rome,
Et de la clergie la some,
Qui ore est en France venue.
Diex doinst qu'ele i soit retenue,
Et que li lius li abelisse
Tant que de France n'isse
L'onor qui s'i est arestée!

'Now by this book you will learn that first Greece had the renown for chivalry and letters: then chivalry and the primacy in letters passed to Rome, and now it is come to France. God grant it may be kept there; and that the place may please it so well, that the honour which has come to make stay in France may never depart thence!'

Yet it is now all gone, this French romance-poetry, of which the weight of substance and the power of style are not unfairly represented by this extract from Christian of Troyes. Only by means of the historic estimate can we persuade ourselves now to think that any of it is of poetical importance.

But in the fourteenth century there comes an Englishman nourished on this poetry, taught his trade by this poetry, getting words, rhyme, metre from this poetry; for even of that stanza which the Italians used, and which Chaucer derived immediately from the Italians, the basis and suggestion was probably given in France. Chaucer (I have already named him) fascinated his contemporaries, but so too did Christian of Troyes and Wolfram of Eschenbach. Chaucer's power of fascination, however, is enduring; his poetical importance does not need the assistance of the historic estimate; it is real. He is a genuine source of joy and strength, which is flowing still for us and will flow always. He will be read, as time goes on, far more generally than he is read now. His language is a cause of difficulty for us; but so also, and I think in quite as great a degree, is the language of Burns. In Chaucer's case, as in that of Burns, it is a difficulty to be unhesitatingly accepted and overcome.

If we ask ourselves wherein consists the immense superiority of Chaucer's poetry over the romance-poetry – why it is that in passing from this to Chaucer we suddenly feel ourselves to be in another world, we shall find that his superiority is both in the substance of his poetry and in the style of his poetry. His superiority in substance is given by his large, free, simple, clear yet kindly view of human life – so unlike the total want, in the romance-poets, of all intelligent command of it. Chaucer has not their helplessness; he has gained the power to survey the world from a central, a truly human point of view. We have only to call to mind the Prologue to *The Canterbury Tales*. The right comment upon it is Dryden's: 'It is sufficient to say, according to the proverb, that *here is God's plenty*.' And again: 'He is a perpetual fountain of good sense.' It is by a large, free, sound representation of things, that poetry, this high criticism of life, has truth of substance; and Chaucer's poetry has truth of substance.

Of his style and manner, if we think first of the romance-poetry and then of Chaucer's divine liquidness of diction, his divine fluidity of movement, it is difficult to speak temperately. They are irresistible, and justify all the rapture with which his successors speak of his 'gold dew-drops of speech'. Johnson misses the point entirely when he finds fault with Dryden for ascribing to Chaucer the first refinement of our numbers, and says that Gower also can show smooth numbers and easy rhymes. The refinement of our numbers means something far more than this. A nation may have versifiers with smooth numbers and easy rhymes, and yet may have no real poetry at all. Chaucer is the father of our splendid English poetry; he is our 'well of English undefiled', because by the lovely charm of his diction, the lovely charm of his movement, he makes an epoch and founds a tradition. In Spenser, Shakespeare, Milton, Keats, we can follow the tradition of the liquid diction, the fluid movement, of Chaucer; at one time it is his liquid diction of which in these poets we feel the virtue, and at another time it is his fluid movement. And the virtue is irresistible.

Bounded as is my space, I must yet find room for an example of Chaucer's virtue, as I have given examples to show the virtue of the great classics. I feel disposed to say that a single line is enough to show the charm of Chaucer's verse; that merely one line like this –

O martyr souded* in virginitee!

has a virtue of manner and movement such as we shall not find
in all the verse of romance-poetry; but this is saying nothing. The
virtue is such as we shall not find, perhaps, in all English poetry,
outside the poets whom I have named as the special inheritors of
Chaucer's tradition. A single line, however, is too little if we
have not the strain of Chaucer's verse well in our memory; let us
take a stanza. It is from *The Prioress's Tale*, the story of the
Christian child murdered in a Jewry:

> My throte is cut unto my nekke-bone
> Saidè this child, and as by way of kinde
> I should have deyd, yea, longè time agone;
> But Jesu Christ, as ye in bookès finde,
> Will that his glory last and be in minde,
> And for the worship of his mother dere
> Yet may I sing *O Alma* loud and clere.

Wordsworth has modernised this Tale, and to feel how delicate
and evanescent is the charm of verse, we have only to read Wordsworth's first three lines of this stanza after Chaucer's –

> My throat is cut unto the bone, I trow,
> Said this young child, and by the law of kind
> I should have died, yea, many hours ago.

The charm is departed. It is often said that the power of liquidness and fluidity in Chaucer's verse was dependent upon a free, a
licentious dealing with language, such as is now impossible; upon
a liberty, such as Burns too enjoyed, of making words like *neck*,
bird, into a dissyllable by adding to them, and words like *cause
rhyme*, into a dissyllable by sounding the *e* mute. It is true that
Chaucer's fluidity is conjoined with this liberty, and is admirably
served by it; but we ought not to say that it was dependent upon
it. It was dependent upon his talent. Other poets with a like

* The French *soudé*: soldered, fixed fast.

liberty do not attain to the fluidity of Chaucer; Burns himself does not attain to it. Poets, again, who have a talent akin to Chaucer's, such as Shakespeare or Keats, have known how to attain to his fluidity without the like liberty.

And yet Chaucer is not one of the great classics. His poetry transcends and effaces, easily and without effort, all the romance-poetry of Catholic Christendom; it transcends and effaces all the English poetry contemporary with it; it transcends and effaces all the English poetry subsequent to it down to the age of Elizabeth. Of such avail is poetic truth of substance, in its natural and necessary union with poetic truth of style. And yet, I say, Chaucer is not one of the great classics. He has not their accent. What is wanting to him is suggested by the mere mention of the name of the first great classic of Christendom, the immortal poet who died eighty years before Chaucer – Dante. The accent of such verse as

In la sua volontade è nostra pace . . .

is altogether beyond Chaucer's reach; we praise him, but we feel that this accent is out of the question for him. It may be said that it was necessarily out of the reach of any poet in the England of that stage of growth. Possibly; but we are to adopt a real, not a historic, estimate of poetry. However we may account for its absence, something is wanting, then, to the poetry of Chaucer, which poetry must have before it can be placed in the glorious class of the best. And there is no doubt what that something is. It is the σπουδαιότης, the high and excellent seriousness, which Aristotle assigns as one of the grand virtues of poetry. The substance of Chaucer's poetry, his view of things and his criticism of life, has largeness, freedom, shrewdness, benignity; but it has not this high seriousness. Homer's criticism of life has it, Dante's has it, Shakespeare's has it. It is this chiefly which gives to our spirits what they can rest upon; and with the increasing demands of our modern ages upon poetry, this virtue of giving us what we can rest upon will be more and more highly esteemed. A voice from the slums of Paris, fifty or sixty years after Chaucer, the voice of poor Villon out of his life of riot and crime, has at its happy moments (as, for instance, in the last stanza of *La Belle*

*Heaulmière**) more of this important poetic virtue of seriousness than all the productions of Chaucer. But its apparition in
Villon, and in men like Villon, is fitful; the greatness of the
great poets, the power of their criticism of life, is that their virtue
is sustained.

To our praise, therefore, of Chaucer as a poet there must be
this limitation; he lacks the high seriousness of the great classics,
and therewith an important part of their virtue. Still, the main
fact for us to bear in mind about Chaucer is his sterling value
according to that real estimate which we firmly adopt for all
poets. He has poetic truth of substance, though he has not high
poetic seriousness, and corresponding to his truth of substance
he has an exquisite virtue of style and manner. With him is born
our real poetry. . . .

S o u r c e : 'The Study of Poetry' (1880), reprinted in *Essays
in Criticism, Second Series* (1888).

* The name *Heaulmière* is said to be derived from a head-dress (helm) worn as a
mark by courtesans. In Villon's ballad, a poor old creature of this class laments
her days of youth and beauty. The last stanza of the ballad runs thus:

> Ainsi le bon temps regretons
> Entre nous, pauvres vieilles sottes.
> Assises bas, à croppetons,
> Tout en ung tas comme pelottes;
> A petit feu de chenevottes
> Tost allumées, tost estainctes.
> Et jadis fusmes si mignottes!
> Ainsi en prend à maintz et maintes.

'Thus amongst ourselves we regret the good time, poor silly old things, low-seated
on our heels, all in a heap like so many balls, by a little fire of hemp-stalks, soon
lighted, soon spent. And once we were such darlings! So fares it with many and
many a one.'

PART TWO

Twentieth-century Criticism

G. L. Kittredge

CHAUCER'S DISCUSSION
OF MARRIAGE (1912)

We are prone to read and study the *Canterbury Tales* as if each
tale were an isolated unit and to pay scant attention to what we
call the connecting links – those bits of lively narrative and dialogue that bind the whole together. Yet Chaucer's plan is clear
enough. Structurally regarded, the *Canterbury Tales* is a kind of
Human Comedy. From this point of view, the Pilgrims are the
dramatis personae, and their stories are only speeches that are
somewhat longer than common, entertaining in and for themselves (to be sure), but primarily significant, in each case, because they illustrate the speaker's character and opinions, or
show the relations of the travellers to one another in the pro-
gressive action of the Pilgrimage. In other words, we ought not
merely to consider the general appropriateness of each tale to
the character of the teller : we should also inquire whether the
tale is not determined, to some extent, by the circumstances – by
the situation at the moment, by something that another Pilgrim
has said or done, by the turn of a discussion already under way.

Now and then, to be sure, this point is too obvious to be over-
looked, as in the squabble between the Summoner and the Friar
and that between the Reeve and the Miller, in the Shipman's
intervening to check the Parson, and in the way in which the
gentles head off the Pardoner when he is about to tell a ribald
anecdote. But, despite these unescapable instances, the general
principle is too often blinked or ignored. Yet its temperate application should clear up a number of things which are
traditionally regarded as difficulties, or as examples of heedless-
ness on Chaucer's part.

Without attempting to deny or abridge the right to study and
criticize each tale in and for itself – as legend, romance,
exemplum, fabliau, or what-not – and without extenuating the

results that this method has achieved, let us consider certain tales in their relation to Chaucer's structural plan – with reference, that is to say, to the Pilgrims who tell them and to the Pilgrimage to which their telling is incidental. We may begin with the story of Griselda.

This is a plain and straightforward piece of edification, and nobody has ever questioned its appropriateness to the Clerk, who, as he says himself, has traveled in Italy and had heard it from the lips of the laureate Petrarch. The Clerk's 'speech', according to the General Prologue, was 'sowning in moral vertu', so that this story is precisely the kind of thing which we should expect from his lips. True, we moderns sometimes feel shocked or offended at what we style the immorality of Griselda's unvarying submission. But this feeling is no ground of objection to the appropriateness of the tale to the Clerk. The Middle Ages delighted (as children still delight) in stories that exemplify a single human quality, like valor, or tyranny, or fortitude. In such cases, the settled rule (for which neither Chaucer not the Clerk was responsible) was to show to what lengths this quality may conceivably go. Hence, in tales of this kind, there can be no question of conflict of duties, no problem as to the point at which excess of goodness becomes evil. It is, then, absurd to censure a fourteenth-century Clerk for telling (or Chaucer for making him tell) a story which exemplifies in this hyperbolical way the virtue of fortitude under affliction. Whether Griselda could have put an end to her woes, or ought to have put an end to them, by refusing to obey her husband's commands is *parum ad rem*. We are to look at her trials as inevitable, and to pity her accordingly, and wonder at her endurance. If we refuse to accept the tale in this spirit, we are ourselves the losers. We miss the pathos because we are aridly intent on discussing an ethical question that has no status in this particular court, however pertinent it may be in the general forum of morals.

Furthermore, in thus focusing attention on the morality or immorality of Griselda's submissiveness, we overlook what the Clerk takes pains to make as clear as possible – the real lesson that the story is meant to convey – and thus we do grave injustice to that austere but amiable moralist. The Clerk, a student of 'Aristotle and his philosophye', knew as well as any of us that every virtue may be conceived as a mean between two extremes.

Even the Canon's Yeoman, an ignorant man, was aware of this principle:

> That that is overdoon, it wol nat preve
> Aright, as clerkes seyn, – it is a vyce.   (G. 645–6)

Chaucer had too firm a grasp on his *dramatis personae* to allow the Clerk to leave the true purport of his parable undefined. 'This story is not told,' says the Clerk in substance, 'to exhort wives to imitate Griselda's humility, for *that* would be beyond the capacity of human nature. It is told in order that every man or woman, in whatever condition of life, may learn fortitude in adversity. For, since a woman once exhibited such endurance under trials inflicted on her by a mortal man, a fortiori ought we to accept patiently whatever tribulation God may send us. For God is not like Griselda's husband. He does not wantonly experiment with us, out of inhuman scientific curiosity. God *tests* us, as it is reasonable that our Maker should test his handiwork, but he does not *tempt* us. He allows us to be beaten with sharp scourges of adversity, not, like the Marquis Walter, to see if we can stand it, for he knoweth our frame, he remembereth that we are dust: all *his* affliction is for our better grace. Let us live, therefore, in manly endurance of the visitations of Providence.'

And then, at verse 1163, comes that matchless passage in which the Clerk (having explained the *universal* application of his parable – having provided with scrupulous care against any misinterpretation of its serious purport) turns with gravely satiric courtesy to the Wife of Bath and makes the *particular* application of the story to her 'life' and 'all her sect'.

Here one may appreciate the vital importance of considering the *Canterbury Tales* as a connected Human Comedy – of taking into account the Pilgrims in their relations to one another in the great drama to which the several narratives are structurally incidental. For it is precisely at this point that Professor Skeat notes a difficulty. 'From this point to the end', he remarks, 'is the work of a later period, and in Chaucer's best manner, though unsuited *to the coy Clerk.*' This is as much as to say that, in the remaining stanzas of the Clerk's Tale and in the Envoy, Chaucer has violated dramatic propriety. And, indeed, many readers have detected in these concluding portions Chaucer's own personal revulsion of feeling against the tale that he had suffered the Clerk to tell.

Now the supposed difficulty vanishes as soon as we study vss. 1163–1212, not as an isolated phenomenon, but in their relation to the great drama of the Canterbury Pilgrimage. It disappears when we consider the lines in what we may call their dramatic context, that is (to be specific), when we inquire what there was in the situation to prompt the Clerk, after emphasizing the serious and universal moral of Griselda's story, to give his tale a special and peculiar application by annexing an ironical tribute to the Wife of Bath, her life, her 'sect', and her principles. To answer this question we must go back to the Wife of Bath's Prologue.

The Wife of Bath's Prologue begins a group in the *Canterbury Tales*, or, as one may say, a new act in the drama. It is not connected with anything that precedes. Let us trace the action from this point down to the moment when the Clerk turns upon the Wife with his satirical compliments.

The Wife had expounded her views at great length and with all imaginable zest. Virginity, which the Church glorifies, is not required of us. Our bodies are given us to use. Let saints be continent if they will. She has no wish to emulate them. Nor does she accept the doctrine that a widow or a widower must not marry again. Where is bigamy forbidden in the Bible, or octogamy either? She has warmed both hands before the fire of life, and she exults in the recollection of her fleshly delights:

> But lord Crist! whan that it remembreth me
> Upon my youthe and on my iolitee,
> It tikleth me aboute myn herte rote;
> Unto this day it doth myn herte bote
> That I have had my world as in my time! (D. 469–73)

True, she is willing to admit, for convention's sake, that chastity is the ideal state. But it is not *her* ideal. On the contrary, her admission is only for appearances. In her heart she despises virginity. Her contempt for it is thinly veiled, or rather, not veiled at all. Her discourse is marked by frank and almost obstreperous animalism. Her whole attitude is that of scornful, though good-humored, repudiation of what the Church teaches in that regard.

Nor is the Wife content with this single heresy. She maintains also that wives should rule their husbands, and she enforces this doctrine by an account of her own life, and further illustrates it by her tale of the knight of King Arthur who learned that

> Wommen desiren to have sovereyntee
> As wel over hir housband as hir love,
> And for to been in maistrie him above,   (D. 1038–40)

and who accepted the lesson as sound doctrine. Then, at the end of her discourse, she sums up in no uncertain words :

> And Iesu Crist us sende
> Housbandes meke, yonge, and fresshe abedde,
> And grace to overbyde hem that we wedde;
> And eek I preye Iesu shorte her lyves
> That wol nat be governed by her wyves.   (D. 1258–62)

Now the Wife of Bath is not *bombinans in vacuo*. She addresses her heresies not to *us* or to the world at large, but to her fellow-pilgrims. Chaucer has made this point perfectly clear. The words of the Wife were of a kind to provoke comment – and we have the comment. The Pardoner interrupts her with praise of her noble preaching :

> 'Now, dame,' quod he, 'by God and by seint Iohn,
> Ye been a noble prechour in this cas!'   (D. 164–5)

The adjective is not accidental. The Pardoner was a judge of good preaching : the General Prologue describes him as 'a noble ecclesiaste' (A. 708), and he shows his ability in his own sermon on Covetousness. Furthermore, it is the Friar's comment on the Wife's preamble that provokes the offensive words of the Summoner, and that becomes thereby the occasion for the two tales that immediately follow in the series. It is manifest, then, that Chaucer meant us to imagine the *dramatis personae* as taking a lively interest in whatever the Wife says. This being so, we ought to inquire what effect her Prologue and Tale would have upon the Clerk.

Of course the Clerk was scandalized. He was unworldly and an ascetic – he 'looked holwe and therto sobrely'. Moral virtue was his special study. He had embraced the celibate life. He was grave, devout, and unflinchingly orthodox. And now he was confronted by the lust of the flesh and the pride of life in the person of a woman who flouted chastity and exulted that she had 'had her world as in her time'. Nor was this all. The woman was an heresiarch, or at best a schismatic. She set up, and aimed to establish, a new and dangerous sect, whose principle was that the wife should rule the husband. The Clerk kept silence for the moment. Indeed, he had no chance to utter his sentiments, unless he interrupted – something not to be expected of his quiet ('coy') and sober temperament. But it is not to be imagined that his thoughts were idle. He could be trusted to speak to the purpose whenever his opportunity should come.

Now the substance of the Wife's false doctrines was not the only thing that must have roused the Clerk to protesting answer. The very manner of her discourse was a direct challenge to him. She had garnished her sermon with scraps of Holy Writ and rags and tatters of erudition, caught up, we may infer, from her last husband. Thus she had put herself into open competition with the guild of scholars and theologians, to which the Clerk belonged. Further, with her eye manifestly upon this sedate philosopher, she had taken pains to gird at him and his fellows. At first she pretends to be modest and apologetic – 'so that the clerkes be nat with me wrothe' (D. 125) – but later she abandons all pretense and makes an open attack:

> 'For trusteth wel, it is an impossible
> That any clerk wol speken good of wyves,
> But-if it be of holy seintes lyves,
> Ne of noon other wommen never the mo.   (D. 688–91)
>
> .   .   .   .
>
> The clerk, whan he is old, and may noght do
> Of Venus werkes worth his olde sho,
> Than sit he doun, and writ in his dotage
> That wommen can not kepe hir mariage.'   (D. 707–10)

And there was more still that the Wife made our Clerk endure. Her fifth husband was, like him, 'a clerk of Oxenford' – surely this is no accidental coincidence on Chaucer's part. He had abandoned his studies ('had left scole'), and had given up all thought of taking priest's orders. The Wife narrates, with uncommon zest, how she intrigued with him, and cajoled him, and married him (though he was twenty and she was forty), and how finally she made him utterly subservient to her will – how she got 'by maistrie al the soveraynetee'. This was gall and wormwood to our Clerk. The Wife not only trampled on his principles in her theory and practice, but she pointed her attack by describing how she had subdued to her heretical sect a clerk of Oxenford, an alumnus of our Clerk's own university. The Wife's discourse is not malicious. She is too jovial to be ill-natured, and she protests that she speaks in jest ('For myn entente nis but for to pleye', D. 192). But it none the less embodies a rude personal assault upon the Clerk, whose quiet mien and habitual reticence made him seem a safe person to attack. She had done her best to make the Clerk ridiculous. He saw it; the company saw it. He kept silent, biding his time.

All this is not speculation. It is nothing but straightforward interpretation of the text in the light of the circumstances and the situation. We can reject it only by insisting on the manifest absurdity (shown to be such in every headlink and endlink) that Chaucer did not visualize the Pilgrims whom he had been at such pains to describe in the Prologue, and that he never regarded them as associating, as looking at each other and thinking of each other, as becoming better and better acquainted as they jogged along the Canterbury road.

Chaucer might have given the Clerk a chance to reply to the Wife immediately. But he was too good an artist. The drama of the Pilgrimage is too natural and unforced in its development under the master's hand to admit of anything so frigidly schematic. The very liveliness with which he conceived his individual *dramatis personae* forbade. The Pilgrims were interested in the Wife's harangue, but it was for the talkative members of the company to thrust themselves forward. The Pardoner had already interrupted her with humorous comments before she was fully under way and had exhorted her to con-

tinue her account of the 'praktike' of marriage. The Friar, we
may be confident, was on good terms with her before she began :
she was one of those 'worthy wommen of the toun' whom he
especially cultivated. He, too, could not refrain from comment :

> The Frere lough, whan he had herd al this :
> 'Now, dame,' quod he, 'so have I ioye or blis,
> This is a long preamble of a tale!'   (D. 829–31)

The Summoner reproved him, in words that show not only his
professional enmity but also the amusement that the Pilgrims
in general were deriving from the Wife's disclosures. They
quarreled, and each threatened to tell a story at the other's expense. Then the Host intervened roughly, calling for silence and
bidding the Wife go ahead with her story. She assented, but not
without a word of good-humored, though ironical, deference to
the Friar :

> 'Al redy, sir,' quod she, 'right as yow lest,
> If I have licence of this worthy Frere.'   (D. 854–5)

And, at the very beginning of her tale, she took humorous vengeance for his interruption in a characteristic bit of satire at the
expense of 'limitours and other holy freres' (D. 864–81). This
passage, we note, has nothing whatever to do with her tale. It
is a side-remark in which she is talking at the Friar, precisely as
she has talked at the Clerk in her Prologue.

    The quarrel between the Summoner and the Friar was in abey-
ance until the Wife finished her tale. They let her end her story
and proclaim her moral in peace – the same heretical doctrine
that we have already noted, that the wife should be the head of
the house. Then the Friar spoke, and his words are very much to
our present purpose. He adverts in significant terms both to the
subject and to the manner of the Wife's discourse – a discourse,
we should observe, that was in effect a doctrinal sermon illustrated (as the fashion of preachers was) by a pertinent *exemplum* :

> 'Ye have here touched, al-so moot I thee,
> In scole-matere greet difficultee.'   (D. 1271–2)

She has handled a hard subject that properly belongs to scholars.
She has quoted authorities, too, like a clerk. Such things, he says,
are best left to ecclesiastics :

> 'But, dame, here as we ryden by the weye,
> Us nedeth nat to speken but of game,
> And lete auctoritees, on Goddes name,
> To preching and to scole eek of clergye.' (D. 1274-7)

This, to be sure, is but a device to 'conveyen his matere' – to lead
up to his proposal to 'telle a game' about a summoner. But it
serves to recall our minds to the Wife's usurpation of clerkly functions. If we think of the Clerk at all at this point (and assuredly
Chaucer had not forgotten him), we must feel that here is another prompting (undesigned though it be on the Friar's part)
to take up the subject which the Wife has (in the Clerk's eyes) so
shockingly maltreated.

Then follows the comic interlude of the Friar and the Summoner, in the course of which we may perhaps lose sight of the
serious subject which the Wife had set abroach – the status of
husband and wife in the marriage relation. But Chaucer did
not lose sight of it. It was a part of his design that the Host should
call on the Clerk for the first story of the next day.

This is the opportunity for which the Clerk has been waiting.
He has not said a word in reply to the Wife's heresies or to her
personal attack on him and his order. Seemingly she has
triumphed. The subject has apparently been dismissed with the
Friar's words about leaving such matters to sermons and to school
debates. The Host, indeed, has no idea that the Clerk purposes
to revive the discussion; he does not even think of the Wife in
calling upon the representative of that order which has fared so
ill at her hands.

> 'Sir clerk of Oxenford,' our hoste sayde,
> 'Ye ryde as coy and stille as doth a mayde
> Were newe spoused, sitting at the bord;
> This day ne herde I of your tonge a word.
> I trowe ye studie aboute som sophyme.' (E. 1-5)

Even here there is a suggestion (casual, to be sure, and, so far as the Host is concerned, quite unintentional) of *marriage*, the subject which is occupying the Clerk's mind. For the Host is mistaken. The Clerk's abstraction is only apparent. He is not pondering syllogisms; he is biding his time.

'Tell us a tale,' the unconscious Host goes on, 'but don't preach us a Lenten sermon – tell us som mery thing of aventures.' 'Gladly,' replies the demure scholar. 'I will tell you a story that a worthy *clerk* once told me at Padua – Francis Petrarch, God rest his soul!'

At this word *clerk*, pronounced with grave and inscrutable emphasis, the Wife of Bath must have pricked up her ears. But she has no inkling of what is in store, nor is the Clerk in any hurry to enlighten her. He opens with tantalizing deliberation, and it is not until he has spoken more than sixty lines that he mentions marriage. 'The Marquis Walter,' says the Clerk, 'lived only for the present and lived for pleasure only' –

> 'As for to hauke and hunte on every syde,
> Wel ny al othere cures leet he slyde;
> And eek he nolde, and that was worst of alle,
> Wedde no wyf, for noght that may bifalle.'   (E. 821–4)

These words may or may not have appeared significant to the company at large. To the Wife of Bath, at all events, they must have sounded interesting. And when, in a few moments, the Clerk made Walter's subjects speak of 'soveraynetee', the least alert of the Pilgrims can hardly have missed the point:

> 'Boweth your nekke under that blisful yok
> Of soveraynetee, noght of servyse,
> Which that men clepeth spousaille or wedlok.'
>
>   (E. 113–15)

'Sovereignty' had been the Wife's own word:

> 'And whan that I hadde geten unto me
> By maistrie al the soveraynetee.'   (D. 817–18)

'Wommen desyren to have sovereyntee
As wel over hir housband as hir love,
And for to been in maistrie him above.' (D. 1038–40)

Clearly the Clerk is catching up the subject proposed by the Wife.
The discussion is under way again.

Yet, despite the cheerful view that Walter's subjects take of
the marriage yoke, it is by no means yet clear to the Wife of Bath
and the other Pilgrims what the Clerk is driving at. For he soon
makes Walter declare that 'liberty is seldom found in marriage',
and that, if he weds a wife, he must exchange freedom for
servitude. Indeed, it is not until vss. 351–7 are reached that
Walter reveals himself as a man who is determined to rule his wife
absolutely. From that point to the end there is no room for doubt
in any Pilgrim's mind: *the Clerk is answering the Wife of Bath*;
he is telling of a woman whose principles in marriage were the
antithesis of hers; he is reasserting the orthodox view in opposition to the heresy which she had expounded with such zest and
with so many flings and jeers at the clerkly profession and
character.

What is the tale of Griselda? Several things, no doubt – an
old *märchen*, an *exemplum*, a *novella*, what you will. Our present concern, however, is primarily with the question what it
seemed to be to the Canterbury Pilgrims, told as it was by an
individual Clerk of Oxford at a particular moment and under
the special circumstances. The answer is plain. To them it was a
retort (indirect, impersonal, masterly) to the Wife of Bath's
heretical doctrine that the woman should be the head of the man.
It told them of a wife who had no such views – who promised ungrudging obedience and kept her vow. The Wife of Bath had
railed at her husbands and badgered them and cajoled them:
Griselda never lost her patience or her serenity. On its face, then,
the tale appeared to the Pilgrims to be a dignified and scholarly
narrative, derived from a great Italian clerk who was dead, and
now ulitized by their fellow-pilgrim, the Clerk of Oxford, to
demolish the heretical structure so boisterously reared by the Wife
of Bath in her prologue and her tale.

But Chaucer's Clerk was a logician – 'unto logik hadde he longe
ygo'. He knew perfectly well that the real moral of his story was

not that which his hearers would gather. He was aware that
Griselda was no model for literal imitation by ordinary woman-
kind. If so taken, his tale proved too much; it reduced his argument *ad absurdum*. If he let it go at that, he was playing into his
opponent's hands. Besides, he was a conscientious man. He could
not misrepresent the lesson which Petrarch had meant to teach
and had so clearly expressed – the lesson of submissive fortitude
under tribulation sent by God. Hence he does not fail to explain
this moral fully and in unmistakable terms, and to refer distinctly
to Petrarch as authority for it :

> And herkeneth what this auctor seith therfore.

> This storie is seyd, nat for that wyves sholde
> Folwen Griselde as in humilitee,
> For it were importable, though they wolde;
> But for that every wight, in his degree,
> Sholde be constant in adversitee
> As was Grisilde; therfor Petrark wryteth
> This storie, which with heigh style he endyteth.

> For, sith a womman was so pacient
> Un-to a mortal man, wel more us oghte
> Receyven al in gree that God us sent;
> For greet skile is, he preve that he wroghte.
> But he ne tempteth no man that he boghte,
> As seith seint Iame, if ye his pistel rede;
> He preveth folk al day, it is no drede,

> And suffreth us, as for our exercyse,
> With sharpe scourges of adversitee
> Ful ofte to be bete in sondry wyse;
> Nat for to knowe our wil, for certes he,
> Er we were born, knew al our freletee;
> And for our beste is al his governaunce :
> Lat us than live in vertuous suffrance.   (E. 1141–62)

Yet the Clerk has no idea of failing to make his point against
the Wife of Bath. And so, when the tale is finished and the proper

Petrarchan moral has been duly elaborated, he turns to the Wife (whom he has thus far sedulously refrained from addressing) and distinctly applies the material to the purpose of an ironical answer, of crushing force, to her whole heresy. There is nothing inappropriate to his character in this procedure. Quite the contrary. Clerks were always satirizing women – the Wife had said so herself – and this particular Clerk had, of course, no scruples against using the powerful weapon of irony in the service of religion and 'moral vertu'. In this instance, the satire is peculiarly poignant for two reasons : first, because it comes with all the suddenness of a complete change of tone (from high seriousness to biting irony, and from the impersonal to the personal); and secondly, because, in the tale which he has told, the Clerk has incidentally refuted a false statement of the Wife's, to the effect that

> 'It is an impossible
> That any clerk wol speke good of wyves,
> But if it be of holy seintes lyves,
> Ne of noon other womman never the mo.'   (D. 688–91)

Clerks *can* 'speak well' of women (as our Clerk has shown), when women deserve it; and he now proceeds to show that they can likewise speak well (with biting irony) of women who do *not* deserve it – such women as the Wife of Bath and all her sect of domestic revolutionists.

It now appears that the form and spirit of the conclusion and the Envoy are not only appropriate to clerks in general, but peculiarly and exquisitely appropriate to this particular clerk under these particular circumstances and with this particular task in hand – the duty of defending the orthodox view of the relations between husband and wife against the heretical opinions of the Wife of Bath : 'One word in conclusion, gentlemen. There are few Griseldas now-a-days. Most women will break before they will bend. Our companion, the Wife of Bath, is an example, as she has told us herself. Therefore, though I cannot sing, I will recite a song in honor, not of Griselda (as you might perhaps expect), but of the Wife of Bath, of the sect of which she aspires to be a doctor, and of the life which she exemplifies in practice –

> '. . . . for the wyves love of Bathe,
> Whos lif and al hir secte God mayntene
> In high maistrye, and elles were it scathe.'   (E. 1170–2)

Her *way of life* – she had set it forth with incomparable zest. Her *sect* – she was an heresiarch or at least a schismatic. The terms are not accidental : they are chosen with all the discrimination that befits a scholar and a rhetorician. They refer us back (as definitely as the words 'Wife of Bath' themselves) to that prologue in which the Wife had stood forth as an opponent of the orthodox view of subordination in marriage, as the upholder of an heretical doctrine, and as the exultant practicer of what she preached.

And then comes the Clerk's Envoy, the song that he recites in honor of the Wife and her life and her sect, with its polished lines, its ingenious rhyming, and its utter felicity of scholarly diction. Nothing could be more in character. To whom in all the world should such a masterpiece of rhetoric be appropriate if not to the Clerk of Oxenford? It is a mock encomium, a sustained ironical commendation of what the Wife has taught :

'O noble wives, let no clerk ever have occasion to write such a story of you as Petrarch once told me about Griselda. Follow your great leader, the Wife of Bath. Rule your husbands, as she did; rail at them, as she did; make them jealous, as she did; exert yourselves to get lovers, as she did. And all this you must do whether you are fair or foul [with manifest allusion to the problem of beauty or ugliness presented in the Wife's story]. Do this, I say, and you will fulfil the precepts that she has set forth and achieve the great end which she has proclaimed as the object of marriage : that is, *you will make your husbands miserable, as she did!*'

> 'Be ay of chere as light as leef on linde,
> And lat him care and wepe and wringe and waille !'
>   (E. 1211–12)

And the Merchant (hitherto silent, but not from inattention) catches up the closing words in a gust of bitter passion :

> 'Weping and wayling, care and other sorwe
> *I* know ynough on even and amorwe,'
> Quod the Merchant, 'and so don othere mo
> That wedded ben.' (E. 1213–16)

The Clerk's Envoy, then, is not only appropriate to his character and to the situation : it has also a marked dynamic value. For
it is this ironical tribute to the Wife of Bath and her dogmas that,
with complete dramatic inevitability, calls out the Merchant's *cri
du cœur*. The Merchant has no thought of telling a tale at this
moment. He is a stately and imposing person in his degree, by
no means prone (so the Prologue informs us) to expose any holes
there may be in his coat. But he is suffering a kind of emotional
crisis. The poignant irony of the Clerk, following hard upon the
moving story of a patient and devoted wife, is too much for him.
He has just passed through his honeymoon (but two months
wed!) and he has sought a respite from his thraldom under color
of a pilgrimage to St. Thomas.

> 'I have a wyf, the worste that may be!' (E. 1218)

She would be an overmatch for the devil himself. He need not
specify her evil traits : she is bad in every respect.

> 'There is a long and large difference
> Bitwix Grisildis grete pacience
> And of my wyf the passing crueltee.' (E. 1223–5)

The Host, as ever, is on the alert. He scents a good story :

> 'Sin ye so muchel knowen of that art,
> Ful hertely I pray yow tell us part.' (E. 1241–2)

The Merchant agrees, as in duty bound, for all the Pilgrims take
care never to oppose the Host, lest he exact the heavy forfeit
established as the penalty for rebellion. But he declines to relate
his own experiences, thus leaving us to infer, if we choose – for
nowhere is Chaucer's artistic reticence more effective – that his
bride has proved false to him, like the wife of the worthy Knight
of Lombardy.

Ans so the discussion of marriage is once more in full swing.
The Wife of Bath, without intending it, has opened a debate in
which the Pilgrims have become so absorbed that they will not
leave it till the subject is 'bolted to the bran'.

The Merchant's Tale presents very noteworthy features, and
has been much canvassed, though never (it seems) with due
attention to its plain significance in the Human Comedy of the
Canterbury Pilgrimage. In substance, it is nothing but a tale of
bawdry, one of the most familiar of its class. There is nothing
novel about it except its setting, but that is sufficiently remarkable. Compare the tale with any other version of the Pear-Tree
Story – their name is legion – and its true significance comes out
in striking fashion. The simple fabliau devised by its first author
merely to make those laugh whose lungs are tickle o' the sere, is so
expanded and overlaid with savage satire that it becomes a complete disquisition on marriage from the only point of view which
is possible for the disenchanted Merchant. Thus considered, the
cynicism of the Merchant's Tale is seen to be in no way surprising,
and (to answer another kind of comment which this piece has
evoked) in no sense expressive of Chaucer's own sentiments, or
even of Chaucer's momentary mood. The cynicism is the Merchant's. It is no more Chaucer's than Iago's cynicism about love
is Shakspere's.

In a word, the tale is the perfect expression of the Merchant's
angry disgust at his own evil fate and at his folly in bringing that
fate upon himself. Thus, its very lack of restraint – the savagery of
the whole, which has revolted so many readers – is dramatically
inevitable. The Merchant has schooled himself to hide his debts
and his troubles. He is professionally an adept at putting a good
face on matters, as every clever business man must be. But when
once the barrier is broken, reticence is at an end. His disappointment is too fresh, his disillusion has been too abrupt, for him to
measure his words. He speaks in a frenzy of contempt and hatred.
The hatred is for women; the contempt is for himself and all
other fools who will not take warning by example. For we
should not forget that the satire is aimed at January rather than
at May. That egotistical old dotard is less excusable than his
young wife, and meets with less mercy at the Merchant's hands.

That the Merchant begins with an encomium on marriage

which is one of the most amazing instances of sustained irony in
all literature, is not to be wondered at. In the first place, he is
ironical because the Clerk has been ironical. Here the connection is remarkably close. The Merchant has fairly snatched the
words out of the Clerk's mouth ('And lat him care and wepe and
wringe and waile' – 'Weping and wayling, care and other sorwe'),
and his mock encomium on the wedded state is a sequel to the
Clerk's mock encomium on the Wife of Bath's life and all her
sect. The spirit is different, but that is quite proper. For the
Clerk's satire is the irony of a logician and a moral philosopher,
the irony of the intellect and the ethical sense : the Merchant's
is the irony of a mere man, it is the irony of passion and personal
experience. The Clerk is a theorist – he looks at the subject from a
point of philosophical detachment. The Merchant is an egotist –
he feels himself to be the dupe whose folly he depicts. We may
infer, if we like, that he was a man in middle age and that he had
married a young wife.

There is plenty of evidence that the Merchant has been an
attentive listener. One detects, for instance, a certain similarity between January and the Marquis Walter (different as they are) in
that they have both shown themselves disinclined to marriage.
Then again, the assertion that a wife is never weary of attending a
sick husband –

> 'She nis nat wery him to love and serve,
> Thogh that he lye bedrede til he sterve' –   (E. 1291–2)

must have reminded the Pilgrims of poor Thomas, in the Summoner's Tale, whose wife's complaints to her spiritual visitor had
precipitated so tremendous a sermon. But such things are trifles
compared with the attention which the Merchant devotes to the
Wife of Bath.

So far, in this act of Chaucer's Human Comedy, we have
found that the Wife of Bath is, in a very real sense, the dominant
figure. She has dictated the theme and inspired or instigated the
actors; and she has always been at or near the center of the stage.
It was a quarrel over her prologue that elicited the tale of the
Friar and that of the Summoner. It was she who caused the Clerk
to tell of Griselda – and the Clerk satirizes her in his Envoy. 'The

art' of which the Host begs the Merchant to tell is *her* art, the
art of marriage on which she has discoursed so learnedly. That
the Merchant, therefore, should allude to her, quote her words,
and finally mention her in plain terms is precisely what was to be
expected.

The order and method of these approaches on the Merchant's
part are exquisitely natural and dramatic. First there are
touches, more or less palpable, when he describes the harmony
of wedded life in terms so different from the Wife's account of
what her husbands had to endure. Then – after a little – comes a
plain enough allusion (put into January's mouth) to the Wife's
character, to her frequent marriages, and to her inclination to
marry again, old as she is :

> 'And eek thise olde widwes, God it wot,
> They conne so muchel craft on Wades boot,
> So muchel broken harm, whan that hem leste,
> That with hem sholde I never live in reste!
> For sondry scoles maken sotil clerkis :
> Wommen of many scoles half a clerk is.'   (E. 1423–8)

Surely the Wife of Bath was a woman of many schools, and her
emulation of clerkly discussion had already been commented on
by the Pardoner and the Friar. Next, the Merchant lets Justinus
quote some of the Wife's very words – though without naming
her: 'God may apply the trials of marriage, my dear January,
to your salvation. Your wife may make you go straight to heaven
without passing through purgatory.'

> 'Paraunter she may be your purgatorie!
> She may be Goddes mene, and Goddes whippe;
> Than shal your soule up to hevene skippe
> Swifter than doth an arwe out of the bowe.'
>
>   (E. 1670–3)

This is merely an adaptation of the Wife of Bath's own language
in speaking of her fourth husband :

> 'By God, in erthe I was his purgatorie,
> For which I hope his soule be in glorie.'   (D. 489–90)

Compare also another phrase of hers, which Justinus echoes:
'Myself have been the whippe' (D. 175). And finally, when all
the Pilgrims are quite prepared for such a thing, there is a frank
citation of the Wife of Bath by name, with a reference to her exposition of marriage :

> 'My tale is doon : – for my wit is thinne.
> Beth not agast herof, my brother dere.
> *But lat us waden out of this matere:*
> *The Wyf of Bathe, if ye han understonde,*
> *Of marriage, which we have on honde,*
> *Declared hath ful wel in litel space.*
> Fareth now wel, God have yow in his grace.'
>
>   (E. 1682–8)

Are the italicized lines a part of the speech of Justinus, or are
they interpolated by the Merchant, in his own person, in order to
shorten Justinus' harangue? Here is Professor Skeat's comment :
'These four parenthetical lines interrupt the story rather awkwardly. They obviously belong to the narrator, the Merchant,
as it is out of the question that Justinus had heard of the Wife of
Bath. Perhaps it is an oversight.' Now it makes no difference
whether we assign these lines to Justinus or to the Merchant, for
Justinus, as we have seen, has immediately before quoted the
Wife's very words, and he may as well mention her as repeat her
language. Either way, the lines are exquisitely in place. *Chaucer*
is not speaking, and there is no violation of dramatic propriety
on *his* part. It is not Chaucer who is telling the story. It is the
Merchant. And the Merchant is telling it as a part of the discussion which the Wife has started. It is dramatically proper, then,
that the Merchant should quote the Wife of Bath and that he
should refer to her. And it is equally proper, from the
dramatic point of view, for Chaucer to let the Merchant make
Justinus mention the Wife. In that case it is the Merchant – *not
Chaucer* – who chooses to have one of his characters fall out of his
part for a moment and make a 'local allusion'. Chaucer is responsible for making the *Merchant* speak in character; the
Merchant, in his turn, is responsible for *Justinus*. That the Merchant should put into the mouth of Justinus a remark that

Justinus could never have made is, then, not a slip on Chaucer's part. On the contrary, it is a first-rate dramatic touch, for it is precisely what the Merchant might well have done under the circumstances.

Nor should we forget the exquisitely comic discussion between Pluto and Proserpine which the Merchant has introduced near the end of his story. This dialogue is a flagrant violation of dramatic propriety – not on Chaucer's part, however, but on the Merchant's. And therein consists a portion of its merit. For the Merchant is so eager to make his point that he rises superior to all artistic rules. He is bent, not on giving utterance to a masterpiece of narrative construction, but on enforcing his lesson in every possible way. And Chaucer is equally bent on making him do it. Hence the Queen of the Lower World is brought in, discoursing in terms that befit the Wife of Bath (the presiding genius of this part of the *Canterbury Tales*), and echoing some of her very doctrines. The Wife had said :

> 'Thus shal ye speke and bere hem wrong on honde;
> For half so boldely can ther no man
> Swere and lyen as a womman can.
> I say nat this by wyves that ben wyse,
> But-if it be whan they hem misavyse.
> A wys wyf, if that she can hir good,
> Shal beren him on hond the cow is wood,
> And take witnesse of his owene mayde.'   (D. 226–33)

Now hear Proserpine :

> 'Now, by my modres sires soule I swere,
> That I shal yeven hir suffisaunt answere,
> And alle wommen after, for hir sake;
> That, though they be in any gilt ytake,
> With face bold they shulle hemself excuse,
> And bere hem doun that wolden hem accuse.
> For lakke of answere noon of hem shal dyen.
> Al hadde man seyn a thing with bothe his yen,
> Yit shul we wommen visage it hardily,
> And wepe, and swere, and chyde subtilly,
> So that ye men shul been as lewed as gees.'   (E. 2265–75)

And note that Pluto (who is as fond of citing authorities as the Wife's last husband) yields the palm of the discussion to Proserpine:

> 'Dame,' quod this Pluto, 'be no lenger wrooth;
> I yeve it up.'   (E. 2311–12)

This, too, was the experience of the Wife's husbands:

> 'I ne owe hem nat a word that is not quit.
> I broghte it so aboute by my wit
> That they moste yeve it up, as for the beste.'   (D. 425–7)

The tone and manner of the whole debate between Pluto and his queen are wildly absurd if regarded from the point of view of gods and goddesses, but in that very incongruity resides their dramatic propriety. What we have is not Pluto and Proserpine arguing with each other, but the Wife of Bath and one of her husbands attired for the nonce by the cynical Merchant in the external semblance of King Pluto and his dame.

The end of the Merchant's Tale does not bring the Marriage Chapter of the *Canterbury Tales* to a conclusion. As the Merchant had commented on the Clerk's Tale by speaking of his own wife, thus continuing the subject which the Wife had begun, so the Host comments on the Merchant's story by making a similar application:

> 'Ey, Goddes mercy,' seyde our Hoste tho,
> 'Now such a wyf I pray God kepe me fro!' (E. 2419–20)

'See how women deceive us poor men, as the Merchant has shown us. However, *my* wife is true as any steel; but she is a shrew, and has plenty of other faults.' And just as the Merchant had referred expressly to the Wife of Bath, so also does the Host refer to her expressly: 'But I must not talk of these things. If I should, it would be told to her by some of this company. I need not say by whom, "sin wommen connen outen swich chaffare".' (E. 2419–40). Of course the Host points this remark by looking at the Wife of Bath. There are but three women in the company. Neither the highborn and dainty Prioress nor the pious nun who accompanies her is likely to gossip with Harry Baily's spouse. It is the Wife, a woman of the Hostess's own rank and temper, who will tattle when the party returns to the Tabard. And so we find the Wife of Bath still in the foreground, as she has been, in one way or another, for several thousand lines.

But now the Host thinks his companions have surely had enough of marriage. It is time they heard something of love, and with this in view he turns abruptly to the Squire, whom all the Pilgrims have come to know as 'a lovyer and a lusty bachiler'.

> 'Squier, com neer, if it your wille be,
> And sey somewhat of *love*; for certes ye
> Connen theron as muche as any man.'   (F. 1–3)

The significance of the emphasis on *love*, which is inevitable if the address to the Squire is read (as it should be) continuously with the Host's comments on marriage, is by no means accidental.

There is no psychology about the Squire's Tale – no moral or social or matrimonial theorizing. It is pure romance, in the mediaeval sense. The Host understood the charm of variety. He did not mean to let the discussion drain itself to the dregs.

But Chaucer's plan in this Act is not yet finished. There is still something lacking to a full discussion of the relations between husband and wife. We have had the wife who dominates her husband; the husband who dominates his wife; the young wife who befools her dotard January; the chaste wife who is a scold and stirs up strife. Each of these illustrates a different kind of marriage – but there is left untouched, so far, the ideal relation, that in which love continues and neither party to the contract strives for the mastery. Let this be set forth, and the series of views of wedded life begun by the Wife of Bath will be rounded off; the Marriage Act of the Human Comedy will be concluded. The Pilgrims may not be thinking of this; but there is at least *one* of them (as the sequel shows) who has the idea in his head. And who is he? The only pilgrims who have not already told their tales are the yeoman, two priests, the five tradesmen (haberdasher, carpenter, weaver, dyer, and tapicer), the parson, the plowman, the manciple, and the franklin. Of all these there is

but one to whom a tale illustrating this ideal would not be inappropriate – the Franklin. To him, then, must Chaucer assign
it, or leave the debate unfinished.

At this point, the dramatic action and interplay of characters
are beyond all praise. The Franklin is not brought forward in
formal fashion to address the company. His summons is incidental
to the dialogue. No sooner has the Squire ended his chivalric
romance, than the Franklin begins to compliment him :

> 'In feyth, squier, thou hast thee well yquit
> And gentilly. I preise wel thy wit,'
> Quod the frankeleyn, 'considering thy youthe.
> So felingly thou spekest, sir, I allow the !
> As to my doom, there is noon that is here
> Of eloquence that shal be thy pere,
> If that thou live : God yeve thee good chaunce
> And in vertu sende thee continuance,
> For of thy speche I have great deyntee !'   (F. 673–81)

'You have acquitted yourself well and *like a gentleman* !' *Gentillesse*, then, is what has most impressed the Franklin in the tale
that he has just heard. And the reason for his enthusiasm soon
appears. He is as we know, a rich freeholder, often sheriff in his
county. Socially, he is not quite within the pale of the gentry, but
he is the kind of man that mayhope to found a family, the kind of
man from whose ranks the English nobility has been constantly
recruited. And that such is his ambition comes out naïvely and
with a certain pathos in what he goes on to say : 'I wish my son
were like you' :

> 'I have a sone, and, by the Trinitee,
> I hadde lever than twenty pound worth lond,
> Though it right now were fallen in myn hond,
> He were a man of swich discrecioun
> As that ye been ! Fy on possessioun
> But-if a man be vertuous with-al !
> I have my sone snibbed, and yet shal,
> For he to vertu listeth nat entende;
> But for to pleye at dees, and to despende,

> And lese al that he hath, in his usage;
> And he hath lever talken with a page
> Than to commune with any gentil wight
> Ther he mighte lerne gentillesse aright.' (F. 682–94)

It is the contrast between the Squire and his own son, in whom his hopes are centered, that has led the Franklin's thoughts to *gentillesse*, a subject which is ever in his mind.

But the Host interrupts him rudely: 'Straw for your gentillesse! It is your turn to entertain the company':

> 'Telle on thy tale withouten wordes mo!' (F. 702)

The Franklin is, of course, very polite in his reply to this rough and unexpected command. Like the others, he is on his guard against opposing the Host and incurring the forfeit:

> 'I wol yow nat contrarien in no wise,
> As fer as that my wittes wol suffise.' (F. 705–6)

Here, then, as in the case of the Merchant, the Host has taken advantage of a spontaneous remark on some Pilgrim's part to demand a story. Yet the details of the action are quite different. On the previous occasion, the Merchant is requested to go on with an account of his marriage, since he has already begun to talk about it; and, though he declines to speak further of his own troubles, he does continue to discuss and illustrate wedlock from his own point of view. In the present instance, on the contrary, the Host repudiates the topic of *gentillesse*, about which the Franklin is discoursing to the Squire. He bids him drop the subject and tell a story. The Franklin pretends to be compliant, but after all, he has his own way. Indeed, he takes delicate vengeance on the Host by telling a tale which thrice exemplifies *gentillesse* – on the part of a knight, a squire, and a clerk. Thus he finishes his interrupted compliment to the Squire, and incidentally honors two other Pilgrims who have seemed to him to possess the quality that he values so highly. He proves, too, both that *gentillesse* is an entertaining topic and that it is not (as the Host has roughly intimated) a theme which he, the Franklin, is ill-equipped to handle.

For the Franklin's Tale is a gentleman's story, and he tells it
like a gentleman. It is derived, he tells us, from 'thise olde *gentil*
Britons' (F. 709–15). Dorigen lauds Arveragus' *gentillesse* toward her in refusing to insist on soveraynetee in marriage (F.
754–5). Aurelius is deeply impressed by the knight's *gentillesse*
in allowing the lady to keep her word, and emulates it by releasing her :

> Fro his lust yet were him lever abyde
> Than doon so heigh a churlish wrecchednesse
> Agaynes franchyse and alle gentillesse.   (F. 1522–4)

> I see his grete gentillesse.   (F. 1527)

> Thus can a squyer don a gentil dede
> As wel as can a knyght, withouten drede.   (F. 1543–4)

> Arveragus, of gentillesse,
> Had lever dye in sorwe and in distresse
> Than that his wyf were of her trouthe fals.
>   (F. 1595–7)

And finally, the clerk releases Aurelius, from the same motive of
generous emulation :

> This philosophre answerde, 'Leve brother,
> Everich of yow dide gentilly til other.
> Thou art a squyer, and he is a knight;
> But God forbede, for his blisful might,
> But-if a clerk coude doon a gentil dede
> As wel as any of yow, it is no drede !'   (F. 1607–12)

Thus it appears that the dramatic impulse to the telling of
the Franklin's Tale is to be found in the relations among the
Pilgrims and in the effect that they have upon each other – in
other words, in the circumstances, the situation, and the interplay of character.

It has sometimes been thought that the story, either in subject or in style, is too fine for the Franklin to tell. But this

objection Chaucer foresaw and forestalled. The question is not whether this tale, thus told, would be appropriate to a typical or 'average' fourteenth-century franklin. The question is whether it is appropriate to this particular Franklin, under these particular circumstances, and at this particular juncture. And to this question there can be but one answer. Chaucer's Franklin is an individual, not a mere type-specimen. He is rich, ambitious socially, and profoundly interested in the matter of *gentillesse* for personal and family reasons. He is trying to bring up his son as a gentleman, and his position as 'St. Julian in his country' has brought him into intimate association with first-rate models. He has, under the special circumstances, every motive to tell a gentleman's story and to tell it like a gentleman. He is speaking under the immediate influence of his admiration for the Squire and of his sense of the inferiority of his own son. If we choose to conceive the Franklin as a mediaeval Squire Western and then to allege that he could not possibly have told such a story, we are making the difficulty for ourselves. We are considering – not Chaucer's Franklin (whose character is to be inferred not merely from the description in the General Prologue but from all the other evidence that the poet provides) – not Chaucer's Franklin, but somebody quite different, somebody for whom Chaucer has no kind of responsibility.

In considering the immediate occasion of the Franklin's Tale, we have lost sight for a moment of the Wife of Bath. But she was not absent from the mind of the Franklin. The proper subject of his tale, as we have seen, is *gentillesse*. Now that (as well as marriage) was a subject on which the Wife of Bath had descanted at some length. Her views are contained in the famous harangue delivered by the lady to her husband on the wedding night : 'But for ye speken of swich gentillesse', etc. (D. 1109–76). Many readers have perceived that this portentous curtain-lecture clogs the story, and some have perhaps wished it away, good as it is in itself. For it certainly seems to be out of place on lips of the *fée*. But its insertion is (as usual in such cases) exquisitely appropriate to the teller of the tale, the Wife of Bath, who cannot help dilating on subjects which interest her, and who has had the advantage of learned society in the person of her fifth husband. Perhaps no *fée* would have talked thus to her knightly bridegroom on such an occasion; but it is quite in character for the Wife of Bath to use the *fée* (or anybody else) as a mouthpiece for her own ideas, as the Merchant had used Proserpine to point his satire. Thus the references to Dante, Valerius, Seneca, Boethius, and Juvenal — so deliciously absurd on the lips of a *fée* of King Arthur's time — are perfectly in place when we remember who it is that is reporting the monologue. The Wife was a citer of authorities — she makes the *fée* cite authorities. How comical this is the Wife did not know, but Chaucer knew, and if we think he did not, it is our own fault for not observing how dramatic in spirit is the *Canterbury Tales*.

A considerable passage in the curtain-lecture is given to the proposition that 'such gentillesse as is descended out of old rich-esse' is of no value: 'Swich arrogance is not worth an hen' (D. 1109 ff.). These sentiments the Franklin echoes:

> 'Fy on possessioun
> But-if a man be vertuous withal!'   (F. 686–7)

But, whether or not the Wife's digression on *gentillesse* is linger-ing in the Franklin's mind (as I am sure it is), one thing is per-fectly clear: the Franklin's utterances on marriage are spoken under the influence of the discussion which the Wife has precipitated. In other words, though everybody else imagines that the subject has been finally dismissed by the Host when he calls on the Squire for a tale of *love*, it has no more been dismissed in fact than when the Friar attempted to dismiss it at the begin-ning of his tale. For the Franklin has views, and he means to set them forth. He possesses, as he thinks, the true solution of the whole difficult problem. And that solution he embodies in his tale of *gentillesse*.

The introductory part of the Franklin's Tale sets forth a theory of the marriage relation quite different from anything that has so far emerged in the debate. And this theory the Franklin arrives at by taking into consideration both *love* (which, as we remember, was the subject that the Host had bidden the Squire treat of) and *gentillesse* (which is to be the subject of his own story).

Arveragus had of course been obedient to his lady during the

period of courtship, for obedience was well understood to be the
duty of a lover. Finally, she consented to marry him –

> To take him for hir housbande and hir lord,
> Of swich lordshipe as men han over her wyves.
>
> (F. 742–3)

Marriage, then, according to the orthodox doctrine (as held by
Walter and Griselda) was to change Arveragus from the lady's
servant to her master. But Arveragus was an enlightened and
chivalric gentleman, and he promised the lady that he would
never assert his marital authority, but would content himself with
the mere name of sovereignty, continuing to be her servant and
lover as before. This he did because he thought it would ensure
the happiness of their wedded life.

> And for to lede the more in blisse hir lyves,
> Of his free wil he swoor hir as a knight,
> That never in al his lyf he, day ne night,
> Ne sholde up-on him take no maistrye
> Agayn hir wil, ne kythe hir ialousye,
> But hir obeye, and folwe hir wil in al,
> As any lovere to his lady shal;
> Save that the name of soveraynetee,
> That wolde he have for shame of his degree.
>
> (F. 744–52)

But, just as Arveragus was no disciple of the Marquis Walter,
so Dorigen was not a member of the sect of the Wife of Bath.
She promised her husband obedience and fidelity in return for his
gentillesse in renouncing his sovereign rights.

> She thanked him, and with ful greet humblesse
> She seyde, 'Sire, sith, of your gentillesse,
> Ye profre me to have so large a reyne,
> Ne wolde never God bitwixe us tweyne,
> As in my gilt, were outher werre or stryf.
> Sir, I wol be your humble trewe wyf,
> Have heer my trouthe, till that myn herte breste.'
>
> (F. 753–9)

This, then, is the Franklin's solution of the whole puzzle of matrimony, and it is a solution that depends upon love and *gentillesse* on both sides. But he is not content to leave the matter in this purely objective condition. He is determined that there shall be no misapprehension in the mind of any Pilgrim as to his purpose. He wishes to make it perfectly clear that he is definitely and formally offering this theory as the only satisfactory basis of happy married life. And he accordingly comments on the relations between his married lovers with fulness, and with manifest reference to certain things that the previous debaters have said.

The arrangement, he tells the Pilgrims, resulted in 'quiet and rest' for both Arveragus and Dorigen. And, he adds, it is the only arrangement which will ever enable two persons to live together in love and amity. Friends must 'obey each other if they wish to hold company long'.

> 'Love wol nat ben constreyned by maistrye;
> Whan maistrie comth, the god of love anon
> Beteth hise winges, and farewel! he is gon!
> Love is a thing as any spirit free;
> Wommen of kinde desiren libertee,
> And nat to ben constreyned as a thral;
> And so don men, if I soth seyen shal.
> Loke who that is most pacient in love,
> He is at his avantage al above.
> Pacience is an heigh vertu certeyn;
> For it venquisseth, as thise clerkes seyn,
> Thinges that rigour sholde never atteyne.
> For every word men may nat chyde or pleyne.
> Lerneth to suffre, or elles, so moot I goon,
> Ye shul it lerne, wher-so ye wole or noon.' (F. 764–78)

Hence it was that this wise knight promised his wife 'suffraunce' and that she promised him never to abuse his goodness.

> Heer may men seen an humble wys accord;
> Thus hath she take hir servant and hir lord,
> Servant in love, and lord in mariage;
> Than was he bothe in lordship and servage;

> Servage? nay, but in lordshipe above,
> Sith he hath bothe his lady and his love;
> His lady, certes, and his wyf also,
> The which that lawe of love accordeth to.   (F. 791–8)

The result, the Franklin adds, was all that could be desired. The knight lived 'in blisse and in solas'. And then the Franklin adds an encomium on the happiness of true marriage :

> 'Who coude telle, but he had wedded be,
> The ioye, the ese, and the prosperitee
> That is bitwixe an housbonde and his wyf?'   (F. 803–5)

This encomium echoes the language of the Merchant :

> 'A wyf! a Seinte Marie! *benedicite!*
> How mighte a man han any adversitee
> That hath a wyf? Certes, I can nat seye!
> The blisse which that is bitwixe hem tweye
> Ther may no tonge telle or herte thinke.'   (E. 1337–41)

The Franklin's praise of marriage is sincere; the Merchant's had been savagely ironical. The Franklin, we observe, is answering the Merchant, and he answers him in the most effective way – by repeating his very words.

And just as in the Merchant's Tale we noted that the Merchant has enormously expanded the simple *fabliau* that he had to tell, inserting all manner of observations on marriage which are found in no other version of the Pear-Tree Story, so also we find that the Franklin's exposition of the ideal marriage relation (including the pact between Arveragus and Dorigen) is all his own, occurring in none of the versions that precede Chaucer. These facts are of the very last significance. No argument is necessary to enforce their meaning.

It is hardly worth while to indicate the close connection between this and that detail of the Franklin's exposition and certain points that have come out in the discussion as conducted by his predecessors in the debate. His repudiation of the Wife of Bath's doctrine that men should be 'governed by their wives' is express, as well as his rejection of the opposite theory. Neither party should lose his liberty; neither the husband nor the wife should be a thrall. Patience (which clerks celebrate as a high virtue) should be mutual, not, as in the Clerk's Tale, all on one side. The husband is to be both servant and lord – servant in love and lord in marriage. Such servitude is true lordship. Here there is a manifest allusion to the words of Walter's subjects in the Clerk's Tale :

> That blisful yok
> Of sovereynetee, noght of servyse,   (E. 113–14)

as well as to Walter's rejoinder :

> 'I me reioysed of my libertee,
> That selde tyme is founde in mariage ;
> Ther I was free, I moot been in servage.'
> (E. 145–7)

It was the regular theory of the Middle Ages that the highest type of chivalric love was incompatible with marriage, since marriage brings in mastery, and mastery and love cannot abide together. This view the Franklin boldly challenges. Love *can* be consistent with marriage, he declares. Indeed, without love (and perfect, *gentle* love) marriage is sure to be a failure. The difficulty about mastery vanishes when mutual love and forbearance are made the guiding principles of the relation between husband and wife.

The soundness of the Franklin's theory, he declares, is proved by his tale. For the marriage of Arveragus and Dorigen was a brilliant success :

> Arveragus and Dorigene his wyf
> In sovereyn blisse leden forth hir lyf.
> Never eft ne was ther angre hem bitwene ;
> He cherisseth hir as though she were a quene ;
> And she was to him trewe for evermore.
> Of this two folk ye gete of me na-more.   (F. 1551–6)

Thus the whole debate has been brought to a satisfactory conclusion, and the Marriage Act of the Human Comedy ends with the conclusion of the Franklin's Tale.

Those readers who are eager to know what Chaucer thought about marriage may feel reasonably content with the inference that may be drawn from his procedure. The Marriage Group of Tales begins with the Wife of Bath's Prologue and ends with the Franklin's Tale. There is no connection between the Wife's Prologue and the group of stories that precedes; there is no connection between the Franklin's Tale and the group that follows. Within the Marriage Group, on the contrary, there is close connection throughout. That act is a finished act. It begins and ends an elaborate debate. We need not hesitate, therefore, to accept the solution which the Franklin offers as that which Geoffrey Chaucer the man accepted for his own part. Certainly it is a solution that does him infinite credit. A better has never been devised or imagined.

S O U R C E : *Modern Philology*, IX (1911–12)

E. T. Donaldson

CHAUCER THE PILGRIM (1954)

Verisimilitude in a work of fiction is not without its attendant dangers, the chief of which is that the responses it stimulates in the reader may be those appropriate not so much to an imaginative production as to an historical one or to a piece of reporting. History and reporting are, of course, honorable in themselves, but if we react to a poet as though he were an historian or a reporter, we do him somewhat less than justice. I am under the impression that many readers, too much influenced by Chaucer's brilliant verisimilitude, tend to regard his famous pilgrimage to Canterbury as significant not because it is a great fiction, but because it seems to be a remarkable record of a fourteenth-century pilgrimage. A remarkable record it may be, but if we treat it too narrowly as such there are going to be certain casualties among the elements that make up the fiction. Perhaps first among these elements is the fictional reporter, Chaucer the pilgrim, and the role he plays in the Prologue to the *Canterbury Tales* and in the links between them. I think it time that he was rescued from the comparatively dull record of history and put back into his poem. He is not really Chaucer the poet – nor, for that matter, is either the poet, or the poem's protagonist, that Geoffrey Chaucer frequently mentioned in contemporary historical records as a distinguished civil servant, but never as a poet. The fact that these are three separate entities does not, naturally, exclude the probability – or rather the certainty – that they bore a close resemblance to one another, and that, indeed, they frequently got together in the same body. But that does not excuse us from keeping them distinct from one another, difficult as their close resemblance makes our task.

The natural tendency to confuse one thing with its like is perhaps best represented by a school of Chaucerian criticism, now outmoded, that pictured a single Chaucer under the guise of a wide-eyed, jolly, rolypoly little man who, on fine Spring morn-ings, used to get up early, while the dew was still on the grass, and go look at daisies. A charming portrait, this, so charming, indeed, that it was sometimes able to maintain itself to the exclusion of any Chaucerian other side. It has every reason to be charming, since it was lifted almost *in toto* from the version Chaucer gives of himself in the Prologue to the *Legend of Good Women*, though I imagine it owes some of its popularity to a rough analogy with Wordsworth – a sort of *Legend of Good Poets*. It was this version of Chaucer that Kittredge, in a page of great importance to Chaucer criticism, demolished with his assertion that 'a naïf Collector of Customs would be a paradoxical monster'. He might well have added that a naïve creator of old January would be even more monstrous.

Kittredge's pronouncement cleared the air, and most of us now accept the proposition that Chaucer was sophisticated as readily as we do the proposition that the whale is a mammal. But unhappily, now that we've got rid of the naïve fiction, it is easy to fall into the opposite sort of mistake. This is to envision, in the *Canterbury Tales*, a highly urbane, literal-historical Chaucer setting out from Southwark on a specific day of a specific year (we even argue somewhat acrimoniously about dates and routes), in company with a group of persons who existed in real life and whom Chaucer, his reporter's eye peeled for every idiosyncrasy, determined to get down on paper – down, that is, to the last wart – so that books might be written identifying them. Whenever this accurate reporter says something especially fatuous – which is not infrequently – it is either ascribed to an opinion peculiar to the Middle Ages (sometimes very peculiar), or else Chaucer's tongue is said to be in his cheek.

Now a Chaucer with tongue-in-cheek is a vast improvement over a simple-minded Chaucer when one is trying to define the whole man, but it must lead to a loss of critical perception, and in particular to a confused notion of Chaucerian irony, to see in the Prologue a reporter who is acutely aware of the significance of what he sees but who sometimes, for ironic emphasis, interprets the evidence presented by his observation in a fashion directly contrary to what we expect. The proposition ought to be expressed in reverse : the reporter is, usually, acutely unaware of the significance of what he sees, no matter how sharply he sees it. He is, to be sure, permitted his lucid intervals, but in general he is the victim of the poet's pervasive – not merely sporadic – irony. And as such he is also the chief agent by which the poet achieves his wonderfully complex, ironic, comic, serious vision of a world which is but a devious and confused, infinitely various pilgrimage to a certain shrine. It is, as I hope to make clear, a good deal more than merely fitting that our guide on such a pilgrimage should be a man of such naïveté as the Chaucer who tells the tale of 'Sir Thopas.' Let us accompany him a little distance.

It is often remarked that Chaucer really liked the Prioress very much, even though he satirized her gently – very gently. But this is an understatement: Chaucer the pilgrim may not be said merely to have liked the Prioress very much – he thought she was utterly charming. In the first twenty-odd lines of her portrait (A. 118 ff.) he employs, among other superlatives, the adverb *ful* seven times. Middle English uses *ful* where we use *very*, and if one translates the beginning of the portrait into a kind of basic English (which is what, in a way, it really is), one gets something like this: 'There was also a Nun, a Prioress, who was very sincere and modest in the way she smiled; her biggest oath was only "By saint Loy"; and she was called Madame Eglantine. She sang the divine service very well, intoning it in her nose very prettily, and she spoke French very nicely and elegantly' – and so on, down to the last gasp of sentimental appreciation. Indeed, the Prioress may be said to have transformed the rhetoric into something not unlike that of a very bright kindergarten child's descriptive theme. In his reaction to the Prioress Chaucer the pilgrim resembles another – if less – simple-hearted enthusiast: the Host, whose summons to her to tell a tale must be one of the politest speeches in the language. Not 'My lady prioresse, a tale now!' but, 'as curteisly as it had been a mayde',

> My lady Prioresse, by youre leve,
> So that I wiste I sholde yow nat greve,
> I wolde demen that ye tellen sholde
> A tale next, if so were that ye wolde.
> Now wol ye vouche sauf, my lady deere? (B.² 1637–41)

Where the Prioress reduced Chaucer to superlatives, she reduces the Host to subjunctives.

There is no need here to go deeply into the Prioress. Eileen Power's illustrations from contemporary episcopal records show with what extraordinary economy the portrait has been packed with abuses typical of fourteenth-century nuns. The abuses, to be sure, are mostly petty, but it is clear enough that the Prioress, while a perfect lady, is anything but a perfect nun; and attempts to whitewash her, of which there have been many, can only proceed from an innocence of heart equal to Chaucer the pilgrim's and undoubtedly directly influenced by it. For he, of course, is quite swept away by her irrelevant *sensibilité*, and as a result misses much of the point of what he sees. No doubt he feels that he has come a long way, socially speaking, since his encounter with the Black Knight in the forest, and he knows, or thinks he knows, a little more of what it's all about: in this case it seems to be mostly about good manners, kindness to animals, and female charm. Thus it has been argued that Chaucer's appreciation for the Prioress as a sort of heroine of courtly romance *manquée* actually reflects the sophistication of the living Chaucer, an urbane man who cared little whether amiable nuns were good nuns. But it seems a curious form of sophistication that permits itself to babble superlatives; and indeed, if this is sophistication, it is the kind generally seen in the least experienced people – one that reflects a wide-eyed wonder at the glamor of the great world. It is just what one might expect of a bourgeois exposed to the splendors of high society, whose values, such as they are, he eagerly accepts. And that is precisely what Chaucer the pilgrim is, and what he does.

If the Prioress's appeal to him is through elegant femininity, the Monk's is through imposing virility. Of this formidable and important prelate the pilgrim does not say, with Placebo,

> I woot wel that my lord kan moore than I:
> What that he seith, I holde it ferme and stable,
>
> (E. 1498–9)

but he acts Placebo's part to perfection. He is as impressed with the Monk as the Monk is, and accepts him on his own terms and at face value, never sensing that those terms imply complete condemnation of Monk *qua* Monk. The Host is also impressed by the Monk's virility, but having no sense of Placebonian propriety (he is himself a most virile man) he makes indecent jokes about it. This, naturally, offends the pilgrim's sense of decorum : there is a note of deferential commiseration in his comment, 'This worthy Monk took al in pacience' (B. 3155). Inevitably when the Monk establishes hunting as the highest activity of which religious man is capable, 'I seyde his opinion was good' (A. 183). As one of the pilgrim's spiritual heirs was later to say, Very like a whale; but not, of course, like a fish out of water.

Wholehearted approval for the values that important persons subscribe to is seen again in the portrait of the Friar. This amounts to a prolonged gratulation for the efficiency the deplorable Hubert shows in undermining the fabric of the Church by turning St. Francis' ideal inside out :

> Ful swetely herde he confessioun,
> And pleasaunt was his absolucioun.   (A. 221-2)

> For unto swich a worthy man as he
> Acorded nat, as by his facultee,
> To have with sike lazars aqueyntaunce.   (A. 243-5)

It is sometimes said that Chaucer did not like the Friar. Whether Chaucer the man would have liked such a Friar is, for our present purposes, irrelevant. But if the pilgrim does not unequivocally express his liking for him, it is only because in his humility he does not feel that, with important people, his own likes and dislikes are material : such importance is its own reward, and can gain no lustre from Geoffrey, who, when the Friar is attacked by the Summoner, is ready to show him the same sympathy he shows the Monk (see D. 1265-7).

Once he has finished describing the really important people on the pilgrimage the pilgrim's tone changes, for he can now concern himself with the bourgeoisie, members of his own class for whom he does not have to show such profound respect. Indeed, he can even afford to be a little patronizing at times, and to have his little joke at the expense of the too-busy lawyer. But such indirect assertions of his own superiority do not prevent him from giving substance to the old cynicism that the only motive recognized by the middle class is the profit motive, for his interest and admiration for the bourgeois pilgrims is centered mainly in their material prosperity and their ability to increase it. He starts, properly enough, with the out-and-out money-grubber, the Merchant, and after turning aside for that *lusus naturae*, the non-profit-motivated Clerk, proceeds to the Lawyer, who, despite the pilgrim's little joke, is the best and best-paid ever; the Franklin, twenty-one admiring lines on appetite, so expensively catered to; the Gildsmen, cheered up the social ladder, 'For catel hadde they ynogh and rente' (A. 373); and the Physician, again the best and richest. In this series the portrait of the Clerk is generally held to be an ideal one, containing no irony; but while it is ideal, it seems to reflect the pilgrim's sense of values in his joke about the Clerk's failure to make money: is not this still typical of the half-patronizing, half-admiring *un*understanding that practical men of business display towards academics? But in any case the portrait is a fine companion-piece for those in which material prosperity is the main interest both of the characters described and of the describer.

Of course, this is not the sole interest of so gregarious – if shy – a person as Chaucer the pilgrim. Many of the characters have the additional advantage of being good companions, a faculty that receives a high valuation in the Prologue. To be good company might, indeed, atone for certain serious defects of character. Thus the Shipman, whose callous cruelty is duly noted, seems fairly well redeemed in the assertion, 'And certeinly he was a good felawe' (A. 395). At this point an uneasy sensation that even tongue-in-cheek irony will not compensate for the lengths to which Chaucer is going in his approbation of this sinister seafarer sometimes causes editors to note that *a good felawe* means 'a rascal'. But I can find no evidence that it ever meant a rascal. Of course, all tritely approbative expressions enter easily into ironic connotation, but the phrase *means* a good companion, which is just what Chaucer means. And if, as he says of the

Shipman, 'Of nyce conscience took he no keep' (A. 398), Chaucer the pilgrim was doing the same with respect to him.

Nothing that has been said has been meant to imply that the pilgrim was unable to recognize, and deplore, a rascal when he saw one. He could, provided the rascality was situated in a member of the lower classes and provided it was, in any case, somewhat wider than a barn door : Miller, Manciple, Reeve, Summoner, and Pardoner are all acknowledged to be rascals. But rascality generally has, after all, the laudable object of making money, which gives it a kind of validity; if not dignity. These portraits, while in them the pilgrim, prioress-like conscious of the finer aspects of life, does deplore such matters as the Miller's indelicacy of language, contain a note of ungrudging admiration for efficient thievery. It is perhaps fortunate for the pilgrim's reputation as a judge of men that he sees through the Pardoner, since it is the Pardoner's particular tragedy that, except in Church, every one can see through him at a glance; but in Church he remains to the pilgrim 'a noble ecclesiaste' (A. 708). The equally repellent Summoner, a practising bawd, is partially redeemed by his also being a good fellow, 'a gentil harlot and a kynde' (A. 647), and by the fact that for a moderate bribe he will neglect to summon : the pilgrim apparently subscribes to the popular definition of the best policeman as the one who acts the least policely.

Therefore Chaucer is tolerant, and has his little joke about the Summoner's small Latin – a very small joke, though one of the most amusing aspects of the pilgrim's character is the pleasure he takes in his own jokes, however small. But the Summoner goes too far when he cynically suggests that purse is the Archdeacon's hell, causing Chaucer to respond with a fine show of righteous respect for the instruments of spiritual punishment. The only trouble is that his enthusiastic defense of them carries *him* too far, so that after having warned us that excommunication will indeed damn our souls –

> But wel I woot he lyed right in dede :
> Of cursyng oghte ech gilty man him drede,
> For curs wol slee right as assoillyng savith –
>
> (A. 659–61)

he goes on to remind us that it will also cause considerable inconvenience to our bodies: 'And also war hym of a *Significavit*' (A. 662). Since a *Significavit* is the writ accomplishing the imprisonment of the excommunicate, the line provides perhaps the neatest – and most misunderstood – Chaucerian anticlimax in the Prologue.

I have avoided mentioning, hitherto, the pilgrim's reactions to the really good people on the journey – the Knight, the Parson, the Plowman. One might reasonably ask how his uncertain sense of values may be reconciled with the enthusiasm he shows for their rigorous integrity. The question could, of course, be shrugged off with a remark on the irrelevance to art of exact consistency, even to art distinguished by its verisimilitude. But I am not sure that there is any basic inconsistency. It is the nature of the pilgrim to admire all kinds of superlatives, and the fact that he often admires superlatives devoid of – or opposed to – genuine virtue does not inhibit his equal admiration for virtue incarnate. He is not, after all, a bad man; he is, to place him in his literary tradition, merely an average man, or mankind: *homo*, not very *sapiens* to be sure, but with the very best intentions, making his pilgrimage through the world in search of what is good, and showing himself, too frequently, able to recognize the good only when it is spectacularly so. Spenser's Una glows with a kind of spontaneous incandescence, so that the Red Cross Knight, mankind in search of holiness, knows her as good; but he thinks that Duessa is good, too. Virtue concretely embodied in Una or the Parson presents no problems to the well-intentioned observer, but in a world consisting mostly of imperfections, accurate evaluations are difficult for a pilgrim who, like mankind, is naïve. The pilgrim's ready appreciation for the virtuous characters is perhaps the greatest tribute that could be paid to their virtue, and their spiritual simplicity is, I think, enhanced by the intellectual simplicity of the reporter.

The pilgrim belongs, of course, to a very old – and very new – tradition of the fallible first person singular. His most exact modern counterpart is perhaps Lemuel Gulliver who, in his search for the good, failed dismally to perceive the difference between the pursuit of reason and the pursuits of reasonable horses: one may be sure that the pilgrim would have whinnied with the best of them. In his own century he is related to Long Will of *Piers Plowman*, a more explicit seeker after the good, but just as unswerving in his inability correctly to evaluate what he sees. Another kinsman is the protagonist of the *Pearl*, mankind whose heart is set on a transitory good that has been lost – who, for very natural reasons, confuses earthly with spiritual values. Not entirely unrelated is the protagonist of Gower's *Confessio Amantis*, an old man seeking for an impossible earthly love that seems to him the only good. And in more subtle fashion there is the teller of Chaucer's story of *Troilus and Cressida*, who, while not a true protagonist, performs some of the same functions. For this unloved 'servant of the servants of love' falls in love with Cressida so persuasively that almost every male reader of the poem imitates him, so that we all share the heartbreak of Troilus and sometimes, in the intensity of our heartbreak, fail to learn what Troilus did. Finally, of course, there is Dante of the *Divine Comedy*, the most exalted member of the family and perhaps the immediate original of these other first-person pilgrims.

Artistically the device of the *persona* has many functions, so integrated with one another that to try to sort them out produces both oversimplification and distortion. The most obvious, with which this paper has been dealing – distortedly, is to present a vision of the social world imposed on one of the moral world. Despite their verisimilitude most, if not all, of the characters described in the Prologue are taken directly from stock and recur again and again in medieval literature. Langland in his own Prologue and elsewhere depicts many of them : the hunting monk, the avaricious friar, the thieving miller, the hypocritical pardoner, the unjust stewards, even, in little, the all-too-human nun. But while Langland uses the device of the *persona* with considerable skill in the conduct of his allegory, he uses it hardly at all in portraying the inhabitants of the social world : these are described directly, with the poet's own voice. It was left to Chaucer to turn the ancient stock satirical characters into real people assembled for a pilgrimage, and to have them described, with all their traditional faults upon them, by another pilgrim who records faithfully each fault without, for the most part, recognizing that it is a fault and frequently felicitating its possessor for possessing it. One result – though not the only result –

is a moral realism much more significant than the literary realism which is a part of it and for which it is sometimes mistaken; this moral realism discloses a world in which humanity is prevented by its own myopia, the myopia of the describer, from seeing what the dazzlingly attractive externals of life really represent. In most of the analogues mentioned above the fallible first person receives, at the end of the book, the education he has needed: the pilgrim arrives somewhere. Chaucer never completed the *Canterbury Tales*, but in the Prologue to the Parson's Tale he seems to have been doing, rather hastily, what his contemporaries had done: when, with the sun nine-and-twenty degrees from the horizon, the twenty-nine pilgrims come to a certain – unnamed – *thropes ende* (I. 12), then the pilgrimage seems no longer to have Canterbury as its destination, but rather, I suspect, the Celestial City of which the Parson speaks.

If one insists that Chaucer was not a moralist but a comic writer (a distinction without a difference), then the device of the *persona* may be taken primarily as serving comedy. It has been said earlier that the several Chaucers must have inhabited one body, and in that sense the fictional first person is no fiction at all. In an oral tradition of literature the first person probably always shared the personality of his creator: thus Dante of the *Divine Comedy* was physically Dante the Florentine; the John Gower of the *Confessio* was also Chaucer's friend John Gower; and Long Will was, I am sure, someone named William Langland, who was both long and wilful. And it is equally certain that Chaucer the pilgrim, 'a popet in an arm t'enbrace' (B.[2] 1891), was in every physical respect Chaucer the man, whom one can imagine reading his work to a courtly audience, as in the portrait appearing in one of the MSS. of *Troilus*. One can imagine also the delight of the audience which heard the Prologue read in this way, and which was aware of the similarities and dissimilarities between Chaucer, the man before them, and Chaucer the pilgrim, both of whom they could see with simultaneous vision. The Chaucer they knew was physically, one gathers, a little ludicrous; a bourgeois, but one who was known as a practical and successful man of the court; possessed perhaps of a certain diffidence of manner, reserved, deferential to the socially imposing persons with whom he was associated; a bit absent-minded, but affable and, one supposes, very good company – a good fellow; sagacious and highly perceptive. This Chaucer was telling them of another who, lacking some of his chief qualities, nevertheless possessed many of his characteristics, though in a different state of balance, and each one probably distorted just enough to become laughable without becoming unrecognizable : deference into a kind of snobbishness, affability into an over-readiness to please, practicality into Babbittry, perception into inspection, absence of mind into dimness of wit; a Chaucer acting in some respects just as Chaucer himself might have acted but unlike his creator the kind of man, withal, who could mistake a group of stock satirical types for living persons endowed with all sorts of superlative qualities. The constant interplay of these two Chaucers must have produced an exquisite and most ingratiating humor – as, to be sure, it still does. This comedy reaches its superb climax when Chaucer the pilgrim, resembling in so many ways Chaucer the poet, can answer the Host's demand for a story only with a rhyme he 'lerned longe agoon' (B.² 1899) – 'Sir Thopas', which bears the same complex relation to the kind of romance it satirizes and to Chaucer's own poetry as Chaucer the pilgrim does to the pilgrims he describes and to Chaucer the poet.

Earlier in this paper I proved myself no gentleman (though I hope a scholar) by being rude to the Prioress, and hence to the many who like her and think that Chaucer liked her too. It is now necessary to retract. Undoubtedly Chaucer the man would, like his fictional representative, have found her charming and looked on her with affection. To have got on so well in so changeable a world Chaucer must have got on well with the people in it, and it is doubtful that one may get on with people merely by pretending to like them : one's heart has to be in it. But the third entity, Chaucer the poet, operates in a realm which is above and subsumes those in which Chaucer the man and Chaucer the pilgrim have their being. In this realm prioresses may be simultaneously evaluated as marvelously amiable ladies and as prioresses. In his poem the poet arranges for the moralist to define austerely what ought to be and for his fictional representative – who, as the representative of all mankind, is no mere fiction – to go on affirming affectionately what is. The two points of

104

view, in strict moral logic diametrically opposed, are somehow made harmonious in Chaucer's wonderfully comic attitude, that double vision that is his ironical essence. The mere critic performs his etymological function by taking the Prioress apart and clumsily separating her good parts from her bad; but the poet's function is to build her incongruous and inharmonious parts into an inseparable whole which is infinitely greater than its parts. In this complex structure both the latent moralist and the naïve reporter have important positions, but I am not persuaded that in every case it is possible to determine which of them has the last word.

SOURCE: *PMLA*, LXIX (1954)

NOTE

Quotations from Chaucer in this paper are made from F. N. Robinson's text (Cambridge, Mass., 1933). Books referred to or cited are G. L. Kittredge, *Chaucer and His Poetry* (Cambridge, Mass., 1915) p. 45; Eileen Power, *Medieval People* (London, 1924) pp. 59–84. Robinson's note to A. 650 records the opinion that *a good felawe* means a 'rascal'. The medieval reader's expectation that the first person in a work of fiction would represent mankind generally and at the same time would physically resemble the author is commented on by Leo Spitzer in an interesting note in *Traditio*, IV (1946) 414–22.

Arthur W. Hoffman

CHAUCER'S PROLOGUE TO
PILGRIMAGE: THE TWO VOICES (1954)

Criticism of the portraits in Chaucer's General Prologue to the
Canterbury Tales has taken various directions : some critics have
praised the portraits especially for their realism, sharp in-
dividuality, adroit psychology, and vividness of felt life; others,
working in the genetic direction, have pointed out actual
historical persons who might have sat for the portraits; others,
appealing to the light of the medieval sciences, have shown the
portraits to be filled, though not burdened, with the lore of
Chaucer's day, and to have sometimes typical identities like case
histories. Miss Bowden,[1] in her recent study of the Prologue,
assembles the fruits of many earlier studies and gives the text an
impressive resonance by sketching historical and social norms and
ideals, the facts and the standards of craft, trade, and profession,
so that the form of the portraits can be tested in the light of possible conformities, mean or noble, to things as they were or to
things as they ought to have been.

It is not unlikely that the critics who have explored in these
various directions would be found in agreement on one commonplace, a metaphor which some of them indeed have used,
the designation of the portraits in the General Prologue as
figures in a tapestry. It is less likely that all of the critics would
agree as to the implications of this metaphor, but it seems to me
that the commonplace deserves to be explored and some of its
implications tested. The commonplace implies that the portraits
which appear in the General Prologue have a designed together-
ness, that the portraits exist as parts of a unity.

Such a unity, it may be argued, is partly a function of the
exterior framework of a pilgrimage to Canterbury; all the portraits are portraits of pilgrims :

At nyght was come into that hostelrye
 Wel nyne and twenty in a compaignye,
 Of sondry folk, by aventure yfalle
 In felaweshipe, and pilgrimes were they alle. (A. 23–6)[2]

But the unity of the Prologue may be also partly a matter of internal relationships among the portraits, relationships which are
many and various among 'sondry folk'. One cannot hope to survey all of these, but the modest objective of studying some of the
aesthetically important internal relationships is feasible.

If one begins with the unity that is exterior to the portraits, the
unity that contains them, one faces directly the question of the
nature of pilgrimage as it is defined in this dramatic poem. What
sort of framework does the Prologue in fact define? Part of the
answer is in the opening lines, and it is not a simple answer because the definition there ranges from the upthrust and burgeon-
ing of life as a seasonal and universal event to a particular out-
pouring of people, pilgrims, gathered briefly at the Tabard Inn
in Southwark, drifting, impelled, bound, called to the shrine of
Thomas a Becket at Canterbury. The pilgrimage is set down in
the calendar of seasons as well as in the calendar of piety; nature
impels and supernature draws. 'Go, go, go,' says the bird; 'Come,'
says the saint.

In the opening lines of the Prologue springtime is characterized
in terms of procreation, and a pilgrimage of people to Canterbury is just one of the many manifestations of the life thereby
produced. The phallicism of the opening lines presents the
impregnating of a female March by a male April, and a marriage of water and earth. The marriage is repeated and varied
immediately as a fructifying of 'holt and heeth' by Zephirus, a
marriage of air and earth. This mode of symbolism and these
symbols as parts of a rite of spring have a long background of
tradition; as Professor Cook[3] once pointed out, there are eminent
passages of this sort in Aeschylus and Euripides, in Lucretius, in
Virgil's *Georgics*, in Columella, and in the *Pervigilium
Veneris*, and Professor Robinson cites Guido delle Colonne,
Boccaccio, Petrarch, and Boethius. Zephirus is the only overt
mythological figure in Chaucer's passage, but, in view of the
instigative role generally assigned to Aphrodite in the rite of

spring, she is perhaps to be recognized here, as Professor Cook suggested, in the name of April, which was her month both by traditional association and by one of the two ancient etymologies.[4] Out of this context of the quickening of the earth presented naturally and symbolically in the broadest terms, the Prologue comes to pilgrimage and treats pilgrimage first as an event in the calendar of nature, one aspect of the general springtime surge of human energy and longing. There are the attendant suggestions of the renewal of human mobility after the rigor and confinement of winter, the revival of wayfaring now that the ways are open. The horizon extends to distant shrines and foreign lands, and the attraction of the strange and faraway is included before the vision narrows and focusses upon its English specifications and the pilgrimage to the shrine at Canterbury with the vows and gratitude that send pilgrims there. One way of regarding the structure of this opening passage would emphasize the magnificent progression from the broadest inclusive generality to the firmest English specification, from the whole western tradition of the celebration of spring (including, as Cook pointed out, such a non-English or very doubtfully English detail as 'the droghte of March') to a local event of English society and English Christendom, from natural forces in their most general operation to a very specific and Christian manifestation of those forces. And yet one may regard the structure in another way, too; if, in the calendar of nature, the passage moves from general to particular, does it not, in the calendar of piety, move from nature to something that includes and oversees nature? Does not the passage move from an activity naturally generated and impelled to a governed activity, from force to *telos*? Does not the passage move from Aphrodite and *amor* in their secular operation to the sacred embrace of 'the hooly blisful martir' and of *amor dei*?

The transition from nature to supernature is emphasized by the contrast between the healthful physical vigor of the opening lines and the reference to sickness that appears in l. 18. On the one hand, it is physical vitality which conditions the pilgrimage; on the other hand, sickness occasions pilgrimage. It is, in fact, rather startling to come upon the word 'seeke' at the end of this opening passage, because it is like a breath of winter across the landscape of spring. 'Whan that they were seeke' may, of course, refer literally to illnesses of the winter just past, but, in any event, illness belongs symbolically to the inclement season. There is also, however, a strong parallelism between the beginning and end of this passage, a parallelism that has to do with restorative power. The physical vitality of the opening is presented as restorative of the dry earth; the power of the saint is presented as restorative of the sick. The seasonal restoration of nature parallels a supernatural kind of restoration that knows no season; the supernatural kind of restoration involves a wielding and directing of the forces of nature. The Prologue begins, then, by presenting a double view of the Canterbury pilgrimage : the pilgrimage is one tiny manifestation of a huge tide of life, but then, too, the tide of life ebbs and flows in response to the power which the pilgrimage acknowledges, the power symbolized by 'the hooly blisful martir'.

After l. 18 the process of particularizing is continued, moving from 'that seson' just defined to a day and to a place and to a person in Southwark at the Tabard, and thence to the portraits of the pilgrims. The double view of pilgrimage is enhanced and extended by the portraits where it appears, in one aspect, as a range of motivation. This range of motivation is from the sacred to the secular and on to the profane – 'profane' in the sense of motivations actually subversive of the sacred. All the pilgrims are, in fact, granted an ostensible sacred motive; all of them are seeking the shrine. The distances that we are made aware of are both *within* some of the portraits, where a gulf yawns between ostensible and actual motivation, and *between* the portraits, where the motivation of the Knight and the Parson is near one end of the spectrum, and the motivation of the Summoner and the Pardoner near the other end. There is such an impure but blameless mixture as the motivation of the Prioress; there is the secular pilgrimage of the Wife of Bath, impelled so powerfully and frankly by Saint Venus rather than drawn by Saint Thomas, and goaded by a Martian desire to acquire and dominate another husband; in the case of the Prioress, an inescapable doubt as to the quality of *amor* hesitates between the sacred and secular, and in the case of the thoroughly secular Wife of Bath, doubt hesitates between the secular and the profane while the portrait shows the ostensible motive that belongs to all the pilgrims shaken without ever being subverted, contradicted perhaps, brazenly opposed, but still acknowleged and offered, not, at any rate, hypocritically betrayed. In the area of motivation, the portraits seem to propose, ultimately, a fundamental, inescapable ambiguity as part of the human condition; prayer for the purification of motive is valid for all the pilgrims. And the pilgrims who move, pushed by impulse and drawn by vows, none merely impelled and none perfectly committed, reflect, in their human ambiguity, the broad problem of origins and ends, the stubbornness of matter and the power of spirit, together with ideas of cosmic resolution and harmony in which source and end are reconciled and seen to be the same, the purposes of nature and supernature found to be at one, the two restorative powers akin, the kinds of love not discontinuous, Saint Venus and Saint Thomas different and at odds yet not at war, within the divine purpose which contains both.

The portraits of the Knight and the Squire have a particular interest. The relationships between these two portraits are governed by and arise out of the natural relationship of father and son. Consanguinity provides the base for a dramatic relationship, and at the same time is the groundwork for a modestly generalized metaphor of age and youth. Each portrait is enhanced and defined by the presence of the other: the long roll of the Knight's campaigns, and the Squire's little opportunity ('so litel space'), a few raids enumerated in one line; a series of past tenses, a history, for the Knight, and for the Squire a present breaking forth in active participles; the Knight not 'gay', wearing fustian soiled by his coat of mail, 'bismotered', the Squire bright and fresh and colorful; the Knight meek and quiet – or so the portrait leaves him – beside the Squire, who sings and whistles all the day. The Knight's love is an achieved devotion, a matter of pledges fulfilled and of values, if not completely realized, yet woven into the fabric of experience (ideals – 'trouthe', 'honour', 'fredom', 'curteisie'). The Squire is a lover, a warm and eager lover, paying court to his lady and sleeping no more than the nightingale. In the one, the acquired, tutored, disciplined, elevated, enlarged love, the piety; and in the other, the love channelled into an elaborate social ritual, a parody piety, but still emphatically fresh and full of natural impulse. One cannot miss the creation of the Squire in conventional images of nature, the meadow, the flowers, the freshness like May, the lover like the nightingale – comparisons that are a kind of re-emergence of the opening lines of the Prologue, the springtime surge of youthful, natural energy that animates the beginning. 'Go, go, go', the bird's voice, is a major impulse in the portrait of the Squire and in the Squire's pilgrimage; the Knight's pilgrimage is more nearly a response to the voice of the saint. Yet the Squire is within the belt of rule, and learning the calendar of piety. The concluding couplet of the portrait

> Curteis he was, lowely and servysable,
> And carf biforn his fader at the table.   (A. 99–100)

has the effect of bending all the youth, energy, color, audibleness, and high spirit of the Squire to the service of his father, the Knight, and to attendance on his pilgrimage, with perhaps a suggestion of the present submitting to the serious and respected values served and communicated by the past, the natural and the imposed submitting of the son to his natural father, and beyond him to the supernatural goal, the shrine to which the father directs his pilgrimage.

The portraits of the Knight and the Squire represent one of the ways in which portraiture takes into account and develops the double definition of pilgrimage which is established at the beginning. The double definition of pilgrimage is involved in a different way in the portrait of the Prioress; there it appears as a delicately poised ambiguity. Two definitions appear as two faces of one coin. Subsequently, when the portrait of the Prioress is seen together with the portraits of the Monk and the Friar, a sequence is realized, running from ambiguity to emphatic discrepancy, and the satire that circles the impenetrable duality of sacred and secular impulse in the case of the Prioress, knifes in as these impulses are drawn apart in the case of the Monk and strikes vigorously in the still wider breach that appears in the case of the Friar. What is illustrated within the portraits is amplified by a designed sequence.

The delicate balance in the picture of the Prioress has been generally recognized and has perhaps been only the more clearly exhibited by occasional seesawing in the critical interpretation of the portrait in which the satiric elements are sometimes represented as heavy, sometimes as slight, sometimes sinking the board, and sometimes riding light and high. There is, perhaps, no better illustration of the delicacy of the balance than the fact that the Prioress's very presence on a pilgrimage, as several commentators have pointed out, may be regarded as the first satiric touch. The very act of piety is not free from the implication of imperfection; the Prioress is obligated to a cloistered piety that serves and worships God without going on a journey to seek a shrine, and prioresses were specifically and repeatedly enjoined from going on pilgrimages. Prioresses did, nevertheless, go as pilgrims, so that Chaucer's Prioress is not departing from the norm of behavior of persons in her office so much as she is departing from the sanctioned ideal of behavior.[5] In the case of the Prioress, the blemish is sufficiently technical to have only faint satiric coloring; it is not the notable kind of blemish recognized in all times and all places. Nevertheless, it is precisely this kind of hint of a spot that places the Prioress at one end of a sequence in which the more obviously blemished Monk and Friar appear. If we pose a double question – What kind of woman is the Prioress, and what kind of prioress is the woman? – the portrait responds more immediately to the first part of the question, and leaves the answer to the second part largely in the area of implication. The portrait occupies forty-five lines, and more than three-fourths of the lines have to do with such matters as the Prioress's blue eyes, her red mouth, the shape of her nose and width of her forehead, her ornaments and dress, her table manners, her particular brand of French, her pets and what she fed them, and her tenderness about mice. It is, of course, one of the skilful arts of these portraits to work with surfaces and make the surfaces convey and reveal what lies beneath, but it should be observed that in the case of the Parson – or even in the case of the Knight – a character is arrived at almost entirely without physical and superficial detail. One need not take the emphatic surface in the portrait of the Prioress as necessarily pejorative in its implication; it need not follow that the Prioress is a shallow and superficial person, and, in consequence, sharply satirized. But the portrait does seem, by means of its emphasis on surfaces, to define the Prioress as woman, and strongly enough so that tension between the person and her office, between the given human nature and the assumed sacred obligation is put vividly before us, and rather as the observation of a fact than as the instigation of a judgment. In the cases of the Monk and the Friar, the tension is so exacerbated that judgment is, in the case of the Monk, incited, and in the case of the Friar, both incited and inflamed to severity.

In the portrait of the Prioress the double view of pilgrimage appears both in an ambiguity of surfaces, and in an implied inner range of motivation. In the surfaces there is a sustained hovering effect: the name, Eglentyne, is romance, and 'simple and coy' is a romance formula, but she *is* a nun, by whatever name, and 'simple' and 'coy', aside from their romance connotations, have meanings ('simple' and 'modest') appropriate enough to a nun; there are the coral beads and the green gauds, but they *are* a rosary; there are the fluted wimple and the exposed forehead, but the costume *is* a nun's habit; there is the golden brooch shining brightly, but it *is* a religious emblem. Which shall be taken as principal, which as modifying and subordinate? Are the departures or the conformities more significant of her nature? Are her Stratford French and her imitation of court manners more important than the fact that she sings well and properly the divine service? Do we detect vanity in her singing well, or do we rely on what she sings and accept her worship as well performed – to the glory of God? The ambiguity of these surface indications leads into the implied range of motivation; this implied range has been generally recognized in the motto – '*Amor vincit omnia*' – on the Prioress's golden brooch, and the implications set up in the portrait as a whole seem to be clustered and tightly fastened in this ornament and symbol.

The motto itself has, in the course of history, gone its own double pilgrimage to the shrine of Saint Venus and to sacred shrines; the original province of the motto was profane, but it was drawn over to a sacred meaning and soon became complexly involved with and compactly significant of both. Professor Lowes comments on the motto as it pertains to the Prioress:

Now is it earthly love that conquers all, now heavenly; the phrase plays back and forth between the two. And it is precisely that happy ambiguity of the convention – itself the result of an earlier transfer – that makes Chaucer's use of it here . . . a master stroke. *Which of the two loves does 'amor' mean to the Prioress?* I do not know; but I think she thought she meant love celestial.[6]

Professor Lowes, presumably, does not really expect to see the matter concluded one way or the other and finds this very inconclusiveness, hovering between two answers, one of the excellences of the portrait. There is, however, a certain amount of illumination to be gained, though not an answer to the question as formulated by Professor Lowes, by asking the question another way and considering an answer in terms that lie outside of the Prioress's motivation. Put the question in this form: Which of the two loves does the *portrait* in the context of the Prologue mean by *amor*? The answer to this question, of course, is *both*. On the one hand, profane love or the love of earthly things does overcome all; the little vanities and pretensions, the love of color and decoration and dress, the affection squandered in little extravagances towards pets, the pity and tender emotion wasted upon a trapped mouse – the multiplicity of secular, impulsive loves threatens to and could ultimately stifle the dedication to the celestial love. This answer is, in fact, a version of the Prioress's character and motivation sometimes offered. It actually implies one half of the view of pilgrimage – the natural powers that move people and that may usurp the whole character. But the other answer – celestial love conquers all things – also applies to the portrait, though it is not very easily arrived at in terms of the Prioress's motivation. Here we are dealing with the ostensible meaning of the motto, the ideal meaning of the motto as worn by a prioress – what it ought to mean in terms of her office. And, no matter what the impurity of the Prioress's motives, no matter what she means or thinks she means by the motto, the motto does, in the calendar of piety, mean that God's love is powerful over all things, powerful in this case over the vanity that may be involved in the wearing of the brooch, powerful over all the shallowness and limitation and reduction and misdirection of love that the Prioress may be guilty of, powerful over all her departures from or misunderstandings of discipline and obligation and vow, powerful over all inadequacy, able to overcome the faults of God's human instruments and make this woman's divine office valid. The motto, and the portrait of which it is the conclusion, appreciate both the secular impulses and the sacred redemptive will, but there is no doubt which love it is that is crowned with ultimate power.

Chaucer has found ways, as in the case of the Prioress, of making an ideal or standard emerge within a portrait. The standard may be ambiguously stated or heavily involved in irony, but it is almost always present, and nowhere with greater effectiveness than in the most sharply satiric portraits. This, I take it, is the effect of the formula of worthiness which is applied to so many of the pilgrims. A character is declared to be 'worthy' or 'the best that ever was' of his craft or profession or office, and frequently under circumstances that make the statement jarring and the discrepancy obvious. There is a definite shock, for example, when Friar Huberd is declared to be a 'worthy lymytour', or the Pardoner 'a noble ecclesiaste'. Even when the satiric thrust has two directions, striking both at the individual and at the group to which he belongs, the implication has nevertheless been lodged in the portrait that there could be, for example, a worthy friar, or a pardoner who was indeed a noble ecclesiastic. The reader is, as it were, tripped in the act of judging and reminded that if he condemns these figures, if they appear culpable, there must be some sort of standard by which they are so judged, by which they appear so.

Chaucer has also adopted the method of including ideal or nearly ideal portraits among the pilgrims. There are, for example, the Knight and the Plowman, figures at either end of the secular range, and among the clerical figures there is the Parson. A host of relative judgments, of course, are set up by devices of sequence and obvious pairing and contrasting of portraits. It is the ideal portraits, however, that somehow preside over all these judgments and comparisons, and it is to them that the relative distinctions are presented for a kind of penultimate judgment. Prioress, Monk, and Friar, and all the other clerical figures are reckoned with the Parson who is, in fact, made to speak in an accent of judgment upon the clerical figures who go astray – '. . . if gold ruste, what shal iren do?' (We may remember the

Prioress's shining gold brooch, the Monk's gold pin, and, among the secular figures, the Physician who so doubly regarded gold as a sovereign remedy.)

Chaucer has used an interesting device for undergirding the ideal portrait of the Parson. He employs consanguinity with metaphorical effect. After the assertions which declare that the Parson 'first . . . wroghte, and afterward . . . taughte', the actualizing of Christian ideals is supported by the representation of the Parson as brother to the Plowman. It is the Parson's Christian obligation to treat men as brothers, and the portrait abundantly affirms that he does so. Making him actually the brother of the Plowman brilliantly insists that what supernature calls for is performed by the Parson and, more than that, comes by nature to him.[7] The achieved harmony both comes from above and rises out of the ground; sacred and secular are linked, the shepherd of souls and the tiller of the soil. This is a vantage point from which the conflicts of secular and sacred, of nature and supernature, are seen in a revealing light, a point at which one sees reflected in the clear mirror of ideal characters and an actual–ideal relationship the fundamental double view of pilgrimage established in the beginning.

The double definition of pilgrimage is differently but nonetheless revealingly illuminated by the portraits of another fraternizing pair, the Summoner and Pardoner, who conclude the sequence of pilgrims. The illumination here is not clarified by way of ideal characters but somehow refracted and intensified by the dark surfaces upon which it falls. The darkness is most visible in connection with the theme of love, which appears here in a sinister and terrible distortion. The hot and lecherous Summoner, the type of sexual unrestraint, is represented as harmonizing in song with the impotent Pardoner, the eunuch; the deep rumbling voice and the thin effeminate voice are singing, 'Com hider, love, to me!' The song, in this context, becomes both a promiscuous and perverted invitation and an unconscious symbolic acknowledgment of the absence of and the need for love, love that comes neither to the grasping physical endeavor of the Summoner nor to the physical incapacity of the Pardoner – nor to their perverted spirits. Love has been treated in the Prologue from the beginning as dual in character, a matter both of

the body and the spirit, the *amor* symbolized by Venus, sung by
the Squire, equivocally illustrated by the Prioress, lustily
celebrated by the Wife of Bath; and the *amor dei*, the love
shadowily there beyond all the secular forms of love, a hovering
presence among the pilgrims and sometimes close, as to the
Knight and the Parson and the Plowman, and symbolized in the
saint's shrine which is the goal of all of them. On this view, the
song of the Summoner and the Pardoner is a superb dramatic
irony acknowledging the full extent of their need and loss, the
love of God which they ought to strive for, the love which they
desperately need.

The office which each of these men is supposed to fulfill
should be taken into account. The Summoner is, ostensibly, an
instrument through whom divine justice, in a practical way,
operates in the world. There are, in the portrait, a few touches
that may be reminders of the ultimate source of his authority and
function: his *'Questio quid iuris'*, though it is represented
satirically as the sum and substance of his knowledge, and posed
as a question, *is* legitimately the substance of his knowledge – his
province is law, especially the divine law; *'Significavit'* is the
opening word of a legal writ, a dreaded worldly pronouncement
of divine judgment, excommunication; he is physically a fearful figure from whom children run (not the divine love which
suffers them to come), and some of the physical details may be
reminders of noble and awesome aspects of divine justice – his
'fyr-reed cherubynnes face' and the voice described in a
significant analogy as like a trumpet, 'Was nevere trompe of half
so greet a soun'. The Pardoner, on the other hand, is the ostensible instrument of divine mercy and love. Many of the pardoners,
as Miss Bowden points out, went so far as to pretend to absolve
both *a poena* and *a culpa*, thereby usurping, in the pretended
absolution *a culpa*, a function which theological doctrine reserved
to God and His grace. In any case, their legitimate functions were
an appeal for charity and an extension of God's mercy and love.
The Pardoner, it should be observed, is, compared to the Summoner, an attractive figure. We may be reminded of the superior
affinity of the Pardoner's office by the veil which he has sewed
upon his cap, the copy of St. Veronica's veil which is supposed
to have received the imprint of Christ's face.[8]

The justice and love[9] of which the Summoner and Pardoner
are emissaries are properly complementary and harmoniously,
though paradoxically and mysteriously, related, so that the advances that are being made both of persons and of values are, in a
very serious sense, proper to this pair. The radical physical distinctness of Summoner and Pardoner is at this level the
definition of two aspects of supernature; there is the same employment of physical metaphor here that there is in the portraits
of the Parson and the Plowman, but with the difference that
light comes out of darkness, and out of the gravest corruption of
nature the supernatural relationship emerges clarified in
symbol. The Summoner cannot finally pervert, and the
Pardoner's impotence cannot finally prevent; the divine justice
and love are powerful even over these debased instruments –
Amor vincit omnia. Beyond their knowing, beyond their power
or impotence, impotently both Pardoner and Summoner appeal
for the natural love – melody of bird-song and meadows of
flowers – and both pray for the celestial love, the ultimate pardon
which in their desperate and imprisoned darkness is their only
hope : 'Com hider, love, to me !'

The exterior unity achieved by the realistic device and
broadly symbolic framework of pilgrimage is made stronger and
tighter in the portraits, partly by local sequences and pairings, but
most impressively by the illustration, the variation and enrichment by way of human instances, of a theme of love, earthly and
celestial, and a general complex intermingling of the consideration of nature with the consideration of supernature. The note
of love is sounded in different keys all through the portraits :

The Knight   . . . he loved chivalrie,
                    Trouthe and honour, fredom and curteisie
                                                      (A. 45–6)

The Squire   A lovyere and a lusty bacheler . . . (A. 80)

                    So hoote he lovede that by nyghtertale
                    He sleep namoore than dooth a nyghtyngale.
                                                      (A. 97–8)

The Prioress   . . . *Amor vincit omnia.* (A. 162)

The Monk   A Monk . . . that lovede venerie, . . . (A. 166)

He hadde of gold ywroght a ful curious pyn;
A love-knotte in the gretter ende ther was.
(A. 196–7)

A fat swan loved he best of any roost. (A. 206)

The Friar   In love-dayes ther koude he muchel help . . .
(A. 258)

Somewhat he lipsed, for his wantownesse, . . .
(A. 264)

The Clerk   For hym was levere have at his beddes heed
Twenty bookes, clad in blak or reed,
Of Aristotle and his philosophie,
Than robes riche, or fithele, or gay sautrie.
(A. 293–6)

The Frankelyn Wel loved he by the morwe a sop in wyn;
To lyven in delit was evere his wone,
For he was Epicurus owene sone . . . (A. 334–6)

The Physician He kepte that he wan in pestilence.
For gold in phisik is a cordial,
Therefore he lovede gold in special. (A. 442–4)

The Wife of   Of remedies of love she knew per chaunce,
Bath   For she koude of that art the olde daunce.
(A. 475–6)

The Parson   But rather wolde he yeven, out of doute,
Unto his povre parisshens aboute
Of his offryng and eek of his substaunce.
(A. 487–9)

. . . Cristes loore and his apostles twelve
He taughte, but first he folwed it hymselve.
(A. 527–8)

The Plowman With hym ther was a Plowman, was his
brother, . . . (A. 529)

> Lyvynge in pees and parfit charitee.
> God loved he best with al his hoole herte
> At alle tymes, thogh him gamed or smerte,
> And thanne his neighebor right as hymselve.
>
> (A. 532-5)

The Summoner
    and
the Pardoner   ... 'Com hider, love, to me!' (A. 672)

The theme of restorative power attends upon the theme of love. It is, of course, announced at the beginning and defined in terms both of nature and supernature. Both the Physician, concerned with natural healing, and the Pardoner, the agent of a supernatural healing, appear under the rubric of 'Physician, heal thyself'. The worldly Physician is disaffected from God; the Pardoner is naturally impotent. Serious inadequacy in either realm appears as counterpart of inadequacy in the other. It is the Parson who both visits the sick and tends properly to the cure of souls; he works harmoniously in both realms, and both realms are in harmony and fulfilled in him.

The pilgrims are represented as affected by a variety of destructive and restorative kinds of love. Their characters and movement can be fully described only as mixtures of the loves that drive and goad and of the love that calls and summons. The pilgrims have, while they stay and when they move, their worldly host. They have, too, their worldly Summoner and Pardoner who, in the very worst way, move and are moved with them. Nevertheless, the Summoner and Pardoner, who conclude the roll of the company, despite and beyond their appalling personal deficiency, may suggest the summoning and pardoning, the judgment and grace which in Christian thought embrace and conclude man's pilgrimage and which therefore, with all the corrosions of satire and irony, are also the seriously appropriate conclusion to the tapestry of Chaucer's pilgrims.

S o u r c e : *Journal of English Literary History*, xxi (1954).

NOTES

1. Muriel Bowden, *A Commentary on the General Prologue to the Canterbury Tales* (New York, 1948).

2. All references to the text of the *Canterbury Tales* are to *The Poetical Works of Chaucer*, ed. F. N. Robinson (Cambridge, Mass., 1933).

3. Albert S. Cook, 'Chaucerian Papers – 1 : 1 Prologue 1–11', *Transactions of the Connecticut Academy of Arts and Sciences*, XXIII (New Haven, 1919) 5–21.

4. Cook, 5–10.

5. The relevance of the ideal sanctioned character of an office to the portrait of a person will appear again strikingly in the case of the Summoner and the Pardoner.

6. John Livingston Lowes, *Convention and Revolt in Poetry* (Boston and New York, 1919) p. 66.

7. There is, of course, plenty of actual basis for representing a parson as a son of the soil; the connection is not merely an artistic and symbolic device.

8. Later, in telling his story, the Pardoner acknowledges that his pardons are inferior versions of the supreme pardon which is Christ's. See the Pardoner's Tale, C. 915–18.

9. This statement of the symbolic values behind the Summoner and the Pardoner is not a disagreement with, but merely an addition to, the point made by Kellogg and Haselmayer (Alfred L. Kellogg and Louis A. Haselmayer, 'Chaucer's Satire of the Pardoner', *PMLA*, LXVI (1951) 215–77, when they assert : 'In this paradox, this ironic portrait of justice and crime singing in close harmony, we reach the center of Chaucer's satire' (p. 275). There is, indeed, the strongest satiric impact in this affiliation of the man who should apprehend the wrongdoer with the criminal. In addition, however, if we are to see beyond the Summoner's disabilities to his representation of justice, we see in parallel vision beyond the Pardoner's disabilities a representation of love.

William Frost

AN INTERPRETATION OF CHAUCER'S
KNIGHT'S TALE (1949)

In his recent article, 'A Reinterpretation of Chaucer's Theseus'
[*Review of English Studies*, xxiii (1947) 289–96], Professor
Henry J. Webb undertakes to demonstrate that the Theseus of
the Knight's Tale is more of a villain that has commonly been
believed. It is his contention that Chaucer, in reworking his
source material, emphasized or added to 'those traits in the
character of Theseus which were ignoble or cruel'; and that the
poet's frequent use of the adjective 'noble' in conjunction with
Theseus's name is to be interpreted as ironic (pp. 289, 296).
Part of Mr. Webb's argument is based on Theseus's actions in
the Tale (his destruction of Thebes, pillaging of the Theban
country-side, imprisonment of Palamon and Arcite without asking ransom, and release of Arcite without releasing Palamon);
part is based on the character of Theseus as it appears in other
legends about him (notably in the story of his desertion of
Ariadne, which Chaucer recounts in *The Legend of Good
Women*).

Mr. Webb's reinterpretation appears to me partial, mislead-
ing, and incomplete. To deal with the second class of evidence
first, it is a moot question how closely the Theseus of the Knight's
Tale is to be identified with the Theseus of the Ariadne story.
Mr. Webb, if I understand him correctly, supposes that the
Ariadne episode occurred *later* in Theseus's life than the events
of the Tale; thus he says that Theseus's character 'soon suffered
a change' (p. 289), and speaks of Arcite's release as having 'foreshadowed the deed which eventually damned the duke' (p. 294).
But it is clear from l. 980 of the Knight's Tale that the conquest
of the Minotaur, which led immediately to the betrayal of
Ariadne, had taken place *before* the Palamon and Arcite story.
Probably long before; for in the Knight's Tale Theseus is no
longer a young man [he says that he has been a lover 'ful yore

agon' (1813)]; while according to Chaucer's version of the Ariadne story he was sent to Crete at the age of twenty-three (*L.G.W.* 2075).

But even setting chronology aside, how closely are we to identify the Theseuses of the two stories? I would suggest that they be kept quite distinct. In the Legend of Ariadne, one more woeful tale of a woman abandoned by her lover, Chaucer is using the figure of Theseus for a purpose utterly unlike his purpose in the Knight's Tale; and, furthermore, the circumstances of the two stories are not compatible with each other if the two are taken as relating episodes in the life of the same man. Egeus, Theseus's father, drowns at the end of Chaucer's Ariadne legend (*L.G.W.* 2178), probably as a kind of poetic penalty for his son's faithlessness to that heroine; but in the Knight's Tale – many years later – Egeus is still alive, though aged, and has a speaking part (2837–52). All that remains, in the Knight's Tale, of the whole Cretan business is a single passing reference to the heroic glories of Theseus's early youth.

As for Theseus's actions in the Tale, Mr. Webb reviews several of them in the light of various medieval treatises on chivalry with the object of showing that the Duke was at times an abnormally cruel and arbitrary ruler. Here his argument would have more point, I think, if Theseus were an historical English duke rather than a figure in a poem. As a figure in a poem he is entitled to be regarded first of all in the light of the full literary context in which he appears; but Mr. Webb omits entirely any consideration of such an important part of that context as, for example, Theseus's 'cheyne of love' speech (2987 ff.). When Chaucer calls his Friar 'noble' in his description of him in the Prologue (208 ff.) it is clear from the preceding lines (which have strongly implied that the Friar is a great seducer of women) that the praise is ironic; but we have no corresponding reason, in the text of the Knight's Tale itself, for interpreting the praise of Theseus in a similarly ambiguous light.

I agree entirely with Mr. Webb when he calls Theseus one of the most complex characters delineated anywhere in the *Canterbury Tales*; but for an understanding of his complexities nothing less than a review of the entire poem as an artistic unit will adequately serve.[1]

The labours of modern medievalists have clarified for us much of the intellectual, historical, and literary materials which went into the creation of the poem Chaucer put into the mouth of his Knight and dignified as the first of the *Canterbury Tales*. Thanks to historical scholarship we now know not only that its immediate source was in Boccaccio rather than 'Stace of Thebes and thise bookes olde' (as the Knight rather vaguely puts it) but also just what Chaucer imitated from the Italian's *Teseide*, what he left out, and where he got much of what he added. Arcite's 'maladye of Hereos' has been diagnosed by Professor Lowes with an erudition no doubt few fourteenth-century physicians could have commanded; Chaucer's use of the *Teseide* (in the Knight's Tale and elsewhere) has been related to his general development as a poet by Professor R. A. Pratt; Professor B. A. Wise has traced the inspiration of some passages in the Tale back to 'Stace of Thebes' himself; Professors B. L. Jefferson and H. R. Patch have derived many ideas in the poem from the tradition of Boethius. The mysteries of Chaucerian astrology have been clarified by Professor W. C. Curry; a number of writers have dealt with the conventions of courtly love embodied in the story; and the close relation of the military aspects of the Tale to actual fourteenth-century warfare has been established: indeed, the latest suggestion is that the tournament at the climax of the plot may have been inspired by a real tournament Chaucer probably witnessed in London.[2]

In short, we know something of Chaucer's experiences, library, tastes, opinions, and methods of composition; as well as, by inference, something of the point of view of his earliest audience – we can dimly imagine how it felt to read the Knight's Tale in the 1390s. But on the Tale as a tale – except for widespread comments that it is, generally speaking, a good one – much less has been written and very little agreement been reached. What may be the point of the story is frequently debated, votes having been registered for the Tale as allegory, as a riddle, as a pseudo-epic (marred by omission of too much of Boccaccio's material), and as a piece of realism (marred by an excess of epic machinery). Who should be considered the hero is even questioned, some preferring Palamon, some Arcite, others finding little to choose between them. Among these latter is Professor Root,[3] who feels that the descriptions (of battles, temples, May, &c.), 'with occasional passages of noble reflection', are the 'flesh and blood' of the poem, 'of which the characters and action are merely the skeleton framework'.[4] 'What is the Knight's Tale', he asks, 'but a splendidly pictured tapestry, full of color and motion?'[5] It is my purpose to attempt, in terms of the Tale itself, an answer to Mr. Root's question.

I

The Knight's Tale develops from three widening concentric circles of interest: the merely human interest of the rivalry between two young heroes, both noble and both in love, for the hand of a heroine who has no apparent preference between them; the ethical interest of a conflict of obligations between romantic love and military comradeship; and finally the theological interest attaching to the method by which a just providence fully stabilizes a disintegrating human situation.

As important as the problems of the plot is the atmosphere in which they are worked out, the world of the Knight's Tale. This world, being an amalgam of legendary Athens, fourteenth-century England, and the never-never land of chivalric romance, presents to us that curious double relationship to any imaginable real world which most great art – the *Odyssey, Hamlet, Paradise Lost, Faust* – seems to attain; that is, a simultaneous relationship (the delight of readers and despair of historians) of nearness and distance. Anyone called 'Theseus, Duke of Athens' must surely be a classical hero refracted through a medieval lens; so we suppose, only to discover that there was a living 'Duke of Athens' at the time Chaucer wrote.[6] But whether classical, realistic, or chivalric, the atmosphere of the Tale has three abiding attributes: it is predominantly noble, predominantly tragic, and deeply infused with a sense of significance transcending both human beings and their material environment. In this essay I shall consider first the problems of the story, then the general characteristics of the universe in which the story happens.

II

The problem of who shall win the hand of the fair Emelye, Duke Theseus's young sister, is intensified throughout the Knight's Tale by systematic and delicately balanced parallelism in the presentation of the rival heroes, Palamon and Arcite. At no point is either allowed to take the centre of the stage or the initiative in setting the plot in motion without the other at once having an equal opportunity. If the two knights are together they are spoken of as a pair: 'This Palamon and his felawe Arcite' (1031); if events separate them the spotlight shifts impartially from one to the other:

> Now wol I stynte of Palamon a lite,
> And lete hym in his prisoun stille dwelle,
> And of Arcita forth I wol yow telle. . . .   (A. 1334–6)

> . . . And in this blisse lete I now Arcite
> And speke I wole of Palamon a lite. . . .   (A. 1449–50)

Moreover, the two knights have much in common: besides being noble, young, and passionately in love, besides being kinsmen, compatriots, and sworn blood-brothers, they are equally valorous:

> There nas no tygre in the vale of Galgopheye
> Whan that hir whelp is stole whan it is lite,
> So crueel on the hunte as is Arcite
> For jelous herte upon this Palamon.
> Ne in Belmarye ther nys so fel leon,
> That hunted is, or for his hunger wood,
> Ne of his praye desireth so the blood,
> As Palamon to sleen his foo Arcite. . . .   (A. 2626–33)

If Arcite despairs at being exiled from Athens and the sight of Emelye, Palamon despairs at being still imprisoned and helpless to win her. If Palamon breaks faith with Theseus by escaping from prison, Arcite merits equal punishment for returning to Athens in disguise. At the final tourney, for which each has prepared by prayer and sacrifice to a patron deity, each is seconded by a confederate champion, warlike and exotic : Palamon by 'Lygurge hymself, the grete kyng of Trace' (2129), with his white wolfhounds; Arcite by 'the grete Emetreus, the kyng of Inde' (2156), an eagle on his wrist and tame lions and leopards all about him.

So ostensibly impartial is the presentation of the heroes, in fact, that it is no wonder that some Chaucerians – Professor Hulbert, for example[7] – have failed to see any significant distinction between them. The teller of the tale himself never obviously sides with one or the other; to Theseus they are an identical pair of infatuated fools; and even Emelye expresses no preference between 'Palamon, that hath swich love to me' (2314) and 'Arcite, that loveth me so soore' (2315). Finally, as the lines I have been quoting demonstrate, the concurrent stories of the two heroes are narrated in a poetry marked by all manner of rhetorical parallelism.[8]

I am sure myself that the heroes are significantly differentiated from each other, and that a valid preference between them is implied by the poem; but they are certainly not individualized in the manner of such rival protagonists of later storytelling as Richard II and Bolingbroke, or Dobbin and George Osborne. Much of the beauty of the Knight's Tale, and of its appropriateness to the man who tells it, resides in a certain formal regularity of design. Thus the May-songs of Emelye and Arcite, redolent of youth, freshness, and spontaneity, come at two crucial points in the plot; while early May is also the time of the final contest that will make one hero happy and the other glorious. Thus the Tale begins with a wedding, a conquest, and a funeral; and ends with a tournament, a funeral, and a wedding.

III

A conflict between love and comradeship in the hearts of the two knights is the emotional focus of the story, the poetry of which

develops each of the conflicting elements as a constituent of the
world in which the story takes place. Comradeship implies war :
Palamon and Arcite are first introduced, side by side, 'both in
oon armes', on the field of battle. Chaucer created the military
elements of the poem by fusing his own knowledge of contemporary warfare with a classical tradition that stretches back through
Boccaccio and Statius to the ancient Greeks. The mixture is
rich, allusive, and concrete :

> The rede statue of Mars, with spere and targe,
> So shyneth in his white baner large,
> That alle the feeldes glyteren up and doun;
> And by his baner born is his penoun
> Of gold ful riche, in which there was ybete
> The Mynotaur, which that he slough in Crete.
> Thus rit this duc, thus rit this conquerour,
> And in his hoost of chivalrie the flour . . .   (A. 975–82)

These lines are from a description of Theseus, the dominant
figure of the poem and, significantly, the man who unites in his
person successes in war and love alike. 'He conquered al the regne
of Femenye' (866), symbolic homeland of Ypolita, Amazon
queen and Theseus's bride. For neither of the two knights, it
finally develops, will such a double triumph be possible; one is
to have victory in battle, the other to marry Emelye.

In a drama involving conquest, tourneying, and hand-to-
hand combat ankle-deep in blood, comradely loyalty is, of course,
a fitting plot-motif; and the outward similarity between
Palamon and Arcite enhances the violence of their rupture. They
are, moreover, sworn blood-brothers – into Palamon's mouth is
put a picture of the relation between them as it has been up to the
beginning of the tale and ought, ideally, to continue (1129–40).
Since the re-establishment of this normal, desirable, and exemplary relation is to be a part of the denouement, it is noteworthy that immediately after the break between the two
knights there occurs a symbolic allusion to one of the most famous
instances of fellowship in ancient legend. Scarcely have Palamon
and Arcite quarrelled for the first time than Perotheus arrives
in Athens and is described as follows :

> A worthy duc that highte Perotheus,
> That felawe was unto duc Theseus
> Syn thilke day that they were children lite. . . .
> So wel they lovede, as olde bookes sayn,
> That whan that oon was deed, soothly to telle,
> His felawe went and soughte hym doun in helle. . . .
>
> (A. 1191–3, 1198–1200)

And we are reminded of a great myth celebrated in classical poetry – in Horace, for example:

> . . . Theseus leaves Pirithöus in the chain
> The love of comrades cannot take away.[9]

This reference to Theseus's journey to the underworld is, by the way, one classical detail Chaucer *added* to what he took from the *Teseide*.[10]

Romantic love, which drives Palamon and Arcite apart, enters the poem most notably in the praise each lover accords Emelye, the illness and despair each undergoes, and Palamon's prayer in the temple of Venus. Romantic love, however, implying as it does chivalry, courts of love, and the idealization of woman, invests the figure of Theseus also. Despite his mockery of the lovers the Duke has been, he says, a 'servant' in his time. He is, moreover, a general who undertakes a new war to avenge insults done to ladies; an absolute ruler who allows his punishment of self-acknowledged culprits to be deflected by the merciful intervention of his wife and sister; a devastator of 'wall and sparre and rafter' in conquered Thebes, but also an umpire who forbids fatal bloodshed at the tournament over which he presides. Thus if the Knight's Tale develops a conflict between an ethic of battle and an ethic of love, nevertheless in the figures of Theseus, Ypolita, and Perotheus we are presented with an emblem of the two kinds of value reconciled and in accord.

We are also presented, in the minds of Palamon and Arcite, with two views of the same situation, Palamon being the spokesman of the greater idealism.[11] The contrast comes first in the way each regards Emelye. In Boccaccio both saw her as Venus; in Chaucer Palamon alone, in the following metaphor charged with religious overtones, makes that identification:

> Venus, if it be thy wil
> Yow in this gardyn thus to transfigure,
> Bifore me, sorweful, wrecched creature . . .
>
> (A. 1104–6)

Arcite emphatically differs, and seeks to use the difference as an argument for his own priority; he says to Palamon,

> Thyn is affeccioun of hoolynesse,
> And myn is love, as to a creature . . . .   (A. 1158–9)

Or, as Dryden translated the lines:

> Thine was devotion to the blest above;
> I saw the woman, and desired her love. . . .
>
> (*Palamon and Arcite*, I, 319–20)

It is a conflict, not between love and love, but between devotion and desire.[12]

This is the first instance of a significant divergence between the rivals; a second follows at once in their attitude toward the law of comradeship. Each, naturally, cites this law as binding on the other; but it is Arcite, not Palamon, who ultimately repudiates it for them both, in the lines:

> And therfore, at the kynges court, my brother,
> Ech man for hymself, ther is noon other.   (A. 1181–2)

The third and crucial divergence comes on the morning of the tournament when Arcite prays to Mars for a victory in arms which he thinks will be the means of possessing Emelye, while Palamon prays to Venus for Emelye herself.

Thus to Arcite the situation presents itself throughout as a practical problem of satisfying a desire by pursuit of the logical means to attain it. When he compares himself and Palamon, quarrelling in prison over Emelye, to the two dogs who fought over a bone till both lost it (1177–80) he resembles Theseus at the latter's most pragmatic moment (1798–1812); and on his return to Athens as Philostrate Arcite sets on foot the most

elaborate scheme either lover ever conceives of to gain his object.
Palamon, on the other hand, though fully as fervent as his rival,
includes his passion in a wider conception of Venus-worship; and,
far from prizing victory or any other means of success, puts his
love for Emelye above life itself (2254–8). In thus extending beyond the grave his love resembles the devoted comradeship of
Theseus and Perotheus.

    Even the language used about him by the teller of the Tale dis-
tinguishes Palamon's experience from that of his comrade: his
imprisonment while Arcite is free is spoken of as a 'martyrdom'
(1460),[13] and with 'hooly herte' he makes a 'pilgrymage' to the
temple of Venus (2214–15).[14]

    It seems to me, then, that the outcome of the tale is fully
justified by what has gone before – that Palamon wins Emelye
because he is worthier of her, in terms of the story, than is Arcite.
By this I would not imply either that Arcite is base or that the
loser wins nothing; half the interest of the final solution is in the
reconciliation between the two knights and the comments of
Theseus on Arcite's fate. If it be thought that the evidence on
which I have sought to make a distinction between the knights
is too slender to support one, then I can plead in defence that
the slightest parts of the poem are often charged with a significance only apparent in the light of the whole. When Arcite, for
example, on being given his liberty complains that 'We witen
nat what thing we preyen heere' (1260), his words are full of an
irony (because of his later prayer to Mars) greater than his
immediate circumstances presuppose.

                                    IV

The justice of the solution in relation to the two knights would
be incomplete, however, if that solution were not brought by
justifiable procedure. The course of events is determined to some
extent by the knights themselves, more largely by Theseus, and
ultimately by the various divinities, especially Saturn, and the
supernatural power that they represent. Of the human figures in
the story that of Theseus is most dominant – indeed, so much
so as to seem, in comparison to Palamon, Arcite, and Emelye,

almost superhuman. Theseus is both the guardian of Emelye and the legal possessor of the persons of the knights from the moment they are brought before him, more dead than alive, after the battle at Thebes. Later he releases Arcite, and Palamon escapes; but before either has had a chance to advance his cause with Emelye the Duke comes upon them and takes them prisoner again. At this point the poem implicitly associates him with the destiny and divine foreknowledge which, according to the teller of the Tale, lie behind all human events and situations :

> . . . And forth I wole of Theseus yow telle.
> The destinee ministre general,
> That executeth in the world over al
> The purveiaunce that God hath seyn biforn
> So strong it is that, though the world had sworn
> The contrarie of a thing by ye or nay,
> Yet sometyme it shall fallen on a day
> That falleth nat eft withinne a thousand yeer. . . .
> This mene I now by myghty Theseus. . . .   (A. 1662 ff.)

Theseus is the executant of destiny. On the morning of the final tourney he sits in a window of his palace overlooking the crowd and 'arrayed right as he were a god in trone' (2529). As a personality he is appropriately impressive : terrifying in action, philosophical in outlook; richly experienced yet detached in point of view; warmly sympathetic to misfortune[15] yet mockingly ironical at the expense of youthful enthusiasm. From the moment when he gives orders that the captured knights be imprisoned to the moment when he arranges the final nuptials of Emelye and Palamon he dominates the plot without ever being a partisan. Thus his pronouncements, and especially his long speech in the final scene, carry peculiar weight.

Destiny proper is represented first by the three divinities to whom the rivals, and Emelye, appeal; then by Saturn, who settles the issue among the divinities; and ultimately by a Divinity – 'the sighte above' (1672), 'the Firste Moevere' (2987) – beyond all particular divinities. This ultimate godhead, 'the which is prince and cause of alle thing' (3036), is identified by Theseus with 'Juppiter'; but the conception of him given by Theseus's speech as a whole sets him significantly apart from those other representatives of the classical pantheon who figure in the Knight's Tale. These – Mars, Diana, and the rest – are as much stars as gods;[16] and being stars they are the particular manifestations of Fortune, or Destiny, which is the agent, ultimately, of Providence. In *Paradise Lost* the pagan deities are assimilated to Christian story by their banishment to hell as rebel angels; in the Knight's Tale they still reign in the physical heavens, but reign as deputies of a transcendent sovereign.[17]

                                   V

When the Knight had finished his Tale Chaucer records that it won the general applause of the pilgrims, and the unanimous approval of the gentlefolk among them : 'And namely the gentils everichon' (3113). This last statement we can readily believe; for the Tale is wholeheartedly aristocratic, both in subject-matter and attitude. All the principal figures are of high birth; Arcite, for example, mortified by his disguise as a poor squire, reflects on his lineage in the following lines :

> Allas, ybroght is to confusioun
> The blood roial of Cadme and Amphioun, –
> Of Cadmus, which that was the firste man
> That Thebes bulte, or first the toun bigan,
> And of the citee first was crouned kyng.
> Of his lynage am I and his ofspryng
> By verray ligne, as of the stok roial. . . . (A. 1545–51)

Theseus represents the full exercise of a sovereignty the material prerogatives of which are made, at several points, very explicit. 'Ful lik a lord' the Duke rides to the lists through a city which is said to be 'Hanged with clooth of gold, and nat with sarge' (2568–9). For the building of the temples beside the 'noble theatre' he has employed all the architects and artisans in the country, regardless of expense : the temple of Mars 'coste largely of gold a fother' (1908). The limitlessness of his wealth is initially apparent when he demands no ransom for his royal prisoners – a circumstance so remarkable in dukes that it is referred to more than once.

Even persons who appear only briefly in the action are of rank : the suppliant Theban women at the beginning of the poem are all duchesses and queens. Even disguised as Philostrate, a mere hewer of wood and bearer of water, Arcite

> . . . was so gentil of condicioun
> That thurghout al the court was his renoun.
>
> (A. 1431–2)

The recurrent occasions of life for people of such condition as this are ceremonious, their actions at such times being imbued with the piety of ancient ritual. Arcite, even though he has rejected the code that binds him to his blood-brother, insists on returning to Athens, after finding the escaped Palamon, for food and weapons for his rival. The poem as a whole presents in affectionate detail three major ceremonial events : the prayers at the temples, the elaborate formalities of the tournament, and Arcite's funeral. Even the period of mourning for Arcite is apparently of prescribed duration (2967–8).

The action takes place, then, in an idealized aristocratic universe, magnanimous, munificent, and ceremonial. Theseus is the ideal conquering governor, Palamon the ideal lover, Emelye the emblem of vernal innocence. The story ends, too, with its ideal lover at last

> . . . in alle wele,
> Lyvynge in blisse, in richesse, and in heele. . . .
>
> (A. 3101–2)

Yet the view of the universe taken by the Tale is a tragic view, and the condition of man presented by the teller is also tragic.

The most direct, simple, and uncompromising expression of this tragic view comes in the words of Egeus, Theseus's father, after the accident to Arcite proves fatal. Egeus (who makes only this single brief appearance in the story) has been taken by some critics for a dotard; however that may be, his speech, of which I will quote the final lines, has central importance :

> This world nys but a thurghfare ful of wo,
> And we been pilgrymes, passynge to and fro.
> Deeth is an ende of every worldly soore.   (A. 2847–9)

The sentiment is a commonplace, of course, which could doubtless be matched, if not duplicated, a thousand times in the
literature of Chaucer's age and of preceding periods; it nevertheless has power in the Knight's Tale because that poem, although its plot is concerned with success in love and its setting
pictures aristocratic splendours, presents on the whole such an
abiding and various image of 'every worldly soore'. Man, the
teller might be saying, whatever his station in life, is the victim of
arbitrary, cruel, and often ironical mischance. The Theban ladies
are summarily widowed by civil wars; Thebes sacked by Athens;
the knights jailed by Theseus; while noble Arcite slowly and painfully dies of a fall from his horse because, nature having abandoned him, medicine is consequently useless –

> And certeinly, ther Nature wol nat wirche,
> Fare wel phisik ! go ber the man to chirche !
>
>   (A. 2759–60)

It is not only the events of the story which provide a rich reference for Palamon's bitter questioning of the 'crueel goddes' in
the following lines :

> What is mankynde moore unto you holde
> Than is the sheep that rouketh in the folde?
> For slayn is man right as another beest
> And dwelleth eek in prison and arreest,
> And hath siknesse and greet adversitee. . . .
>
>   (A. 1307–11)

As tragically impressive as the events I have mentioned is the
image of the human condition implied by the great descriptions
of the temples of Venus, Mars, and Diana (especially by that of
Mars) and by the speech of Saturn detailing his own influence
on mortal affairs. These passages, among the most admired in
Chaucer, are generally treated as set-pieces, in detachment from

context. Actually they are an organic part of the Tale, for they symbolically extend the misfortunes and griefs of the central characters and at the same time provide a background against which these same misfortunes and griefs will seem less extraordinary. This extension supports the view of human life taken by Egeus and Palamon in the lines I have just quoted, and by Arcite and Theseus in lines I shall presently discuss.

The picture of the temple of Venus refers, it is true, to both the delights and the sorrows she causes; but it begins and ends with the sorrows – 'ful pitous to biholde' – and it emphasizes the follies of lovers : 'the folye of kyng Salomon. . . . The riche Cresus, kaytyf in servage' (1942, 1946). The temple of Diana, which represents innocence and a kind of divine beneficence and is associated with Emelye, is described more naïvely as a collection of wonders merely; but even here the most vivid pictures are of the hounds devouring Actaeon 'for that they knewe hym naught' (2068), and of a woman in the throes of a difficult childbirth. The images inspired by Mars and Saturn give an inclusive and uncompromising panorama of existence as a moral hell and a cosmic chaos. The sow devours the baby 'right in the cradel' (2019); the man-eating wolf rends his victim at the foot of Mars's statue, to the glory of the god; the glance of Saturn is 'the fader of pestilence' (2469); images of manslaughter, arson, suicide, treason, murder, and rapine make up the decorations of Mars's temple.

This last edifice is built like a dungeon, as the following lines show :

> The dore was al of adamant eterne,
> Yclenched overthwart and endelong
> With iren tough; and for to make it strong,
> Every pyler, the temple to sustene,
> Was tonne-greet, of iren bright and shene . . .
>
> (A. 1990–4)

Imprisonment is a symbol of great importance to the poem; it is significant that Arcite's long-desired release from captivity leads first to exile and then despair, then to a strenuous life of practical expedients crowned by illusive victory and sudden death. His epitaph is spoken by Theseus (the original imprisoner of the knights) in these words :

> ... goode Arcite, of chivalrie the flour,
> Departed is with duetee and honour
> Out of this foule prisoun of this lyf. . . .
>
> (A. 3059–61)

For Arcite release from prison has been no more than escape into a larger prison, until the final release of death. 'What is this world?' asks the dying knight, whom devices and expedients can help no longer –

> What is this world? What asketh men to have?
> Now with his love, now in his colde grave
> Allone, withouten any compaignye?   (A. 2777–9)

But although the picture of 'this world' implied by the Mars and Saturn passages is chaotic and hideous enough, such a view of human existence is by no means the total effect left by the Knight's Tale. To begin with, the very presence of the gods, whether astrological or theological, gives a degree of order and significance to the lives of mortals. A trio of divinities accounts for the misery of Palamon : as Palamon puts it,

> ... I moot been in prisoun thurgh Saturne,
> And eek thurgh Juno, jalous and eek wood,
> That hath destroyed wel ny al the blood
> Of Thebes with his waste walles wyde;
> And Venus sleeth me on that oother syde
> For jalousie and fere of hym Arcite.   (A. 1328–33)

And a conflict of divinities accounts for the death of Palamon's rival. Nothing exists in this human world but has its source, significance, and guidance from above – a kind of guidance symbolized most concretely by the traditional device of Mercurie's appearance to advise Arcite to go to Athens. Thus the very vicissitudes of life fall into an ultimate pattern decipherable by wisdom and philosophy; even the destructive divinities are still divine.

More important still, beyond these destructive divinities governs the Firste Moevere of Theseus's final elegy. This speech is the climax of the poem. Here Theseus sets forth in general terms what the particulars of the story have been leading to. Human decay and corruption (the accident to Arcite, the violence and pestilence symbolized by Mars and Saturn, the follies in which Venus has a share) proceed under the laws of an ultimate Providence, which has fixed a term to the existence of finite things. Man's proper wisdom is not to cry out against the 'faire cheyne of love' which binds the universe, but nobly to accept his destiny – to 'take it weel . . . that to us alle is due' (3043–4). Hence the importance of Arcite: his nobility, his education, his tragedy. His death was not meaningless to him since it empowered him to reassert his proper relation to Palamon and to do his friend the service he might have done at the beginning. As Theseus says,

> . . . And certeinly a man hath moost honour
> To dyen in his excellence and flour,
> Whan he is siker of his goode name;
> Thanne hath he doon his freend, ne hym, no shame.
>
> (A. 3047–50)

And after Arcite's funeral, the decent period of mourning, and Theseus's elegy, stability can be established by the harmonious union of Emelye and Palamon, who incidentally represent the formerly warring countries, Thebes and Athens.

VI

Such a tale is clearly suited to the Knight of Chaucer's prologue who tells it, a man of high rank, wide travel, and ingenuous loyalty to the ideas of his class and age. The lessons of the Tale, if such they mày be called, imply a pious and logical mind in the instructor, a deep acceptance of Christian faith and chivalric standards, and an heroic disposition to face the vicissitudes and disasters of a dangerous calling. That they had been faced in fact we have been assured by the prologue :

At Alisaundre he was whan it was wonne.
Ful ofte tyme he hadde the bord bigonne
Aboven alle nacions in Pruce;
In Lettow hadde he reysed and in Ruce,
No Cristen man so ofte of his degree.
In Gernade at the seege eek hadde he be
Of Algezir, and riden in Belmarye.
At Lyeys was he and at Satalye,
Whan they were wonne; and in the Grete See
At many a noble armee hadde he be.   (A. 51–60)

To present the mind and heart of this Knight is an important
function of the Tale. Though hardly a dramatic monologue
in the Shakespearian or Browningesque sense of the term, the
Tale is nevertheless a dramatic utterance both externally (in the
light of its setting) and internally. Scarcely has the Knight
finished his story of Palamon and Arcite, and won the applause
of all the pilgrims (especially of the gentlefolk), than the
drunken Miller is pushing forward, interrupting the Host's attempted introduction of the Monk as second narrator, and insisting loudly on *his* tale instead. The Miller's Tale (as everyone
knows) is perhaps the most elaborate improper story in English
literature – the most elaborate and in many ways the grossest.
It represents an artistic antithesis to the Knight's Tale, being
also a tale of the rivalry of two suitors for a young woman. But
whereas Palamon and Arcite worshipped the maiden Emelye
with an introspective ardour that seemed almost its own reward,
Nicholas and Absolon pursue the lickerish Alisoun for the simple
object of cuckoldry just (to use Chaucer's simile) as a cat pursues a mouse. Instead of the international and even cosmological
background of the Knight's Tale, the scene of the Miller's Tale
is small-town, domestic, and bourgeois. Its plot embodies a kind of
crude justice meted out by circumstances both to successful and
to attempted adultery. The manners of chivalry are burlesqued
in the figure of the genteel parish-clerk-and-barber Absolon;
while Christianity enters the story as a ready means of duping an
illiterate and credulous husband. The contrast to the Knight's
Tale could hardly be more complete. It is as if the Miller, growing more and more restive in the moral stratosphere as the

leisurely Knight's Tale winds to its ceremonious and philosophical conclusion, were unable to keep silent after the Knight's final words about the young couple :

> For now is Palamon in alle wele,
> Lyvynge in blisse, in richesse, and in heele,
> And Emelye hym loveth so tendrely,
> And he hire serveth al so gentilly,
> That nevere was ther no word hem bitwene
> Of jalousie or any oother teene. . . .   (A. 3101–6)

What a picture of married life ! The Miller will show that there is another side to *that* story ! –

> By armes, and by blood and bones,
> I kan a noble tale for the nones,
> With which I wol now quite the Knyghtes tale
>
> (A. 3125–7)

says the Miller.

The Miller's Tale, then, is the principal external means by which the Knight's Tale is made dramatic and given a certain artistic distance both from the reader and from the poet of the *Canterbury Tales*. There are also internal and ironical means of accomplishing the same object, and they are fully employed. I refer, of course, to such occasions as when Theseus remarks that the lover who loses Emelye may as well 'go pipen in an yvy leef' (1838); or when the women of Athens (with all the sensibilities of modern cinema addicts) lament the death of Arcite because, as they put it, he had 'gold ynough, and Emelye' (2836); or when the species of trees that make up Arcite's funeral pyre are listed with no more ceremony of adjective than it is now customary to give the names in a telephone directory. The very ingenuousness of the Knight as a commentator on his own story may sometimes give rise to the pleasantest irony : the reader must smile at the speaker, while his heart warms to him. I shall close this essay with one example of such irony, an example which illustrates also the pitfalls into which even a learned Chaucerian may occasionally slip.

The pathetic death of Arcite is a matter of intense grief to his

comrade-in-arms and his intended bride. 'Shrighte Emelye, and
howleth Palamon' (2817); and Theseus carries away the prostrate heroine. At this point the Knight who tells the story em-
barks on a generalization, in the following terms:

> What helpeth it to tarien forth the day
> To tellen how she weep bothe eve and morwe?
> For in swich cas wommen have swich sorwe,
> Whan that hir housbondes ben from hem ago,
> That for the moore part they sorwen so,
> Or ellis fallen in swich maladye,
> That at the laste certeinly they dye.   (A. 2820–6)

'Coming from the author of the Wife of Bath,' remarks H. B.
Hinckley in his *Notes on Chaucer*,[18] 'these words can only be construed as satire, or as insincerity. Was it such a passage as this –
a passage which is certainly out of place – that prompted Matthew Arnold's celebrated saying that Chaucer lacked "high
seriousness"?'

The Knight, however, is neither insincere, satirical, nor the
author of the Wife of Bath; and it is probably a measure of our
present distance from the Victorian critics that the irony of
Chaucer, his constant perception of personal and spiritual in-
compatibilities in a complex humanity, is the very quality that
gives him, in our eyes, his seriousness as a poet and a critic of life.

S O U R C E : *Review of English Studies*, xxv (1949).

NOTES

1. A method of critical procedure similar to Mr. Webb's
(namely, examination of selected parts divorced from any treatment of the poem as a whole) renders equally open to attack, in my
judgement, the conclusions about the personalities of Palamon and
Arcite reached recently by Professor A. H. Marckwardt, *Characterization in Chaucer's Knight's Tale*, University of Michigan
Contributions in Modern Philology, No. 5 (1947).
2. See the notes to the Tale in *The Complete Works of Chaucer*,

ed. F. N. Robinson (Cambridge, Mass., 1933) pp. 770 ff. for Lowes,
Wise, Patch, and Curry; also B. L. Jefferson, *Chaucer and . . .
Boethius* (Princeton, 1917); Johnstone Parr, 'The Date and Revision
of Chaucer's Knight's Tale', *PMLA* LX (1945) 307–24; and R. A.
Pratt, 'Chaucer's Use of the *Teseide*'. *PLMA*, LXII (1947) 598–
621, especially 613–20.

3. See R. K. Root, *Poetry of Chaucer* (Cambridge, Mass., 1922)
pp. 163–73. Mr. Root discriminates between the temperaments of
the two knights, but concludes that 'the reader of the tale . . . is
unable to decide on which he would wish the ultimate success to
light' (p. 170).

4. Root, p. 172.

5. Root, p. 37.

6. See H. R. Patch, 'Chauceriana', *Englische Studien*, LXV
(1930–1) 354 *n.*; cited by Robinson in a note on A. 860.

7. J. R. Hulbert, 'What was Chaucer's Aim in the Knight's Tale?',
Studies in Philology, XXVI (1929) 375 ff.

8. At one point rhetorical parallelism may possibly extend beyond
the two knights and bracket Palamon and Emelye: compare
ll. 2212 and 2273.

9. *Odes*, IV. 7. The translation is from Housman's *Collected Poems*
(New York, 1940) p. 164.

10. See B. A. Wise, *Influence of Statius upon Chaucer* (Baltimore,
1911) p. 88.

11. For some aspects of the following comparison of Palamon
and Arcite I am indebted to my friend Mr. Douglas Knight.

12. Contrast the language of Arcite's prayer to Mars (especially
the verb 'usedest') : 'For thilke hoote fir / In which thow whilom
brendest for desir,/Whan that thou usedest the beautee/Of faire
yonge, fresshe Venus free' (2383–6) with that of Palamon's
prayer to Venus : 'For thilke love thow haddest to Adoon' (2224).

13. Cf. also l. 1562, where Arcite says that Theseus 'martireth'
Palamon in prison.

14. By far the most interesting discussion of Palamon and Arcite
I have seen in print is that of Professor H. N. Fairchild in his
article 'Active Arcite, Contemplative Palamon', *Journal of English
and Germanic Philology*, XXVI (1927) 285–93. His allegorical interpretation has been called 'somewhat forced' by Robinson in his
edition of Chaucer (p. 772), and it must be admitted that several
of Fairchild's comments do not seem fully warranted by the text of
the poem. We have no reason to suppose, for example, that Arcite
goes a-maying because he is 'stirred by the vague uneasiness of the

active man' (Fairchild, p. 289), especially when the poem says that he 'litel wiste how ny that was his care' (1489). But Fairchild's article, in contrast to some other discussions of the subject, is fully alive to possible symbolic values in Chaucer's presentation of the knights.

15. I take his imprisonment of the two knights without asking ransom to be simply part of the *donnée* of the story as it came to Chaucer – and not, without further explanation of motive than the poet gives us, an implication that Theseus lacks chivalry.

16. See W. C. Curry, *Chaucer and the Medieval Sciences* (Oxford, 1926) chapter VI.

17. The position of 'Juppiter' is made ambiguous by his brief appearance during the quarrel between Venus and Mars, of which it is said that 'Juppiter was bisy it to stente' (2442); Saturn finally resolves the strife. In the light of the poem as a whole it appears that Saturn is the logical deity to devise the catastrophe which causes Arcite's death; and the passage in question need not be taken to imply either that Saturn is superior in power to the divine disputants or that Jupiter was, or would have been, unable to settle matters. Nothing in the passage seems inconsistent with the idea of Saturn representing one aspect, or agent, of Jupiter's omnipotence.

18. (Northampton, Mass., 1907) p. 113.

E. T. Donaldson

IDIOM OF POPULAR POETRY IN
THE MILLER'S TALE (1950)

A poet who abandons the poetic idiom of his time and nation
and devises one entirely new in its place creates for the would-be
critic of his language a difficult problem. Criticism of the language of poetry can exist only through comparison with contemporary and earlier writings, and when, as sometimes happens,
the critic cannot find between these and the work of the
innovator enough similarity even to reflect the differences, he has
to resort, in lieu of criticism, to merely quoting the innovator
admiringly. With Chaucer the problem is even greater than with
Milton, Shakespeare, Wordsworth, or Eliot. For while we may
at least be sure that they were brought up in an English
literary tradition from which they more or less consciously revolted, the disquieting suspicion always arises that Chaucer, bred
if not born in a culture predominantly continental, may not have
been very much aware of the literary tradition from which he was
presumably in revolt; and this means that anyone who, in search
of comparisons with Chaucer's diction, goes to the most prolific of the vernacular literary traditions, the romance, or to the
closely related lyric, must consider himself to be in danger of
wasting his time.[1]

But Chaucer did, after all, write in English, however continental his background may have been, and it stands to reason
that diligent search will reveal at least a few correspondences with
the popular English poetic diction of his day. Complete analysis
of his own vocabulary is now – and has been for some time – possible through use of the Chaucer *Concordance*;[2] in this one can
study all the contexts of every word he ever used, and hence can
try to determine the values he placed upon the words he
appropriated from the conventional vocabulary of popular
poetry. It is the evaluation of these borrowings that I have under-

taken; but since the job is a tricky one at best, I have thought it advisable to begin with those words which, while common in contemporary romance and lyric, occur only a very few times in Chaucer and are therefore to be suspected of carrying a rather special sort of weight. Only by such drastic limitation of the subject can it be treated at all in the time allotted.

In approaching the problem of evaluation there are two subordinate poems that I have found to be of some help. The first is Fragment A of the Middle English translation of the *Roman de la Rose*. That this is really Chaucer's work cannot be entirely proved. Most scholars think it is,[3] and I have little doubt that it is. But even if it is not, it is at least the sort of poem we should suppose him to have written in his poetic immaturity. For while it is not nearly so free as Chaucer's mature works are from that conventional diction – those clichés – by which the whole vernacular tradition was infected,[4] it nevertheless frequently has that quality, common to all Chaucer's indisputable works, of uniting perfectly simple English words with extraordinary ease into genuinely poetic language of a kind that makes the phrase 'poetic diction' seem entirely too high-flown to be apt. Whether it is by Chaucer or not, its diction, occasionally but not consistently conventional, seems to represent a half-way point between popular English poetry and the *Canterbury Tales*. I find it critically illuminating, therefore, in comparing the Fragment with the *Canterbury Tales*, to observe how the mature Chaucer places in new and sometimes startling contexts words which a poet of somewhat less refined taste (probably the young Chaucer) had used flatly in time-honored contexts.

Rather firmer help is offered by Chaucer's 'Sir Thopas'. For this parody, while a criticism of vernacular conventions of every sort, is above all a criticism of standard English poetic diction. Therefore, if we find – as we do – words that Chaucer makes fun of in 'Sir Thopas' showing up in seemingly innocent contexts elsewhere in his work, we shall have at least a small area in which to exercise criticism of Chaucer's idiom. Let me confess at once that the total critical yield from the words of this sort that I have noticed is not great and that it makes possible, not a wider appreciation of Chaucer's more serious poetry, but of some of his comic effects. In this paper I shall deal largely with the effect upon the Miller's Tale of certain words introduced from the vernacular poetic tradition. It goes almost without saying that this effect is ironical and that more irony is not the sole product I should have wished to achieve from my investigation. Still, this is only a beginning, and 'after this I hope ther cometh moore' – if not from me, from better critics. The following is therefore presented as an example of a technique by which it may be possible to arrive at a better understanding of Chaucer's poetic idiom.

Since in the Miller's Tale I shall be dealing with ironical context, I shall start with an illustration of an ironical use of conventional idiom that is, thanks to the brilliant work of Professor Lowes, known to every Chaucerian. Lowes has demonstrated that the key to the portrait of the Prioress is in the second line, which, in describing her smiling as 'ful symple and coy', endows her with a pair of qualities that were also those of innumerable heroines of Old French romance.[5] It is, incidentally, a measure of Chaucer's gallicization, as well as of his tact with a lady who likes to speak at least a sort of French, that these conventional words, along with most of the others in her characterization, are not commonly applied to ladies in Middle English romance. Furthermore, Lowes shows that in describing her person – gray eyes, delicate soft red mouth, fair forehead, nose *tretys* – Chaucer borrows from stock French descriptions of ladies details that were full of courtly reminiscences for the cultivated reader of the time, though with impeccable taste he foregoes the complete physical catalogue that an Old French heroine would feel herself entitled to. If Lowes had wished to reinforce his point, whose delicacy needs no reinforcement, he could have gone on to examine Chaucer's own works for the reappearance of the words used to describe the Prioress. He would have found, for instance, that 'coy' is used of no other woman in Chaucer, though it appears in the stereotype 'as coy as a maid', used only of men. 'Simple', as Lowes does observe, is also the attribute of Blanche the Duchess – Chaucer's most serious conventional portrait; but it is applied further to three romantic ladies in the first fragment of the *Roman*, and, in Chaucer's mature work, it is used twice of Criseide, perhaps in a delicate attempt to be suggestive about her manner without being communicative about her character.

It is worthy of note that the Prioress' nose *tretys* is foreshadowed by the face *tretys* of Lady Beauty in the English *Roman*; but the word is otherwise non-Chaucerian. Further, while ladies' noses receive full treatment in the translation of the *Roman*, elsewhere the only female nose mentioned is the stubby one that the miller's daughter inherited from her father in the Reeve's Tale – 'With kamus nose, and eyen greye as glas', an interesting mutation, incidentally, on the Prioress, 'Hir nose tretys, hir eyen greye as glas'. And of all the women in Chaucer, only the Prioress and Alison, heroine of the Miller's Tale, have mouths or foreheads worthy of note : a case, perhaps, of the Colonel's Lady and Judy O'Grady. Finally, if one had time one might, I think, profitably investigate the words 'fetys' and 'fetisly', both used in describing the Prioress, but elsewhere appearing only in contexts which render highly suspect the particular sort of elegance they suggest.[6] In any case, the Prioress' portrait is a masterpiece of idiomatic irony, though the idiom is that of French poetry rather than of English.

With this much preliminary let us turn to the Miller's Tale. Upon this, Chaucer's worst ribaldry, it is generally agreed that he lavished his greatest skill, and in particular upon his description of the three principal characters – Alison, Absolon, and *hende* Nicholas, and upon their dialogue with one another. One of the devices he used most skillfully was that of sprinkling these characterizations and conversations with clichés borrowed from the vernacular versions of the code of courtly love – phrases of the sort we are accustomed to meet, on the one hand, in Middle English minstrel romances and, on the other, in secular lyrics such as those preserved in Harley MS 2253 – but phrases that are not encountered elsewhere in the serious works of Geoffrey Chaucer. The comic effect of this imported courtly diction will, I hope, be understood as we go along. At the start it is necessary to bear in mind only that by the fourteenth century at least, the aim and end of courtly love was sexual consummation, however idealized it may have been made to appear, and that of the various factors upon which the *ars honeste amandi* depended for its idealization the conventional language associated with it was not the least important.

The key to the matter, as one might expect, is in the constant epithet applied to the hero of the Miller's Tale – that is, in hende Nicholas' almost inseparable *hende*. Any one who has done even cursory reading in popular English poetry of Chaucer's time – and before and after – will heartily agree with the *Oxford Dictionary*'s statement that 'hende' is 'a conventional epithet of praise, very frequent in Middle English poetry'. Originally it seems to have meant no more than 'handy, at hand'; but it gradually extended its area of signification to include the ideas of 'skillful, clever' and of 'pleasant, courteous, gracious' (or 'nice', as the *Oxford Dictionary* says with what I take to be exasperated quotation marks); and it simultaneously extended its area of reference to include, under the general sense 'nice', almost every hero and heroine, as well as most of the rest of the characters siding with the angels, in Middle English popular poetry. Thus, the right of the Squire of Low Degree to the hand of the King's Daughter of Hungary is established by the minstrel poet's exclamation :

> The squir was curteous and hend,
> Ech man him loved and was his frend.

And another poet boasts of Sir Isumbras,

> Alle hym loffede, that hym seghe :
> Se hende a man was hee ![7]

Such examples could be multiplied indefinitely. Indeed, the average popular poet could no more do without 'hende' than he could do without the lovers whose endless misadventures gave him his plots, since unless a lover was 'hende', he or she was no proper exponent of courtly love. We should, therefore, have a right to expect the adjective to modify such Chaucerian characters as Troilus and Criseide, Arveragus and Dorigen, Palamon, Arcite, and Emily. But in Chaucer's indisputable works the word, while it is used eleven times with Nicholas, appears only twice elsewhere, and it is applied to none of the more serious characters, such as those just mentioned. The translator of Fragment A of the *Roman* had, to be sure, used it twice to describe amiable folk associated with the garden of the Rose; but thereafter it is spoken only by the Host, that distinguished exponent of bourgeois good manners, when he calls upon the Friar to be 'hende' to the Summoner; and by Alice of Bath, who expresses with it the charm possessed by her fifth-husband-to-be, jolly Jankin, who is a spiritual sibling of Nicholas' if there ever was one. It is clear from these usages, as well as from the even more eloquent lack of its use in any genuinely courtly context, that for Chaucer 'hende' had become so déclassé and shopworn as to be ineligible for employment in serious poetry.

But by the same token it was highly eligible for employment in the Miller's Tale. Nicholas is, after all, a hero of sorts, and he deserves to be as 'hende' as any other self-respecting hero-lover. But in the present context the word mocks the broad meaning 'nice' that is apparent in non-Chaucerian contexts. Indeed, its constant association with Nicholas encourages one to feel that here 'hende' does not so much define Nicholas as he defines it. Furthermore, he defines it in a way that is surprisingly true to the less usual senses of the word, for Nicholas turns out to be a good deal less romantically 'nice' than he is realistically 'clever, skillful'. He even represents the earliest meaning of the word, 'at hand, handy'; for the Miller, analyzing his love-triangle in proverbial terms, remarks that always the 'nye slye' (the sly dog at hand, Nicholas) displaces the 'ferre leeve' (the distant charmer, Absolon). But most important, in Nicholas as in other heroes, the quality of being 'hende' is the cause of his success in love. In the quotations given above we learn that it was because they were 'hende' that Sir Isumbras and the Squire of Low Degree were generally beloved. Nicholas is also lovable, but his lovableness is of the rather special sort that would appeal to a woman of Alison's tastes and morals. In short, the coupling of word and character suggests in Nicholas nothing more than a large measure of physical charm that is skillful at recognizing its opportunities and putting itself to practical sexual use; and this is a sorry degradation for an adjective that had been accustomed to modify some of the nicest people in popular poetry, who now, as a result of Nicholas, begin to suffer from guilt by association.

A somewhat similar aspect of Nicholas' character is reflected in the line that tells us,

Of deerne love he koude and of solas. (A. 3200)

For his aptitude at *derne love*, 'secret love', Nicholas must have been the envy of a good many young men in contemporary English poetry. For instance, in the Harley MS we meet several swains whose unsuccessful involvement in secret love affairs is their chief source of poetic woe.

> Lutel wot hit any mon
> hou derne loue may stonde,

grumbles one of these before going on to explain with what agonies and ecstasies it is attended.[8] Such lyricists were probably apt to pretend to themselves that the secretive line of conduct suggested by the phrase 'derne love', while it may have made things difficult, was nevertheless one of the ennobling conditions imposed upon them by the courtly code. Chaucer, however, seems to have felt otherwise, for while many of his heroes experience 'secree love', none besides Nicholas is ever 'derne' about it. Elsewhere Chaucer does not even use the common adjective to modify other nouns besides 'love', apparently feeling that its reputation had been ruined by the company it had kept so long. Even in Old English, of course, the word was ambiguous, reflecting sometimes justified secrecy and sometimes secret sin; and among the moral lyrics of the Harley MS there is one whose author makes it clear that for him 'derne dedes' are dirty deeds.[9] From his avoidance of the adjective it appears that Chaucer also subscribed to such an opinion. Moreover, the modern reader of the Harley love lyrics will probably sympathize with him, for it sometimes seems that, whatever the lovers pretended, they respected the principle of 'derne love' more because of its value in protecting them from outraged husbands or fathers than from any courtly ideal of preserving their lady's good name.[10] Thus, long before Chaucer's time 'derne love' was already in potentiality what it becomes in actuality in Nicholas, a device for getting away with adultery, if not really a sort of excuse for indulging in it. Therefore Nicholas' aptitude parodies an ideal already devalued through misuse in the vernacular; and since even at its most exalted the courtly code of secrecy might be described as crassly practical, his aptitude also parodies that of more genuinely courtly lovers than the Harley lyricists.

Turning to Nicholas' rival, jolly Absolon, one may find further instances of this technique of Chaucer's. What Absolon lacks in the way of Nicholas' 'hendeness' he tries to make up with his own 'joly-ness'. The epithet 'joly' is not as consistently used with Absolon as 'hende' is with Nicholas, and since it has a wide variety of meanings and is common in Chaucer, it may not be so readily classified. Suffice it to say that it is generally in the mouths of bourgeois characters and that in the senses 'handsome' and 'pretty' it modifies men or women with equal frequency. But it is, perhaps, the secret of Absolon's ill-success that all his jollification makes rather for prettiness than for masculine effectiveness. One recalls that Sir Thopas, though a sturdy hero, possesses some of the charms of a typical medieval heroine, and the Miller seems to suggest by several of the terms in his portrait of Absolon that the latter had somehow or other fallen across the fine line which in medieval poetry separated feminine beauty from that of beardless youths. For in his description he uses words that a minstrel poet would normally apply to a pretty girl. For instance,

His rode was reed, his eyen greye as goos,   (A. 3317)

and the gray eyes will remind us of the Prioress, as well as of countless other medieval heroines and, it must be granted, a number of heroes, though not in Chaucer, who reserves gray eyes for ladies. But in possessing a 'rode' – that is, a peaches-and-cream complexion recommended by fourteenth-century Elizabeth Ardens, Absolon places himself in the almost exclusive company of Middle English damsels.[11] The complexion of truly manly males of the time was, after all, generally obscured by a good deal of beard, and hence apt to remain unsung. It is significant that the only other 'rode' in all Chaucer belongs to Sir Thopas, a feminine feature that contrasts startingly with the saffron beard of that curiously constituted creature. Absolon further distinguishes himself (from his sex, I fear) by being the only character in Chaucer to be associated with the adjective 'lovely', which is applied to the looks he casts upon the ladies of the parish and to no other thing Chaucerian, though to hundreds of things, especially things feminine, in popular poetry.[12]

Readers of the latter would naturally expect the flesh of this pretty fellow to be

> As whit as is the blosme upon the rys, (A. 3324)

and it comes as a surprise that it is not Absolon's flesh, but his surplice, that is described in these terms. But the line, either in much the same form or, if one wants pink flesh, with the variation 'as reed as rose on ris', is one of the clichés found almost inevitably in descriptions of women.[13] For instance, the variant form is applied to Lady Beauty's flesh in the *Roman* fragment. But in what we are sure is Chaucer's work there is elsewhere no such phrase – indeed, there is elsewhere no such thing as a 'ris', 'spray', at all. When he quietly transfers the conventional descriptive phrase from the body to the clothing that covers it – in this case Absolon's surplice – Chaucer is, of course, creating the humor of surprise; but more important, the trick enables him to evoke for the reader the hackneyed context, with all its associations, in which the phrase usually appears, while at the same time the poet can make literal use of the phrase's meaning in his own more realistic description. There is an even more effective example of this economy in the portrait of Alison, to which I shall now turn.

The pretty heroine of the tale exemplifies most brilliantly Chaucer's reduction of the worn-out ideal, expressed by the worn-out phrase, to its lowest common denominator of sexuality.

> Fair was this yonge wyf, and therwithal
> As any wezele hir body gent and smal. (A. 3233–4)

Now the weasel, as Lowes has observed,[14] is Chaucer's own fresh image, and its effectiveness is obvious. But the fact that Alison's body is 'gent and smal' – shapely and delicate – makes her the sister of every contemporary vernacular heroine who is worthy of having a lover.[15] Lady Beauty, paragon of embraceable women in the *Roman*, is in a similar way shapely –

> Gente, and in hir myddill small –

and it is natural that Sir Thopas should be 'fair and gent'. Posibly with Sird Thopas 'gent' has its non-physical sense of 'highborn, noble', but in view of the fact that the poet later commends his 'sydes smale' – an item of female beauty – one may detect in the word at least a suggestion of ambiguity. On the other hand, while many lovely women in Chaucer's known works are 'gentil', none besides Alison is 'gent'. His third and last use of the adjective is in the *Parliament of Fowls*, where it describes, appropriately enough, the 'facounde gent', the 'noble' eloquence, of the down-to-earth goose (a sort of female Miller in feathers) who speaks so uncourtly of the tercel eagles' love dilemma. Thus, in applying the stale adjective 'gent' to Alison's body the Miller seems to be regarding her from a point of view less ideal and esthetic than realistic and pragmatic.

As in the case of the Prioress, Chaucer's restraint (I suspect that here it is only a teasing sort of restraint) prevents him from listing – except for one startling detail – the other conventional charms of Alison's body. We might expect from the Miller that our heroine would be – as Lowes has said – 'anatomized in good set similes as inescapable as death', as, for instance, is Annot of the Harley lyric 'Annot and John'.[16] But the reader who wants this is doomed to disappointment, for what he gets is less of Alison's body than of her wardrobe. Several of the conventional terms, however, that one expects to meet in corporeal catalogues are still present, even though they are applied only to her clothing. Her sides, to be sure, are not like the Harley Fair Maid of Ribblesdale's,

> Whittore then the moren-mylk,[17]

but her apron is, a quality it shares in Chaucer only with the silk purse of the pink-and-white fleshed Franklin. This same apron lies, moreover,

> Upon hir lendes, ful of many a goore.   (A. 3237)

Now 'gore', which meant originally a triangular piece of land and later (as here) a triangular strip of cloth, hence by synecdoche a skirt or apron, is obviously a technical word, and the fact that Chaucer used it only twice may not be significant. But when one recalls the number of vernacular ladies – including Alison's namesake in the Harley lyrics – who were 'geynest vnder gore', or 'glad vnder gore',[18] one may, perhaps, become suspicious. To be sure, scholars assure us that these phrases, along with such variants as 'worthy under wede', 'lovesome under line', 'semely under serk', are merely stereotyped superlatives and presumably have no sexual connotation.[19] But in their literal meanings they could have such a connotation, and in their origin they probably did have. For instance, the poet of *Gawain and the Green Knight* speaks of the lady of the castle as 'lufsum vnder lyne' only when Gawain is being subjected by her to the most powerful sexual temptation. And inasmuch as Chaucer, violating his self-imposed restraint, takes pains to mention the 'lendes' (the loins), a word that appears a little later in a frankly sexual context[20] – that are hidden beneath the 'gores' of Alison's apron, it is possible that his employment of the word 'gore' is evocative as well as technical; that he is, indeed, by providing a sort of realistic paraphrase of the conventional expression, insinuating what the lover of the Harley Alison really had in mind when he called his mistress 'geynest vnder gore'. This is only a possibility, and I should not want to insist upon it. But the possibility becomes stronger when we recall Chaucer's other use of the word[21] – in Sir Thopas' dream,

> An elf-queene shal my lemman be
> And slepe under my goore.   (B.[2] 1978–9)

Whatever 'gore' means here – presumably cloak – its context is unmistakable.

Nowhere does Chaucer's idiom devaluate with more devastating effect the conventional ideal to the level of flat reality than in two sentences occurring near the end of Alison's portrait. Like many a lyric and romance poet the Miller discovers that he is not clever enough to describe the total effect his lady produces – indeed, he doubts that any one is clever enough. The poet of the *Life of Ipomedon* was later to remark of a lady,   .

> In all this world is non so wyse
> That hir goodnesse kan devyse,

while the Harley Alison's lover had already asserted,

> In world nis non so wyter mon
> That al hire bounte telle con.[22]

True to the convention, the Miller exclaims of his Alison,

> In al this world, to seken up and doun,
> There nys no man so wys that koude thenche
> So gay a popelote, or swich a wenche.   (A. 3252–4)

But the Miller's mind is not on the 'bounte' (excellence) or 'goodnesse' of Alison; and his crashing anticlimax, ending with the word 'wenche', which, in Chaucer, when it does not mean servant-girl means a slut,[23] is a triumph of the whole process we have been examining. Another occurs a little later. Once more the Miller is following convention, this time comparing Alison to a flower. John had said of Annot in the Harley lyric,

> The primerole he passeth, the peruenke of pris,[24]

and the Miller also begins his comparison with the cowslip, the 'primerole':

> She was a prymerole, a piggesnye.   (A. 3268)

But the accompanying item is no longer a 'pervenke of pris', an excellent periwinkle, but a 'piggesneye', something which, while it may be also a flower (perhaps, appropriately enough, a cuckoo flower),[25] remains, unmistakably, a pig's eye. Beneath the Miller's remorseless criticism the Blanchefleurs and even the Emilys of Middle English romance degenerate into the complacent targets of a lewd whistle.

In their conversation with Alison the two clerks talk like a couple of Harley lyricists.[26] But Absolon, fated to accomplish more words than deeds, naturally has the richer opportunity to speak in the vernacular of love – or rather, to quote Absolon, of love-longing.

> Ywis, lemman, I have swich love-longynge,
> That lik a turtel trewe is my moornynge,   (A. 3705–6)

he laments outside her window. Love-longing was, of course, a common complaint, positively epidemic in the Middle Ages, and most of Chaucer's lovers have at least occasional attacks of it. But as with certain modern diseases, its name seems to have varied with the social status of its victim, and in Chaucer only Absolon and Sir Thopas are afflicted with it under that name. They are therefore in a tradition that includes knights as illustrious as Sir Tristram, not to mention those rustics the Harley lovers,[27] but fails to include Aurelius, Arcite, Troilus, or even the less admirable Damian. The inference is that for Chaucer the phrase 'love-longing' implied a desire of the flesh irreconcilable with courtly idealism, though fine for Absolon. Absolon is also following popular tradition when he introduces the figure of the legendarily amorous turtle-dove into his declaration : 'like a turtle true is my mourning.' Ordinarily, however, it is the lady who is the dove, a 'trewe tortle in a tour'[28] – faithful and remote in her tower, but curiously inarticulate, considering that she is a dove and that doves are rarely silent. Thus, the conventional image is reset in a context that is more natural and in this case more genuinely poetic. Another simile of Absolon's for conveying his distress –

I moorne as dooth a lamb after the tete –   (A. 3704)

is the Miller's own audacious contribution to the language of love, and demonstrates the ease with which Chaucer, employing a sort of merciless logic, can move from a wholly conventional image involving animals to one wholly original and wholly devastating.

Elsewhere, Absolon keeps closer to what we should expect. Alison, for instance is his 'swete brid' or 'brïd' – that is, his sweet bird, bride, or possibly even 'burd' (maiden): as in the romances and love lyrics it is often difficult to tell which of the three the lover means, or whether he is himself altogether sure.[29] In the other works of Chaucer birds are clearly birds, brides clearly brides, and 'burd' does not occur except once of a lady in the *Roman*. Perhaps, however, it is only fair to observe that Chaucer's avoidance elsewhere of this trite form of endearment results in a use of 'dear heart' and of the substantive 'swete' so excessive as to amount to a triteness of Chaucer's own devising.

Continuing in the lyrical tradition even after the shame of his débacle, Absolon calls Alison his 'deerelyng' – the only instance in Chaucer of this indestructible term.[30] But Absolon's lyricism reaches its highest point, naturally, before his disillusionment when, close to what he mistakes for the Promised Land – in this case the shot-window of the carpenter's bower – he begs for Alison's favors – that is, for her 'ore' (mercy), as lyric poets usually expressed it. A Harley poet describing a similar crisis in his relations with his mistress reports,

> Adoun y fel to hire anon
> Ant cri[d]e, 'Ledy, thyn ore!'[31]

And much earlier, according to Giraldus Cambrensis, a priest of Worcestershire had so far forgotten himself at the altar as to displace the liturgical response 'Dominus vobiscum' with the lyrical refrain 'Swete lamman, dhin are'.[32] Thus, Absolon was conforming to a very old tradition when, about to receive his kiss, he

> doun sette hym on his knees,
> And seyde, 'I am a lord at alle degrees;
> For after this I hope ther cometh moore :
> Lemman, thy grace, and sweete bryd, thyn oore!'
>
> (A. 3723–6)

'Ore', the venerable word that is so often in the mouths of love-sick swains in Middle English, occurs in Chaucer only here. And the immediate similarity but impending difference between Absolon's situation and the situation of the average lyric lover epitomizes the technique we have been examining.

One final illustration of Chaucer's use – or abuse – of conventional idiom will suffice. Every reader of medieval romance knows that sooner or later the poet is going to describe a feast, if not a literal feast of food, at least a metaphorical one of love; and readers of English romances, including, in this case, Chaucer's own, can anticipate with some accuracy the terms in which the feast is going to be described – all the mirth and minstrelsy, or mirth and solace, or bliss and solace, or bliss and revelry, or revelry and melody by which the occasion will be distinguished. In the Miller's Tale the feast is, of course, of the metaphorical kind, consisting in the consummation of an adulterous love; and the obscene Miller, with his vast talent for realism, adapts the hackneyed old phrases most aptly to the situation. The carpenter, snug if uncomfortable in his kneading trough on high, is alternating groans with snores – 'for his head mislay' – while Alison and Nicholas are in his bed below.

> Ther was the revel and the melodye;
> And thus lith Alison and Nicholas
> In bisynesse of myrthe and of solas.   (A. 3652–4)

At this feast the carpenter's snores furnish the 'melodye', while his wife and her lover experience the 'solas' – that seemingly innocent word for delight which here receives the full force of Chaucer's genius for devaluation – the completion of a logical process that began when we first heard it said of 'hende' Nicholas that

> Of deerne love he koude and of solas.   (A. 3200)

It is, of course, true that the idiom I have been examining is just what we should expect of the Miller's cultural background – and of that of his characters[33] – and it would be possible to dispose of it by simply labeling it 'verisimilitude'. But verisimilitude seems to me among the least important of artistic criteria, and I refuse to believe that the courtly idiom in the Miller's Tale accomplishes nothing more than that. Perhaps I should have made a larger effort than I have to distinguish the Miller from Chaucer, and my interchanging of their names must have grated on some ears. But as I see it, much of Chaucer's irony in the *Canterbury Tales* becomes operative in the no man's land that exists between the poet Chaucer – who if he read his poems aloud must have been a very personal fact to his own audience – and the assigned teller of the tale, whether the Miller, the Knight, or, in 'Sir Thopas', Chaucer the pilgrim. The irony produced by the use of popular poetic idiom in the Miller's Tale becomes operative in this no man's land and operates in several directions. First, the idiom tends to make of the tale a parody of the popular romance, rather like 'Sir Thopas' in effect, though less exclusively literary. Then, too, it reinforces the connection between the Miller's Tale and the Knight's truly courtly romance that the Miller's Tale is intended to 'quite' (to repay); for it emphasizes the parallelism between the two different, though somehow similar, love-rivalries, one involving two young knights in remote Athens, the other two young clerks in contemporary Oxford. And in so far as it does this, it tends to turn the tale into a parody of all courtly romance, the ideals of which are subjected to the harshly naturalistic criticism of the fabliau. But finally, while doing its bit in the accomplishment of these things, the idiom Chaucer borrows from popular poetry contributes to the directly humorous effect of the Miller's Tale, and that is probably its chief function.[34]

SOURCE: *English Institute Essays*, ed. A. S. Downer (New York, 1950).

NOTES

1. The researches of Laura H. Loomis in recent years have, however, done much to justify such comparison by demonstrating Chaucer's familiarity with the native romance tradition. See 'Chaucer and the Auchlinleck MS. . .', in *Essays and Studies in Honor of Carleton Brown* (New York, 1940) pp. 111–28; 'Chaucer and the Breton Lays of the Auchinleck MS', *Studies in Philology* XXXVIII (1941) 14–33; and her study of 'Sir ,Thopas' in *Sources and Analogues to Chaucer's Canterbury Tales*, ed. W. F. Bryan and Germaine Dempster (Chicago, 1941) pp. 485–559.

2. Ed. J. S. P. Tatlock and A. G. Kennedy (Washington, 1927).

3. For a summary of scholarly opinions on the authorship of the Fragment see Joseph Mersand, *Chaucer's Romance Vocabulary* (New York, 1939) p. 60, n. 7.

4. See, for instance, the old poetic word 'swire' (neck); and the conventional alliterative phrases *styf in stour* and *byrde in bour*. Quotations from Chaucer are from F. N. Robinson's edition (Cambridge, Mass., 1933).

5. J. L. Lowes, 'Simple and Coy . . .', *Anglia*, xxxiii (1910) 440–51.

6. Aside from Fragment A of the *Roman*, where the words are common, they are normally used only by lower-class speakers; the only exceptions are in the portraits of the Prioress and the Merchant.

7. *Squyr of Lowe Degre*, ed. W. E. Mead, ll. 3–4; *Sir Ysumbras*, ed. G. Schleich, ll. 17–18; for examples of many of the characteristics discussed here, see W. C. Curry, *The Middle English Ideal of Personal Beauty* (Baltimore, 1916).

8. See *The Harley Lyrics*, ed. G. L. Brook (Manchester, 1948) 32.1–2; also 3.36 and 9.43 (references are to poem and line numbers).

9. See *O.E.D.*, 'dern', and Brook, 2.5–11.

10. See Brook, 24.17–20.

11. For examples see Curry, pp. 92–4. In contexts not concerned with romantic love or lovers this word, as well as others discussed here, was commonly employed without regard to gender.

12. For an example see Brook, 14.32. *O.E.D.*, 'lovely', records the word at *Anel.* 142, but Skeat and Robinson read 'lowly'.

13. Curry, p. 94; also Brook, 3.11, 5.32.

14. *Geoffrey Chaucer* (Oxford, 1934) p. 177.

15. Curry, p. 102.

16. See Lowes, *Geoffrey Chaucer*, p. 177; Brook, 3.11–20.

17. Brook, 7.77; also Curry, p. 81.

18. Brook, 4.37, 3.16.

19. See *O.E.D.*, 'gore', *sb.* 2, 2; *Sir Gawain and the Green Knight*, ed. J. R. R. Tolkien and E. V. Gordon (rev. edn : Oxford, 1930) note on l. 1814.

20. 'And [Nicholas] thakked hire aboute the lendes weel.'

21. In MS Harley 7334, A. 3322 reads : 'Schapen with goores in the newe get', which Tatlock regarded as a possible Chaucerian revision : see Robinson's textual note on the line.

22. *Lyfe of Ipomydon*, ed. E. Koelbing, ll. 123–4; Brook, 4.26–7.

23. In his thorough study of the dialect of the Reeve's Tale in *Transactions of the Philological Society* (London) for 1934, p. 52, J. R. R. Tolkien observes that 'wench' 'was still a respectable and literary word for "girl" in Chaucer's time, and was probably in pretty general use all over the country.' But it was not a respectable word in Chaucer's eyes (except in the sense 'servant-girl'), as a study of his uses will quickly reveal; see the Manciple's definition, H. 211–22.

24. Brook, 3.13; cf. 14.51–3.

160   E. T. DONALDSON

25. See J. M. Manly's note, citing an *English Dialect Dictionary* definition for Essex, in his edition of *C.T.* (New York, 1928) p. 560.

26. One is frequently tempted to suggest that Chaucer had the Harley lyrics in mind when he was composing *M.T.*, but in view of the poor conditions that existed for the preservation of secular lyrics, to associate Chaucer with a few survivals seems too large an economy. Particularly close correspondences may be noted with the lyric 'De Clerico et Puella' (Brook, 24), a dramatic dialogue in which a maiden initially repulses a clerk's plea of secret love: notice especially the third stanza, where she rebukes him ('Do wey, thou clerc, thou art a fol') and warns him of the consequences if he should be caught in her bower, and compare Alison's initial resistance ('Do wey youre handes') and her warning (A. 3294–7); further, the Harley lyric's window where the two had kissed 'fyfty sythe' (l. 23), and the carpenter's shot window. But the situation is, of course, a very old one (see *Dame Sirith*), and the Harley lyric may go back remotely to the same source from which Chaucer's immediate source stems.

27. See Brook, 4.5; *Sir Tristrem*, ed. E. Koelbing, l. 1860.

28. Brook, 3.22; cf. 9.3.

29. The Harley lyrics have 'burde', maiden (Brook, 3.1., 5.36), 'brudes', maidens (6.39), 'brid', maiden? (14.17), and 'brid', bird for maiden (6.40). In the *King's Quair*, stanza 65, 'bridis' rhymes with 'bydis' (abides), but clearly means 'birds'.

30. See, for instance, *William of Palerne*, ed. W. W. Skeat, l. 1538.

31. Brook, 32.16–17.

32. *Opera*, ed. J. S. Brewer, II (London, 1862) 120.

33. According to L. A. Haselmayer, 'The Portraits in Chaucer's Fabliaux', *Review of English Studies*, XIV (1938) 310–14, conventionalized portraits existed – though in only a vestigial form – in the French fabliaux with which Chaucer was acquainted. It was perhaps from these that Chaucer got the idea of using conventional poetic idiom in ironic contexts.

34. Since this was written, Fr. Paul E. Beichner has in a delightful paper fully demonstrated the effeminacy of Absolon and its traditional nature; see 'Absolon's Hair', *Mediaeval Studies*, XII (1950) 222–33.

Tony Slade

IRONY IN THE WIFE OF
BATH'S TALE (1969)

A feature of much criticism of the Wife of Bath's Tale has been a
tendency to view it against a background of supposed Arthurian
romances, and some critics have gone so far as to suggest that it
is exactly this Arthurian element which gives the tale its appeal
and interest.[1] Allied with this branch of Chaucerian criticism
has been the suggestion that 'only a small part of [the tale's] significance lies in its expression of character'.[2] Yet although most
discussions of the tale have centred on the analogues of the story
and the loathly lady motif (often to such an extent that the Wife
of Bath herself seems to have been forgotten), one or two critics
have suggested that this interest in the background to the
tale is not of much immediate use in evaluating the particularly
literary appeal of the story as Chaucer tells it. J. F. Roppolo in
particular makes out an interesting case for emphasizing the importance of the character of the knight in his attempt to suggest
that the tale has more unity than some former critics have held.[3]
Roppolo's discussion of the knight's role in the tale is continued
by F. G. Townsend, who goes on to suggest the importance not
only of the 'nameless knight' but also of the fact that the tale
does illustrate the character of Dame Alison, and that moreover
the tale cannot be properly understood unless we remember that
it is Alison who is telling the story which 'is the expression of
her hopes and dreams'.[4] Quite rightly in my opinion Townsend
adds that it is unfortunate that 'Chaucer's use of the very
common transformation motif has focussed attention on the tale
and its analogues, and obscured its real function, which is to prolong the self-revelation of the Wife to the very end of the
episode'. In this present discussion I wish to take Townsend's
thesis a stage further to show that by looking at the tale as an
example of the Wife's character the story does take on a unity

which it might otherwise seem to lack, in that certain apparent irrelevancies in it (notably the sermon on 'gentilesse') have an essentially ironic function in a tale of superb comedy and character portrayal. My suggestion is that by interpreting the Wife of Bath's Tale primarily as an expression of her personality, and by playing down the Arthurian element, we shall be able to see in it an example of Chaucer's ironic genius at its very best.

To do this it is important to remember that although the tale is, as Townsend has argued, an expression of the Wife's character, it is ultimately told by Chaucer himself. That is, the Wife is telling the story on one level whilst Chaucer is telling it on another, so that the usual ironic situation of a statement being made which one audience takes at its face value, and another (more sophisticated) audience at its ironic level, is considerably complicated here by the fact that at times Dame Alison is commenting ironically on the story she is telling (for example, her comments on the friars at the beginning) while at other times Chaucer himself is commenting ironically on her views and reactions. The Wife's character has already been exposed in some detail in her Prologue, which rambles around the theme of 'sovereynetee' in marriage : her tone is coarse and garrulous, and there is little evidence of that sort of delicate poetic beauty which some critics have professed to find in the Tale itself (I shall refer to this in more detail later). The main features of her character are common sense and a pre-occupation with sex, and an important element in both Prologue and Tale is her desire to explain life in terms of her own values. This leads her to tell a traditional story of the 'loathly lady' in a wholly typical and individual way, which is totally distinct in tone from all the other surviving versions. The Wife's version has none of the naive and fairy-tale elements of the analogues, for on the contrary its tone is largely (though not entirely) adult, aggressive, matter-of-fact, and sexually pre-occupied. She is telling the story because she wishes to make a moral point which has relevance in the world as she sees it, but in telling it in the way she does she exposes much of her own character.

The tone of the whole story is well struck from the beginning. At the end of her Prologue the Friar has rudely (but perhaps understandably) called her to task for rambling on :

> 'Now dame,' quod he, 'so have I joye or blis,
> This is a long preamble of a tale!'   (D. 830–1)

The Summoner comes to her aid and argues with the Friar, but
at the beginning of her tale the Wife shows that she is well able
to look after herself with a masterly attack on the friars in the
opening passage:

> In th'olde dayes of the Kyng Arthour,
> Of which that Britons speken greet honour,
> Al was this land fulfild of fayerye.
> The elf-queene, with hir joly compaignye,
> Daunced ful ofte in many a grene mede.
> This was the olde opinion, as I rede;
> I speke of manye hundred yeres ago.
> But now kan no man se none elves mo,
> For now the grete charitee and prayeres
> Of lymytours and othere hooly freres,
> That serchen every lond and every streem,
> As thikke as motes in the sonne-beem,
> Blessynge halles, chambres, kichenes, boures,
> Citees, burghes, castels, hye toures,
> Thropes, bernes, shipnes, dayeryes –
> This maketh that ther ben no fayeryes.
> For ther as wont to walken was an elf,
> Ther walketh now the lymytour hymself
> In undermeles and in morwenynges,
> And seyth his matyns and his hooly thynges
> As he gooth in his lymytacioun.
> Wommen may go now saufly up and doun.
> In every bussh or under every tree
> Ther is noon oother incubus but he,
> And he ne wol doon hem but dishonour.
>
> (D. 857–81)

It is worth looking closely at this whole introductory passage because it does appear to have been misconstrued by some critics.
Close textual analysis of Middle English poetry is notoriously
open to abuse because it is difficult to assess what overtones were
carried by words in Chaucer's time, but it does seem unjustifiable

to me to see in the passage 'a consciousness of the ancient
nature religion of Britain as having been desecrated, uprooted
and supplanted by the new ecclesiastical order' as John Speirs
asserts, nor is it by any means clear 'that the Wife's sympathy is
with the old nature cults, with "the elf-queene, with her joly
compaignye" . . .'.[5] It seems just as wrong to view this passage in
this way as it is to assume from the reference to the 'fayerye'
that the Wife's Tale is in any important sense a legendary tale of
wonder.[6] An important feature of the Tale is its bareness of description. The descriptive element is reduced to a minimum, and
we have only the bare essentials of the scene. The reference to
Arthur would seem at first to place the Tale firmly in the
tradition of Arthurian romance, but in reality this is simply a set
introduction similar to many folk-songs and ballads which
usually have little or nothing to do with any romance tradition.
In view of the imminent attack on the friars, however, there does
appear to be a sardonic touch in the phrase 'fulfild of fayerye',
where 'fulfild' could almost be rendered as 'filled to overflowing'
or even 'chock-a-block', and in the phrase 'ful ofte' with its
slightly comic suggestion of 'all the time, everywhere you looked'.
In any case, it seems wrong to regard these lines simply as the
Wife's expression of lament for the lost world of Faery Britain,
partly because this sort of sentimentality is not typical of her
character (her sentimentality is of a different sort, and is not
revealed until the end of the Tale), and partly because such an
interpretation implies a dramatic change of tone in the following lines with the attack on the sexual conduct of the friars. The
Wife in this case is consciously employing the irony, with the
magnificent, almost surrealist, image of the friars 'as thikke as
motes in the sonne-beem' searching for alms and women. At the
same time the Wife's own loquaciousness is implied by Chaucer
in the lines which seem at first to be merely a list –

> Blessynge halles, chambres, kichenes, boures,
> Citees, burghes, castels, hye toures,
> Thropes, bernes, shipnes, dayeryes . . .   (D. 869–71)

but which have the point of being those places which the friars
are 'blessing with their presence' because women will be found

in them. The friars have chased out the 'fayerye' (who has now become an incubus, in any case, with its additional sexual implication) and women can now go about safely, apart from the threat of dishonour posed by the friars themselves. Apart from this last sting in the tail, however, a notable feature of the tone of this section is that the irony is not vicious or hostile, and the Wife does not give the impression of being morally outraged by the friars' behaviour.

This tone of tolerant sexual irony is continued in the rape episode, which has received considerable attention from commentators. The late Professor G. H. Gerould has aptly emphasized the point of the 'grotesque absurdity of beginning a tale of "gentilesse" with rape',[7] and unless we remember the Wife's own character the episode does raise certain problems. Again it is the tone of the story as the Wife tells it which is all-important. Everything is described in a matter-of-fact way, and one gets the impression that she is not worried by the fact of rape in the sense that we might be : the woman is merely a figure in the piece, and she is 'fair game' to the 'lusty bacheler' (one can imagine the Wife's lips curling around the phrase). What is wrong in the Wife's eyes is not related necessarily to whether the woman is a peasant or a lady, but the fact that the act was committed 'maugree hir heed' (D. 887). In the Wife's eyes it is the domination of the man over the woman which is the knight's real offence, and it is for this that he has to undergo his test. We have to accept the episode in terms of the Wife's own values, which ironically appear humorous as the scene shifts to Arthur's court. This court is far removed from the world of Arthurian romance or 'gentilesse', however, for it is one where the women hold sway. Although the knight should have been beheaded for his offence 'the queene and othere ladyes mo' (D. 894) – almost certainly because he is a 'lusty bacheler' – persuade Arthur to hand him over to them. Arthur is a shadowy, unimportant figure in all this, but he knows his place according to the Wife's viewpoint, which is to give in to his wife's demands on the subject even if it involves ignoring the law of the land. The off-hand, matter-of-fact, way in which this is implied by the Wife should not blind us to the ironically humorous comment which Chaucer is implying all this time upon her assumptions and attitudes.

The Queen's motivation in saving the knight's life is not discussed by the Wife, who assumes it to be self-evident. The knight's
reaction to his reprieve, however, is not one of joy or steadfast
resolve to do better when he is told to go and search for
the answer to the question of what it is that women most desire :

> Wo was this knyght, and sorwefully he siketh;
> But what! he may nat do al as hym liketh.
>
> (D. 913–14)

Although he is a knight he has still to learn that he cannot do just
as he pleases, but it is worth noting now that the lesson he is to be
taught is hardly a profoundly moral one : it is that he has to accept women's 'sovereynetee' over men, and the lesson goes no
deeper than this in spite of the discussions on 'gentilesse' and
proper behaviour which are to follow later in the Tale. The ensuing search for an answer to the question is described very much
in terms of the Wife's own values, and she is unable to keep her
own views out of the discussion. The things which are suggested
as answers to the knight are almost all accepted as serious
answers by her : women want riches, honour, a good time, fine
clothes, sex, to be often married and widowed, to be flattered, to
be free and irresponsible, and lastly to be regarded as stable and
capable of keeping a secret. Only with this last suggested answer
does she seriously disagree, and it is in keeping with her argu-
mentative and dogmatic nature that she should ramble off the
main point of the narrative, just as it is in keeping with
her character that in doing so she should misquote a story from
Ovid in an attempt to prove her point. This illogicality is
typical of her, and the digression (comparatively brief here)
should also prepare us for a similar situation later in the Tale in
the sermon on 'gentilesse'.

She then returns to the narrative with the description of the
knight meeting with the old hag in what is for a moment a
typical fairy-tale setting of a tale of wonder. Yet the 'wondrous'
elements of the scene are not dwelt on, and the bareness of description is apparent in the economic handling of the episode
(D. 989–99). The old hag and the knight strike a bargain in which
he promises to do the next thing she asks him in return for the

answer to the question he has been set. Quickly the scene shifts
back to the Court of Love at Arthur's palace, where the assembled
wives, girls, and widows (the widows being especially wise, adds
the often-widowed Wife) are all immediately and without dispute satisfied with the knight's answer that women most of all
desire to have mastery over their men. In comparison with some
other versions of the story this section is hurried on by the narrator, for the knight does not experiment by suggesting other
possible answers before he states the right one, as there is only one
obvious answer according to the Wife in any case. Yet although
the knight has given the right answer it is apparent from his
shocked reaction to the old hag's request that he should marry
her that he has still not learnt his lesson. He tries to back out of
his earlier agreement in a realistic and understandable fashion :

> This knyght answerde, 'Allas! and weylawey!
> I woot right wel that swich was my biheste.
> For Goddes love, as chees a newe requeste! . . .
>
> (D. 1058–60)

Eventually, however, he is forced to marry the old hag, and in a
scene of rich comedy he is taken off to the marriage bed – 'he was
with his wyf abedde *ybroght*' (D. 1084). The humour of this
episode, which we are sharing with the Wife, is magnificent,
where the knight 'walweth and he turneth to and fro', whilst
his old wife lies smiling by his side. The comedy is aided by the
relish and understanding which the Wife has for the knight's
predicament, and the old hag taunts him with superb irony :

> 'Oh deere housebonde, *benedicitee*!
> Fareth every knyght thus with his wyf as ye?
> Is this the lawe of kyng Arthures hous?
> Is every knyght of his so dangerous? . . .'
>
> (D. 1087–90)

Only a hundred lines have been used to get to this point from
the old hag's first introduction into the story (D. 998), which
has up to this section moved swiftly, with only slight digressions
typical of the Wife's character. Now, however, the story is put

on one side whilst the hag gives her reluctant husband a long
and sententious sermon.

The humour we have noticed in this 'bedroom-scene' preceding the sermon is humour which the Wife of Bath intends us to
share with her, although at times throughout her tale we have
been laughing at her assumptions as well as with her jokes. Now,
however, the tone of the tale changes: the Wife becomes serious
in showing the reluctant knight persuaded by what to her are
logical and morally admirable arguments, whilst the reader and
Chaucer himself continue to regard the narration ironically. The
knight, stung by the hag's taunting of his behaviour in bed, ill-
naturedly and in desperation draws her attention to three things
which upset him:

> Thou art so loothly, and so oold also,
> And therto comen of so lough a kynde,
> That litel wonder is thogh I walwe and wynde.
>
> (D. 1100–2)

It is surely obvious that the first two of these objections – that she
is ugly and old – are the more serious, yet it is the third and least
important (though not unimportant) objection which the hag
enlarges on somewhat illogically for over one hundred lines. The
point is reached only by grasping that Chaucer is aware of the
illogicality of the argument whilst the Wife herself is perfectly
serious in repeating ideas which have become, by the time she is
telling them, commonplaces of Christian and other literature.
It is true that some of the ideas on 'gentilesse' which the hag
expresses are similar to some of Chaucer's own favourite themes,
but the manner in which these ideas are expressed here surely
suggests that they are not meant to be taken as seriously as some
modern critics have done. Kemp Malone has sensibly summed up
the way in which the other pilgrims would have reacted to the
Wife's arguments as a whole (although his emphasis on the
poetic qualities of the sermon would be different from mine):

The Wife of Bath's unorthodox extension of the principle of female
sovereignty from love affairs to married life undoubtedly struck our
forefathers as funny. They did not take it seriously, and the so-
called debate on the subject which modern men of learning with

extraordinary *naïveté* have read into the *Canterbury Tales* is not really there. The Clerk, in the second ending tacked on to his tale, pokes fun at the Wife of Bath's kind of matrimony but he makes no effort whatever to refute her views. To him and to all the other pilgrims these views are merely amusing and need no refutation. The pilgrims, if not the modern scholars, take the Wife for the comic character that Chaucer meant her to be.[8]

In the sermon the argument is intentionally questionable. Germaine Dempster has brought out the problem of lines D. 1159–62,[9] and although James Winny has made an interesting alteration to the Robinson text in his edition of the Wife of Bath's Prologue and Tale (Cambridge, 1965) to avoid this problem, it seems possible that the illogicality of these lines is as intentional as the inconsistency of the hag discoursing at length on the theme of 'gentilesse' when the knight has raised other more pressing objections which are dismissed peremptorily at the end of her speech. W. P. Albrecht effectively confirms this general reading of the sermon in agreeing with J. F. Roppolo on the ironic fact that the Wife cannot qualify under her own (and to her serious) definitions of 'gentilesse'. As Albrecht points out, the Wife's 'method of disputation must have been pretty transparent to several of the pilgrims',[10] and he goes on to support Roppolo's arguments for the useful function of the sermon within the Tale.

Even so, some qualifications to Roppolo's article (to which I referred at the beginning of this paper) need to be made, for although the 'gentilesse' sermon certainly has a structural value within the Tale it is surely not simply in the way in which he goes on to define it. Primarily Roppolo's argument centres around the change in the knight's character which takes place as a result of the force and eloquence of the hag's speech, and he even goes so far as to quote (p. 267) an earlier critic (R. K. Root, *The Poetry of Chaucer*) to the effect that 'we are held captive by the spell of [the Lady's] poetry, and at the conclusion of the speech are not surprised to find that the speaker is of wondrous beauty'. This seems to be patently ridiculous. The Wife of Bath herself is certainly intending us to read the sermon in this way, but there seems to be little that is critically admirable in the poetry of this section. It is not only that 'the Lady's argument contains nothing original in ideas and outlook',[11] but also that

the poetry itself is commonplace and laboured. The knight is
persuaded not by the spell of the poetry or the logic of the argument, but largely because the speech goes on for so long that he is
willing to accept anything to stop the flow of talk. He is offered
the chance of making a choice between having her either old,
ugly, yet a good wife on the one hand, or young and attractive,
though licentious, on the other. This choice is not the usual one
in the other versions of the folk-tale, but it is typical of the Wife
of Bath's values and a repetition of the hag's concluding argument in the sermon proper, when she briefly deals with the
knight's fundamental complaints about her age and ugliness by
saying that in that case he need have no fear of becoming a
cuckold (otherwise implicitly assumed by the Wife to be a distinct
probability). However, the knight does not make the choice, but
tells her to do what she thinks best, in a comment which is filled
with wearisome and heavy irony :

> 'My lady and my love, and wyf so deere,
> I put me in youre wise governance . . .'   (D. 1230–1)

An element of irony is surely present in the effusion of sentiment
of 'my love', 'wyf so deere', and particularly in 'wise' (for the
knight has seen through her arguments as scholastically weak) –
an irony which Chaucer intends but which neither the Wife nor
the hag (fortunately for her husband) themselves detect. The
Wife suggests that the knight is giving in for what to her are the
right reasons of the hag's persuasive arguments, but Chaucer himself leaves some comic doubt as to the real motivation. One
result of the long sermon has been to swing the reader's sym-
pathies behind the knight and his unpleasant predicament, but
the sermon as a whole has an essentially dramatic function in the
Tale and is not simply 'dragged in as a makeweight'.[12]

In conclusion we might note that the ironic handling of the
Wife's character is continued in the last few lines of her tale,
where her sentimentality is clearly apparent. By this time she is
perfectly serious in suggesting that the knight now deserves the
sexual prize he gains when the hag changes into a young, beautiful, and yet virtuous woman. It is in one sense a typical ending
to a romantic love story which middle-aged women like the Wife

admire. Her sentimental ending is rather funny, but she is not so overwhelmed by the sentimentality that it has drastically altered her real nature, for in the last lines (D. 1258 ff.) she gives a parting insight into the vigour of her character which her tale has so marvellously brought out:

> . . . and Jhesu Crist us sende
> Housbondes meeke, yonge, and fressh abedde,
> And grace t'overbyde hem that we wedde;
> And eek I praye Jhesu shorte hir lyves
> That wol nat be governed by hir wyves;
> And olde and angry nygardes of dispence,
> God sende hem soone verray pestilence!

SOURCE: *Modern Language Review*, LXIV (1969)

NOTES

1. Notably S. Eisner, *A Tale of Wonder* (Wexford, 1957).

2. D. S. Brewer, *Chaucer* (London, 1961), p. 130.

3. 'The Converted Knight in Chaucer's Wife of Bath's Tale', *College English*, XII (1951) 263–9.

4. 'Chaucer's Nameless Knight', *Modern Language Review*, XLIX (1954) 1–4.

5. *Chaucer the Maker* (London, 1962) pp. 147–8. Even so fine a commentator as G. H. Gerould talks of 'the momentary and lovely glimpse of the dancing elf-queen' (*Chaucerian Essays*, Princeton, 1952, p. 79).

6. For a well-argued opposite view, see Kemp Malone's article, 'The Wife of Bath's Tale', *Modern Language Review*, LVII (1962) 481–91.

7. Gerould, p. 75.

8. Malone, pp. 489–90.

9. ' "Thy Gentilesse" in the Wife of Bath's Tale, D. 1159–62', *Modern Language Notes*, LVII (1942) 173–6.

10. 'The Sermon on "Gentilesse" ', *College English*, XII (1951) 459.

11. Winny, p. 26. But note that my interpretation of the Tale as a whole, and of the function of the 'gentilesse' sermon within it, is almost entirely opposed to that put forward in Mr. Winny's introduction.

12. Paull F. Baum, *Chaucer: A Critical Appreciation* (Durham, N.C., 1958) p. 133.

John Burrow

IRONY IN THE MERCHANT'S TALE (1957)

The Merchant's Tale is usually classed as a 'fabliau tale', and the classification has its point. But it has perhaps drawn attention away from those qualities which distinguish the Merchant's Tale from the rest of Chaucer's 'fabliaux'. These are qualities which it shares, not with the comic tales of the Miller or the Summoner, but with the moral fable of the Pardoner – the persistent irony, the seriousness which informs even the farcical climax. This climax (the gulling of January in the 'pear-tree episode') is no more simply comic than the death of the Pardoner's rioters. It is much more closely realised than, for example, the dénouement of the Miller's Tale; and Chaucer, in filling out the fabliau form in this way, makes something new. The French fabliaux may be cruel, but they are also casual – one gets just enough about, for example, the duped husband to make the joke, and no more. The comic effect depends on the preservation of the skeletal bareness of the story. The reader is never allowed to get near enough, as it were, to be seriously involved. In contrast, the Merchant's Tale is full of 'close-ups':

> ... Januarie hath faste in armes take
> His fresshe May, his paradys, his make.
> He lulleth hire, he kisseth hire ful ofte,
> With thikke brustles of his berd unsofte,
> Lyk to the skyn of houndfyssh, sharp as brere,
> For he was shave al newe in his manere. (E. 1821–6)

The clarity of the observation is given a sharp point, here, by the simile of the dogfish, and by the ironic comment in the last line. The reader is forced to visualise the scene, as never in the French fabliau, to grasp its human reality; and in the process the moral issues, with which the French authors were not concerned (Bédier called them 'amoral'), come alive.

Unlike the other 'fabliau tales', but like the Pardoner's Tale, the story of January and May faces up to the moral issues it raises. This involves a radical modification of the fabliau method. The treatment of January's dream life (his 'fantasye') recalls, not the carpenter or the miller, but the Pardoner's rioters with their dreams of wealth :

> This yongeste which that wente to the toun
> Ful ofte in herte he rolleth up and doun
> The beautee of thise floryns newe and brighte.
>
> (C. 837–9)

> Heigh fantasye and curious bisynesse
> Fro day to day gan in the soule impresse
> Of Januarie aboute his mariage.
> Many fair shap and many a fair visage
> Ther passeth thurgh his herte nyght by nyght.
>
> (E. 1577–81)

But it is the distinguishing characteristic of the Merchant's Tale that the ironic contrast between the dream and the reality, the self-centred and insecure 'heigh fantasye' of the old knight and the predictable course of his marriage, should be pointed insistently at every turn. In the Pardoner's Tale there is a strong general dramatic irony. The rioters pursue their own downfall; and they ignore the old man, as January ignores Justinus. But there is nothing like the accumulation of local irony which marks the Merchant's Tale.

Take, for example, the opening passage of the poem (E. 1245–1398) where January, in what is really an internal monologue, persuades himself that he will find permanent 'ioye and blisse' in marriage with a young wife. The general irony of this is clear. The mistake would have been as obvious to a medieval reader as the rioters' mistake about the gold ('But mighte this gold be caried from this place . . . than were we in heigh felicitee'). But the point is made more heavily – January's dotage is much more ridiculous than anything in the Pardoner's Tale. He turns pro-

verbial and biblical lore inside out in a way that places him
decisively in the moral scheme of the poem – 'Old fissh and yong
flessh wolde I have ful fayn', 'Do alwey so as wommen wol
thee rede'. These lines, and lines like them, suggest the proverbs
of which they are distortions (elsewhere in Chaucer – 'Wom-
menes conseils been ful ofte colde' 'Men sholde wedden after hir
estaat, For youthe and elde is often at debaat'). One more
quotation will illustrate the tone of the poem's opening:

> Alle othere manere yiftes hardily
> As londes, rentes, pasture or commune,
> Or moebles, alle been yiftes of fortune,
> That passen as a shadwe upon a wal.
> But drede nat, if pleynly speke I shal,
> A wyf wol laste, and in thyn hous endure,
> Wel lenger than thee list, paraventure.   (E. 1312–18)

The last line makes a joke out of what is obviously a philosophical blunder. It is interpolated into the sequence of January's
thoughts to point the irony, like an aside in an Elizabethan
play. January is subjected to the most unblinking scrutiny
throughout the poem. His fantastic thoughts and desires, his
slack skin and his bristles, are all rendered in unsparing detail;
and every detail carries a point, strengthening the general with a
local irony:

> Adoun by olde Januarie she lay
> That sleep til that the coughe hath him awaked.
> (E. 1956–7)

(This technique is familiar from the General Prologue, where
the poetry is all detail – of behaviour or dress or appearance – and
the ironies depend on the implications of the details). The insistent irony, and the answering choice of detail, expose the
characters of the poem in a brilliant light, which makes the Pardoner's Tale feel almost kindly by comparison.

Now, although Chaucer was by no means always 'gentle
Chaucer', he was not characteristically a destructive poet. His

irony, as in the portrait of the Prioress, is often so fleeting as to be genuinely ambiguous, at least to the modern reader; his tone is most often that of Theseus in the Knight's Tale – 'The god of love, a benedicite, How mighty and how greet a lord is he' – and can modulate easily, as in the same speech of Theseus, into a sympathetic generalization – 'A man moot be a fool, or yong or oold, I woot it by myself ful yore agon'. It is an irony which does justice to its victims; the destructive or critical impulse does not work unchecked. Of course, there is no *a priori* reason why the Merchant's Tale should not be an exception to this generalization; it might be argued that a ruthless almost hysterical story was called for at this point in the 'Marriage Group' from the disillusioned Merchant. But I want to suggest that the 'corrosive, destructive, even hopeless quality' which Mr. Patch, and other critics, found in this poem, and with which I have so far been concerned, is not the whole story; and that, if it were, the poem would not be as good as it is. The Merchant's Tale is not only a poem of clarity, critical observation, and disgust – a medieval *Madame Bovary*. There is an opposing impulse, an impulse to approach and understand, which appears in a tendency to *generalize*. This I consider to be a feature of all Chaucer's best narrative poetry.

Take one line from the description of January's marriage – 'tendre youthe hath wedded stouping age'. The point is a critical one again (it is the old fish and young flesh theme) but there is no mistaking the genuine lyrical note. There is generalization, but it is not the dry generalization of a proverb inside out. A generosity about the line contrasts sharply with the nagging irony we have been noting. The gentle contrast between 'stouping' and 'tendre' is not like the sharp and disgusting physical contrast between January's bristly chin and May's 'tendre face' in the description of the wedding night from which a passage has already been quoted. There is a generous lyrical note about the line which we find again in the introduction of Bacchus and Venus into the wedding festivities :

> Bacus the wyn hem skynketh al aboute,
> And Venus laugheth upon every wight,
> For Januarie was bicome hir knyght,

    And wolde bothe assayen his corage
    In libertee and eek in mariage;
    And with hire fyrbrond in hire hand aboute
    Daunceth biforn the bryde and all the route.

                                    (E. 1722–8)

There is malice in the equating of liberty with marriage; but
hardly, it seems, any mock heroic effect in the introduction of
Bacchus and Venus. January's marriage takes on a festal dignity in the archaic 'skynketh', and the last buoyant couplet.
There is another finer couplet on this theme a little later :

    So sore hath Venus hurt hym with hire brond
    As that she bar it daunsing in hire hond.   (E. 1777–8)

(Here the 'daunsing' can refer either to Venus, or to the torch; it
effectively goes with both.) The effect of such lines as these is to
dignify the emotions involved by setting them in the general context of human feelings represented by the gods. It will be clear
from these examples that there is nothing thin or abstract about
the generalization. It is done concretely, and is felt as a sort of
lyrical expansiveness in the verse (an effect I do not find in the
Pardoner's Tale).

   There is, further, a perceptible drift towards allegory in the
poem. The names January and May, Justinus and Placebo, suggest this. At one point there is a significant reference to what for
Chaucer was the allegory par excellence, the *Romance of the
Rose* :

    He made a gardyn, walled al with stoon,
    So fair a gardyn woot I nowher noon.
    For, out of doute, I verraily suppose
    That he that wroot the Romance of the Rose
    Ne coude of it the beautee wel devyse . . .

                                     (E. 2029–33)

The garden, which is here being introduced, plays an important part in the poem. As it serves to dignify and strengthen
January's feelings by generalizing them, and to counter the 'cor-

rosive' irony to which they are exposed, it may fittingly be considered here.

January's desire for a young wife is presented from the start as 'fantasye' – self deception (the word is a favourite of Chaucer's, occurring very frequently in *Troilus and Criseyde*). But it is associated equally, in a series of contexts at the beginning of the poem, with the image of the earthly paradise, the general fantasy of the great good place. 'Wedlock' January thinks 'is so esy and so clene, That in this world it is a paradys' . . . 'Wyf is mannes help and his confort, His paradys terrestre and his desport'. Then at the wedding 'Ianuarie hath faste in armes take His fresshe May, his paradys, his make'. Marriage is like the earthly paradise quite specifically in being at once 'esy' and 'clene' – delightful and morally irreproachable. Desire and duty are at one in marriage, as January points out to May on their wedding night – 'Blessed be the yok that we be inne, For in our actes we mowe do no sinne.'

It is true that January's 'heigh fantasye' is made to look ridiculous in the poem. When he worries lest he should have 'myn hevene in erthe here' and pay for it later, Justinus remarks :

> Dispeire yow noght, but have in youre memorie,
> Paraunter she may be youre purgatorie.
> She may be Goddes mene, and Goddes whippe,
> Thanne shal youre soule up to hevene skippe
> Swifter than dooth an arwe out of a bowe.
>
> (E. 1669–73)

But it is not only ridiculous. It draws strength from association with the image of the earthly paradise (or the garden of Genesis as is clear from E. 1325–32). January's 'fantasye' is broadened by these allusions to include a general human fantasy; it is not only the delusion of a besotted *senex amans*. Here again the generalizing lends dignity and significance to the action of the poem, contributing to the reader's sense of an intelligible and meaningful narrative progression.

It seems clear that in this progression January's garden in the second part of the poem takes over from the image of the 'paradys terrestre' in the first. It is in fact the paradys of his sexual

fantasy realised; in the poem the garden has something approaching a symbolic status (as gardens often have in medieval literature). The opening of the description has already been quoted.
It goes on :

> Ne Priapus ne myghte nat suffise,
> Though he be god of gardyns, for to telle
> The beautee of the gardyn and the welle
> That stood under a laurer alwey grene.   (E. 2034–7)

The *Romance of the Rose* has already been explicitly introduced
into the description, and the well under the laurel is certainly
meant to recall the well in the garden of the *Romance* which, in
Chaucer's translation, lies 'under a tree, Which tree in Fraunce
men cal a pyn'. The laurel must have been substituted for the
pine to link the garden with January's erotic fantasies. It is meant
to recall his earlier boast :

> Though I be hoor, I fare as dooth a tree
> That blosmeth er the fruyt ywoxen bee;
> And blosmy tree nys neither drye ne deed.
> I feele me nowhere hoor but on myn heed;
> Myn herte and alle my lymes been as grene
> As laurer thurgh the yeer is for to sene.   (E. 1461–6)

This suggests that Chaucer is considering more than the narrative necessities in organising the detail of the tale. There is a
further suggestion of the sexual significance of the garden in the
introduction of Priapus here. The repetition, through the opening description (E. 2029–37), of the words 'garden' and
'beauty' gives to the lines an emphatic, almost incantatory, ring,
which disposes the reader to look for 'meanings', as if it were the
garden of the *Parlement* or of Dante's *Purgatorio*. It is in this
garden of love, for such it clearly seems to be, that January
'payes his wyf hir dette'. He guards it as jealously as if it were May
herself, and walls it off, like the garden of Guillaume Lorris, with
stone.

January goes blind, and the extravagance of his jealousy (it is
'outrageous') is noted in the best fabliau manner – although not

without gestures of sympathy ('O Januarie, what myghte it thee availle, Thogh thou myghte se as fer as shippes saille?'). His fantasy, no longer associated with the solid and persuasive ideal image of the fertile garden of love, becomes almost imbecile ('He nolde suffre hir for to ryde or go, But if that he had hand on hire alwey'). But, with the opening of the final scene in the garden, the tone changes again:

> ... in a morwe unto this May seith he :
> 'Rys up, my wyf, my love, my lady free,
> The turtles voys is herd, my dowve sweete,
> The wynter is goon with all his reynes weete.
> Com forth now with thyne eyen columbyn,
> How fairer been thy brestes than is wyn.
> The gardyn is enclosed al aboute.
> Com forth my white spouse! . .   (E. 2137–44)

This very striking passage, as Skeat pointed out, is a mosaic of phrases from the *Song of Solomon*. It is beautifully timed. The strong impersonal lyric note re-establishes January's passion, bringing out the essential intelligibility of his behaviour, making sense of him again after the fabliau comedy of the preceding passage. And the garden, the symbolic home of his ideal of fertility and privacy, gains a further reference. 'The gardyn is enclosed al aboute' recalls, from the *Song of Solomon*: 'A garden enclosed is my sister, my spouse; a spring shut up, a fountain sealed'. Chaucer has turned this metaphor into a literal statement about January's walled garden, and it might seem that the resulting line would sit oddly in the middle of the passage, which in general preserves the elaborately metaphoric style of the biblical original. That it seems quite natural suggests how the literal garden of Chaucer's poem has itself gathered a kind of metaphorical significance.

This is not to deny that there is meant to be some kind of mock-heroic effect in the passage, although I think it is faint. The passage primarily works in the other direction, resisting the 'corrosive' irony. Chaucer certainly damps the Solomon passage down with his comment 'Swiche olde lewed wordes used he' (where 'lewed' seems to mean 'lecherous' rather than 'ignorant').

But the final effect is rather of pathos than of irony. As January speaks, Damyan slips in through the gate and hides behind a bush; and January, 'blynd as is a stoon', follows him in with May. He *is* presented as pathetic, absurd, and repulsive (there is more pathos in him as the poem progresses, though this never involves any sort of moral concession towards him on the author's part). But he is not only the object of ironic sympathy and contempt. Chaucer makes out of his sexual 'fantasye' something that the reader can feel is real and intelligible, by extending the poem's field of reference beyond the range of its narrative particularities, drawing on the common literary experience of his culture. The *Romance of the Rose* and the Bible were the obvious common points of reference (knowledge of the Italian poets was much more restricted), and these works are very much present in the Merchant's Tale.

This width of reference seems to me to be a general characteristic of Chaucer's best poetry. It is this which marks the Merchant's Tale off from the two other fabliau tales which are sometimes associated with it – the Friar's Tale and the Summoner's Tale. These poems have in common with the Merchant's Tale a quality of destructive wit (which appears at its best in the ironically observed speeches of the Friar to Thomas) and of farcical popular humour (which appears in the dénouements of the poems). The anecdotes are filled out with ironic detail. The Friar comes to see Thomas:

> . . . fro the bench he droof awey the cat,
> And leyde adoun his potente and his hat,
> And eek his scrippe, and sette hym softe adoun.

> (D. 1775–7)

The Friar's smooth impudence is superbly conveyed in the rhythm and even the rhyme of these lines. It is comedy – more obviously comedy than the close-up of January sitting up in bed which was quoted earlier. The first part of the Summoner's Tale is brilliantly successful. But if we compare the poem as a whole with the Merchant's Tale we may feel that it lacks solidity. The Friar is taken at his face value – the common satiric type of the corrupt cleric. The tone of the poem never modulates from the ironic and critical; the method is exclusively mimetic. It is 'poetry of the surface'. We find these qualities in the Merchant's Tale too. But January's behaviour is not only observed, it is explored (the key word, I have suggested, is 'fantasye'). It is traced back to a compelling sexual fantasy, which is linked, through the garden, with the fantasies of the Earthly Paradise, the *Song of Songs*, and the *Romance of the Rose*. There is a lyrical expansiveness ('tendre youthe hath wedded stouping age') in the poem, where the anecdote is being generalized in this way. The particularity of the Summoner's Tale is invigorating (at least in the earlier part); but in the end the poem does not add up to much. It remains an extended anecdote.

It seems obvious that the quality in the Merchant's Tale which is being described bears some relation to Allegory. The allegorical suggestions of the names January and May, Placebo and Justinus, are apparent enough. The reader of *Piers Plowman* will recognise in the system of cross-references which links January's garden with other gardens, and all these gardens with the theme of sexual fantasy, a familiar technique. It bears little relation to the strict allegorical method, which some critics detect in *Piers* – the method of four-level meaning deriving, ultimately, from biblical interpretation; but neither does most medieval allegory. Usually the technique is loose, flexible, and intermittent. The equations may for a time be very fixed and clear ('Petrus id est Christus'); but they may equally well amount to nothing more than a casual cross-reference. Only on a too rigid definition could the part played by the allegorical method in the Merchant's Tale be ignored. Its story is not in itself allegorical; neither is the story of the Eighteenth Passus of *Piers Plowman* (the story of the crucifixion and resurrection) with which, technically, the poem has something in common. In both, allegory is at work generalising and equating (Christ is Light is Piers; January is Age, his garden is Adam's and Solomon's and Lorris'). In both, allegorical figures can enter the story without anomaly (Mercy, Peace, Truth and Righteousness; Venus and Bacchus).

The point here is that this generalizing impulse (characteristic of allegory) exists side by side in Chaucer with the ironic or satiric impulse (characteristic of fabliau) which tends to isolate its object and particularize it. It is this dual impulse which makes the Merchant's Tale a saner and more balanced poem than the conventional account might suggest. It is unlike the Summoner's Tale in having a significance beyond its anecdotal content, in having a 'meaning'. The irony is controlled (and this is surely characteristic of Chaucer) by a recognition that January's case illustrates general human weakness – a suggestion that is rigidly excluded in the treatment of the Summoner's Friar. It is a knowledge of 'fantasye' which informs the poem and gives it its moral framework within which the irony works. This knowledge appears in the unobtrusively allegorical treatment of the story, notably of the garden. The poem owes as much to the allegory as to the fabliau, bringing to the anecdotal clarity of the latter a scope and significance which belong to the former tradition. This seems to be one of the secrets of Chaucer's best narrative poems. They grow in the mind without losing the precision of their outline.

SOURCE: *Anglia*, LXXV (1957).

Robert B. Burlin

THE ART OF CHAUCER'S
FRANKLIN (1967)

Modern criticism of the *Canterbury Tales* has greatly sharpened
our image of many of the pilgrims, and clarified, though perhaps
not settled, the theoretical issue of the dramatic propriety of the
tale to its teller. In the specific instance of the Franklin, however, a
fundamental disagreement persists. The critical record contains
wildly divergent estimates. Early in this century, Robert K. Root,
thinking of the Franklin's autobiographical statements, compared him to a 'Toledo oil-magnate' bewailing 'the vicious ten-
dencies of the son whom he is lavishly maintaining at Yale or
Harvard'.[1] Yet the English critic, Raymond Preston, has recently
given him academic status : 'a comfortable don of an ancient
college, careful to be wise and not too serious, and telling his
story with mellow vinous satisfaction'.[2]

Perhaps the most significant attempt to reconcile 'The
Character and Performance of Chaucer's Franklin'[3] was made
by R. M. Lumiansky. Like Root, he gives us a socially minded
individual, by nature belonging to the 'everyday, practical
world', yet aspiring to the rarefied atmosphere of the 'gentils'.
Rebuffed by the Host, the Franklin offers meek apologies and
shameless flattery, yet is unable to abandon his preoccupation
with the idea of 'gentillesse'. In the Tale and particularly in the
character of Dorigen, Lumiansky sees the same clash of social
values : the sophisticated, aristocratic ideal of courtly love
against the practical bourgeois insistence upon a perfect, happy
marriage. Thus the character and performance of the Franklin
exhibit a consistent uncertainty of response to conflicting social
demands.

The opposing (and, I believe, 'orthodox') point of view has,
however, been restated by Roland Blenner-Hassett,[4] who paints a
formal portrait of the wise and dignified Franklin in legal garb –

a man of perfect self-possession consorting with a professional Lawyer for whom certainty is a prime requisite. This critic more or less identifies the Franklin with Chaucer himself, on the basis of similar technical background and professional experience, and the brusque treatment accorded both men by the Host. Finally, the 'semi-legal language' of the Franklin is said to invest his tale with an 'added seriousness' which makes it a 'fitting summation, artistically and intellectually, of the problems raised in the so-called Marriage Group of Tales'.[5]

Where some readers, then, have found conflicting motivations and a tale full of incongruities, others see dignity and high seriousness. Clearly, this radical disagreement over the Franklin points either to failure on Chaucer's part or to complex purposes which have not yet been fully articulated. There seems to be ample justification for reopening the entire case and exploring the second of these alternatives: the possibility of multiple intentions on the part of the poet. A firm distinction between the art of the Franklin and that of his creator will lead inevitably to thematic considerations of some consequence to a full understanding of Chaucer's poetry.

One major difficulty in assessing the Franklin's character is the obscurity of the portrait in the General Prologue. It is partly an obscurity imposed by the passage of time. Even the meaning of the term, 'franklin', has been in dispute. The *N.E.D.* had relegated that rank to a position in society 'next below the gentry', but G. H. Gerould[6] has substantially established that the franklin in Chaucer's day was of a sufficiently exalted position to be considered 'gentil'. Yet Lumiansky, wishing (as I do) to stress the Franklin's social aspirations, ignores Gerould's evidence and reverts to Kittredge's estimate:

> Socially, he is not quite within the pale of the gentry, but he is the kind of man that may hope to found a family, the kind of man from whose ranks the English nobility has been constantly recruited.[7]

Some confusion arises from the slipperiness of the word 'gentry', which Kittredge seems to equate with the aristocracy. The modern English use, however, first appearing in the late sixteenth century,[8] designates the class immediately below the nobility, and it is here no doubt that Gerould would place the Franklin. Such a class depends not on title, but on the appearance of gentility, on an established position in society, the result of wealth and political ability over a number of generations; it would, therefore, be accessible to the bourgeois in a way that the nobility would not. The *Canterbury Tales* alone provides sufficient evidence that a 'gentry' class in this sense existed in the fourteenth century, and that they commanded considerable power and prestige.

The Franklin, though a man of ample means and political prestige, clearly does not belong to that order of society for which 'gentilesse', in its primary sense[9] at least, is assured by birth. Moreover, the perpetuation of those gifts which the Franklin abundantly possesses is by no means guaranteed. Political and social abilities are not hereditary, and wealth, unlike a title, can be consumed in a single generation. It is just such a prospect which the Franklin has painfully before him in the person of a young son who

> to vertu listeth nat entende;
> But for to pleye at dees, and to despende
> And lese al that he hath, is his usage.
> And he hath levere talken with a page
> Than to comune with any gentil wight
> Where he myghte lerne gentilesse aright.
>
> (F. 689–94)

The Franklin himself professes belief in a 'vertu' which exceeds in value all the material wealth he possesses. This 'gentilesse' is not simply social rank, but a nobility of manner which can be learned and imitated, so that, in all but title, the son of a franklin might become indistinguishable from the son of a knight.

But there is a telling betrayal in the Franklin's words to the Squire :

> I have a sone, and by the Trinitee,
> I hadde levere than twenty pound worth lond,
> Though it right now were fallen in myn hond,
> He were a man of swich discrecioun
> As that ye been !   (F. 682–6)

'Discrecioun' and 'gentillesse' are not, the Franklin realizes, qualities that can be bought, but he automatically and naturally thinks in such terms. He is a man used to buying what he wants. The precision and the immediacy with which he envisions the twenty pound worth of land falling at that moment into his hand expose him as one more at ease when exchange takes the tangible form of land or currency than with the exchange of ideas or mere words, where values are more difficult to ascertain. Yet it is just these intangibles which attract the man who is so exceedingly comfortable in other ways. The Franklin, who is a St. Julian of hospitality as well as a frequent and popular office holder, is, because of this fatal attraction, an unhappy father. The vigour and passion with which the Franklin lauds the young Squire and abuses his own son betray the uneasiness of his paternal relationship. But even as the father reveals his attempts to lead his son toward 'vertu' and 'gentillesse', he unconsciously stresses with equal force that he is leading him *from* sins of prodigality. The motives are clearly not distinguished in the Franklin's mind; the preservation of a tangible power and the acquisition of intangible but socially esteemed virtues contend for prominence. These words of the Franklin, then, support the description of one comfortably ranking with the 'landed gentry', but uncomfortably unsure of real gentility.

It is his exchange of words with the Host, however, which most strikingly confirms our notion of the Franklin's social insecurity. Precisely at the word 'gentillesse', the Host can bear no more and puts an end to the old man's confessions. Harry Bailly has heard a great deal about 'gentillesse' in the last tales, ever since the Wife dragged the issue into her story by its heels. It may well be that he has heard too much precious debate on the subject by members of the pilgrimage who are manifestly trying to compensate for want of good birth and good breeding. It is perhaps the Franklin's use of such terms that the Host finds particularly offensive; that, as Nevill Coghill suggests, he 'could see at a glance that there was a penny short in the shilling of the Franklin's gentility'.[10] In any case, the Host, using the familiar pronoun, treats him with unusual rudeness. The Franklin's social position seems not to permit him a rebuke; nor is he lofty enough to withdraw in a huff as the Monk does. He replies with a humble, elaborate submission which would certainly be far from 'the realities of social intercourse', as Kemp Malone implies,[11] were the Franklin truly to be considered of untouchable social respectability.

Perhaps the most serious objection to my estimate of the Franklin's social position is the portrait in the General Prologue. Scholars have almost unanimously found it an approving depiction of a white-bearded gentleman endowed with a sanguine and generous disposition and considerable prestige accruing from the high offices he has held. This view is difficult to refute. The Chaucerian attitude toward the representatives of the moneyed class is in general cold and impersonal. In the case of the professional men – the Merchant, the Lawyer, the Physician – there is, however, clear negative evidence of unscrupulous money-grubbing. In most of the other portraits there is a recognized code of behavior – the chivalric ideal, the monastic rule – against which the pilgrim is measured. But there is no indication of the Franklin's dishonesty, and no established ideal of conduct is alluded to, if indeed one was available.

Yet twenty-one of the thirty lines devoted to the Franklin in the General Prologue are given over to the elaboration of something like an ideal – the wholly worldly philosophy of Epicurus,

> That heeld opinioun that pleyn delit
> Was verray felicitee parfit.   (A. 337–8)

And the pilgrim Chaucer is at great pains to convince us that his new friend is the true and perfect representative of this 'opinioun'. Most scholars have allowed themselves to be convinced without perhaps carefully assessing what they were being convinced of, for the ideals of Epicurus are hardly of the sort which could be granted any serious validity in the theocentric world of the Middle Ages.[12] This is not to say that Chaucer might not have found something to admire in the sumptuous completeness of the Franklin's devotion, but it seems unlikely that he would have shared his narrator's enthusiasm for such unabashed materialism. It is only Chaucer the pilgrim who warmly embraces excellence of performance without questioning the virtue of the action itself.

This distinction is reinforced by the tone of the portrait. Every kind of verbal extravagance is lavished upon the man whose primary concern is the splendid display of unsurpassed wealth and taste. He is not merely an epicurean; he is the legitimate heir of the founder of the cult. The rhetorical superlatives heaped upon his gastronomic stores (A. 342–6) nicely complement the excessive vigilance of the Franklin's activities as host, and even the images playfully emphasize the absorption of the man in good food (A. 345, 358–9). Equally suggestive is the juxtaposition of details. The enumeration of the Franklin's high offices follows directly, without syntactical connection, upon the description of his 'table dormant'. Lumiansky has pointed out that an epicurean delight in pure pleasure is a rare trait in one whose 'important public offices' proclaim him a man 'of outstanding ability and industry'. He concludes that possibly 'good hard work is more important in Chaucer's Franklin than his love of food, drink and pleasure; if so, his lavish hospitality becomes in some respects play acting'.[18] Some such interpretation would help explain another curious juxtaposition – the companionship of the Franklin with the Sergeant of the Law. Such pairings in the General Prologue seem to reflect a kind of propriety, and the Sergeant is a worthy companion in terms of wealth and social prestige. But the worthiness of his portrait as a whole is unquestionably flawed by a recurrent element of false-seeming. It is not unlikely, then, that their association is meant to call attention to an element of incongruity in the Franklin's behavior, though hardly one of calculated deception as in the Lawyer's. In short, the evidence of the General Prologue may well be taken to support the image of an otherwise sober, capable man of practical affairs who is innocently infatuated with an aristocratic performance which he can imitate but not quite fully understand.

This estimate of the Franklin's character is immediately reinforced by the opening of the tale itself. The first thing the narrator tells us is that it is a Breton lay, a form which in his mind has an aristocratic pedigree :

> Thise olde *gentil* Britouns in hir dayes
> Of diverse aventures maden layes.   (F. 709–10)

He seems, further, to have 'deliberately emphasized the ancient air of his own Breton lay', as J. S. P. Tatlock long ago pointed out.[14] Not only do we have the pagan atmosphere of ancient deities and heathenish arts of magic, but also such conscious archaisms as 'Armorik' (729), 'Briteyne' (for England, 810), and the Latin forms of Arveragus and Aurelius. A study of the sources, however, indicates that, whereas the prologue and the descriptions of the geographical and topographical locale are elaborately designed to give the impression of a Breton tale and a Breton setting, the plot itself belongs to an Italian tradition and is perhaps directly indebted to Boccaccio.[15] The Breton veneer, then, seems to reflect a conscious procedure on the part of the poet.

A purpose behind this generic pretension is suggested by the literary status of the Breton lay at the time of the composition of the *Canterbury Tales*. Laura Hibbard Loomis, in an article on the Breton lays in English, has indicated that manuscript evidence implies that in the latter half of the fourteenth century 'the lays were not in vogue, that they were not being recopied by scribes, and were not, presumably, being discussed by contemporary literati'.[16] The literary genre, which is so evidently imposed upon the plot of the Franklin's Tale, may well have seemed as faded and outmoded to Chaucer's audience as the Arthurian romances of the Victorian poets to the public of Pound and Eliot. Mrs. Loomis speaks of the 'noble but old fashioned tastes of the whitebearded Franklin', but it may well be that Chaucer intended the choice of literary mode to represent a conscious attempt on the part of the Franklin to attract the attention and admiration of the aristocratic members of his audience with the most 'refined' sort of tale he could resurrect from his somewhat fossilized memory. He offers a tale which he considers in the best taste, but it is the taste of a previous generation. In emphasizing this generic choice, Chaucer may have been consciously adding to his portrait of a man slightly out of touch with the ways of the nobility, here making a conspicuous attempt to close the gap.

The imitation of noble ways is nowhere more apparent than in the Franklin's use of rhetoric. It is precisely the high manner of the telling that he admires in the performance of the young Squire and considers to be the true manifestation of his 'gentil-

lesse'. He praises the youth for his 'wit', predicts that he will soon
have no peer 'of eloquence', and wishes him continuance 'in
vertu', that is, in these rhetorical accomplishments.[17] Furthermore,
he asserts that the only way to 'lerne gentillesse aright' is 'to
comune with any gentil wight' (F. 693–4), to attend to and then
imitate the elegant discourse of courtly circles. The final compliment paid to the Squire by the Franklin is to do just that, to
pattern his style in the prologue after that of the Squire, which
he has evidently heard with delight and with profit.

One of the devices used repeatedly by the Squire is the formula
of 'affected modesty'.[18] The pose of the plain, blunt man ('Thyng
that I speke, it moot be bare and pleyn', 720) is appropriated
by the Franklin to serve a dual purpose. It will pacify the Host
and the other 'lewed' men who will take it seriously, but at the
same time it will appeal to the 'gentils' who recognize it as a
highly learned device. The Franklin, in fact, extravagantly calls
attention to his learning in the very act of disclaiming it. He
refers directly to 'Marcus Tullius Scithero', the great foster-
parent of medieval rhetoric, and indirectly to Persius, 'that most
rhetorical of Latin poets'.[19] And, in his witty play on three meanings of the word 'colours', he exhibits ostentatious proficiency in
the rhetorical color, or figure of speech, called *traductio*.[20] Indeed, there is very little true modesty in the Franklin's professions, though it may be true that, as he says, his 'spirit feeleth
noght of swich mateere' (727).

The flow of rhetoric by no means stops with the Franklin's
prologue. Benjamin S. Harrison claims to have discovered
'at least 70 rhetorical forms which correspond to the Latin
colors'.[21] Though many of these colors are common tricks of
speech which pass unnoticed in everyday conversation, the
medieval man of letters, intensively trained in rhetorical
forms, would have been conscious of using them, whether he had
sought after them, as the handbooks recommend, or not. Chaucer
was able to avoid drawing attention to them in the low comic
tales, where rhetorical colors were considered inappropriate. In
the aristocratic tales, the abundance of rhetoric seems to be a
part of the world of the poem, whether the theme be profoundly
philosophic like the Knight's or superficially 'gentil' like the
Squire's. The mannered style of the narration seems to be per-

fectly wedded to the mannered behavior of the characters, and both are natural projections of the rank and education of the narrator. Not so with the Franklin. He seems almost as uncomfortably conscious of the way in which he is telling his tale as he is of its meaning. Both consequently are forced upon our attention.

Many rhetorical passages obtrude because of their sheer bulk alone: the extensive *sententia* (F. 761–86), for example, which comes too late and too long to be merely a graceful way of opening the tale,[22] yet manages to interrupt just as the tale is getting under way; the formal descriptive pieces, of the garden (901–17), of the apparitions of the 'tregetour' (1139–51 and 1189–1208), of the 'colde, frosty seson of Decembre' (1245–55),[23] particularly notable for its elegant and irrelevant *circuito* in the figure of Janus, and for the anachronistic cries of 'Nowel' in this predominantly pagan setting; the detailed and highly technical recitation of astrological procedure (1273–93), which is prefaced by 'I ne kan no termes of astrologye' and is punctuated by grumblings against the very idea of such 'supersticious cursednesse'; and finally, most telling for sheer lengthiness, the string of twenty-two *exempla* in the forty-eight hour marathon complaint of Dorigen (1364–1456).

Transitions are often noticeably abrupt and, unlike those in the Knight's Tale, convey the impression of a narrator uneasy about the behavior of his noble characters and with the rhetorical requirements of his chosen genre.[24] One passage in particular calls for comment. It is the notorious example of *expolitio*[25] which follows the first interview between Dorigen and Aurelius:

> But sodeynly bigonne revel newe
> Til that the brighte sonne lost his hewe:
> For th'orisonte hath reft the sonne his lyght!
> This is as muche to seye as it was nyght!   (F. 1015–18)

Critics have chosen to interpret this matter-of-fact statement as Chaucer's satiric 'sly comment' on his own rhetoric. Manly[26] appropriately cites the inanity of the rhetorical handbooks on the matter of *periphrasis* or *circumlocutio*. Geoffroi de Vinsauf, for example, seems unable to distinguish between amplification for its own sake – mere bombast or dishonesty – and the use of such figures for their poetic extension of the 'plain sense' through implication and connotation.[27] But if there is an apparent naiveté or pedantic stupidity in these lines, then the fault must be that of the Franklin and his rhetorical pretensions. He either feels compelled to explain his figure in simple terms to those who are less informed than he; or he has launched himself on a bit of fancy, Italianate description and, not quite knowing where to go with it, decides to sink the whole matter.

However one chooses to reconstruct this little crisis in the Franklin's narrative, it has dramatic validity only if one accepts some such interpretation of the Franklin's character as I have been trying to suggest here; it would be quite impossible, for example, to attribute to him the amused detachment of the Nun's Priest. The way in which the Franklin feels called upon to tell his tale points to the same kind of person we found in the links and prologues – a man of considerable ability and virtue who is markedly over-reaching. His rhetorical practice indicates that he is a man for whom the art is not instinctive and easy. Nor does he seem to be sure of its essential value or purpose. The Franklin's success is considerable, but he is betrayed by the occasional clumsiness or excess, and by the intermittent grumblings of the practical man of good common sense and solid Christian virtues who feels that the whole business is perhaps a bit foolish and a bit undignified for one of his age and position.

The Franklin's greatest rhetorical blunder, for which Chaucer has taken all the blame and some faint praise, is the Complaint of Dorigen. Manly, elsewhere so sensitive to the satiric use of excessive rhetoric, felt that the tale, otherwise so 'finely told, is nearly spoiled by one hundred lines of rhetorical example'. 'What reader', he concludes, 'modern or medieval, would not have been more powerfully and sympathetically affected if Chaucer with the psychological insight displayed in *Troilus and Criseyde*, had caused his distressed and desperate heroine to express the real feelings appropriate to her character and situation?'[28]

It would indeed be difficult to contend that the Complaint is not a blemish upon a 'fine tale', if the tale were in fact as fine as the Franklin wished it to appear. Nor can the passage be written off as rhetorical parody, 'a *reductio ad absurdum* of the use of *exempla*' as Manly was later to propose.[29] As parody, this monstrous intrusion is more of a bore than an absurdity. Here, as in the similar excursions of the Wife of Bath's Prologue and Tale and in the debate of the cock and hen in the Nun's Priest's Tale, Chaucer has not only made his rhetorical parody subtly appropriate to the speaker, but has given it a saving comic grace in the immediate narrative context.

The character of Dorigen must occupy our attention before the dramatic right or wrong of her Complaint can be decided. Lumiansky argues that the device of the formal complaint, characteristic of the world of courtly love, as well as the 'noble choice of suicide rather than dishonour',[30] can be explained by the fact that Dorigen, the noble wife, enters the story somewhat incongruously as a courtly love heroine and retains something of that role throughout. James Sledd,[31] on the other hand, maintains that the Complaint is a 'deliberate bit of rhetorical extravagance, intended as an assurance that all shall yet go well' : as a heroine, Dorigen belongs to the realm of tragicomedy, where the outcome is potentially tragic, but is turned aside 'not to the ludicrous but to the pleasant'. The tone of the Complaint insures that the audience will remain sufficiently detached from the painful emotions of the character and avoids just such pathos as Manly once required. The tale, as Sledd sees it, is a 'tragicomedy with a moral – a serious but pleasant story of recognizably human people'.

But Sledd has the Franklin in better control of his rhetoric than I would allow. He interprets the obtrusive rhetoric, as well as the numerous intrusions into the tale of the Franklin *in propria persona*, as deliberate attempts on his part to allay the fears and disengage the emotions of his audience. If my interpretation of the character of the Franklin is correct, such rhetorical suavity is out of the question. Furthermore, the impression one gets from the Complaint is not that of a deliberate manipulation of the audience by the teller, but of a conspicuous lack of control on the part of the narrator as well as the actor.

My own understanding of the dramatic values of the Complaint has been aided immeasurably by Mrs. Dempster's picture of Chaucer at work on his copy of Jerome. Having looked hard

at the poet's use of his sources, she discovered with satisfaction
that he treated them 'with a degree of *negligence* and *rape,* not to
say boredom, of which we find very few other instances in his
works'.[32] Though we may differ with her conclusions, Mrs.
Dempster's study is of great value in determining the way in
which the Complaint was assembled and the degree of seriousness involved in the process. The choice of *exempla* begins with
appropriate selection and careful elaboration, but concludes in
a crescendo of hasty inconclusiveness and irrelevance. The first
seven *exempla* (F. 1368–1418) are treated in some detail and
are all virgins and wives who sacrificed life to maintain chastity.
They seem to have been drawn from memory or from Jerome
directly with deliberate concern for aptness to the particular situation. But after what professes to be a conclusion at lines 1419–25,
the *exempla* begin again, coming now with increasing rapidity
until with the concubine of Alcibiades (F. 1439–41), appropriateness is abandoned. The rest of the Complaint proceeds with ever
increasing brevity and decreasing relevance, until in the final
couplet no less than three heroines of antiquity are forced to find
accommodation. Of the magnificent impertinence of these
histories to Dorigen's problem, Mrs. Dempster remarks:
'Valeria's glory had consisted in refusing to remarry, Rhodo-
gune's, in killing her nurse, and Bilia's, in never remarking on the
smell of her husband's breath!' The study of sources has shown
that after composing what would have passed as a respectable
complaint, Chaucer deliberately returned to Jerome several
times. Adding one *exemplum* after another, he finally abandoned
all pretense to cogency and threw them all in, with a disregard
for relevance which must have amused him greatly. If this was
'negligence and rape', it was clearly undertaken with the purpose
of destroying any hope of pathos or serious concern on Dorigen's
behalf.

Even without reference to the sources, one can sense the humor
of the monologue. The air of dogged intensity in the opening line
(1367) is followed by the simple righteousness and enthusiasm
for authority of the first *exempla* (esp. 1377–8 and 1402–3).
Dorigen has to wrestle with the temptation to unpack the whole
bag of more than a thousand stories (1412–13); she allows herself one more, then determines to conclude (1422 ff.); but finds

herself betrayed by a rhyme into just one more, and the bag rips open. She rushes through the second half of the Complaint desperately attempting to pile up names until there is scarcely enough breath to get through the final couplet :

> The same thyng I seye of Bilyea,
> Of Rodogone, and eek Valeria. (F. 1455–6)

One is quite convinced that Dorigen can go on in this way for two days without intermission, and it is equally evident that she has no intention of committing suicide. She is the sort of woman who loves to indulge her emotions and knows how to make the most of a melodramatic situation. What the Franklin had intended to be a noble parade of dignified authorities collapses into the garrulousness of an attractive, but hysterical, rather silly woman. Where Sledd has chosen to find a tragicomic situation produced by the Franklin, I prefer to see the Franklin's stiff tragedy developed simultaneously with Chaucer's high comedy.

Of course, such a characterization of Dorigen would be untenable, were it not that from the beginning, in spite of the best intentions of the Franklin, there is something awkward about her 'nobility'. The opening description of the courtship and the marriage 'trouthe' is too formalized – in the evocation of courtly love as well as in the rhetoric – to throw light on the characters. The casual metamorphosis of a courtly love knight and mistress into man and wife is, however, sufficient to put us on our guard. But once Arveragus sets off to war and Dorigen is left alone, we have a good opportunity to estimate this 'faireste' lady of such 'heigh kynrede'. She performs not with the stately tragic grace the Franklin had probably hoped to dramatize, but with a curious lack of propriety, with a somewhat mechanical excessiveness by which Chaucer has made of her an engaging heroine in a high comic mode. Again the Franklin's uncertainty about the manners of gentility and in the use of rhetoric has been put to work by the poet for his own complex artistic purposes :

> For his absence wepeth she and siketh,
> As doon thise noble wyves whan hem liketh.
> She moorneth, waketh, wayleth, fasteth, pleyneth . . .
>   (F. 817–19)

One cannot help but catch an unconscious suggestion on the part
of the practical, sensible Franklin that this sort of behavior (whose
worth he accepts only on faith) is the prerogative of an idle
class, a useless but ornamental activity to be indulged at will by
those who have nothing better to do. The sudden and rather
stiff list of verbs in line 819 (rhetorically an *articulus*) acknowledges, however, that this kind of thing certainly does fill up one's
time.

The monumental 'hevynesse' of Dorigen is industriously opposed by the host of friends who try to bring her back to society
and good sense. But the task seems as difficult as removing the
rocks from the Brittany coast. The juxtaposition of sensible social
behaviour and Dorigen's conspicious display of grief makes her
actions seem something less than truly dignified, somewhat too
much in the proper manner, inappropriately stylized, and
rather silly. The woodenness of her determination to play unflinchingly the role of a devoted noble wife convinces us of her
simplicity, but it is not until we observe her treatment of the
squire Aurelius that we fully appreciate the scope of her
irrational, almost giddy femininity. At first there is dazed terror
in her voice when she replies to his confession. She becomes conscious of his existence for the first time, just as the terrifying black
rocks only took form for her when she saw them as a threat to her
stubborn search for happiness.

> She gan to looke upon Aurelius :
> 'Is this youre wyl', quod she, 'and sey ye thus?
> Nevere erst', quod she, 'ne wiste I what ye mente.'
>
> (F. 979–81)

The shock and incredulity with which she begins, modulates to
the fierce tenacity which she has previously demonstrated. She
seems about to wish Aurelius to hell with the rocks, when she
suddenly recollects herself in the garden world of play. Rashly
she makes her promise, obsessed with all she sees that prevents
her happiness. The 'trouthe' she plights, with the identical
legalistic phrase she offered to Arveragus (F. 759), combines a
slightly cruel revenge on the importunate Aurelius with her
irrational *idée fixe*, those 'grisly rokkes blake'. The promise is

not only self-contradictory; it is also somewhat haughty and
malicious – professing to be motivated by pity ('Syn I you se so
pitously complayne'), but pitiless in its intentional absurdity.
Dorigen concludes with the moral indignation of a franklin:

> What deyntee sholde a man han in his lyf
> For to go love another mannes wyf,
> That hath hir body whan so that hym liketh?

> (F. 1003–5)

But our sympathy has turned to the badly treated squire who
is left to face a 'sodeyn deth horrible', while Dorigen rejoins the
mirth and company of her friends. The folly of her woe has
driven him to raving, and we are fully prepared to enjoy the
spectacle of this haughty woman writhing in turn through her
exempla-ridden complaint. The values and sentiments which the
Franklin had hoped to dramatize cannot be contained in his
peculiarly ignoble *personae*. By such frequent reversals in our
sympathy (from Dorigen to her well-meaning friends to the
squire), we have been spared the Franklin's heavy tragic involvement and are preserved in a splendid comic detachment.

The invitation to detachment, dramatically extended in the
figure of Dorigen, is equally apparent in the other major
characters. Aurelius is a bundle of clichés, conventional notions
and emotions, cold and distant echoes of the Knight's Tale and
Troilus.[33] He loves, moans, suffers, pines, and wastes away in
tactful silence, according to the rules, and never insults his lady
by doing any of these things for a shorter period than two years.

Our acquaintance with Arveragus is brief but impressively
formal and stiff. His actions are noticeably only those of a proper
knight, a conventional counterpart for the courtly heroine and
wife: 'Servant in love, and lord in mariage' (F. 793). From the
beginning his every action betrays a meticulous concern for two
ideals which soon find themselves awkwardly in conflict:
'gentillesse' (754) in his personal, and 'degree' (752) in his
social relationships. It is the second of these, his lofty consciousness of his position and rank in society, which determines him to
abandon his wife and give equal time to his knightly duties. 'A

yer and moore' of 'blisful lyf' is judiciously balanced with 'a yer
or tweyne' (809) of service at arms in England, a duty which
he seems to embrace with equal pleasure, with 'al his lust' (812).
Obviously, this nice devotion to 'degree' is necessary to the plot;
Arveragus must be got out of the way. But the Franklin has
handled it so that the trip to England appears a bit too suddenly dutiful, too business-like in its attention to the prescribed
demands upon knighthood. Perhaps it is again the Franklin's
bewilderment over the strange ways of the nobility which leads
him to justify Arveragus' behavior with reference to a written
source: 'the book seith thus' (813). The narrator seems to feel
that the demands of knighthood would be as pressing as those
of commerce and as strictly regulated as those of the shire. In
fact, one is hardly surprised to find that, when next Dorigen is
in need of her lord and master, 'out of towne was goon Arveragus'
(1351), no doubt busy once again about the business of being a
knight.

The 'gentillesse' of Arveragus is equally automatic and consciously *comme il faut*. When Dorigen rehearses her shattering
tale, the husband not only replies without hesitation: 'Is ther
oght elles, Dorigen, but this?' (1469), but he does so with a
somewhat astounding display of 'glad chiere, in freendly wyse'
(1467). One begins to suspect that, like Shaw's Octavius, he
regards 'the world as a moral gymnasium built expressly to
strengthen [his] character in'.[34] His decision is immediate, unfaltering, and mechanically 'gentil'. Not until he has pronounced his *sententia* upon 'trouthe', does he exhibit the
humanity of bitter tears, shattering the noble image with a command of secrecy (upon threat of death) and with his desire to
keep up appearances. His feelings are efficiently compartmental-
ized; his stiffly principled nobility and his real but less exalted
emotions never quite meet.[35] But the bravado of his 'gentillesse'
is more than its own reward; it releases a cascade of imitation
and promotes the *embarras de gentillesse* in which the tale
tumbles to a conclusion.

Thus, Dorigen, Aurelius, and Arveragus are all elegant but
artificial puppets pieced together from bits of faded romances,
from clichés of character and conventions of courtly behavior.
Behind them lurks a reality which is, however, not their own but

that of their narrator. It reveals a sensibility perhaps less refined and idly extravagant in emotion and ideas, but more practical, prejudiced in favor of common morality and the familiar virtues of Holy Church, and above all, more fundamentally human. It is this reality, the everpresent personality of the Franklin, which gives the lie to the posturing and the self-conscious nobility of his characters, who in turn owe their very existence to his own self-consciousness before the 'gentil' pilgrims of Chaucer's complexly creative *dramatis personae* in the *Canterbury Tales*.

I have examined the Franklin's narrative manner in considerable detail because I believe it not only important for its own sake but essential to an estimation of what the poem is really about. If the Franklin's Tale is in fact the work of two creators, of Chaucer and Chaucer's Franklin, then the thematic possibilities of the narrative are obviously multiplied. It was clear that in the handling of the rhetoric and character, the intentions of the teller were not those of the poet. The purposes of the two creators diverge, though they are often expressed in a single phrase or gesture.

The Franklin's intentions are not difficult to isolate. They are twofold and part of a drama of ideas in the sequence of tales initiated by the Wife of Bath. The Franklin begins his tale with an explicit exposition of his concept of the ideal marriage. In reply to the Wife's advocacy of female sovereignty and to the Clerk's demonstration of wifely submission to her wedded lord, the Franklin proposes a compromise of mutual obedience and equal mastery. Neither love nor liberty is compromised; each partner remains unconstrained in spite of the bonds of marriage. Furthermore, the initial success of the experiment, the 'blisse' and 'solas' (802) of Arveragus and Dorigen, is offered as an antidote to the grim cynicism of the Merchant's depiction of 'wepyng and waylyng, care and oother sorwe' (E. 1213) to be found in wedded life.

But as the story unfolds, a second, less explicit purpose reveals itself – a working definition of the noble ideal of 'gentillesse'. Here again, the Franklin takes his cue from the Wife of Bath, who devoted much of her tale to a digression on that 'verray

gentillesse' which comes not of birth but of God's grace alone
(D. 1162 ff.). To prolong the discussion of this theme, to which
the Franklin, as we have seen, is extraordinarily responsive, he
drags his characters through all the absurdities of his plot, from
the rash promise to the magical illusions, in order to establish a
dilemma which can only be resolved by the gracious operation of
'gentillesse', specifically in terms of its two most significant com-
ponents, 'trouthe' and 'fredom'. The drama of the tale is a
result of the two conflicting 'trouthes' of Dorigen, the vow of
fidelity to Arveragus and the promise to Aurelius. The necessity
of keeping one's plighted word, no matter what the circumstances, is one of the prime requisites of knighthood :

> Trouthe is the hyeste thyng that man may kepe.
>
> (F. 1479)

The acceptance of the requirements of 'trouthe' on the part of
Arveragus enables him to exercise the equally fundamental virtue
of 'fredom'. He generously sacrifices what is most precious to
him, his wife's purity, that she may be true to her word. Aurelius
and the 'Orliens' clerk follow suit in making what obviously seem
to the Franklin to be equally generous sacrifices, to demonstrate
that 'gentillesse' and 'fredom' are not the exclusive prerogatives
of knighthood. The structural weight given to the exposition of
these virtues is increased by the conclusion of the tale in a
demande d'amour :

> Which was the mooste fre, as thynketh yow?   (F. 1622)

The concern with an ideal marriage has been replaced by a
broader but no less idealistic theme.

That 'gentillesse', 'trouthe', and 'fredom' were in reality
serious, valid ideals for Chaucer's audience and for the poet himself is fully demonstrated by their prominence in the portrait of
the Knight in the General Prologue : 'Trouthe and honour, fredom and curteisie' (A. 46). But the Wife of Bath's Tale with its
ungainly digression and ill-mannered 'gentil' squire indicates
equally well that these terms could be comically misdirected by
the poet to inappropriate hands. Just as the Franklin's noble

actors are much nearer the real thing than the grotesque imitation of the Wife, so, too, his handling of these abstractions is more artful and profound. But nevertheless, the flaws in the Franklin's narrative are to be reckoned with in a final estimation of the poem's substance. They force us to consider that the ideals which the tale treats so prominently are those of the Franklin and not necessarily at this moment the poet's primary concern. What is true in the case of the quixotic ideal of a marriage conceived in courtly love[36] must also hold for the loftier, more encompassing ideal of 'gentillesse', though it is at other times demonstrably Chaucerian.

Isolation of the Franklin's simple notion of what his tale is about makes it immediately clear that his two themes are not quite adequate to cover all the material in his narration. The 'prayers' of Dorigen and Aurelius, as they are elaborated by the Franklin, are not structurally necessary to the plot. The removal of the rocks is effected by magical illusion with no suggestion of the assistance of a deity. The two prayers, identical in petition but conflicting in motive, and the irony of their fulfillment seem to belong to another narrative structure – one, for example, like that of the Knight's Tale, which is similar to this in pattern, but whose conclusion clearly focuses upon the intervention of the gods and the philosophical issues raised by the precarious relationship between humanity and divinity. The Franklin's Tale, as far as its themes of marriage and 'gentillesse' are concerned, could well have dispensed with such metaphysical implication.[37]

Dorigen's prayer, or first 'complaint' as it might better be called, grows out of her excessive grief and defines the intensity of her *idée fixe*, the black rocks. Her hysteria leads her to absurdities which are clearly beyond the scope of the tale as the Franklin envisions it. She challenges the very order of the Universe, the reasonableness of Creation; she turns the amorous problem into a metaphysical issue. She invokes an unmistakably Christian God and not the pagan pantheon of the rest of the poem :

> Eterne God, that thurgh thy purveiaunce
> Ledest the world by certain governaunce, . . .

> (F. 865–6)

All things are reputed to have a purpose, but she can find nothing in the rocks except 'a foul confusion of werk' (F. 869–70).
They are a source of grief to all the orders of Creation, destroying its fairest creature, man. She acknowledges that there is another way of looking at things :

> I woot wel clerkes wol seyn as hem leste,
> By argumentz, that al is for the beste,
> Though I ne kan the causes nat yknowe.
>
> (F. 885–7)

But in her wild protest she throws disputation of clerks to the
winds and demands that the rocks be sunk into hell for her husband's sake. Her last words, 'thise rokkes sleen myn herte for the
feere' (893), indicate, however, that her grief is basically self-
centered and wilful.

This complaint, then, becomes more than just a wife's lament.
It is a piece of metaphysical foolishness in the course of which
the theological reply to such protests is clearly stated. The black
rocks loom for Dorigen as symbols of all that in the human
condition is adverse to human happiness. Such adversities, as the
Church obviously has told her, can be overcome not by violent
rebellion, but by faith in divine purveyance and a patient acceptance of the world as we find it. Our perception is humanly
limited; only God can know final purpose.

For Aurelius, too, the rocks come to represent the sole obstacle
to personal happiness, but his prayer is more devious. He avoids
calling upon the chaste goddess of the moon directly to aid his
lustful cause. Going over her head, he calls upon Apollo to lead
her astray in an incestuous, cosmic intrigue which will draw the
earth's waters above the rocks. The powers invoked in these two
prayers are thus appropriate to both the nature of the cause and
the justice of the complaint: Dorigen's love is sanctified and
holy; Aurelius', adulterous and pagan. Dorigen inveighs against
divine Providence; Aurelius, his personal amorous fate. But in
each case the intense distaste for the black rocks is loosed by a
dissatisfaction with things as they are and an inability to suffer
patiently the trials of adversity.

An unconscious awareness of the metaphysical implications of these protests is evident in the fact that their conversation is punctuated with oaths invoking God in His office of Creator: 'by God that this world made' (967), 'by thilke God that yaf me soule and lyf' (983), 'by that Lord . . . . that maked me' (1000). We are made forcibly aware that the universal order is being inadvertently questioned and tested by this excitable wife and her pathetically amorous squire. It is now evident why we must remain detached from them as characters and why they are allowed to seem so stiffly comic and absurd. They have, in fact, muddled themselves into an ultimate foolishness of metaphysical dimension, which will be repented at leisure in the complex of events resulting from their prayers. They will be made to see the folly of their ways precisely by having the prayers granted; the dilemmas of grief and obligation which follow the prayers will far exceed those which preceded them.

Yet, though the implications of the story are to be taken seriously, never are the actions or characters invested with a tragic seriousness. They are mannered in a style of high comedy obliquely imposed on them by their overanxious narrator. The begrudging involvement of the Franklin with terms of astrology, Dorigen's run-away rhetoric in the grand Complaint, and the 'fredom' contest which places a wife's virtue on an equal footing with a thousand pounds – all contribute to the high comic tone of a tale which is set in motion by the self-indulgent folly of Dorigen and Aurelius, and reinforced by the book-governed chivalry of Arveragus. In his ingenious art, Chaucer has taken advantage of the limitations of his story-teller to add another dimension to his tale. The Franklin remains a perfectly valid and consistent dramatic creation, and his tale is appropriate to him in both theme and method, but Chaucer has made the poem do more than he permitted the Franklin to see.

The Franklin's myopia is nowhere more apparent than at the opening of the narrative where he indulges in an extended discourse on patience, the very virtue which will be the submerged theme of his tale. His ears still ringing with the debate of the Wife of Bath and the Clerk, the Franklin is only concerned with the narrow problem of patience in love, yet his words are equally appropriate to the larger virtue which his Dorigen so flagrantly neglects:

> Pacience is an heigh vertu, certeyn,
> For it venquysseth, as thise clerkes seyn,
> Thynges that rigour sholde nevere atteyne.
> For every word men may nat chide or pleyne.
> Lerneth to suffre, or elles, so moot I goon,
> Ye shul it lerne, wher so ye wole or noon.   (F. 773–8)

And so indeed Dorigen learns to suffer against her will, because she had unconsciously placed that will, her petty, immediate desires, against the will of God.

There is no surprise in finding this theme of patience in adversity in a poem of Chaucer's. The *locus classicus* is, of course, Boethius's *Consolation*, which Chaucer first translated, then allowed to filter into his serious works of philosophic romance. The theme is particularly crucial to the *Troilus*, and emerges again and again in the *Canterbury Tales*. Witness most notably the complaint of Arcite in the Knight's Tale:

> Allas, why pleynen folk so in commune
> On purveiaunce of God, or of Fortune,
> That yeveth hem ful ofte in many a gyse
> Wel bettre than they kan hemself devyse? (A. 1251–4)

One couplet especially is equally pertinent to the situation of the Franklin's Tale:

> We seken faste after felicitee,
> But we goon wrong ful often, trewely.   (A. 1266–7)

But it is the Clerk's Tale, in dramatic proximity to the Franklin's, which presents the most interesting parallel. Not only is the theme identical, but it, too, arises as an extension of the more limited concern of the tale itself. As in the case of Dorigen, Griselda's example is not to be confined to married life, but applied to human existence in general:

> For, sith a womman was so pacient
> Unto a mortal man, wel moore us oghte
> Receyven al in gree that God us sent; . . .

> And for oure beste is al his governaunce.
> Lat us thanne lyve in vertuous suffraunce.
>
> (E. 1149–51; 1161–2)

If I am correct in my estimation of the Franklin's character and of the submerged theme of his tale, the connection between the two will be immediately apparent. The Franklin's excessive concern for 'gentillesse', for rank and position, is merely another kind of dissatisfaction with things as they are. Like Dorigen, he places personal well-being above a humble respect for the established order. But he is clearly not a vicious man, and accordingly the tone of the tale and the exposition of his limitations are good-humored and kind. The underlying theme of the tale, which recoils upon the teller, is not a deadly sin, as in the Merchant's and Pardoner's, but imperfect virtue. A stern moral purpose, which is never totally absent from the *Canterbury Tales*, forces us to admit that there is something foolish and misdirected in the actions of the Franklin and his heroine, but the comic method gracefully acknowledges that 'Pacience is an *heigh* vertu, certeyn'.

S o u r c e : *Neophilologus*, LI (1967); this reprint incorporates the author's revisions of the original text.

NOTES

1. *The Poetry of Chaucer* (Cambridge, 1906) p. 273.
2. *Chaucer* (London, 1952) p. 274.
3. *University of Toronto Quarterly*, XX (1951) 344–56, reproduced in his *Of Sondry Folk* (Austin, 1955) pp. 180–93.
4. 'Autobiographical Aspects of Chaucer's Franklin', *Speculum*, XXVIII (1953) 791–800.
5. Blenner-Hassett, p. 791.
6. 'The Social Status of Chaucer's Franklin', *P.L.M.A.*, XLI (1926) 262–79.
7. George L. Kittredge, 'Chaucer's Discussion of Marriage', *Modern Philology*, IX (1912) 458; above, p. 83.
8. *N.E.D.*, 'gentry', 2. In Chaucerian usage, the term seems to be synonymous with 'gentillesse' and refers to personal qualities,

polished manners, courtesy, and generosity, not to a social stratum. See esp. the Wife of Bath's Tale, III, 1152-7, where the two are clearly distinguished.

9. See *M.E.D.*, 'gentillesse', 1 (a).

10. *Geoffrey Chaucer* (London, 1956) p. 14. A similar interpretation was suggested by Lumiansky, p. 347, who would read line 695 : 'Straw for *youre* gentillesse'.

11. *Chapters on Chaucer* (Baltimore, 1951) p. 193.

12. Compare Gower, *Mianour de l'omme*, ed. Macaulay, ll. 9529 ff., quoted by D. W. Robertson Jr., *A Preface to Chaucer* (Princeton, 1962) p. 276, as a good summary of the fourteenth-century attitude toward Epicurus.

13. Lumiansky, p. 346.

14. *The Scene of the Franklin's Tale Visited*, Chaucer Society, Second Series, No. 51 (London, 1914) pp. 17-36.

15. See W. F. Bryan and Germaine Dempster, *Sources and Analogues to Chaucer's Canterbury Tales* (Chicago, 1941) pp. 377-97. Mrs. Dempster and J. S. P. Tatlock offer as a 'highly probable' source the story of Menedon in Boccaccio's *Filocolo*.

16. 'Chaucer and the Breton Lays of the Auchinleck MS', *Studies in Philology*, XXXVIII (1941) 14-33; see esp. pp. 16-17.

17. On this translation, see Robinson's note on l. 689. The value of the Squire's rhetorical accomplishments has recently been subjected to considerable scholarly analysis. See Gardner Stilwell, 'Chaucer in Tartary', *Review of English Studies*, XXIV (1948) 177-88; D. A. Pearsall, 'The Squire as Story-Teller', *University of Toronto Quarterly*, XXXIV (1964) 82-92; and Robert S. Haller, 'Chaucer's Squire's Tale and the Uses of Rhetoric', *Modern Philology*, LXII (1964-5) 285-95. All of these critics take the Squire's performance as dramatically appropriate to the youthful aristocrat whose command of rhetoric is superficial and ostentatiously exhibited as a requisite of his social status. Haller (p. 294) concludes his essay with an estimate of the Franklin which is similar to mine : 'The Squire is "gentil" by blood and presumably may outgrow his ideas of the meaning of his degree; but in the meantime he has fed the pretensions of a man whose only qualification for gentillesse is self-indulgence.'

18. See Eleanor Hammond, *English Verse between Chaucer and Surrey* (Durham, NC., 1927) p. 392, and Ernst Robert Curtius, *European Literature and the Latin Middle Ages*, trans. Willard R. Trask (Pantheon Books, 1953) p. 83. Among the modern critics taken in by this pose must be included the revered name of Kit-

tredge, *Chaucer and his Poetry*, p. 210 : 'He is no cloistered
rhetorician . . . Such a man lies under no suspicion of transcendental
theorism nor vague heroics'.

19. J. M. Manly, *Chaucer and the Rhetoricians*, Warton Lecture
on English Poetry XVII (Oxford, 1926) p. 5. The source of the
allusion is the Prologue to the *Satires*, ll. 2–3 :

> Neque in bicipiti somniasse Parnasso
> Memini, ut repente sic poeta prodirem

That this allusion would have been apparent to some of Chaucer's
audience is suggested by the gloss in the MSS. El, Ad³, Hg-Ht, Ch,
En³, Ps, Manly and Rickert, *The Text of the Canterbury Tales*
(Chicago, 1940) III, p. 512, all fifteenth-century manuscripts, some
of them probably quite early in the century.

20.   Defined in the *Ad Herennium* IV, xiv : 'cum idem verbum
ponitur modo in hac, modo in altera re'. See also E. Faral, *Les Arts
Poétiques du XIIe et du XIIIe Siècle* (Paris, 1924) pp. 178, 332,
351, and p. 169 (paranomasia).

21. 'Rhetorical Inconsistency of Chaucer's Franklin', *Studies in
Philology, XXXII* (1935) 55–61 ; see p. 56.

22. Such a procedure was recommended by the handbooks. See,
for example, Geoffroi de Vinsauf, *Poetra Nova*, 11, 180 ff. (Faral,
pp. 202–3), or Matthieu de Vendome, *Ars Versificatoria*, I, 16
(Faral, p. 113).

23.   See Harrison's analysis, pp. 57–8.

24.   See esp. ll. 814–15 ; 1085–6 ; 1554–6.

25.   Defined in the *Ad Herennium* IV, xlii : 'cum in eodem loco
manemus et aliud atque aliud dicere videmur'.

26.   *Chaucer and the Rhetoricians*, p. 13.

27.   The statement that the opening lines of the *Aeneid* mean
nothing more than 'I will describe Aeneas', or that the invocation
by Boethius beginning : 'O qui perpetua mundum ratione gubernas'
is in fact an assertion 'quod nihil aliud est quam, "O Deus",'
actually denies the poetic value of rhetorical colors. The passage
in the Franklin's Tale, like the more evident appeal to rhetorical
authority in the Nun's Priest's Tale (B. 3347–54), reflects the
literalmindedness of the handbooks. The speaker implies that to say
'th'orisonte hath reft the sonne his lyght', 'nihil aliud est quam,
"nox erat".' Eleanor Hammond, *Modern Language Notes*, XXVII
(1912) 91–2, has pointed out that just such a deflationary phrase
actually occurs in a prose passage of Fulgentius which follows
eleven lines of flowery verse describing the coming of night.

28. Manly, p. 20.

29. *The Text of the Canterbury Tales* (Chicago, 1940) vol. II, p. 315.

30. Lumiansky, p. 354.

31. 'Dorigen's Complaint', *Modern Philology*, XLV (1947) 36–45; esp. pp. 42–4.

32. 'Chaucer at Work on the Complaint in the Franklin's Tale', *Modern Language Notes*, LII (1937) 22. Roberts A. Pratt, 'St. Jerome in Jankyn's Book of Wikked Wyves', *Criticism*, V (1963) 316–22, suggests that the Franklin intends Dorigen as a foil for the Wife of Bath and that the additional virtuous *exempla* in her complaint are a critique of the Wife's conduct.

33. J. L. Lowes, 'The Franklin Tale, the *Teeside*, and the *Filocolo*', *Modern Philology*, XV (1918) 689–782, has demonstrated that his portrait is composed of echoes of Boccaccio's *Teseide* and Chaucer's early translations of Boccaccio in the Knight's Tale, and even of Chaucer's own Squire in the General Prologue.

34. *Man and Superman* (Baltimore, Penguin Books, 1952) pp. 68–9.

35. For a similar evaluation of Arveragus, see D. W. Robertson Jr., *A Preface to Chaucer* (Princeton, 1962) pp. 470–2.

36. Gervase Mathew, 'Marriage and Amour Courtois in Late Fourteenth-Century England', *Essays presented to Charles Williams* (Oxford, 1947) pp. 128–35, considers the Franklin's view to be the common English position of the time; but see also Donald R. Howard, 'The Conclusion of the Marriage Group : Chaucer and the Human Condition', *Modern Philology* LVII (1959–60) 223–32.

37. On the philosophical implications of the Tale, see Edwin B. Benjamin, 'The Concept of Order in the Franklin's Tale', *Philological Quarterly*, XXXVIII (1959) 119–24, and Gerhard Joseph, The Franklin's Tale : Chaucer's Theodicy', *Chaucer Review*, I (1966) 20–32.

Ian Bishop

THE NARRATIVE ART OF THE PARDONER'S TALE (1967)

The Pardoner's Tale has often been praised for its dramatic irony, its concentration and the sense of awe that it engenders; it has more than once been described as one of the best short stories in English. The purpose of the present article is to re-examine some of the ways in which Chaucer achieves this result.[1] I do not propose to do this by comparing the tale with its analogues – that has already been done by Mrs. Germaine Dempster among others.[2] I shall rather compare some aspects of Chaucer's narrative technique in this tale with techniques that he employs in some of the most successful of his other short stories. But that is not my principal intent. My main purpose is to suggest that the concentration and the uncanny power of this tale are the result of three things in particular: a threefold economy, a double perspective and a unifying irony.

It is generally agreed that much of the tale's fascination is due to the figure of the 'old man and a povre' who directs the three rioters to the treasure. Yet there has been considerable disagreement about the identity and the significance of this character. In a recent article in *Medium Ævum*,[3] however, John M. Steadman has offered an explanation of his function which is based more firmly upon Chaucer's text than are most of the other interpretations. According to Steadman the old man is not a sinister or a supernatural figure: he is neither the Wandering Jew nor Death in disguise. Moreover, although one of his functions is to act as a *memento mori*, he is not a personification of Elde, one of the traditional messengers of Death. On the other hand, Professor Steadman will not follow W. J. B. Owen to the position of extreme naturalism and argue that he 'is an old man and nothing more'.[4] Whereas Owen maintains that the old man invents the story about Death being under the tree as a convenient means of getting rid of the drunkards who offer him violence,

Steadman argues that, like the hermit in some of the tale's analogues, the old man really has seen the treasure and, in his wisdom, has passed it by because he 'knows the causal relations between cupidity and death'.[5] Steadman regards the old man as a generalized 'notion of aged humanity' and aptly remarks that Chaucer's 'attempt to delineate the general through the particular brings him close to the frontiers of allegory, but he does not actually cross'.[6] The way in which this generalized figure hovers near the frontiers of naturalism and of other modes of presentation is one of the factors that produce the double perspective which I shall discuss later.

The present article is not concerned with the tale's prologue and epilogue or with the relationship between the tale and its teller; it is concerned almost exclusively with the story of 'thise riotoures thre' as it is narrated between C. 661 and 894. Nevertheless, before I proceed to an analysis of the tale proper, it is necessary to say something about the discourse on the sins of the tavern which separates the false start of the story at l. 463 from its true beginning at l. 661. What I have to say about this digression is so obvious that it would be hardly worth mentioning, were it not for the fact that it seems to have escaped the notice of several scholars who have written about this tale and who have offered some extravagant and cumbersome explanations of the presence of this passage.[7]

The digression is, of course, entirely relevant to the *sentence* of the *exemplum* which it interrupts.[8] Although Avarice is the radical sin that is illustrated in the tale, the three sins that are denounced in the digression – drunkenness, swearing and gambling – all contribute to the bringing about of the tale's catastrophe. If the rioters had not been drunk, they would not have set out upon their quest to 'sleen this false traytour Deeth' in the first place. If they had not been so profligate with their oaths, they might have taken more seriously their covenant of brotherhood and might have paid more attention to the solemn, admonitory imprecations of the old man. 'Hasardrye' is obviously related to Avarice, but it is perhaps worth remarking that the habitual desire of each of the revellers to play for the highest possible stakes causes him to plot against one or both of his 'brothers' and so is directly responsible for inducing the internecine catastrophe.

Once the tale proper has begun there is no further interruption : the action moves forward with a relentless logic to what, when it is reached, appears to be the inevitable conclusion – given the rioters' characters and the circumstances in which they find themselves. This rapid, irresistible progression is reinforced by Chaucer's economy in narrative technique. Not only is there an absence of digression, but an economy in three things principally : in characterization, in description and in narrative itself. I shall consider each of these three in turn.

One of Chaucer's happiest methods of adapting his sources was to pay particular attention to distinctive details of characterization. This can be seen even in such a brief narrative as the Prioress's Tale, where the pathos is considerably enhanced by the way in which the 'litel clergeon' is individualized, mainly through his conversation with his more mundane schoolfellow. In the Pardoner's Tale, however, individualization of character is kept to a minimum. The only character to be described in detail is the old man and, as we have already seen, he is a generalized figure, compounded of 'commonplaces' that were traditionally associated with old age. He is sharply contrasted with the 'riotoures thre', but they are themselves hardly individualized at all : any one of them could have played the part of any other. It might be argued that this is simply because they are presented as a trio of 'sworn brothers', who speak and act in concert – 'we thre been al ones' (l. 696) – until they come upon the gold. It might be pointed out in support of this argument that Aleyn and John, the co-operative pair of clerks in the Reeve's Tale, are far less easy to distinguish than are Nicholas and Absalom, the pair of rivals in the Miller's Tale, whose characters are so carefully contrasted.

The clerks in the Reeve's Tale, however, are distinguished at least by name; whereas in the Pardoner's Tale all the characters, whose voices we hear so clearly, remain anonymous. It is true that this is not the only tale in which the characters are anonymous : there is the Prioress's Tale, for example; but, as we have seen, the 'litel clergeon' in that tale is endowed with a distinct personality of his own. What is so striking about the Pardoner's Tale is the combination of anonymity and impersonality. There is other evidence which suggests that this is deliberate on

Chaucer's part. It is uncertain how much importance should be attached to the fact that names are given to the rioters' counterparts in some of the analogues. But it is surely undeniable that it would have been simpler and more convenient for Chaucer if he had referred to the various members of his trio by using personal names, instead of resorting to the slightly clumsy and obtrusively impersonal means of differentiation that we find in the tale: 'the proudeste of the three', 'the worste', 'the yongeste', 'the firste shrewe', 'that oon', 'that oother' . . . What seems to me to clinch the matter is the answer that the servant gives when one of the rioters bids him:

> 'Go bet . . . and axe redily
> What cors is this that passeth heer forby;
> *And looke that thou reporte his name weel.*'
> (C. 667–9. Italics mine.)

But we no more learn the dead man's name than we learn the name of the servant himself – or, indeed, the names of the rioters, the taverner, the old man or the apothecary. The servant informs his master merely: 'He was, pardee, an old felawe of youres.' Three lines later, however, the intention behind all this contrived anonymity becomes clearer. The final line of the master's command has alerted us: we expect to hear a proper name; but the fulfilment of our expectations is delayed and transferred. Instead of hearing the name of the stricken man, we hear the name of his assailant: 'Ther cam a privee theef, men clepeth Deeth. . . .' This is the only proper name we hear – apart from the name of God – until we reach the final episode.[9]

It is perhaps not too fanciful to argue that Death is the only 'character' in the tale who is completely individualized and presented as a complex personality. We are shown several facets of his character: his capriciousness; the arbitrary way in which he strikes or refuses to strike; his stealth and elusiveness; the subtlety and irony of his way of working. We also encounter some of his 'espye[s]' and those who are truly 'of his assent': *not* – as one of the rioters and some modern critics allege – the old man; but plague and heart-attack, and – more pertinently – Drunkenness, Swearing, Gambling and, above all, Avarice.

This 'character study' is communicated to the reader through the dialogue and by means of implication. The only character who is described in detail is the old man, as we have seen, and that description is conveyed mainly through dialogue. In several of his tales Chaucer 'amplifies' his matter by introducing his characters through more or less formal *effictiones*, but also by giving descriptions, either concentrated or dispersed, of the setting and background of the action. In the Pardoner's Tale, however, he is content with a bare minimum of stage properties, which are introduced to indicate a change of scene and to provide a concrete centre around which the characters can group themselves. The rioters meet the old man 'as they wolde han troden over a stile'. He tells them that, if they 'turne up this croked wey', they will find Death under an oak. Nothing is seen of the funeral *cortège* at the beginning of the tale; the clinking of the bell is merely heard 'off stage' – and, incidentally, is all the more alarming for being introduced in the very next couplet after the one in which we are told that the rioters were sitting in the tavern 'Longe erst er prime rong of any belle'. When Romeo wishes to buy 'a dram of poison', Shakespeare indulges in an extended description of the apothecary's shop, but we are vouchsafed no description whatever of the establishment that the youngest rioter visits for his more venomous purpose. On the other hand, Chaucer reports in detail the false arguments that the rioter used to persuade the apothecary to sell him the poison, and then, modulating into *oratio recta*, he tells us precisely what the apothecary said in reply :

> 'And thou shalt have
> A thyng that, also God my soule save,
> In al this world ther is no creature,
> That eten or dronken hath of this confiture
> Noght but the montance of a corn of whete,
> That he ne shal his lif anon forlete;
> Ye, sterve he shal, and that in lasse while
> Than thou wolt goon a paas nat but a mile,
> This poysoun is so strong and violent.'   (C. 859–67)

Chaucer's reporting this conversation in full, while remaining silent about the setting, brings me to the third kind of economy that is noticeable in this tale : what can only be called 'economy of narrative'. It has often been remarked that much of the tale consists of dialogue and that this is mainly responsible for its dramatic quality. But it has another consequence too : the fact that we so seldom hear the narrator speaking *in propria persona* means that plain narrative, when it does occur, is all the more arresting and telling. Before the full effect of this economy can be properly examined, however, it is necessary to observe just how much information about character, motive and circumstance Chaucer manages to convey through almost completely un-annotated dialogue.

The very first exchange sets the pace for the whole tale and subtly introduces two of its most disquieting features. We hear the master's peremptory 'Go bet', but his servant does not obey. There is no need for the serving-boy to leave the tavern in order to satisfy the rioter's inquiry about the meaning of the lich-bell; he knows the answer already : 'It was me toold er ye cam heer two houres' (l. 671). The uneasy sensation of having been anticipated – whether by another character, by events, or by un-seen powers – increases as the tale proceeds. The other disturb-ing feature I have already touched upon : the rioter asks for the dead man's name, but the boy gives him instead the name of his sinister assailant. This is symptomatic of the essential movement of the plot : when the rioters expect to meet Death, they find the treasure; they find Death, 'hwenne [hie] weneþ to libben best'.

From the boy's speech it emerges that he conceives of death in the way that his mother had taught him to do, as a 'privee theef' armed with a spear, who strikes men unexpectedly and goes stealthily on his way. Being but a child,[10] he is not so sophisticated as to know about personification and allegory; he accepts as literally true what his mother had told him : ' "Thus taughte me my dame; I sey namoore." ' The taverner confirms what the boy has said about the activities of Death during the current epidemic of plague. He continues to speak of Death as if he were a real person, following the boy's remark; but he is, presumably, speaking figuratively, whereas the boy was not. Per-haps we are meant to think of him as humouring the boy – with an innkeeper's tact – by continuing to speak in his phrase; to have questioned his conception of Death would, after all, have meant flouting his mother's authority. For the rioters, who are thoroughly drunk by this time (l. 705), the distinction between literal and figurative meanings has become temporarily blurred. Having heard the boy speak of Death as if he were a real person, and then hearing the adult taverner do likewise, they are convinced that he is a palpable public enemy. So they form themselves into a company of 'sworn brothers', like knights errant engaged on a dedicated quest, and resolve to seek out 'this false traytour Deeth' and slay him. The resolution is made to the accompaniment of many great oaths.

When, in the next scene, they meet the old man, they continue to rend 'Cristes blessed body' by their indiscriminate use of oaths. The old man, by contrast, is a courteous figure. He invokes the name of God only three times, and each time the invocation is solemn and deliberate. His last words to the rioters consist of such an invocation :

> 'God save yow, that boghte agayn mankynde,
> And yow amende !' Thus seyde this olde man . . .

But the name of God has become so devalued in their mouths that it rings hollow in their ears. They are so impatient that they can hardly stay to hear the old man's words, let alone to heed them :

> '. . . And yow amende !' Thus seyde this olde man;
> And everich of thise riotoures *ran*
> Til he cam to that tree. . . .   (C. 767-9. Italics mine.)

Within the space of two lines of narrative they have been precipitated into the third scene and transported to the place where the catastrophe is to be played out. After only seven more lines of narrative dialogue is resumed.

The success of some of the best of Chaucer's shorter tales depends upon the way in which, during the final scene, events move towards their end with an astonishing rapidity and seeming inevitability. But the unimpeded flow of the action at the conclusion of these tales is often made possible only because the author has contrived to introduce into the earlier part of his narrative much of the information and most of the stage 'properties' that are required for the enactment of the *dénouement*. This kind of anticipation is well illustrated in the Reeve's Tale, where the fact that the miller has a 'piled skulle' is mentioned in the description of that formidable character with which the tale begins.[11] A few lines later Chaucer smuggles in, by means of a parenthesis, a reference to the existence of the baby *and its cradle* at the moment when his principal purpose is to impress upon his audience the fact that – apart from this insignificant infant – the miller's daughter was his only child.[12] The reader will be able to think of other examples without much difficulty. In the Pardoner's Tale Chaucer goes even further: all the technical details of the murders are conveyed to the reader in advance in the course of the dialogue between the two conspirators and in the account of the youngest rioter's visit to the village. So that when the moment for the catastrophe arrives, there is no need to describe the action in detail; the fate of the three 'sworn brothers' is a foregone conclusion. It follows with an irresistible logic: the rioters are despatched without ceremony in ten lines of summary narrative that are delivered with the coolness and detachment of a mathematician spelling out the *quod erat demonstrandum* at the end of a theorem. The single couplet of misplaced exultation, uttered by one of the homicides, stands out in ironical relief in the middle of this passage where the narrator's own voice has now become dominant:

> What nedeth it to sermone of it moore?
> For right as they hadde cast his deeth bifoore,
> Right so they han hym slayn, and that anon.
> And whan that this was doon, thus spak that oon:
> 'Now lat us sitte and drynke, and make us merie,
> And afterward we wol his body berie.'
> And with that word it happed hym, par cas,
> To take the botel ther the poyson was,
> And drank, and yaf his felawe drynke also,
> For which anon they storven bothe two.   (C. 879–88)

But the theorem has a corollary. Although the narrator refrains from giving a detailed description of the rioters' death, he does not allow us to forget the implications of the apothecary's

words that I have already quoted. The apothecary had recommended his 'confiture' to his customer by emphasizing the speedi-
ness of its action : it would kill any living thing in less time than
it would take you to cover a mile at an ordinary walking pace.
From the point of view of the writhing victims, however, twenty
minutes is a very long time. Chaucer does not describe their death
agony in a series of 'close-ups' as Flaubert does when he recounts
the death of Emma Bovary after she has taken poison. He
prefers implication to description : he 'distances' the scene and
looks at it with the eyes of a coroner reading a pathologist's re-
port that refers him to a standard medical text-book :

> But certes, I suppose that Avycen
> Wroot nevere in no canon, ne in no fen,
> Mo wonder signes of empoisonyng
> Than hadde thise wrecches two er hir endyng (C. 889–92)

The educated contemporary of Chaucer would have recognized
more readily than the modern reader just how much the narrator
has deliberately left unsaid.

The peculiar strength of this tale derives not only from the
kinds of economy and narrative skill that I have examined above,
but also from the presence of a double perspective. Looked at in
objective sobriety, all the events in the story can be accounted for
rationally. We have already considered how the revellers came
to set out on their mission to slay Death. The presence of the
treasure under the tree may seem extraordinary, but there is no
need to resort to supernatural explanations of how it came there.
The old man is not portrayed 'naturalistically' : his characterization embodies too many of the commonplaces traditionally
associated with aged humanity to satisfy the canons of *verismo*
representation. But, as we have seen, it does not follow from this
that he is, in fact, a supernatural being or an allegorical figure.
Finally, the catastrophe can be explained in simple, psychological
terms : the rioters bring their deaths upon themselves as the result
of their habitual sins.

But we also see the action from another point of view. Much
of the dialogue, of which the tale largely consists, is spoken by the
revellers while they are drunk. Inebriation has an effect upon them

not unlike that which sleep exerts upon the narrator of a
mediæval 'dream allegory': they are transported 'In auenture
þer meruayleȝ meuen'; we receive through their drunken eyes a
glimpse of the world of 'Fayerye'. In that world the frontier between the realm of the marvellous and the realm of everyday
experience is opened, so that denizens of the one may mingle
freely with inhabitants of the other. It is an eclectic world in which
giants and dragons live side by side with gods and demi-gods
from various pantheons. Its origins have some associations with
the Kingdom of Death (the classical underworld is easily meta-
morphosed into the fairy kingdom of *Sir Orfeo*); yet it har-
bours not only the shades of the departed, but also shadowy
abstractions, personifications and allegorical figures. Death himself may be encountered walking abroad in this world with many
of the attributes of a human being. Conversely, it is always possible that any human being one encounters there may, in fact,
be a denizen of the 'other realm', who has slipped across the
frontier. When the rioters meet the strange figure 'al forwrapped
save his face', who seems to be too old to belong rightfully to the
land of the living, they are at once suspicious and one of them
accuses him of being Death's 'espye' in league with him 'to sleen
us yonge folk'. Because Chaucer's presentation of the old man
hovers near the frontiers of allegory and personification, the
rioter's allegations seem sufficiently plausible to make the
reader wonder whether there may not be some substance to them.
The fact that this nightmare world is nothing more than a
drunken delusion does not diminish the disturbing effect that it
has upon the atmosphere of the tale.

When the rioters find the treasure, they experience the sober
certainty of waking bliss. The quest that they had embarked upon
in their drunkenness is forgotten: the company of 'sworn
brothers' is no longer inspired by heroic intentions of ridding the
world of a dangerous public enemy. In their sobriety their main
source of inspiration is their avarice. As a direct result of their
avarice they are destroyed; in their last game of 'hasardrye',
Death sweeps the board.

The two points of view from which the action is seen are
brought into a single focus by means of an intertwining irony.
The irony of the rioters' 'finding Death' only after they have

ceased to look for him is not original with Chaucer's version of the tale; but he develops it in a way that would appear to be his own. We have seen how, in the earlier part of the tale, Chaucer builds up the personality of Death, even to the extent of ensuring that he is the only 'character' to be allowed a proper name. We have also noticed how, through the medium of the dialogue, he creates an atmosphere of mystery so that the reader has a sensation of being in the presence of uncanny 'principalities and powers', in spite of the fact that the objective view of the action insists that this is all part of a drunken misapprehension. The *dénouement* reveals that 'principalities and powers' are indeed present, but that Death is not the prime mover. In fact, death is seen in the event to be something quite negative; a thing without personality. We do not hear his hollow laughter at his moment of triumph. The spectre of Death vanishes from the rioters' minds as soon as they find the treasure, but one of them attributes their discovery of it to the benignity of another personified power, Fortune (l. 779). She is the deity in whom these 'hasardours' really believe, rather than the God Whose name they are continually taking in vain. Later the malignant aspect of Fortune, of which the rioters are oblivious, is suggested by the context in which the phrase 'par cas' occurs at l. 885. Meanwhile the narrator indicates in passing (at l. 844) that the real power behind the scenes is neither Fortune nor Death, but 'the feend our enemy' who is intent on trapping promising victims by means of their own sins. The rioters are as deluded in the world of sober calculation as they were in their drunken fantasy.

I remarked earlier that in the last game of 'hasardrye' that the revellers play among themselves, Death steps in and sweeps the board. But Chaucer makes no such explicit comment. It would have been as inappropriate in the context as would any explicit reference to the 'false traytour' or the 'privee theef' with his spear. Nevertheless the naturalistic, objective narrative does happen to show, with tacit irony, how each of the rioters is slain by nothing other than a 'privee theef'[13] and a 'false traytour' – his own 'sworn brother'. When the Pardoner proceeds to his peroration,[14] and points to the *sentence* of his *exemplum*, his theme is not the omnipotence of Death, but the sin of Homicide and the other sins whose 'deadly' consequences are illustrated in the tale.

A further twist that Chaucer gives to the spiral of irony shows
that he realized potentialities in the fable that would have
appealed to a Greek tragedian; yet, at the same time, he in no
way diminishes its propriety within the Christian ethos of his own
day. When the rioters are about to set out on their quest, he
causes them to boast in their drunkenness: 'Deeth shal be
deed'.[15] This piece of $\H{v}\beta\rho\iota\varsigma$ [hubris] will sound to anyone
acquainted with the Scriptures like a blasphemously materialistic
application of St. Paul's promise that 'Death shall be swallowed
up in victory'.[16] It is therefore entirely fitting that when $N\acute{\epsilon}\mu\epsilon\sigma\iota\varsigma$
[Nemesis] follows it should afford a disturbingly *literal* illustra-
tion of another Pauline text: 'the wages of sin is death'.[17]

S O U R C E : *Medium Ævum*, XXXVI (1967).

NOTES
1. The edition to which reference is made and from which all
quotations are taken in the present article is F. N. Robinson, *The
Works of Geoffrey Chaucer*, 2nd edn (Boston, 1957).
2. *Dramatic Irony in Chaucer* (1932; reprinted New York, 1959)
pp. 72–9.
3. 'Old Age and *Contemptus Mundi* in The Pardoner's Tale',
Medium Ævum, XXXIII (1964) 121–30.
4. 'The Old Man in The Pardoner's Tale', *Review of English
Studies*, N.S. II (1951) 49–55.
5. Steadman, p. 127.
6. Steadman, p. 123.
7. For an example of such an explanation see the separate
edition of the tale by Carleton Brown (Oxford, 1935) pp. xv–xx.
Brown's arguments are discussed and rejected by G. G. Sedgewick,
'The Progress of Chaucer's Pardoner, 1880–1940', *Modern
Language Quarterly*, I (1940) 431–58. But Sedgewick's own
solution – that the Pardoner contrives to introduce references to as
many sins as possible, whether relevant to the *exemplum* or not, in
order to affect his audience's consciences – seems to me hardly more
satisfactory.
Scholars who have considered the digression to be irrelevant have
made much of the fact that the Pardoner resumes his narrative at
l. 661 with the words: 'Thise riotoures thre of whiche I telle' – al-

though he has never mentioned them before. A better knowledge of M.E. idiom might have diminished their allegations of inconsistency. The demonstrative was not infrequently used in M.E. to introduce a new subject or character and the simple present was often used, as in O.E., to express futurity (see, for example, *C.T.*, A. 3278, or *Pearl*, l. 524.). The line could therefore be rendered idiomatically as follows : 'The story I am going to tell you concerns three revellers'.

8. This has indeed been acknowledged by a number of scholars. But insufficient emphasis has been placed upon the fact that, according to the logic of Chaucer's version of the tale, the catastrophe could hardly have taken place, if the rioters had not been subject to all three of these sins, as well as to Avarice.

9. See below, p. 217.

10. The taverner refers to him as 'child' at l. 686. The fact that he is referred to as 'this boy' at l. 670 is probably not an indication of his age; the word is employed in its older sense of 'servant'. See E. J. Dobson, 'The Etymology and Meaning of *Boy*', *Medium Ævum*, IX (1940) 121-54.

11. *C.T.*, A. 3935. Cf. 4300-6.

12. A. 3969-72. Cf. 4211 ff.

13. See C. 788-92. They are thieves because the treasure was not theirs in the first place and also because they plot to take it from each other by force. Notice especially the use of 'slyly' (l. 792), 'ful prively' (l. 797), 'subtilly' (l. 798) – a singularly ironical use of the word – and ' "Shal it be conseil?" ' (l. 819).

14. ll. 895 ff.

15. l. 710

16. 1 Cor. 15 : 54. Cf. Hosea 13 : 14. Part of this verse is quoted in *Piers Plowman*, B, xviii, 35, to describe the consequence of the Crucifixion : 'O mors, ero mors tua !'

17. Rom. 6 :23.

Paul G. Ruggiers

THE NUN'S PRIEST'S TALE (1965)

'Toute est pour enseignement' – *Roman de la Rose*

From many points of view the Nun's Priest's Tale may be considered a high-water mark of complex thematic statement in the *Canterbury Tales*. Even with its proliferation of exemplary materials (such as we note in the tales of the Pardoner and Franklin), it constitutes a complex of most that is happy in Chaucer's artistic and intellectual equipment: a grasp of form, a subtle ironical tone, cleverness without slavery in the literary allusions, the subjection of high seriousness to the needs of the form, a casual finesse with rhetorical conventions, a sharpening of the theme of marital dissension, a suiting of moral utterance to the narrator, and a delicate balance between the romantic and comic modes. It is, in short, *sui generis*.

Its meaning has to do, in one sense, with the way in which reason and instinct are embattled (a sentiment common to the fabliaux), but it places these firmly against the larger questions of love, the destinal order, and human responsibility, and casts a final vote in favor of self-control. If this shift of balance to the side of reason suggests survival through canniness, we have, I feel, a merely ironical tale. By adducing the more serious questions of a rational universe, Chaucer widens the theological ambience in which his agents live, and tests the familiar triad of love, crucial adventure, and virtue acquired which are the heart of romance.

Coming as it does after the limited range of the Monk, the tale evinces an intellectual complexity which is its characteristic tone; just how far removed we are from the mechanical world of Venus, or Fame, or Fortuna, or from a vague retributive Justice meting out good and ill through apparent caprice is demonstrated by the tale of a cock, hen and villain fox, all of whom have responsibility in a world they not only must interpret,

but create for themselves. It is a world seen not from the point
of view of tragedy, but of thought and laugh-provoking comedy.
It is comedy that comes as a response to the plea of the serious-
minded Knight, a man of moderate disposition, albeit a slayer
of his foes and a mighty warrior in fifteen battles. The complexity Chaucer attributes to him is not merely a matter of having
such a man cry out for gladsome tales. If we compare his
character in detail with that of the lugubrious and doleful tale-
teller the Monk, we discover new ironies inherent in their
actions.[1] The purely physical details of the Monk's hulking
figure, his fine horses, his taste for fine food and clothes, his
overbearing assertion of service to God outside the monastic
world afford a sharp contrast to the figure of the Knight with
his meek and maidenly deportment, his restraint of tongue, his
avoidance of the signs of wealth, his fruitful activity in defense
of the faith. To attribute to the one a limited vision of the meaning of suffering and to the other a preference for tales with a
happy ending is to point up in yet another way an expanding
complexity of character in the pilgrimage community. Chaucer
is, as it were, focusing his own attitudes upon the perplexities
of tragedy and comedy in preparation for a new kind of tragicomic vision far beyond the Monk's limited range.

In the Monk's Tale, the concept of tragedy, although it does
not entirely omit the role of the will, is more mechanical than
human, the effect of character upon action being restricted
mostly to the defect of 'mysgovernaunce' and to the 'unwar
strook' dealt out by Fortune. We note in it an absence of character
development and the tendency to see human suffering only as
the result of a fall. The form itself prevents a thoughtful interest
in the development of ethos in the agents, in their ability to
argue themselves into or out of situations and in the important
consideration of the degree of human responsibility which the
agents may assume in this life. In all justice to the tales related
by the Monk, we must consider that any long treatment of these
tragedies would conceivably entail a great deal of thought upon
precisely such matters; indeed their defect is their brevity as much
as it is the incompleteness of the whole view regarding Fortune
and man's lot which they imply.[2]

The interruption by the Knight calls for something more in

literature; if not a correction of the view of Fortune in its relations to the law of the Prime Mover such as he himself has already presented in his tale of Palamon and Arcite, at least an amplification of a view of life which allows for quite another way of fictive presentation :

> '. . . whan a man hath been in povre estaat,
> And clymbeth up and wexeth fortunat,
> And there abideth in prosperitee :
> Swich thyng is gladsom, as it thynketh me,
> And of swich thyng were goodly for to telle.'
>
> (B.²3965 9)

To this the Host gives scolding assent. His point of view may not be that of the Knight, a representative of quite another class of society, but he does know that what he has heard has become a heavy burden to the mind, if not an outright bore :

> 'For sikerly, nere clynkyng of youre belles,
> That on youre bridel hange on every syde,
> By hevene kyng, that for us alle dyde,
> I sholde er this han fallen doun for sleep,
> Althogh the slough had never been so deep.'
>
> (B.² 3984–8)

And so the Knight and Host are united in common intention if not in comprehension of the issue at hand. Both have objected to the performance of the Monk, the Knight we presume because he objects to the statement of a not entirely sound view of life (if we may judge him from the story he has told) and because 'litel hevynesse / Is right ynough to muche folk, I gesse'. The Host objects because there is 'no desport ne game' in these tales, and furthermore the reiterated theme has become monotonous. Both views have their healthy side.

The Monk, however, had had his say and declines to relate a tale of hunting; his natural discretion, which has held him back from engaging in badinage with the Host, again urges upon him the better course of keeping his private life to himself. We turn instead to another religious, the 'sweete preest, this goodly man, sir John', who is urged to tell us a happy, cheerful tale. His horse, a jade 'bothe foul and lene', offers a contrast to the sleek berry-brown palfrey of the Monk, whom the Nun's Priest now supersedes. But as we read we see that the paucity and poverty of material goods in the Nun's Priest do not preclude a richness of natural gifts and a depth of cheerful goodness absent from the performance of the materially endowed, self-limiting Monk.

For reasons which we can only surmise, Chaucer has not given explicit details about the person and character of the Nun's Priest. In the Prologue of the Nun's Priest's Tale the Host describes his horse, and in the famous epilogue, regarded by some as a cancelled link, substantially repeats a line and a sentiment which we have already heard him apply to the Monk: 'Thou woldest han been a tredefowel aright' (B.² 3135). We can only conjecture that Chaucer has, by the shift of the line to the previous performance, exhausted one view of the ecclesiastical male and temporarily, at least, abandoned the matter of expanding upon the character of the Nun's Priest. On artistic grounds it seems suitable too to explore the matter of celibacy and marriage (the lives of Monk and Host) immediately following upon the 'Melibee', a natural enough movement from the admonitions of Dame Prudence in that tale to the bodily threats of Goodelief in the Monk's Prologue, and thence to the plight of matrimony in a world from which the best men have escaped. It would seem that Chaucer is by degrees opening the door on the many-faceted subject of marriage, so that when he has finished the Nun's Priest's Tale, there is little reason for him to revert to the matter of priestly celibacy inasmuch as it diverts attention from the subject of the tale itself and repeats elements now applied to the character of the Monk.

Since Chaucer himself has told us little about the character of the Nun's Priest (some deductions may be made from the tone and attitudes of the tale assigned him), critical opinion has perforce to be conjectural. One commentator describes him as 'a handsome, strong, rosy-cheeked youngster, with a sense of humor unequalled in the company', who can 'deftly satirize the personal characteristics and the literary style of his predecessor without for a moment arousing the suspicion of his dignified superior'.[3] Another later writer suggests that he is 'Scrawny, humble, and timid, while at the same time highly intelligent, well-educated, shrewd and witty', and further that he is 'weak in body and fawning in manner'.[4] These are tantalizing surmises; in the end, each reader will feel that the personality of the Nun's Priest is best derived from an examination of the story Chaucer chose to assign him.

As we have said, the tale masterfully integrates many elements which we have seen or noted singly or in combinations in other tales. More important perhaps than these elements taken one by one or in combination is the creation of a frame or envelope in which to contain the moral and quasi-mythic structure. This outer frame presents to us those human agents necessary to provide for the reader some ideal of human behavior, some rule of continence and contentment. The old widow, with her little cottage and her careful economy by which she provides for herself and her two daughters, offers by such details as temperance of diet and exercise and a contented heart an image of temperate law, of self-restraint and self-control, of sobriety and reasonable discretion. It is the widow's yard that is the world, apparently safe and secure, for Chauntecleer and his wives; it is into this world that evil intrudes in the shape of the sly fox; it is to this world that the widow wishes to restore Chauntecleer at the conclusion of his adventure, setting in motion the final boisterous attempt at rescue.[5]

But it is Chauntecleer's plight which holds our interest and for which the outer human frame exists. It is Chauntecleer's character and his virtues or absence of virtues, his self-assurance and braggadocio, his pride, his sensuality, his susceptibility to flattery, and his sly intelligence that engage our minds. The opening description of Chauntecleer, replete with instinctive passion and joy, follows immediately upon the associations of poverty and patient, passionless temperance. Style itself echoes the contrast as Chaucer begins to employ the language of the romantic mode, and what is austere or even pedestrian in the opening of the tale gives way to something courtly, perhaps, and descriptively elevated, with even a momentary flight into lyric: 'My lief is faren in londe!'

This may be considered the high style, in keeping with the poet's intention to parody the purely tragic view of the Monk and to supply a corrective through the device of comedy. Hence the necessity for enhancing the character of the cock so that he may appear to be regal, hence the fall from good fortune, hence the philosophical rumination about the relation of will to necessity, the elevated speeches, apostrophes and exclamations, the comparisons with figures of classical antiquity, and hence the errors in judgment and the final moral tag. The subjects and mannerisms of tragedy must be present, even in ironical contexts, seen in contrast to the subjects and mannerisms of comedy: the world of love and marriage, of domestic quarreling, of deception and jokes, of personal arrogance and instinctive passions, of personal vanity and wishing to be right at all costs, of wit and hairbreadth escape, of chases and rueful laughter. The result is, in its way, like the relation of the Franklin's Tale to the Merchant's Tale, a saner, more humane attitude than the one stated in the previous tale.

A large section of the tale is composed of the debate between Chauntecleer and his beautous paramour Pertelote on the subject of dreams. Their speeches reveal a great deal of their character; Pertelote's lines beginning 'Avoy! Fy on yow, herte-lees!' with their repeated exclamations and questions are full of feminine excitability and concern. Her admonitions are purely domestic: 'For Goddes love, as taak som laxatyf.' Her wisdom is for the most part the wisdom of the home dispenser. Chaucer is clearly enjoying the game. Chauntecleer's long-winded answer, beginning with an elaborate politeness ('Madame, graunt mercy of youre loore.') is a rejoinder of some haughtiness of tone. More than a refutation answering the alleged authority of Cato, the long recital of superior authorities allows us to see Chauntecleer as one of Chaucer's more self-conscious orators, more thoughtful, more playful and sly, more pompous and self-assured. The cock is a narrator of no little skill, constructing his two initial *exempla* with great care as to form and tone and attention to detail. Indeed he is so careful a constructer of plot, with its inevitable conclusions, that the moral statement with which the first one closes tends to overshadow the principal concern with the credibility of dreams:

'O blisful God, that art so just and trewe,
Lo, how that thou bewreyuest mordre alway!

Mordre wol out, that se we day by day.
Mordre is so wlatsom and abhomynable
To God, that is so just and resonable,
That he ne wol nat suffre it heled be,
Though it abyde a yeer, or two, or thre.
Mordre wol out, this my conclusioun.'   (B.² 4240–7)

But the point is made, first through a reluctant believer in
dreams, and then through an actual non-believer who is proved
to be wrong. Thereafter Chauntecleer warms to his task, and in
a rapid mélange of instances drawn from Biblical, literary, and
historical sources, within a space of some 40 lines as compared
with the 126 of the first two *exempla*, he rattles off six additional
stories to refute his wife's authority. His conclusion is inevitable,
a mixture of the tragic assertion with the most bathetic comic
statement :

'Shortly I seye, as for conclusioun,
That I shal han of this avisioun
Adversitee; and I seye forthermoor,
That I ne telle of laxatyves no stoor,
For they been venymous, I woot it weel;
  I hem diffye, I love hem never a deel !'   (B.² 4341–6)

And the action that follows upon this long debate, in which
each agent has but one major speech, bears out this predic-
tion. But before the action there intervenes his love speech to
Pertelote containing its bold and unself-conscious *ludum*, a joke
at the expense of his less tutored wife :

'... *In principio,*
Mulier est hominis confusio, –
Madame, the sentence of this Latyn is,
"Womman is mannes joye and al his blis." '
                                    (B.² 4353–6)

Whether we cheer or blame him in this joke upon his wife-
paramour, the speech is that of the passionate lover, embellished

with sincere regard, expressing gratitude for God's grace, joy and comfort in her companionship, as well as that up-surging confidence that enables him to defy dreams and visions. They have had their quarrel or debate, but their relationship is a happy and natural one elevated by the poet through the language of love. The jest that Chaucer puts in his beak hints at that double-edged truth to which the Middle Ages were dedicated by tradition on the one hand and by human nature on the other: in the beginning Eve was the source of Adam's fall. And yet, Chaucer's humane and comic realism forbids the dour anti-feminist implications[6] and provides a counterpoise in that other truth, that other affirmation, *Amor vincit omnia*.

> 'For whan I feele a-nyght your softe syde,
> Al be it that I may nat on yow ryde,
> For that oure perche is maad so narwe, allas!
> I am so ful of joye and of solas,
> That I diffye bothe sweven and dreem.'   (B.[2] 4357–61)

We see Chauntecleer here in all his pride, hardly deigning to set his foot to the ground, royal as a prince in his hall, says Chaucer, summoning all his wives with a mere cluck.

Up to this point (l. 4376) the narrative has supplied us with a situation which is to be fulfilled in the remaining part of the tale, and with some intellectual attitudes that are to be tested. Chauntecleer's pride has been placed before us not only in the details of his dainty high stepping and his grim lion's look, but in the whole context of his long answer to Pertelote. Chaucer hereafter plays against each other instinct and rational control in much the same way that he assays willfulness and human responsibility in *Troilus and Criseyde*.

With the return to a purely narrative tone in lines 4377 ff., Chaucer seems to take a deep breath before providing the catastrophe foreseen by Chauntecleer in his dream. In the midst of the beauties of May, when Chauntecleer's heart is full of 'revel and solas', he is to discover that the latter end of joy is woe. The Nun's Priest now raises the whole question of destiny and man's freedom as the catastrophe impends, and the fox waits to fall upon the cock. It is a burst of rhetoric in a variety of

tones: the extravagant comic sublime ('O false mordrour . . . /
O newe Scariot, newe Genylon, . . . o Greek Synon, / That
broghtest Troye al outrely to sorwe! / O Chauntecleer . . .')
merges into a more arid statement of simple and conditional
necessity familiar to readers of the *Consolatio*, and finally into
the traditional indictment:

> Wommennes conseils been ful ofte colde;
> Wommannes conseil broghte us first to wo,
> And made Adam fro Paradys to go,
> Ther as he was ful myrie and wel at ese.   (B. ² 4446–9)

In the mouth of the Nun's Priest, such a statement is a kind
of bold impertinence; in Chaucer's mouth it is not less so if we
bear in mind the tradition of oral presentation at court. And
yet it has a kind of arch humor about it. It can be carried off
by welding it fast to the narrative context:

> My tale is of a cok, as ye may heere,
> That tok his conseil of his wyf, with sorwe,
> To walken in the yerd upon that morwe
> That he hadde met that dreem that I yow tolde.
>   (B.² 4442–5)

And so the narrator escapes responsibility both for philosophical
explanation and for the indictment of women. Just how much
involvement we can impute to Chaucer himself, or how much
the poet has made the indictment of women a statement assess-
able only in terms of the priest's character – these are questions
that we solve only with a kind of presumption.

And yet there may be a level of artifice here, a trick of narrative in which the artist-writer stands behind his creations and
allows some of his own personal attitudes to be expressed
through one of his agents, a form of play in which we sometimes discern the remoter *ludum* beyond the situation in which
the agents are involved: Chauntecleer has had his intellectual
fun in deceiving his wife with a Latin tag; Chaucer has had the
Nun's Priest offer us, in Chauntecleer's translation of the Latin,

two definitions of love which threaten to cancel each other out: Adam fell through Eve's counsel and bequeathed to their children similar falls without number; yet in the relationship of Chauntecleer and his wife-paramour there is a certain careless and lovely sensuality, a springtime 'revel and solas', an overtone of one strong tradition that sees the love of woman as the means by which man perfects himself. It constitutes a perennially perplexing ambiguity which man's mind declines to resolve, even if it could.

We pass out of the romantic and sensual into the mutability theme, into a commentary upon the turn of fortune's wheel, with which we have been bludgeoned in the previous performance. The joke becomes more serious; the sarcasm, faintly antifeminist in the priestly attitude towards women's taste in literature, is kindly enough if it is Chaucer's own view; if it is the Priest's, there is a want of decorum in his speaking even in so veiled a fashion before the Prioress, the Nun, and even the Wife of Bath, who can make a moral point herself, with considerably less ambiguity. But in the familiar lines dealing with the opinions of worthy clerks on the problem of evil and the relation of God's foreknowledge to man's free will, the universal problem of the freedom of all men arises, and one feels that it is not the Priest's reluctance to provide a solution, but Chaucer's own disinclination that is expressed in the line, 'I wol nat han to do of swich mateere'. It seems strange that this priest should not know what he believes, when all the other clerical tales stand squarely upon the strong base of assertion. It seems less strange that Chaucer should do what writers have always done in the spirit of play: allowed their creations to toy with notions they themselves would decline.

But the context is comic and philosophical. The elevation of Chauntecleer's fortunes to a level we expect of the epic and tragic has the obvious effect of comic incongruity and disproportion. The narrator's special task is to accommodate the mysteries of the destinal order, dreams, Venus, nature, and the rest to a Divine Foreknowing which yet allows to man significant action and a saving self-knowledge. As the subsequent appearance of the fox makes clear, Chauntecleer's original assertion was correct, and Pertelote was wrong: he will indeed have adversity as a result of his dream. Seduced by the confidence which may be the fruit of love, and following his wife's advice so far as to 'fly down from the beams', Chauntecleer makes obvious the difference between believing with conviction and acting upon that conviction. No matter how bad the advice of Pertelote, Chauntecleer cannot be exempt from the trials and temptations of his temporal existence. Indeed, the trials and temptations are themselves the means by which the Christian comedy achieves its happy goal, the battlefield upon which the soldier's mettle is put to the test.

The test offered by the appearance of the fox is compounded of flattery and deceit which in some measure balances out Chauntecleer's own towards his wife. In both deceptions there is that curious intermingling of instinctive self-preservation with soothing, blandishing flattery. Both deceptions are successful, the fox's more obviously so inasmuch as Chauntecleer's bird nature itself conspires to supplement the fall: like his father's, and presumably every rooster's before him, Chauntecleer's endeavors to match his parent's singing necessitate the closing of the eyes. 'Ah! beware of the betrayal through flattery', cries the Priest, and in an instant, Chauntecleer is caught by his natural enemy.

It is difficult to refrain from pointing up the skill of the rhetorical pattern of complaint beginning with line 4528, 'O destinee, that mayst nat been eschewed!' and passing shortly to 'O Venus, that art goddesse of plesaunce', then to 'O Gaufred, deere maister soverayn', and finally to the capping mock heroics of lamentation in 'O woful hennes, right so criden ye', the quadruple outburst drawing into fearful and wonderful juxtaposition comedy of situation with the inflated sublime of exclamatory closet tragedy. Whatever may be lacking in internal unifying factors is more than adequately compensated by the poetic effort to hold in delicate balance the humble matters of comedy with the elevated, the transporting, and the philosophical matters of tragedy.

The poem draws to its closing act in a burst of vividly detailed activity. All that has been restrained, controlled, elevated gives way in style and subject matter to the hectic demands of a chase. The serenity and moderated quietude of the poor widow's household is dissipated in a flash by the spirit of mobilized rescue spreading like wildfire to 'many another man', and to the dogs, and in further hectic sympathy, to the hogs, cows, ducks and geese, and a swarm of bees. Then in a sudden move out of the excitement of the chase, the Nun's Priest closes in upon his moral goal in the colloquial and familiar tones of admonition : 'Now, goode men, I prey yow herkneth alle' (l. 4592).

The reversal of Fortune by which Chauntecleer's native wit brings about his escape gives us some clue as to the relation of man's reasoned actions to the providential plan. The flattery by which he himself deceived his wife was superseded by that of the fox; now again, the laying on of flattery and praise for the sake of personal safety wins the cock his freedom; the fox's last attempt with unctuous and specious humility to win back his loss is deservedly unsuccessful, and Chauntecleer's answer to his enemy is a famous locus in Chaucerian moral statement :

'Thou shalt namoore, thurgh thy flaterye,
Do me to synge and wynke with myn ye;
For he that wynketh, whan he sholde see,
Al wilfully, God lat him nevere thee !'
    'Nay,' quod the fox, 'but God yeve hym meschaunce,
That is so undiscreet of governaunce
That jangleth whan he sholde holde his pees.'
    Lo, swich it is for to be reccheles
And necligent, and truste on flaterye.

    .   .   .   .

Taketh the moralite, goode men.   (B.² 4619–30)

Not only Chauntecleer, but the fox as well has come to a kind of wisdom that goes beyond the use of wit : both of them must observe a law of governance; both of them must come to rueful admissions of their failure to recognize the advantages of self-control. In the famous lines quoted above, both have learned through error.

The Nun's Priest's Tale thus raises the questions of human responsibility and destiny in the manner of tragedy or the moral romance but dismisses them, as a kind of impertinence, in favor of man's ability to learn from daily experience, in the manner of

an ironic comedy. Its subject matter is a weighing of two sides
of the ledger of man's serious and comic interests.

A host of questions is set in motion in contexts domestic and
destinal. Insofar as the questions can be confronted, they challenge the facile view of tragedy set up by the Monk. The answers,
insofar as they are given, are couched in the terms of ironic
affirmation : man is responsible for errors in judgment; from the
errors flows self-knowledge. And about chance, or love, or destiny,
the least said the better.

One level of its meanings can be described by the word 'quiz-
zical'.[7] They arise out of the complex picture of man seen as willful and self-loving, yet amiable and capable of loving others;
created in the divine image but somehow all-too-human;
responsible for his actions yet somehow controlled by forces beyond himself. To assert that man is free and at the same time that
he is not is in effect to make us accept both assertions as true. To
offer the view that love yields joy and then that it offers sorrow, or to hold in balance the philosophy of Boethius and
Bradwardine with a world of laxatives and remedies for ague,
is in essence to concentrate our gaze upon the disparities in the
experience of fallen man and to confess to a certain helplessness
in the human condition.

On another more accessible level of meaning we encounter the
ironist's pronouncements to those who must pick their way
through the obstacles of life : beware of flattery which destroys
self-control, blinds us to what we should see, and loosens our
tongues when we should be still. The lesson spoken at the close
by cock and fox is securely anchored to the real world of ex-
pedience in which there are errors in judgment, flattery, negligence, lack of governance, and an uneasy acceptance of another.
Whether the promulgator of those pedestrian truths is the inscrutable Sir John pronouncing so knowledgeably on life and love
or Chaucer speaking through a mask, a sane hope pervades them :
the hope for rational creatures accepting the appalling truth of
their day-to-day responsibility within (it is devoutly wished) a
rational universe.

The final plight of Chauntecleer demonstrates the relation of
instinct to rational control, of thoughtless vanity to presence of
mind, of foolish pride to a just humility. The 'happy' ending,

with the rivals standing hand in hand, so to speak, reciting what
wisdom they have achieved, reveals some truths in miniature,
truths mundane and pedestrian, but truths nonetheless.[8]

S O U R C E : *The Art of the Canterbury Tales* (Madison,
1965).

NOTES

1. See R. E. Kaske, 'The Knight's Interruption of the Monk's
Tale', *Journal of English Literary History*, xxiv (1957) 249–63.
2. Still useful is Theodore Spencer, 'The Story of Ugolino in
Dante and Chaucer', *Speculum*, ix (1934) 295–301.
3. Samuel B. Hemingway, 'Chaucer's Monk and Nun's Priest',
Modern Language Notes, xxxi (1916) 479–83.
4. Robert M. Lumiansky, 'The Nun's Priest in the *Canterbury
Tales*', *PMLA*, lxviii (1953) 896–906.
5. Needless to say this interpretation is somewhat willful, an
insistence that the opening section has pertinence to the whole tale.
Paull F. Baum, *Chaucer: A Critical Appreciation* (Durham, N.C.,
1958) p. 134, sees it as a false start. See Mortimer J. Donovan,
'The *Moralite* of the Nun's Priest's Sermon', *Journal of English and
Germanic Philology*, lii (1953) 505, for the identification of the
widow with the Church.
6. But see Arthur T. Broes, 'Chaucer's Disgruntled Cleric',
PMLA, lxxviii (1963) 156–62; Charles A. Owen Jr, 'The
Crucial Passages in Five of the *Canterbury Tales* : A Study in Irony
and Symbol', *Journal of English and Germanic Philology* lii (1953)
309; and J. Burke Severs, 'Chaucer's Originality in the Nun's
Priest's Tale', *Studies in Philology*, xliii (1946) 37.
7. Two articles have opened up a new avenue of inquiry into the
function of the fable as a literary type : Stephen Manning, 'The
Nun's Priest's Morality and the Medieval Attitude toward Fables',
Journal of English and Germanic Philology, lix (1960) 403–16;
and R. T. Lenaghan, 'The Nun's Priest's Fable', *PMLA*, lxxviii
(1963) 300–7.
8. Charles Muscatine, *Chaucer and the French Tradition*,
(University of California Press, 1957) p. 242, offers salutary warning : 'Unlike fable, the Nun's Priest's Tale does not so much make
true and solemn assertions about life as it tests truth and tries out

solemnities. If you are not careful, it will try out your solemnity too; it is here, doubtless, trying out mine. . . . The shifting style and succession of topics never rest long enough to serve a single view or a single doctrine or an unalterable judgment. . . . None of the targets of the poem's parodies are demolished, or even really hit at the center. There are senses in which the solemnities of courtly love, science, marriage, authority, eloquence, tragedy, the Monk, and the Tale of Melibee are funny, but the Nun's Priest's Tale does not make us feel that they are always funny . . . it offers no conclusion but that sublunary values are comically unstable. . . . In the Nun's Priest's Tale, as altogether in the mature Chaucer, we are compelled to respect the conservative conclusion because the question has been so superbly well confronted. . . . The Chaucerian mixed style illuminates the tale's microcosmic contradictions, just as it expresses, in large, the great capaciousness of Chaucer's humane vision.'

D. W. Robertson Jr, *A Preface to Chaucer* (Princeton, 1962) p. 281, notes with insight that Chaucer's humor, 'which is based on the confident acceptance of a Providential order underlying the apparent irrationality of the world and its inhabitants, is sometimes more profound and more persuasive than any "highly serious" discourse couched in the grand style can possibly be. True humor . . . requires an intellectual approach which permits a sense of detachment, not the detachment of the egoist or of the self-styled sophisticate, but the detachment of a man whose faith is unshaken by the shortcomings of society and whose love for his fellows enables him to regard both their pettiness and his own with a certain equanimity.'

Charles Muscatine

THE CANON'S YEOMAN'S TALE (1957)

The abruptness of the Canon's arrival among the pilgrims, his
equally abrupt flight, and the breathless, vehement urgency of his
Yeoman's subsequent discourse, have led most critics from the
poem to the facts that may have inspired it. Tyrwhitt's conjecture – 'that some sudden resentment had determined Chaucer to
interrupt the regular course of his work, in order to insert
a Satire against the Alchemists' – has not been generally accepted.
But scholarship still tends to class the poem as a 'current event'.
If not autobiographical, it is journalistic, and something like bio-
graphical interest still lurks in the much debated question of
Chaucer's attitude toward alchemy. Was Chaucer a credulous,
medieval dupe, or an initiate into alchemical mysteries, or was he
modern, a skeptic? Speculation on questions such as this has
robbed the poem of the critical interest due it. The story is widely
regarded as a good one, a good piece of realism, and not much
more.[1] Let it be admitted that there is hardly another poem of
Chaucer's that seems so compact of fact, so little ulterior in its
design. Its surface argument is determinedly simple; it is a warning against alchemy. Its materials are so solid as to seem to defy
further 'interpretation'. If there is a philosophical pattern to the
Canterbury Tales, this seems to be its one unassimilable lump.
I am emboldened to present the following rather hypothetical
reading partly by the conviction that journalism is un-
Chaucerian, partly by the virtual absence of previous literary
criticism, and partly by the enigmatic nature of the poem itself.
The reader will have to judge how much to allow in it for the
peculiar preoccupations of our own age,[2] and how much for my
own conviction that Chaucer's realism is ultimately symbolic.

The poem divides itself into three parts which do not quite
coincide with the formal, textual divisions. The first part (the
Prologue and *prima pars* of the text, i.e. G. 554–971) describes
the arrival of the Canon and Yeoman, the Canon's flight and

the Yeoman's revelation of their alchemical activities. Its style is
dramatic : all of the *prima pars* is, indeed, dramatic monologue.
The second part (*pars secunda* to G. 1387) is the Yeoman's tale
proper, of another swindling canon-alchemist. The narrative
here, though it contains some rhetorical formalism, is so highly
dramatized with interjections and asides that it harmonizes
closely with the tone of the first part. In the third part (G. 1388–
1481)[3] the stance of the narrator changes. Whereas before he has
been represented as unlearned, and his very proverbs are
accredited to hearsay,[4] now his voice carries its own authority.
He cites Arnaldus de Villanova and the rather mysterious
'Senior' without embarrassment, and ends with a sober, philosophical statement that deepens the context of the entire poem.
We must recognize here – what we have seen in the *Roman de la
Rose*, in the *Troilus*, and elsewhere – the convention of philosophical amplification. The characterization of the speaker is suspended in favor of comment on the wider meaning of his
position :

> Thanne conclude I thus, sith that God of hevene
> Ne wil nat that the philosophres nevene
> How that a man shal come unto this stoon,
> I rede, as for the beste, lete it goon.
> For whoso maketh God his adversarie,
> As for to werken any thyng in contrarie
> Of his wil, certes, never shal he thryve,
> Thogh that he multiplie terme of his lyve.
> And there a poynt; for ended is my tale.   (G. 1472–80)

This philosophical postscript expresses the ruling attitude toward alchemy in the poem. In the light of it, the poem expresses
neither credulity nor skepticism, but rather a distinction between
false alchemy and true, between men's alchemy and God's. The
body of the poem, the first two parts, is an exposure of the
alchemy without God, of faith in earth. Its skepticism is that of
the believer, not of the scientist, who sees in technology another
secular religion, as seductive in its way as the religion of Love :

> This sotted preest, who was gladder than he ?
> Was nevere brid gladder agayn the day,

> Ne nyghtyngale, in the sesoun of May,
> Was nevere noon that luste bet to synge;
> Ne lady lustier in carolynge,
> Or for to speke of love and wommanhede,
> Ne knyght in armes to doon an hardy dede,
> To stonden in grace of his lady deere,
> Than hadde this preest this soory craft to leere.
>
> (G. 1341–9)

The poem's dualism of attitude is conventional. It corresponds to the division of the science between the charlatans and puffers on the one hand, and the philosophers and mystics on the other.[5] Medieval alchemical texts from about the early thirteenth century discuss pro and con the doubts already raised concerning the possibility of transmutation, and the Christian alchemical tradition is full of both practical 'skepticism' and the thoroughly orthodox but hardly credulous notion that to God all things are possible.[6]

As with other philosophical poems of Chaucer, we are more interested in the poetry than in the conclusion. The poetry everywhere evokes a profound sense of the futility, the cursedness, of a soulless striving with matter. The trickery of alchemical swindlers, illustrated by the 'tale' proper, stands also for the nature of the science itself. The chantry priest is swindled by the alchemist in the second part just as the alchemist is swindled by the science in the first. That the victim is a priest and the alchemists also canons may be owing to current events, for all we know.[7] But the poetic effect is to suggest that their activity is a deep apostasy, a treason, a going over to the devil himself. They are Judases (G. 1003). The falseness of mere deceit is not enough to account for the Yeoman's passionate insistence on 'this chanons cursednesse', and the ubiquity of 'the foule feend' in the Yeoman's discourse.[8] The following rhetorical invocation to an undistinguished victim can be anticipated only by our seeing something infernal in 'this chanoun',

> roote of al trecherie,
> That everemoore delit hath and gladnesse –
> Swiche feendly thoghtes in his herte impresse –

How Cristes peple he may to meschief brynge.
God kepe us from his false dissymulynge!
Noght wiste this preest with whom that he delte,
Ne of his harm comynge he no thyng felte.
O sely preest! o sely innocent!
With coveitise anon thou shalt be blent!
O gracelees, ful blynd is thy conceite,
No thyng ne artow war of the deceite
Which that this fox yshapen hath to thee!
His wily wrenches thou ne mayst nat flee.   (G. 1069–81)

Religious overtones are suggested equally by the context. The poem follows the Second Nun's Tale. There is perhaps something more than coincidence in the contrast between St. Cecilia, unharmed in her bath of flames, conquering fire through faith, and the blackened, sweating believers in earth, whose fire blows up in their faces. Cecilia, in her retort to the pagan prefect, curiously anticipates the Yeoman's teaching:

'Ther lakketh no thyng to thyne outter eyen
That thou n'art blynd, for thyng that we seen alle
That it is stoon, that men may wel espyen,
That ilke stoon a god thow wolt it calle.
I rede thee, lat thyn hand upon it falle,
And taste it wel, and stoon thou shalt it fynde,
Syn that thou seest nat with thyne eyen blynde.'
                              (Second Nun's Tale, G. 498–504).

Though ye prolle ay, ye shul it nevere fynde.
Ye been as boold as is Bayard the blynde,
That blondreth forth, and peril casteth noon.
He is as boold to renne agayn a stoon
As for to goon bisides in the weye.
So faren ye that multiplie, I seye.
If that youre eyen kan nat seen aright,
Looke that youre mynde lakke noght his sight.
For though ye looken never so brode and stare,
Ye shul nothyng wynne on that chaffare.
                              (Canon's Yeoman's Tale, G. 1412–21)

The extremely naturalistic characterization of the Yeoman serves the conception of alchemy as a blind materialism. He is a simple, unlearned soul. His greatest gift is a dogged sense of the world of matter. There is not the faintest glimmer of spirituality or mysticism about him. Screened through this personality, everything is lost but the world of rocks and stones. Thus his idiom is ruggedly dramatic. His narrative can be trusted to describe the slightest motions in the physical world:

> But taketh heede now, sires, for Goddes love!
> He took his cole of which I spak above,
> And in his hand he baar it pryvely.
> And whiles the preest couched bisily
> The coles, as I tolde yow er this,
> This chanoun seyde, 'Freend, ye doon amys.
> This is nat couched as it oghte be;
> But soone I shal amenden it,' quod he.
> 'Now lat me medle therwith but a while,
> For of yow have I pitee, by Seint Gile!
> Ye been right hoot; I se wel how ye swete.
> Have heere a clooth, and wipe awey the wete.'
> And whiles that the preest wiped his face,
> This chanoun took his cole – with harde grace!–
> And leyde it above upon the myddeward
> Of the crosselet, and blew wel afterward,
> Til that the coles gonne faste brenne.
> 'Now yeve us drynke,' quod the chanoun thenne;
> 'As swithe al shal be wel, I undertake.
> Sitte we doun, and lat us myrie make.'
> And whan that this chanounes bechen cole
> Was brent, al the lemaille out of the hole
> Into the crosselet fil anon adoun;
> And so it moste nedes, by resoun,
> Syn it so evene aboven it couched was.
> But therof wiste the preest nothyng, alas!
> He demed alle the coles yliche good;
> For of that sleighte he nothyng understood.

(G. 1176–1203)

His commentary, on the other hand, is dully repetitive; it is analysis frustrated and strangled by a limited vision. Blear-eyed, he has come to see only, as his modern counterpart might put it, that alchemy 'don't work':

> 'We blondren evere and pouren in the fir,
>   And for al that we faille of oure desir,
>   For evere we lakken oure conclusioun.'   (G. 670–2)

> For alle oure sleightes we kan nat conclude. (G. 773)

> Noght helpeth us, oure labour is in veyn.   (G. 777)

> For lost is al oure labour and travaille.   (G. 781)

> Al is in veyn, and parde! muchel moore.   (G. 843)

> This is to seyn, they faillen bothe two.   (G. 851)

> The pot tobreketh, and farewel, al is go!   (G. 907)

>   be it hoot or coold, I dar seye this,
> That we concluden everemoore amys.   (G. 956–7)

Beneath the Yeoman's unconscious simplicity, this insistent chorus voices a frustration beyond that of mere mechanical failure. It registers a failure of vision. It says that dealing with matter as matter has no end, that is, no teleology. Medieval philosophical alchemy was nourished on hylozoism, on the feeling that matter was instinct with life. The Yeoman's recitation, however, evokes an opposite feeling, of matter spiritless and contingent, of that primordial impurity, 'corrupt', floterynge', from which only God can raise man.[9] To expect an end, a 'conclusioun', to the cooking of this hopeless stuff is the real irony of the alchemist's failure.

The technical imagery of the poem is very powerful in evoking the feeling of matter as matter. The Yeoman's recitation is dramatically motivated; now that the Canon is gone he will tell all that he can. The ensuing list of materials and equipment answers to a tradition of inventory in the alchemical writings themselves, but, given certain changes of tone, it answers also to the literary convention of the *parade*, the list of wares or drugs vaunted in the *Herberie* and in the *mercator* scenes of the passion plays.[10] Chaucer read alchemy for the matter. The manner belongs more to the tradition of Rutebeuf. Nowhere else in Chaucer is there such a solid, unspiritual mass of 'realism', and nowhere is its artistic function less to be doubted :

> Ther is also ful many another thyng
> That is unto oure craft apertenyng.
> Though I by ordre hem nat reherce kan,
> By cause that I am a lewed man,
> Yet wol I telle hem as they come to mynde,
> Thogh I ne kan nat sette hem in hir kynde :
> As boole armonyak, verdegrees, boras,
> And sondry vessels maad of erthe and glas,
> Oure urynales and oure descensories,
> Violes, crosletz, and sublymatories,
> Cucurbites and alambikes eek,
> And othere swiche, deere ynough a leek.
> Nat nedeth it for to reherce hem alle, –
> Watres rubifiying, and boles galle,
> Arsenyk, sal armonyak, and brymstoon;
> And herbes koude I telle eek many oon,
> As egremoyne, valerian, and lunarie,
> And othere swiche, if that me liste tarie;
> Oure lampes brennyng bothe nyght and day,
> To brynge aboute oure purpos, if we may;
> Oure fourneys eek of calcinacioun,
> And of watres albificacioun;
> Unslekked lym, chalk, and gleyre of an ey,
> Poudres diverse, asshes, donge, pisse, and cley,
> Cered pokkets, sal peter, vitriole,
> And diverse fires maad of wode and cole;
> Sal tartre, alkaly, and sal preparat,
> And combust materes and coagulat;
> Cley maad with hors or mannes heer, and oille
> Of tartre, alum glas, berme, wort, and argoille,
> Resalgar, and othre materes enbibyng,

> And eek of oure materes encorporyng,
> And of oure silver citrinacioun,
> Oure cementyng and fermentacioun,
> Oure yngottes, testes, and many mo.   (G. 784–818)

The Wife of Bath's Prologue, as we have seen, has a notable collection of concrete, material images. But compared to this, it is spiritual and airy. If art and not journalism is at work in the Canon's Yeoman's Tale, this chaos of matter, refuse, excrement, represents the universe of technology.

In the context of this kind of interpretation, the headlong entry of the Canon and Yeoman cannot be read as Chaucer's afterthought. It seems thoroughly, artistically, premeditated. These men are not introduced with the other pilgrims, because they are not within Christian society. They do not go on pilgrimages; they are not headed for Canterbury, or rather, for the City of God that it represents. Their entry is dramatically motivated, to be sure. They see the pilgrims leave town and must therefore gallop to catch up. But Chaucer's emphasis on the haste and the hot sweat, like the Yeoman's stridency of tone, seems to call for a more-than-dramatic explanation. It is very well for the sympathetic Chaucerian Narrator to find an earthy zest in it all: 'But it was joye for to seen hym swete!' (G. 579). We must ask, nevertheless, whether the hot gallop and the high temperature are not at the same time precisely characteristic of the Canon's way of life, the way of technology. The Canon doubtless intends to swindle the pilgrims, but this is only one stage in the greater pursuit:

> 'To muchel folk we doon illusioun,
> And borwe gold, be it a pound or two,
> Or ten, or twelve, or manye sommes mo,
> And make hem wenen, at the leeste weye,
> That of a pound we koude make tweye.
> Yet is it fals, but ay we han good hope
> It for to doon, and after it we grope.
> *But that science is so fer us biforn,*
> *We mowen nat, although we hadden it sworn,*
> *It overtake, it slit awey so faste.'*   (G. 673–82)

The Canon is described as carrying peculiarly little baggage. Dramatically, this is explainable by the traditional poverty of alchemists. Poetically, it says what the Yeoman in a brief moment of reflection says later on :

> I warne you wel, it is to seken evere.
> That futur temps hath maad men to dissevere,
> In trust thereof, from al that evere they hadde.
>
> (G. 874–6)

The pathetic gravity of these lines suggests that the 'al that evere they hadde' is more than money and clothing and a fresh complexion. It is also, perhaps, the spiritual tradition that a community of men takes with it along the way, and that gives purpose and direction to the journey. Marie Hamilton remarks that the Canon was apostate, or else 'guilty of that *instabilitas loci* forbidden to monastics'.[11] Surely his flight, while it is dramatically motivated by 'verray sorwe and shame' (G. 702), poetically symbolizes an apostasy from the human congregation, an instability of place in life. Like the canon of the Yeoman's story, he abides nowhere.

Chaucer could make fun of the complacent ignorance that despises knowledge. The carpenter of the Miller's Tale is a victim of this vice :

> 'I thoghte ay wel how that it sholde be !
> Men sholde nat knowe of Goddes pryvetee.
> Ye, blessed be alwey a lewed man
> That noght but oonly his bileve kan !'   (A. 3453–6)

The Canon's Yeoman's Tale deals with an ignorance that is less funny : that complacent faith in science that despises God. Dante's Hell has its place for those who 'wished to see too far ahead'.[12] Chaucer is no less conservative. In attitude the poem is as medieval as the Knight's Tale. The dogged refusal to admit the intractability of matter, one of the virtues to which we owe so much of our civilization, is here represented by a group of sooty figures sifting and picking for salvage in a pile of refuse. He who cheers them on is a fool. In the light of later history, indeed, the poem is reactionary. This kind of alchemy gave us chemistry. Yet there is still time to judge whether the poem has not a germ of wry prophecy in it, whether already in the fourteenth century an acute consciousness could not have caught the future of technology in a single line :

The pot tobreketh, and farewel, al is go !

SOURCE: *Chaucer and the French Tradition* (California, 1957).

NOTES

1. R. D. French, *A Chaucer Handbook*, 2nd edn (New York, 1947) pp. 327–32, gives a brief résumé of the scholarship, including the quotation from Tyrwhitt. See also Thomas R. Lounsbury, *Studies in Chaucer*, 3 vols. (New York, 1892), II, pp. 389–90, 500–2 (on Chaucer's skepticism); G. L. Kittredge, *Chaucer and His Poetry* (Cambridge, Mass., 1915) p. 17 ('contemporary anecdote'); S. Foster Damon, 'Chaucer and Alchemy', *PLMA*, XXXIX (1924) 782–8 (Chaucer 'a serious student of alchemy'); Paull F. Baum, 'The Canon's Yeoman's Tale', *Modern Language Notes*, XL (1925) 152–4. W. C. Curry, *Chaucer and the Medieval Sciences* (New York, 1926) pp. xix–xxi, issues a useful *caveat* against reading Chaucer's scientific attitudes in his artistic works. Chaucer's interest, he says, 'was evidently centered in the personality of the Canon's Yeoman . . .'.

2. Thus I follow J. Speirs, *Chaucer the Maker* (London, 1951) p. 197 : '. . . the misguided effort . . . exposes itself as a scientific specialist drive, uncontrolled by humane intelligence as to ends, such as we have grown familiar with as a phenomenon of our own day'; and R. Preston, *Chaucer* (London, 1952) p. 282 : 'The evils of competition and applied science, after six centuries, are more completely out of control . . . and of this progress Chaucer observed the beginnings.'

3. This division is recognized by Damon, p. 783, and Baum, pp. 152–3.

4. Canon's Yeoman's Tale, G. 748, 786–9, 819.

5. See J. Read, *The Alchemist in Life, Literature, and Art* (London, 1947) pp. 23–4.

6. See M. Berthelot, *La Chimie au moyen âge*, I (Paris, 1893) pp. 238–9, 281, 344–5; Arthur John Hopkins, *Alchemy, Child of Greek Philosophy* (New York, 1934) pp 213–15; and the illustrative materials printed by John Webster Spargo in W. F. Bryan and Germaine Dempster, *Sources and Analogues to Chaucer's Canterbury Tales* (Chicago, 1941) pp. 691–8.

7. See J. M. Manly, *Some New Light on Chaucer* (New York, 1926) p. 246.

8. Canon's Yeoman's Tale, G. 705, 861, 916–19, 984, 1158–9, 1302–3.

9. See, for example, the Parson's Tale, I. 333; *Boece* III, met. 9.

10. On the alchemical inventory see Berthelot, pp. 14–15; note that the alchemical texts and criticisms printed by Spargo in *Sources and Analogues* occasionally fall into rhetorical cataloguing of 'dirty things'. On the *parade* see P. Abrahams, 'The Mercator-Scenes in Mediaeval French Passion-Plays', *Medium Ævum*, III (1934) 112–23. To this tradition also belongs the Pardoner's preliminary sales talk (C. 347–88).

11. 'The Clerical Status of Chaucer's Alchemist', *Speculum*, XVI (1941) 107.

12. *Inferno*, XX, 38.

SELECT BIBLIOGRAPHY

Note. This bibliography contains no more than a brief personal selection of books and articles. Essays reprinted in this book, and books mentioned in the Introduction, are not listed here.

BIBLIOGRAPHY

D. D. Griffith, *Bibliography of Chaucer 1908–53* (Seattle, 1955), continued by W. R. Crawford, *Bibliography of Chaucer 1954–63* (Seattle, 1967). Comprehensive.

EDITIONS

F. N. Robinson, *The Works of Geoffrey Chaucer*, 2nd edn (Boston and London, 1957). Standard edition.

A. C. Cawley, *Geoffrey Chaucer: Canterbury Tales* (London, 1958). Robinson's text, with marginal and footnote translations.

BOOKS ON CHAUCER AND THE 'CANTERBURY TALES'

Muriel Bowden, *A Commentary on the General Prologue to the Canterbury Tales* (New York, 1948). Very full commentary, giving a wealth of background information.

T. W. Craik, *The Comic Tales of Chaucer* (London, 1964). Detailed analyses.

B. F. Huppé, *A Reading of the Canterbury Tales* (New York, 1964). Wide-ranging consideration of selected tales, emphasising religious aspects.

S. S. Hussey, *Chaucer: An Introduction* (London, 1971). Lively general introduction.

Beryl Rowland (ed.), *Companion to Chaucer Studies* (Toronto, 1968). Summary essays by experts on various topics, with useful bibliographies.

Trevor Whittock, *A Reading of the Canterbury Tales* (Cambridge, 1968). Stimulating examination of thematic patterning.

ARTICLES ON CHAUCER AND THE 'CANTERBURY TALES'

J. V. Cunningham, 'The Literary Form of the Prologue to the *Canterbury Tales*', *Modern Philology*, XLIX (1952). Finds the genesis of the form of the Prologue in the dream-vision tradition.

Dorothy Everett, 'Some Reflections on Chaucer's "Art Poetical" ', *Proceedings of the British Academy*, XXXVI (1950); reprinted in her *Essays on Middle English Literature* (London, 1955). Classic Study of Chaucer's rhetoric.

R. A. Lanham, 'Game, Play, and High Seriousness in Chaucer's Poetry', *English Studies*, XLVIII (1967). Interesting consideration of Chaucer's poems and themes (especially love, war, rhetoric) as 'games'.

R. T. Lenaghan, 'The Nun's Priest's Fable', *PMLA*, LXXVIII (1963). Illuminates Chaucer's poem by examining medieval concepts of fable.

R. A. Pratt, 'The Development of the Wife of Bath', in *Studies in Medieval Literature in Honor of Professor Albert Croll Baugh*, ed. MacEdward Leach (Philadelphia, 1961). Examines the way in which Chaucer puts together and develops the character.

Janette Richardson, 'Hunter and Prey: Functional Imagery in the Friar's Tale', *English Miscellany*, XII (1961). Skilful examination of the way in which Chaucer 'manipulates a cluster of images'.

G. H. Russell, 'Chaucer: The Prioress's Tale', in *Medieval Literature and Civilisation: Studies in Memory of G. N. Garmonsway*, eds. D. A. Pearsall and R. A. Waldron (London, 1969). Argues well for the artistic success of the tale.

NOTES ON CONTRIBUTORS

IAN BISHOP. Lecturer in English, University of Bristol. He is author of *Pearl in its Setting* (Oxford, 1968).

ROBERT B. BURLIN. Professor of English, Bryn Mawr College. He is author of *The Old English Advent: A Typological Commentary* (Yale, 1968).

JOHN BURROW. Fellow and Tutor in English, Jesus College, Oxford, and University Lecturer in English. He is author of *A Reading of Sir Gawain and the Green Knight* (London, 1965), *Geoffrey Chaucer: A Critical Anthology* (London, 1969), and *Ricardian Poetry* (London, 1971).

E. T. DONALDSON. Professor in the Department of English and Comparative Literature, Columbia University. He is author of *Piers Plowman: The C-Text and Its Poet* (Yale, 1949), and *Speaking of Chaucer* (London, 1970). He has edited *Chaucer's Poetry* (New York, 1958).

WILLIAM FROST. Professor of English, University of California. He is author of *Dryden and the Art of Translation* (Yale, 1955), and is an associate editor of the Twickenham edition of Pope's Homer (Yale, 1967).

ARTHUR W. HOFFMAN. Professor of English, Syracuse University. He is author of *John Dryden's Imagery* (Florida, 1962).

G. L. KITTREDGE. Formerly Professor of English, Harvard University, 1894–1936. He is author of *The Language of Chaucer's Troilus* (London, 1894), *Chaucer and His Poetry* (Cambridge, Mass., 1915), and *A Study of Gawain and the Green Knight* (Cambridge, Mass., 1916).

CHARLES MUSCATINE. Professor of English, University of California. He is author of *Chaucer and the French Tradition* (California, 1957), and *Poetry and Crisis in the Age of Chaucer* (Notre Dame, 1972).

PAUL G. RUGGIERS. Professor of English, University of Oklahoma. He is author of *Florence in the Time of Dante* (Oklahoma, 1964), and *The Art of the Canterbury Tales* (Madison, 1965).

TONY SLADE. Senior Lecturer in English, University of Adelaide. He is author of *D. H. Lawrence* (London, 1969).

INDEX